Opportunities and Challenges for Computational Social Science Methods

Enes Abanoz
Ondokuz Mayıs University, Turkey

A volume in the Advances in Human and Social Aspects of Technology (AHSAT) Book Series

IGI Global
PUBLISHER of TIMELY KNOWLEDGE

Published in the United States of America by
IGI Global
Information Science Reference (an imprint of IGI Global)
701 E. Chocolate Avenue
Hershey PA, USA 17033
Tel: 717-533-8845
Fax: 717-533-8661
E-mail: cust@igi-global.com
Web site: http://www.igi-global.com

Library of Congress Cataloging-in-Publication Data

Names: Abanoz, Enes, DATE- editor.
Title: Opportunities and challenges for computational social science methods / Enes Abanoz, editor.
Description: Hershey, PA : Information Science Reference, [2022] | Includes bibliographical references and index. | Summary: "This book focuses on the implementation of computational social science methods and touches upon the opportunities and challenges of this method in social sciences with the goals of suggesting how the infrastructure could be built to gain required skill sets, the tools used in computational social sciences and the methods which have been developed and applied into computational social sciences"-- Provided by publisher.
Identifiers: LCCN 2021027668 (print) | LCCN 2021027669 (ebook) | ISBN 9781799885535 (hardcover) | ISBN 9781799885542 (paperback) | ISBN 9781799885559 (ebook)
Subjects: LCSH: Social sciences--Methodology. | Social sciences--Mathematics--Data processing. | Social sciences--Research--Mathematical models. | Internet in research.
Classification: LCC H61 .O67 2022 (print) | LCC H61 (ebook) | DDC 300.72--dc23
LC record available at https://lccn.loc.gov/2021027668
LC ebook record available at https://lccn.loc.gov/2021027669

This book is published in the IGI Global book series Advances in Human and Social Aspects of Technology (AHSAT) (ISSN: 2328-1316; eISSN: 2328-1324)

British Cataloguing in Publication Data
A Cataloguing in Publication record for this book is available from the British Library.

For electronic access to this publication, please contact: eresources@igi-global.com.

Advances in Human and Social Aspects of Technology (AHSAT) Book Series

Mehdi Khosrow-Pour, D.B.A.
Information Resources Management Association, USA

ISSN:2328-1316
EISSN:2328-1324

MISSION

In recent years, the societal impact of technology has been noted as we become increasingly more connected and are presented with more digital tools and devices. With the popularity of digital devices such as cell phones and tablets, it is crucial to consider the implications of our digital dependence and the presence of technology in our everyday lives.

The **Advances in Human and Social Aspects of Technology (AHSAT) Book Series** seeks to explore the ways in which society and human beings have been affected by technology and how the technological revolution has changed the way we conduct our lives as well as our behavior. The AHSAT book series aims to publish the most cutting-edge research on human behavior and interaction with technology and the ways in which the digital age is changing society.

COVERAGE

- Gender and Technology
- Information ethics
- Technology Dependence
- Philosophy of technology
- ICTs and social change
- Cyber Behavior
- Technology and Freedom of Speech
- ICTs and human empowerment
- Human-Computer Interaction
- Human Rights and Digitization

IGI Global is currently accepting manuscripts for publication within this series. To submit a proposal for a volume in this series, please contact our Acquisition Editors at Acquisitions@igi-global.com or visit: http://www.igi-global.com/publish/.

The Advances in Human and Social Aspects of Technology (AHSAT) Book Series (ISSN 2328-1316) is published by IGI Global, 701 E. Chocolate Avenue, Hershey, PA 17033-1240, USA, www.igi-global.com. This series is composed of titles available for purchase individually; each title is edited to be contextually exclusive from any other title within the series. For pricing and ordering information please visit http://www.igi-global.com/book-series/advances-human-social-aspects-technology/37145. Postmaster: Send all address changes to above address.

Titles in this Series

For a list of additional titles in this series, please visit: http://www.igi-global.com/book-series/

Impact and Role of Digital Technologies in Adolescent Lives
Shaveta Malik (Terna Engineering College, India) Rohit Bansal (Department of Management Studies, Vaish College of Engineering, Rohtak, India) and Amit Kumar Tyagi (Vellore Institute of Technology, Chennai, India)
Information Science Reference • © 2022 • 313pp • H/C (ISBN: 9781799883180) • US $195.00

Applied Ethics in a Digital World
Ingrid Vasiliu-Feltes (University of Miami, USA) and Jane Thomason (University College London, UK)
Information Science Reference • © 2022 • 316pp • H/C (ISBN: 9781799884675) • US $195.00

Multidisciplinary Perspectives on Diversity and Equity in a Virtual World
Emily K. Reeves (Midwestern State University, USA) and Christina Janise McIntyre (Midwestern State University, USA)
Information Science Reference • © 2022 • 317pp • H/C (ISBN: 9781799880288) • US $195.00

Next-Generation Applications and Implementations of Gamification Systems
Filipe Portela (University of Minho, Portugal) and Ricardo Queirós (ESMAD, Polytechnic Institute of Porto, Portugal)
Engineering Science Reference • © 2022 • 281pp • H/C (ISBN: 9781799880899) • US $245.00

Philosophical Issues of Human Cyborgization and the Necessity of Prolegomena on Cyborg Ethics
Ivana Greguric (Faculty of Croatian Studies, University of Zagreb, Croatia)
Information Science Reference • © 2022 • 352pp • H/C (ISBN: 9781799892311) • US $195.00

IGI Global
PUBLISHER of TIMELY KNOWLEDGE

701 East Chocolate Avenue, Hershey, PA 17033, USA
Tel: 717-533-8845 x100 • Fax: 717-533-8661
E-Mail: cust@igi-global.com • www.igi-global.com

Table of Contents

Detailed Table of Contents

Computational social science is regarded as a research method that provides an unprecedented breadth and depth of data to classify and analyze how human interaction occurs and provide a different dimension to studies of collective human behavior. Computational social science refers to computational methods and approaches to study the social sciences, particularly incorporating big data, social network analysis, social media content, and spatial data. The outcomes of computational approaches should help overcome the limitations of existing theory in the field. This chapter focuses on the term computational approach and discusses the opportunities and challenges in the social sciences.

This chapter discusses the challenges and opportunities of incorporating computational social science (CSS) into political science. Using an original dataset of quantitative methods courses offered at the top-40 schools, this study shows that CSS courses are currently underrepresented, but their number is likely to augment because of the competition among schools. Yet, this trend is likely to stay confined to North American and Western European schools. Also, collaboration in CSS requires reconciling research priorities in engineering and physics (prediction) and in political science (explanation). Regarding research, big data does not mitigate concerns about causation and representativeness. But simulations allow studying rare phenomena and phenomena for which experiments are not appropriate. By running thousands of experiments at various combinations of explanatory variables, simulations explore counterfactuals, assess the explanatory power of competing theories, and make forecasts.

The objective of this study was to explore the potential of the opinion mining methodology in sociopolitical research, its techniques, and applications from the field of reflexivity. It is a non-experimental and exploratory study. It concludes that advances in the field of artificial intelligence have provided the sociopolitical sciences with tools that make it possible to approach the dominant trends of opinion in society during specific junctures where decision-making and/or the positioning of an idea, public policy, or social project can be measured in real-time, with broad demographic scopes that can be segmented, bringing the researcher closer to the subject of study with minimum levels of bias. Opinion mining research continues to be dominated by electoral and marketing topics; however, there are potentialities in the research of public policies, social programs, democracy, and governance that are still waiting for the application of opinion mining as a sociopolitical research methodology.

Often we hear that human beings are social creatures who interact with one another. In organizations, employees communicate with one another using both formal and informal networks, but top management are unable to observe and manage these networks. This chapter addresses how social network analysis theory and computational social science can be combined to visualize and map out the relationship structures. The chapter seeks to address how the theory, which is commonly associated with mathematics and sociology disciplines can be used in communication since the research is hardly visible. It breaks down some aspects of the theory and describes another two theories that have developed from it. Finally, for illustration, the chapter applied R Studio software to compute the social structures within a media organization and help realize the benefit of theory in knowledge sharing and employee synergy.

The immense impact of social media on contemporary cultural evolution is undeniable, consequently declaring them an essential data source for computational social science studies. Alongside the advancements in natural language processing and machine learning disciplines, computational social science researchers continuously adapt new techniques to the data collected from social media. Although these developments are imperative for studying the sociological transformations in many communities, there are some inconspicuous problems on the horizon. This chapter addresses issues that may arise from the use of social media data, like biased models. It also discusses various obstacles associated with machine learning methods while also providing possible solutions and recommendations to overcome these struggles from an interdisciplinary perspective. In the long term, this chapter will guide computational social science researchers in their future studies, from things to be aware of with data collection to assembling an accurate experimental design.

One can expect the economics profession to gravitate towards microeconomics after the big data revolution is completed. The term big data refers to unconventionally large data streams from many sources to a bunch of (not necessarily known) recipients. Relying on aggregate relations by disregarding underlying dynamics is a suboptimal when the micro data is available. Via an international organization, all costs could be decreased, and gains could be increased with global optimization of the big data just like the International Space Station (ISS). Big data is a completely new way of practice, and it must develop its own ethical standards. A few economies such as Turkey can be pioneers in terms of big data utilization in economic research if necessary technical, practical, and legal steps are taken.

Preface

Although there is no general definition of computational social science that everyone accepts, an interdisciplinary field definition in which computational tools and techniques are used to expand the methods and approaches used in social science research is accepted by researchers. Computational tools and techniques enable researchers in the social sciences to analyze the unconventional data sources, which are existence an unprecedented scale with innovative methods. These tools and techniques have made it possible to find patterns in sizeable unstructured text, audio, and image data, which was costly and time-consuming for researchers before. Computational methods act as a complementary element to the qualitative and quantitative methods that currently used in the field of social sciences and help find new answers by providing a different perspective on social science research topics such as the mode of social movements, the direction of community polarization, and the effect of robot accounts on misinformation activities. Due to this binding effect of computational methods in social sciences, the number of studies and researchers using these methods is increasing day by day. Focusing on how computational methods are used in social sciences, this book examines tools, general trends, and methods applied in different fields.

Data creation practices have gained momentum with digitalization. Data is the essential element used to define the behaviors and attitudes of individuals in social life, the working practices of institutions and organizations, and the world of things that communicate through sensors. The widespread use of data has naturally led to a significant increase in demand and efforts of researchers working in social sciences to access, analyze and make sense of this data. In this process, in addition to the methods, methods, tools, and techniques used in the field of social sciences, it has become inevitable to adopt new approaches with an interdisciplinary perspective. Thus, studies that include many different approaches such as text mining, network theory, topic modeling, called computational social sciences, have started to be seen rapidly in social sciences. he possibilities, limitations, and usage examples offered by this interdisciplinary approach, which has started to come to the fore in social sciences, have become a subject that attracts the attention of researchers. This study was planned due to this emerging need. It was prepared to set an example for researchers who want to integrate the computational social science approach into their field of study. It is undeniable that the subject and the study are essential in today's social science fields and interdisciplinary studies.

BOOK ORGANIZATION

The book is organized as follows so that those working in the social sciences can understand the computational social science's methods, applications, and approaches and examine sample applications.

The title of the first chapter is 'What Is Computational Communication Research?' This chapter focus on the meaning of the computational methods and their application into the communication field. From a theoretical standpoint, a "computation" is the repeated transmission of information through space (communication) and time (storage), guided by an algorithmic procedure. Computational social science is regarded as a research method that provides an unprecedented breadth and depth of data to classify and analyze how human interaction occurs and provide a different dimension to studies of collective human behavior. Computational social science refers to computational methods and approaches to study the social sciences, particularly incorporating big data, social network analysis, social media content, and spatial data. The outcomes of computational approaches should help overcome the limitations of existing theory in the field. This paper focuses on the term computational approach and discusses the opportunities and challenges in social sciences. For taking advantage of this method, (1) build the infrastructure, skills, and institutional incentives required to use and maintain computational methods and tools; (2) work toward open, transparent, and collaborative research, with sharing and reusing datasets and tools the norm rather than the exception; and (3) continue developing, validating, and critically discussing computational methods in the context of substantive social science questions.

The second chapter is called 'Incorporating Computational Social Science and Political Science.' This chapter discusses the challenges and opportunities of incorporating computational social science (CSS) into political science. Using an original dataset of quantitative methods courses offered at the top-40 schools, this study shows that CSS courses are currently underrepresented; but their number is likely to augment because of the competition among schools. Yet, this trend is likely to stay confined to North American and Western European schools. Also, collaboration in CSS requires reconciling research priorities in engineering and physics (prediction) and political science (explanation). Regarding research, big data does not mitigate concerns about causation and representativeness. But simulations allow studying rare phenomena and phenomena for which experiments are not appropriate. By running thousands of experiments at various combinations of explanatory variables, simulations explore counterfactuals, assess the explanatory power of competing theories, and make forecasts.

The title of the third chapter is 'Opinion Mining in Sociopolitical Research.' The objective of this chapter was to explore the potential of the opinion mining methodology in sociopolitical research, its techniques, and applications from the field of reflexivity. It is a non-experimental and exploratory study. It concludes that advances in the field of artificial intelligence have provided the sociopolitical sciences with tools that make it possible to approach the dominant trends of opinion in society during specific junctures where decision-making and/or the positioning of an idea, public policy, or social project can be measured in real-time, with broad demographic scopes that can be segmented, bringing the researcher closer to the subject of study with minimum levels of bias. Opinion mining research continues to be dominated by electoral and marketing topics; however, there are potentialities in the research of public policies, social programs, democracy, and governance that are still waiting for the application of opinion mining as a sociopolitical research methodology.

The fourth chapter is titled 'Breaking Social Network Analysis in Organization and Interpersonal Communication.' This chapter addresses how Social Network Analysis theory and computational social science can be combined to visualize and map the relationships structures. The chapter seeks to address how the theory, commonly associated with mathematics and sociology disciplines, can be used in communication since the research is visible. It breaks down some aspects of the theory and describes the other two theories developed from it. Finally, for illustration, the chapter applied R Studio software to compute the social structures within a media organization and help realize the benefit of theory in knowledge sharing and employee' synergy.

The title of the fifth chapter is 'Applying Machine Learning to Online Data? Beware! Computational Social Science Requires Care.' This chapter addresses issues that may arise from the use of social media data, like biased models. It also discusses various obstacles associated with machine learning methods while providing possible solutions and recommendations to overcome these struggles from an interdisciplinary perspective. In the long term, this chapter will guide computational social science researchers in their future studies, from things to be aware of with data collection to assembling an accurate experimental design.

The sixth chapter is called 'Generating Big Data in (Micro)Economics.' One can expect the economics profession to gravitate towards microeconomics after the Big Data Revolution is completed. Big Data refers to unconventionally large data streams from many sources to a bunch of (not necessarily known) recipients.

Relying on aggregate relations by disregarding underlying dynamics is suboptimal when the microdata is available. Via an international organization, all costs could be decreased, and gains could be increased with global optimization of the Big Data just like the International Space Station (ISS). Big Data is an entirely new way of practice, and it must develop its own ethical standards. A few economies such as Turkey can be pioneers in Big Data utilization in economic research if necessary technical, practical, and legal steps are taken.

The seventh chapter is titled 'The Virtual Persona Triad: From Self-Presentation to Social Media Mining.' This chapter aims to introduce the virtual persona concept as a mechanism to understand social media users. Emphasis is given to the self-presentation of virtual personas, the perception of physical personas over virtual personas, and the description of three computational frameworks to study virtual personas, what we call here the virtual persona triad.

The eighth chapter is titled 'The Flow of Influence From Two-Step to Network Perspective.' The two-step flow of communication by Paul Lazarsfeld and Elihu Katz is one of the curial theories in the communication science field. The theory focused on the mass media message flow in society and showed that message flowed from opinion leaders to other individuals. Although the study is a groundbreaking masterpiece in its time, significant developments in the mathematical models of contagion theory, simulation technique, empirical data, and digital technologies necessitate a revision of the theory. This chapter focuses on how computational methods can apply to the two-step flow of communication theory and how computational approaches can be handled the less valued or non-evaluable dimensions.

This book provides information about basic concepts and applications to researchers who want to understand computational social science methods, methods, tools, and techniques at a basic level and consider applying this interdisciplinary approach to their fields of study.

Enes Abanoz
Ondokuz Mayis University, Turkey

Introduction

This study focuses on the conceptual definition, usage examples, advantages, and problems encountered in the usage process of computational social science methods, which have become increasingly popular in recent years and have been given examples by many researchers in social sciences. The concept of computational social sciences, in general, describes the phenomenon of computational methods enabled by computer science in social science studies, especially the emergence of big data, the expansion of digitalization, the incorporation of network structure into social life, and the increase in spatial data. In line with this approach, the book combines studies about computational methods that include observation, evaluation, and exemplification efforts of researchers working in different fields of social sciences.

The denominator of these studies is that the striking change in our social world connects individuals, organizations, and institutions and reveals the possibilities created by the digital traces of these structures. These studies include examples of this phenomenon, which provides unprecedented opportunities for the social sciences and enables researchers to make sense of the social behavior of people and organizations through data analysis, social simulation, mathematical modeling, and network analysis. Computational social science methods make it possible to precisely measure human behaviors that were thought to be essentially impossible with the possibilities it provides. Thus, opportunities have emerged to address, re-evaluate, and solve long-standing problems in social sciences from a different perspective. Some of the chapters in the book were created with this approach.

The basic situation that this book wants to create for the readers is the state of mind that computational social science methods can provide the opportunity to approach scientific questions from a different perspective in the current information density. Thus, to convey to the readers the fact that the long-standing challenge of collecting observational data on human activity for the social sciences and manipulating the conditions in which measurements are made can be more easily overcome by researchers (Salganik, 2017). For the first category, computational social science methods make it possible to use digital data at the level of individual and collective human behavior through existing platforms and enable researchers to create new insights. Similarly, the second category provides these platforms as virtual laboratories that allow it to observe on a larger scale, on a broader time interval, and without interfering with the process than is possible in the physical laboratory environment.

Another aspect of this study on computational social science methods can be summarized as the situations that may arise due to available data and design data used in social sciences. Researchers working in social sciences have long been accustomed to working with data collected for research purposes. These data are called designed data. Most researchers work with data not initially created for research purposes in computational social science. This data is also called the found data. What makes computational social science methods so prominent is that a fundamental change in the world drives them. This change is a transition from the analog world to the digital world, and it is a fundamental phenomenon that happens whether social scientists take advantage of it or not. Social scientists come to the fore in this process because data about real people is obtained. This situation causes concepts such as privacy, justice, accountability, and transparency to come to the fore. Computer scientists have been working with digital data for a long time and are generally not interested in anything other than privacy. On the other hand, social scientists have more training and practice in these subjects. Therefore, social scientists have come to the forefront of computational methods.

EXAMPLES FOR COMPUTATIONAL METHOD APPROACHES IN SOCIAL SCIENCES

Communication Sciences

The chapters in this book include how computational methods are applied in social sciences, what they provide, and evaluating possible benefits and disadvantages. Evaluation of the subject through these chapters will be helpful both for revealing the perspective in different disciplines and for the readers to understand the subject. We will start the evaluation with a section that explains the concept of computational social science and its general scientific research approach. Then, we will touch on the possibilities and application examples provided by computational social science methods in the communication field.

The communication process has also been affected, as many individual and social processes have been affected by digitalization. The existence of digital platforms, where researchers can monitor, obtain data, make observations like in a laboratory environment, and contain a large part of the phases of the phenomenon, has paved the way for the increasing use of computational social science methods in communication research. Therefore, communication science is one area that uses these data sources and computational social science methods to provide a better perspective that can help understand the individual and collective level of human actions.

The big and found data structure that emerged in knowledge with digitalization has made it possible to use new methodologies and analyses to establish and test communication theories. These new methodological approaches and analysis methods enable new findings or research questions to emerge, making it possible to formulate theories and develop methodologies. A significant portion of computational social science methods come from computing, biology, and linguistics and can expand and improve methodological approaches used in communication research. These methods are machine learning, topic modeling, and network analysis (Rains, 2020; Windsor, 2020). From the first period of communication studies to the present, the text has been at the center of research topics. Computational social science methods have provided a tool that can reveal hidden patterns in human behavior by obtaining, processing, and analyzing text data, which are more common in social platforms with digitalization.

The theoretical and methodological perspective provided by computational social science methods has increased the tendency to revise existing theories. Therefore, theories such as agenda-setting, two-step flow of influence, and diffusion of innovations, which are of great importance in the field of communication, are discussed again. In particular, the spread of digitalization and social sharing platforms has eliminated the inability to analyze the effect of the social environment on the individual, which is one of the central problematics of communication studies. This made it possible to systematically monitor the social environment, which causes changes in the behavior and attitude of the individual temporally and spatially.

Political Sciences

In terms of policy science, computational social science methods enable big data blending with traditional research methods such as surveys, allowing research designs to differ and providing access to broader information about political phenomena. At the same time, simulation, one of the computational social science methods, offers significant opportunities to study rare historical, social phenomena (e.g., revolutions) or phenomena that cannot be studied using experiments.

Data-driven studies in political science can be divided into two categories, focusing on major cases or processes that consider historical and contextual possibilities. Depending on which of these approaches is used, which discipline will be studied more closely. For example, studies that focus on significant cases are more likely to collaborate with physicists and engineers. In contrast, studies on the process are more likely to collaborate with sociologists and social scientists. At this point, computational social science methods facilitate interdisciplinary studies, finding common points in the study process and interpreting the outputs. In particular, simulation techniques can contribute significantly to the study of policy science. The simulation method is suitable for studying phenomena such as revolutions that rarely occur in real life and testing multiple theories. Another advantage of the simulation method in the testing process is that robust results can be achieved by repeating the experiment thousands or millions of times by changing the parameters within a theoretically validated range. Thus, the predictive power of simulations increases with theoretically determined or designed variables, and more robust predictions are made.

One of the computational social science methods, machine learning, is another method that can be applied to the political science field by analyzing user content, network structure, neural network, text mining to understand public opinion. Current practices of opinion mining are used to minimize bias in determining expressions of polarity or neutrality for a cultural or political product at the socio-political level, both in micro-level and macro-level populations. Opinion mining provides the qualities of a sociopolitical action that affects and can affect the population, the shortcomings, the content of the fragments related to the specific themes it expresses. It is a method for those responsible for public policy and social programs to enable approaches that, once defined, aim to improve levels of manageability, including an approach to social poles.

Economics

Another discipline in which computational social science methods can be applied is economics. The importance of empirical foundations is increasingly recognized in studies conducted in economics. Especially in studies focusing on microeconomics, it comes to the fore in economics using big data and empirical data. With the increase in the availability of big data with digitalization, studies that include more computational social science methods have started to be seen in economics and other disciplines. In particular, it is observed that methods such as deep learning, neural networks, or decision trees can enable the emergence of different dimensions for traditional economics approaches.

The leading role in the application of computational social science methods to economics belongs to big data. The unstructured state of big data, its questionable power of representation, and its biases stand out as some of the problems seen in the discipline. Despite all this, computational social science methods are increasingly being applied in economics, especially in microeconomics.

CONCLUSION

Computational social science methods can provide researchers in different social science fields with the opportunity to test, evaluate, develop and compare existing theories, as well as provide perspectives that were not realized or never thought of before due to impossibility. Computational social science adds a new dimension to scientific studies by providing the opportunity to test new methods, data, and theories on existing methods and approaches. Thus, the applicability of quantitative experimental methods of physical sciences and analytical methods of mathematics to social sciences has increased unprecedentedly.

Another issue that frequently comes to the fore with computational social science methods is the advantages they provide to researchers because the new techniques are faster and cheaper. For example, more valuable results can be obtained by combining the results obtained from the study using computational social science methods with the data obtained by classical methods such as demographic surveys or public opinion polls.

Since people make up a significant portion of big data through social networking platforms, it can be used as a vital research input to study human behavior, perceptions, and attitudes. For this reason, computational methods are increasingly used in social sciences, especially in communication science studies. The use of computational social science methods in communication science research has allowed the fundamental theories in the field of communication to be reconsidered and to evaluate these theories from perspectives that were not possible to examine before.

Computational social science methods are a tool that can be used to reconsider, apply, test and eliminate possible technical and theoretical deficiencies of existing theories and approaches in communication research. Computational social science methods help overcome fundamental limitations in the analysis of the social sciences by taking advantage of digital technologies and moving the discussion from abstractions and metaphors to concrete mechanisms that can be measured and tested (González-Bailón, 2017, p. 95).

Like all techniques applied in social sciences, computational social science methods also bring some problems. One of the problems is that it is hard to know how well this new technique works because it predicts something that was never predicted before. Studies involving computational social science methods tend to use data and results obtained by methods accepted in the field as variables or control variables to overcome this problem. Thus, it is evaluated how well this new method predicts something that could never be predicted before or how well it works. The use of big data in computational social science methods increases the method's applicability to theories in different disciplines while bringing along problems such as data representation and ethical problems. Problems related to the representation power of big data are explained in detail in different parts of the book.

Enes Abanoz
Ondokuz Mayıs University, Turkey

REFERENCES

Rains, S. A. (2020). Big Data, Computational Social Science, and Health Communication: A Review and Agenda for Advancing Theory. *Health Communication*, *35*(1), 26–34. doi:10.1080/10410236.2018.1536955 PMID:30351198

Salganik, M. J. (2017). *Bit by bit: Social research in the digital age*. Princeton University Press.

Windsor, L. C. (2020). Advancing Interdisciplinary Work in Computational Communication Science. *Political Communication*, 1–10. doi:10.1080/10584609.2020.1765915

Chapter 1
What Is Computational Communication Research?

Enes Abanoz
https://orcid.org/0000-0002-4250-1845
Ondokuz Mayıs University, Turkey

ABSTRACT

Computational social science is regarded as a research method that provides an unprecedented breadth and depth of data to classify and analyze how human interaction occurs and provide a different dimension to studies of collective human behavior. Computational social science refers to computational methods and approaches to study the social sciences, particularly incorporating big data, social network analysis, social media content, and spatial data. The outcomes of computational approaches should help overcome the limitations of existing theory in the field. This chapter focuses on the term computational approach and discusses the opportunities and challenges in the social sciences.

INTRODUCTION

To talk about computational social science, we need to look at a very short history of science. The entire history of science has been working on three kinds of problems which are the problem of simplicity, the problem of disorganized complexity, and organized complexity (Weaver, 1948). The problem of simplicity was largely concerned with two variable problems, which are formulated how one variable to another variable relate each other with keeping small number of involved variables. For example, the relation

DOI: 10.4018/978-1-7998-8553-5.ch001

between temperature and pressure, or the relation between population and time. Such as how the population changed over time in a community. The problem of disorganized complexity or the average was emerged with developing powerful techniques of probability theory to deal with a problem in which the number of variables is very large. For example, analyzing the motion of two or even of three balls on a billiard table. With the disorganized complexity, we cannot trace the action of a ball, but with probability theory, some important questions can be answered with useful precision, such as the average of how many balls per second hit a given stretch of rail or on the average how far does a ball move before it is hit by some other ball (Weaver, 1948). The organized complexity is dealing simultaneously with a sizable number of factors that are interrelated into an organic whole; problems in the economic and political sciences cannot be handled with the statistical techniques so effective in describing average behavior. For example, why can one particular genetic strain of microorganism synthesize within its minute body certain organic compounds that another strain of the same organism cannot manufacture complexity (Weaver, 1948). The development of the new type of electronic computing devices has a tremendous impact on science and they make it possible to deal with problems which previously were too complicated, and more importantly, they justify and inspire the development of new methods of analysis applicable to these new problems (Weaver, 1948). Therefore, the quantitative experimental methods and the mathematical analytical methods of the physical sciences are being applied to the social sciences as never before. This and the technological development make the emergence of new methods which allow computational social science today.

Computational social science refers to computational methods and approaches to study the social sciences, particularly incorporating big data, social network analysis, social media content, and spatial data. Therefore, we need to understand the key factor, which is the digital revolution. The digital revolution happened extremely quickly and profoundly. In the late 80s, 99 percent of all information that we had as humankind externally stored, was in analog format, for example, on paper. The digital format of information progressed after the year 2000 and in 2002, for the first time, the word was able to store more digital than analog information. Hard disks made up the lion share of storage in 2007 (52% in total), optical storage contributed more than a quarter (28%), and digital tape roughly 11% (Hilbert & Lopez, 2011, p. 62).The store digital data has doubled every 2.5 years, and as of 2014, the store digital data is around five zettabytes (5×10^{21}bytes).

We have spent most of our daily life in the network, from getting information from different sources and socializing with friends to shopping for our needs and checking medical examination results. All these online actions have left 'digital traces' that provide unprecedented opportunities for researchers to reveal, theorize, and test hypotheses about the way how humans percept, think, believe, behave, and communicate (Lazer et al., 2009; van Atteveldt et al., 2019). This situation led to the emergence of the phenomenon called big data, and the potential of big data helps researchers shed a strong light on human behavior (Abanoz, 2020). The main factors that provide this feature of big data are the significant change in volume, velocity, variety (Rains, 2020). The adjective 'big' refers here less to the size of the datasets and more to their spatial and temporal resolution, meaning that the data are more prosperous than before and that they span several levels of analysis, from the individual to the collective (González-Bailón, 2013, p. 147).

While big data is a tool for computational research used in social, physical, or life sciences, big data should not be considered directly as computational research itself. The original meaning attributed to computational methods by bioinformatics scientists is that the computational approach is and should be different from other types of discovery enterprises by the unique way of marshaling the data and by the analyses it makes possible to provide new and unexpected results (Matei & Kee, 2019). Therefore, the outcomes of computational approaches should help overcome the limitations of existing theory in the field. Even yet, it should focus on the practical problems that might not have a theoretical perspective to accelerate the expansion of research's limits and create new horizons. This brings us to another important point about the computational approaches.

From a theoretical standpoint, a "computation" is the repeated transmission of information through space (communication) and time (storage), guided by an algorithmic procedure (Hilbert & Lopez, 2011, p. 63). A method is executed on a computer does not make it a "computational method"— scholars have used computers to help in their studies for over half a century (van Atteveldt & Peng, 2018). So, what is the research approach in computational social science? Perhaps the emergence of the definition, in this case, can guide us. Computational social science was proposed and defined as a field of inquiry in the Science editorial by a team of social and natural scientists working in the emergent domain of 'network science' (Matei & Kee, 2019). For these scientists, computational social science is regarded as a research method that provides an unprecedented breadth and depth of data to classify and analyze how human interaction occurs and provide a different dimension to studies of collective human behavior.

Society emerges from individuals and different kinds of organizations with different motivations that have been studied in different social science disciplines. The bird's-eye view towards a society shows that there are very stable patterns called the collective current, and each of us contains only a spark of this collective current. Computational tools help us a lot to understand and to attain better this complexity in social emergence.

The scientific method is basically based on three legs, empirical, theoretical, and analytical. Computational social science covers all the three fields; the empirical evidence often is obtained from big data, which is made up of digital trace (what it happened), the theoretical part comes from the simulation of this data (why it happens), and the analytical part emerges between these two processes (how it happens) as shown in Figure 1.

Figure 1. Examples of how computational social sciences cover the empirical, theoretical, and analytical methods

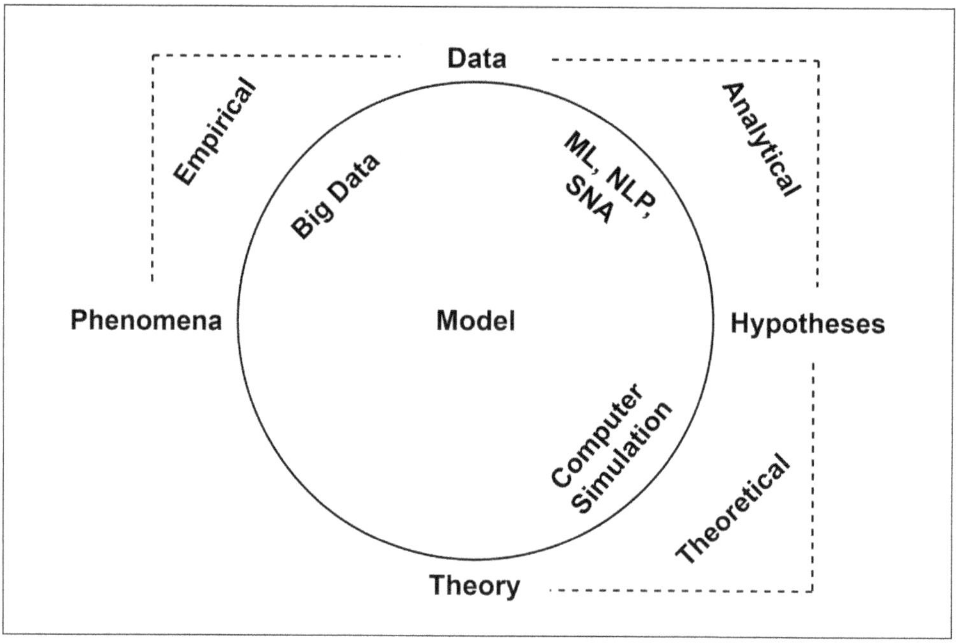

In the empirical approach, researchers start with making observations and research to get evidence about the phenomena and then try to explain the phenomena with empirical evidence to convince the people. In the theoretical approach from the other way around, researchers start with making inferences about a phenomenon based on a few variables and assumptions and then try to prove it with various experiments empirically. The analytical approach overlaps the theoretical and empirical methods where the problem is broken down into small pieces, and research evidence and inference are used together to solve it. As shown in Figure 1: computational social science uses big data for empirical approaches; Machine Learning (ML), Natural Language Processing (NLP), and Social Network Analysis (SNA) for analytical approaches; and computer simulations for theoretical approaches.

EMPIRICAL APPROACH: BIG DATA (GLOBAL DATA SPHERE)

Data is a unit of information that describes a single quality or quantity of an object or phenomenon. Data should not be considered as information in its pure form. For example, while the success grade of each student in a class is a single data, it turns into information when used to find the average of the class using these data. While the success grade of each student is not meaningful on its own, the success average of the class constitutes information that will enable us to make decisions or make sense of many subjects such as the pass-fail, the number of successes, and the general success level. Data can exist in analog or digital format. While analog data represents another type of quantity, it can change over time and constantly exhibits a characteristic (Ferguson & Hebels, 2003). E.g., the process of processing the sound data on the stone record and converting the resulting physical structure into electricity through the gramophone needle is analog data. Digital data, on the other hand, is data that represents a quantity as 0s and 1s in a binary system. E.g., By representing the audio data as 0's and 1's, reaching the data on all devices that can run the binary system and over the internet is digital data.

Digitization of data has led to the creation of the phenomenon called big data, allowing the creation of data in an unprecedented amount, variety, and speed. Big data was first used by NASA employees in 1997 to describe the problem that computer systems face in the data visualization process: often with datasets that are pretty large and have more than main memory, internal and external disk (Cox & Ellsworth, 1997). The three characteristics of big data are defined as 3V: Volume, Variety, and Velocity (Lycett, 2013).

With digitalization, many elements, and relationships of social life, from socializing with friends to the results of routine health screenings, from economic transactions to meeting food needs, began to be realized through network structures. In this way, individuals and institutions have become constant and massive data generators, whether voluntarily or not. As a natural outcome of this process, there was an unprecedented increase in data volume.

We can say that people lead their lives in a lantern surrounded by data, which we can call the data sphere. The diameter of this lantern shows a logarithmic increase day by day depending on the speed of the digitalization process. An essential factor in the proliferation of data is the existence of a wide variety of data types. Data can be structured in many different types and formats, such as text, numbers, images, sounds, and signals, or it can be completely unstructured.

Another factor in the formation of big data is speed. A wide variety and high volume of data are also created in a short time. Data is produced instantaneously by many units such as individuals, institutions, and things. The multiplicity of the number of these input elements naturally leads to a massive amount of data quickly.

The three main structures that make up big data can be classified as machines, humans, and organizations. Machines generate a significant amount of big data online and offline. Especially, the data between sensors, devices, and objects, which are data flow with each other, which is defined as the Internet of things, is an important dimension. Humans' actions that are taken on social media generate uninterrupted and high amounts of data. Organizations are another group that contributes to the creation of big data. Companies, government agencies, and businesses are evaluated under the title of the organization. All the operations performed by these organizations are the elements that provide data formation.

The empirical methods for analysis are based mainly on the path that starts from phenomena to data and then to hypotheses. In this process, mathematical models had used, and data was then collected to fit the models. Big data provides the availability of a large amount of various temporal data coupled with powerful computing resources, which turn mathematical models into more ineffective to solve problems, and became a promising option for the paradigm shifts from the model-driven to the data-driven approach (Cheng et al., 2014; Oliveira et al., 2012). This effect of big data on Science is called a 'fourth paradigm' because it has been used as new algorithmic, computational, and analytical tools in the research process (Bell et al., 2009; Hey et al., 2009). The fourth paradigm has brought a range of methods to allow studying the physics of culture and dealing with the complexity of mass-interaction with enough data and fast enough computers.

The structure of big data causes a transformation in scientific methods from mathematically organized data to algorithmically organized data extracted from different platforms and infrastructures with indexed data structures and traversable networks (Boyd & Crawford, 2012; Mackenzie, 2012; Marres & Weltevrede, 2013). This allows researchers to stroll ''data sets without making the distinction between the level of the individual component and that of the aggregated structure''(Latour et al., 2012, p. 590). Herewith, researchers have been able to use new approaches such as data mining to overcome the crisis of the old approach of empirical methods, and it brings a convergence of the social and natural sciences.

ANALYTICAL APPROACH: ML, NLP, AND SNA

Machine learning can be defined as a computer science branch that mainly focuses on enabling computers to self-learning on prediction and optimization process without outside intervention or being directly programmed (Bonetto & Latzko, 2020; Edgar & Manz, 2017; Samuel, 1959). Computers improve their performance in these tasks through gaining experiences that generally mean fitting data. Therefore, the boundary between statistics and machine learning is vague (Bi et al., 2019). Machine learning is used to test hypothesis-driven inference using big data, which contains various formats and structures to get predictive accuracy over the dataset. Supervised, unsupervised, and semi-supervised methods and support vector machines, Naïve Bayes, neural networks, and k-means clustering algorithms have been used in machine learning to self-learn computers to gain accuracy about hypotheses with the usage of big data (Edgar & Manz, 2017). In the supervised approach, the value of the outcome is known for each observation, and approaches such as linear and logistic regression are used. On the other hand, in unsupervised machine learning, the algorithm aims to identify the genuine relationships within the data without the known outcome existences. In semi-supervised machine learning, the method identifies genuine relationships within data using partially the known outcomes for some observation.

Machine learning uses data to build a parametric model that makes predictions based on the observed system state and finds the best parameters set for the given model to maximize prediction accuracy (Bonetto & Latzko, 2020).

NLP is a computational approach that is based on a set of theories to analyze text so that computer systems understand and manipulate natural languages to perform desired tasks (Chowdhury, 2005; Hirschberg & Manning, 2015). NLP has been used to overcome the vastly large size, general nature, and ambiguity of natural language using statistical parsing methods and language rules (Nadkarni et al., 2011). In addition to statistical methods, NLP includes machine learning methods to make generalized predictions about data using the patterns from training data. Four key factors enabled these developments: (i) a vast increase in computing power, (ii) the availability of very large amounts of linguistic data, (iii) the development of highly successful machine learning (ML) methods, and (iv) a much richer understanding of the structure of human language and its deployment in social contexts (Hirschberg & Manning, 2015, p. 261). With these developments, NLP has been used to build models over large quantities of language data.

SNA is a method that analyzes the relational patterns of nodes (actors) and connections (ties) using a mathematical computation approach (Marin & Wellman, 2011; van der Hulst, 2009). . The method allows to detect and interpret the patterns of social ties such as the social roles, influential actors, positions, power, and dependency mechanisms among actors that sometimes could not be easily seen, grasped, or discovered at first glance in social relations within the network (Wasserman & Faust, 1994). Some theories related to SNA focus on the mathematical form of networks, and they can be studied without the need for empirical data. Researchers take the SNA approach to understand the kinds of outcomes produced by network structure and test hypotheses. They have developed different algorithms and methods for analyzing the relationships and the measuring concepts based on the network structure with statistical analyses.

In all these methods, the problem is divided into small parts, and the conclusions are reached by testing the inferences to solve the problem with these small parts.

THEORETICAL APPROACH: COMPUTER SIMULATION

A *computer simulation* can be defined as "duplication of the essence of a system or activity, that is, the essential characteristic of the system" (Dutton et al., 1971, p. 122). Computer simulations play an essential role in science, and it has a long history that parallels the development of early digital computing. It is difficult sometimes to subject theories to systematic empirical tests because of legal as well as ethical constraints to experimentation with real systems, societies, and human populations (Jacobsen & Bronson, 1995). In addition to this, many systems are constantly changing and making exact replications of them almost impossible. However, the power of computer simulations with combining sample data from these systems provides a new method to overcome these problems. In this way, complex theories can be tested by using computer simulations with the juxtaposition of empirical data and mathematical models. Computer simulations provide the ability to study systems not yet tractable with analytical methods, and can fill the gap between theory and experiment (Heermann, 1990). The outcomes of computer simulation provide a data set produced by the model, which can be used for empirical adequacy for theory.

Computer simulations are enabled more flexibility in design experiments by giving the control power to hold, change, remove, or add over variables. Computer models are of value only if variables are carefully selected and based on analyses of intelligible aspects of realistic phenomena (Federico & Figliozzi, 1981, p. 517). Thus, computer simulations have built upon theory and can assist researchers with relationships among variables comprising a system based on the hypothesis.

OPPORTUNITIES OFFERED BY COMPUTATIONAL METHODS

The echoes of the transformative effect of computational methods, generally observational, theoretical, and experimental aspects of the scientific enterprise and subfields such as biology, physics, and sociology, have been already seen over the past three decades (Hilbert et al., 2019; Lazer et al., 2009). Different disciplines can come up with an innovative approach for subjects that are different from their regular ones. They can have the ability to solve a problem, test a hypothesis, find another perspective, and think out of the box. Seeing a problem from another disciplinary vantage point can unlock new perspectives, as evidenced by the combined efforts of physics and political science in exploring the momentum of social movements (Windsor, 2020, p. 7). Because of this feature, computational methods have been used in research by scholars in different subfields. In recent years, using computational text analysis methods in political science, communication, and sociology have increased remarkably in subjects from understanding political polarization, and sentimental perception to social movements and radicalization. With this situation, many departments in different subfields have developed entire text as-data courses that cover corpus generation, text mining, and text cleaning with programming languages such as R and Python (Windsor, 2020). In addition to this, computational methods have gained institutional support from vital and respected universities such as UPENN, NYU, Northeastern, Harvard, and Oxford for interdisciplinary works. These institutional supports foster research across disparate fields like computer science and engineering, linguistics, psychology, cognitive science, political science, mathematics and statistics, and philosophy (Windsor, 2020).

The computational approach can be used and are applicable as an inductive and deductive method for research designs and answering questions we do not even know how to ask in social science research (Matei & Kee, 2019; Peng et al., 2019).The computational approach can reveal unseen and unthought patterns between points in data, so it can help to overcome and infer the causal relationships that existing theories and empirical research designs have not seen. For example, the two-step flow theory of Katz and Lazarsfeld (2005) has recently been revisited using Twitter data, making it possible to realize the authors' wish that is to trace out all of the interpersonal networks in the community to see how they link up with each other (Hilbert et al., 2019). Also, the computational approach has been playing a pioneering role for experimental research with providing new opportunities such as mobile apps, browser extensions, social media platforms like Facebook and Amazon Mechanical Turk for surveys, field and lab experiments, which create a new and efficient way to analyze actions from individual to the group level (Hilbert et al., 2019; Peng et al., 2019; Salganik, 2017; van Atteveldt & Peng, 2018).

CHALLENGES AND PITFALLS IN COMPUTATIONAL METHODS

Even though computational approaches enable a new level for the communication research field, there are some challenges and pitfalls which can demolish the power of computational approaches, so researchers need to be aware of them. The first and probably the main challenge in computational approaches is the ownership of many required dataset by (social) media companies and other commercial entities that threaten the accessibility of data and the reproducibility of studies (van Atteveldt et al., 2019). Most of the digital traces and big data produced on social media platforms such as Facebook, YouTube, WhatsApp cannot be easily reachable by researchers. A few researchers -who have a co-author from the social media platforms or have the privilege to use data in a certain way- have permission to reach the data. The research coming from these researchers cannot be replicated, tested, or used in complex multidimensional analyses due to no access to the data. The lack of established standards and technical abilities for new methods in computational approaches have also created additional problems for the reproducibility of research.

Another challenge related to data in computational approaches is the representation power of data. Even though the data occurs naturally and untouched, it may not be considered as the general public's actual behavior of interest or expressed attitudes. In societies, many individuals cannot use social media platforms because of technical and economic obstructions. An individual must know how to use social media platforms, need a technological device such as a smartphone, tablet, and computer, and have the economic power to provide the data connection fee. Under these circumstances, the population on social media platforms is generally different from the public, so the representation power of data can be weaker.

Moreover, a dataset collected from social media platforms is not the whole of data in these platforms. For example, data from the protected account in Twitter or closed group activities in Facebook cannot be reachable by researchers even though data collection is permitted from social media platforms. Partial data of all data in any platform is another factor that weakens the representation power of the data.

Maybe the most common pitfall in computational approaches is the required unique skillsets for programming and data handling. There are many off-the-shelf tools and codes for computational methods, and these put the computational approaches at the forefront of the open science philosophy. Researchers can use these tools and codes in their projects, but when it comes to using them in research, they can be very tricky and challenging. Data on online platforms is unstructured and varied. Thus, each case should be thought of separately, and there will be needs for minor tweaks to gather, clean, process, and analyze data.

Finally, another pitfall in computational approaches is neglecting or ignoring the theoretical work due to the omnipresence and size of data and focusing on practical work, especially social science research. Theoretical and practical concerns should be equally existing when computational approaches should be planned to use in a research idea or project (Domahidi et al., 2019; Hilbert et al., 2019). As mentioned before, computational approaches can reveal unseen patterns with many data points, making it easy to understand an ongoing phenomenon in society with the power of theoretical background.

We must also mention that an ethical issue is a rising challenge that has taken the attention of researchers, platforms owners, and users with the more extensive and intensive use of computational approaches. Computational approaches often use publicly available data, and there are sensitive data such as information about the political view, health condition, sexual orientation, ethnicity, and gender. The publication of several controversial large-scale research pieces of computational approach research has caused growing concern on ethical (mis)conduct in research. It has raised the question of how publicly available data can be collected, processed, and published (Niemann-Lenz et al., 2019; van Atteveldt & Peng, 2018). For example, the debacle following AOL's public release of "anonymized" search records of many of its customers highlights the potential risk to individuals and corporations in sharing personal data by private companies (Lazer et al., 2009, p. 722). There are some research and reports about how to pull individual profiles out, even carefully anonymized data. Therefore, researchers should be careful and conscious when using big data with computational methods to prevent ethical issues that can damage both researchers and individuals even if the data was anonymized.

THE ROLE OF COMPUTATIONAL METHODS IN COMMUNICATION SCIENCE

Most of the actions on online networks and leave digital traces are communicative such as likes, comments. In addition to this, social media is seen as having brought with it increased quantification of social interaction, since, for instance, the number of likes that a post has received on Facebook requires no additional operations to be quantified (Törnberg & Törnberg, 2018, p. 4). In this context, communication science is one of the emerging subfields for using these data sources to provide a better perspective that can help understand the individual and collective level of human actions (Hilbert et al., 2019). Therefore, Computational Communication Science (CCS) is the label applied to the emerging subfield that investigates computational algorithms to gather and analyze big and often semi- or unstructured data sets to develop and test communication science theories (van Atteveldt & Peng, 2018). According to the definition by Shah et al. (2015), CCS generally involves: (1) the use of large and complex data sets; (2) 'naturally occurring' data; (3) algorithmic solutions; and (4) allowing the study of human communication by applying and testing communication theory. The large-scale, unstructured, and unprecedented availability of data on social media can be used to uncover psychological and social aspects of behavioral patterns of users with helping of user analytics and algorithms. This approach requires an innovative way to analyze semantic patterns underlying the behaviors on social media. This innovative way can be classified under five activities: data acquisition, classification/prediction, text mining, network analysis, and simulation (Rains, 2020).

New approaches in methodology and analysis can lead to new findings, which can be used to formulate and refine theories, vice versa, a research question can also be used to develop a new methodology. Most computational approaches have been borrowed from various disciplines such as computer, psychology, biology, and linguistic science. Thus, computational approaches can be used to expand and enhance the methodological toolbox in communication research. Computational approaches in communication research can be used to understand the social phenomena by using technics such as machine learning, topic modeling, and network analysis, which increase the power of the questions to look up micro, mezzo, and macro-level of the subject (Rains, 2020; Windsor, 2020). For example, researchers from various sciences such as agenda-setting, two-step flow of information, public perception, and selective exposure have reconsidered communication theories such as psychology, sociology, biology, physics, and computer. Computational approaches in communication research have also focused on text as-data, which is the natural and ubiquity outcome of the communication process on social media platforms such as Twitter, YouTube, and Facebook. With computational approaches, researchers have the power for sorting and binning information in the text as data which is an excellent toolbox to reveal the hidden patterns in human behaviors.

Following the digital breadcrumbs of online social behavior can be considered a new behavior laboratory in communication research. These data are made up of users' actual behavior, which is collected in an inconspicuous way that is better than self-reported data. This can help overcome social desirability problems, and more importantly, it does not rely on people's imperfect estimates of their desires and intentions (van Atteveldt & Peng, 2018, p. 83). In addition, the estimates about users' behaviors do not guarantee to reveal the big picture for the cause-and-effect relationship of behaviors. However, more data points can help researchers to see more clearly. More data points can also be used for a more profound and multidimensional examination of human communication phenomena in various domains or providing enriched perspectives to explicate or test for more complex models across multiple levels. Thus, big data and algorithmic workflows have launched the field of communication to a new level (Hilbert et al., 2019).

Soffer and Geifman (2020) searched the ongoing changes in communication studies, comparing trends in two European media studies journals and three foremost International Communication Association (ICA) journals over the past two decades. They collected the text -title, keywords, and abstracts- of articles published over 23 years (1994-2016). These two researchers applied topic modeling analysis to identify latent themes in the discipline's research agenda as reflected and shaped through these journal outlets (Soffer & Geifman, 2020, p. 3). The result of their research showed that mediazation, which was developed and became routine in communication studies with the rise of digital communication, assumes 'that the media become an integral part of other actors or systems with the effect that the practices of these actors/ systems are increasingly shaped by the media's logic of operation' (Soffer & Geifman, 2020, p. 12).

FUTURE RESEARCH DIRECTIONS

Computational social science has attracted the attention of researchers for the last decades as a scientific method that has been increasingly used with the spread of big data, the ease of access to data, the development of ready-made programs and software, and the increase in the capacity of computers. Along with the advantages of this method, the direction, prevalence, reliability, and reproducibility of developments in social sciences are among the subjects that should be focused on in further studies. Confidentiality of user and private information in research is another research area that is gaining importance as data covers all areas of social life, and not only individuals but also institutions and organizations are integrated into this structure. Ethical concerns and problems, which are the natural result of this situation, come to the fore as a point that should be focused on in future studies.

CONCLUSION

Computational social science adds a new dimension to scientific studies by providing the opportunity to test new methods, data, and theories on existing methods and approaches developed to produce solutions to three fundamental problems that the history of science has studied. Thus, the applicability of quantitative experimental methods of physical science and analytical methods of mathematics to the social sciences has increased unprecedentedly. Computational social science makes it possible to answer questions by applying the methods and approaches used in different scientific fields to the social sciences that could not be answered earlier by addressing the questions focused on social sciences from a different perspective.

The two most important developments that enable to use of the computational method in social sciences are: (1) the creation of content called big data, which humans, machines, and institutions produce, make it possible to understand human behavior and social processes; (2) is the significant technological advance in the data processing capabilities of computers. While the computational method makes it possible to approach scientific problems differently, it provides new possibilities for empirical, theoretical, and analytical approaches, which are the fundamental pillars of science. Thus, a phenomenon has made it possible to use different methods and approaches to answer what happened, why, and how. The computational method makes it possible to use deductive and inductive methods to ask questions that have not been handled differently or unthinkable due to the limitations of research methods and the holistic perspective and to search for answers to these questions. In addition, computational methods enable the application of experimental approaches with the new methods and tools.

Despite the advantages of computational methods, it cannot be ignored that they also have some difficulties and pitfalls in their use in the research process. Some of the main reasons for this situation are the priorities of the companies, which play an essential role in the data production process, in the data production and use process, the restrictions in the data access process, and the representation power of the data. For companies that are the primary decision-makers in creating and using big data, data is not seen as an output to be used in the research process but as a support element in making strategic decisions that will enable more individuals to spend more time on these platforms. Another critical factor is restricting access to the data created by these platforms and institutions by third parties and institutions due to both commercial value and ethical concerns. The fact that some of the created big data can be accessed causes a decrease in the representative power of the data. Another factor that reduces the representative power of data is the limitedness of individuals, institutions, and objects that can be involved in the data creation process. In the process of making sense of a holistic phenomenon, the fact that the decrease in the representative power of the data will lead to a decrease in the representative power of the sample should not be ignored.

Another factor to consider in applying computational methods is the tendency to trivialize theory, which is one of the main components of the scientific research process due to large amounts of big data and technological developments in computer capacity. Although the computational method can define the components of the phenomenon studied in the research process and reveal previously undetected overlaps between these components, the necessity of the existence of the theory for the integrity of the study and the evaluation of the results is an undeniable reality.

Since a significant part of big data is created by people through social sharing platforms, it can be used as a vital research input in examining human behaviors, perceptions, and attitudes. For this reason, computational methods are increasingly used in social sciences and especially in communication science studies. The use of computational methods in communication science research has enabled essential theories in the field of communication to be reconsidered and to evaluate these theories with perspectives that were not possible to examine before. The application of methods and approaches developed in fields such as computer science, psychology, biology, and linguistics to communication studies and theories is also an opportunity provided using computational methods.

Computational approaches open the door to a new world for researchers and carry the research design to a new level in general social sciences. However, these possibilities also make it inevitable to make some necessary changes in individual and institutional dimensions. The first one is that computational approaches require some skillsets to use programming languages such as R and Python, understanding the structure of data on social media platforms, and collaboration practices with researchers other than the researcher's field. The requirement of these skill sets leads to rethinking the changes in educational programs and institutional incentives for developing and maintaining them. Although many institutions have changed or have been changing their curriculum for computational approaches, most schools and departments remain to follow the classical curriculum, which is the better for theoretical approaches. Thus, computational approaches have forced educational changes on an institutional and personal level for gaining the required unique skill sets. For example, Germany and the United States—have already started teaching statistics and data analysis using R starting at the BA level (Niemann-Lenz et al., 2019). At that point, we should say that this does not mean that everyone can (or should) become a programmer for using computational methods in their research, but with the ability to use off-the-shelf tools or tweaking them can be learned with a limited investment in computing skills. On the institutional level, some improvements on scholarship, tenure track, and intellectual recognition process should be made to support scholars to use computational approaches in their research.

It is vital to make progress in at least three areas for getting the benefit of computational approaches in science research (van Atteveldt & Peng, 2018, p. 89): (1) build the infrastructure, skills, and institutional incentives required to use and maintain computational methods and tools; (2) work toward open, transparent, and collaborative research, with sharing and reusing datasets and tools the norm rather than the exception; and (3) continue developing, validating, and critically discussing computational methods in the context of substantive social science questions.

REFERENCES

Abanoz, E. (2020). *The emerge of computational communication at the intersection of communication and computation: Opportunities and challenges*. Academic Press.

Bell, G., Hey, T., & Szalay, A. (2009). Beyond the Data Deluge. *Science*, *323*(5919), 1297–1298. doi:10.1126cience.1170411 PMID:19265007

Bi, Q., Goodman, K. E., Kaminsky, J., & Lessler, J. (2019). What is Machine Learning? A Primer for the Epidemiologist. *American Journal of Epidemiology*, kwz189. Advance online publication. doi:10.1093/aje/kwz189 PMID:31509183

Bonetto, R., & Latzko, V. (2020). Machine Learning. In F. H. P. Fitzek, F. Granelli, & P. Seeling (Eds.), *Computing in Communication Networks* (pp. 135–167). Elsevier. doi:10.1016/B978-0-12-820488-7.00021-9

Boyd, D., & Crawford, K. (2012). Critical questions for big data: Provocations for a cultural, technological, and scholarly phenomenon. *Information Communication and Society*, *15*(5), 662–679. doi:10.1080/1369118X.2012.678878

Cheng, J., Adamic, L., Dow, P. A., Kleinberg, J. M., & Leskovec, J. (2014). Can cascades be predicted? *Proceedings of the 23rd International Conference on World Wide Web - WWW '14*, 925–936. 10.1145/2566486.2567997

Chowdhury, G. G. (2005). Natural language processing. *Annual Review of Information Science & Technology*, *37*(1), 51–89. doi:10.1002/aris.1440370103

Cox, M., & Ellsworth, D. (1997). Application-controlled demand paging for out-of-core visualization. *Visualization*, *97*, 235–244.

Domahidi, E., Yang, J., Niemann-Lenz, J., & Reinecke, L. (2019). Outlining the Way Ahead in Computational Communication Science: An Introduction to the IJoC Special Section on "Computational Methods for Communication Science: Toward a Strategic Roadmap." *International Journal of Communication*, *13*(0), 3876–3884.

Edgar, T. W., & Manz, D. O. (2017). Machine Learning. In Research Methods for Cyber Security (pp. 153–173). Elsevier. doi:10.1016/B978-0-12-805349-2.00006-6

Federico, P.-A., & Figliozzi, P. W. (1981). Computer Simulation of Social Systems. *Sociological Methods & Research*, *9*(4), 513–533. doi:10.1177/004912418100900408

Ferguson, S., & Hebels, R. (2003). Communications and networking. In S. Ferguson & R. Hebels (Eds.), *Computers for Librarians: An Introduction to the Electronic Library* (pp. 197–226). Elsevier Science. doi:10.1016/B978-1-876938-60-4.50013-6

González-Bailón, S. (2013). Social Science in the Era of Big Data. *Policy and Internet*, *5*(2), 147–160. doi:10.1002/1944-2866.POI328

Heermann, D. W. (1990). *Computer Simulation Methods in Theoretical Physics* (2nd ed.). Springer. doi:10.1007/978-3-642-75448-7

Hey, A. J. G., Tansley, S., & Tolle, K. (2009). *The fourth paradigm: Data-intensive scientific discovery* (Vol. 1). Microsoft Research.

Hilbert, M., Barnett, G., Blumenstock, J., Contractor, N., Diesner, J., Seth, F., & González-Bailón, S. (2019). Computational Communication Science: A Methodological Catalyzer for a Maturing Discipline. *International Journal of Communication*, *13*, 3912–3934.

Hilbert, M., & Lopez, P. (2011). The World's Technological Capacity to Store, Communicate, and Compute Information. *Science*, *332*(6025), 60–65. doi:10.1126cience.1200970 PMID:21310967

Hirschberg, J., & Manning, C. D. (2015). Advances in natural language processing. *Science*, *349*(6245), 261–266. doi:10.1126cience.aaa8685 PMID:26185244

Jacobsen, C., & Bronson, R. (1995). Computer-simulations and empirical testing of sociological theory. *Sociological Methods & Research*, *23*(4), 479–506. doi:10.1177/0049124195023004004

Katz, E., & Lazarsfeld, P. (2005). *Personal Influence: The Part Played by People in the Flow of Mass Communications*. Routledge.

Latour, B., Jensen, P., Venturini, T., Grauwin, S., & Boullier, D. (2012). 'The whole is always smaller than its parts' - a digital test of Gabriel Tardes' monads: 'The whole is always smaller than its parts.' *The British Journal of Sociology*, *63*(4), 590–615. doi:10.1111/j.1468-4446.2012.01428.x PMID:23240834

Lazer, D., Pentland, A., Adamic, L., Aral, S., Barabasi, A.-L., Brewer, D., Christakis, N., Contractor, N., Fowler, J., Gutmann, M., Jebara, T., King, G., Macy, M., Roy, D., & Van Alstyne, M. (2009). Computational Social Science. *Science*, *323*(5915), 721–723. doi:10.1126cience.1167742 PMID:19197046

Lycett, M. (2013). 'Datafication': Making sense of (big) data in a complex world. *European Journal of Information Systems*, *22*(4), 381–386. doi:10.1057/ejis.2013.10

Mackenzie, A. (2012). More Parts Than Elements: How Databases Multiply. *Environment and Planning. D, Society & Space*, *30*(2), 335–350. doi:10.1068/d6710

Marin, A., & Wellman, B. (2011). Social Network Analysis: An Introduction. In J. Scott & P. J. Carrington (Eds.), *The SAGE Handbook of Social Network Analysis*. SAGE Publications Inc.

Marres, N., & Weltevrede, E. (2013). Scraping the social?: Issues in live social research. *Journal of Cultural Economics*, *6*(3), 313–335. doi:10.1080/17530350.2013.772070

Matei, S. A., & Kee, K. F. (2019). Computational communication research. *WIREs Data Mining and Knowledge Discovery*, *9*(4), 1–18. doi:10.1002/widm.1304

Nadkarni, P. M., Ohno-Machado, L., & Chapman, W. W. (2011). Natural language processing: An introduction. *Journal of the American Medical Informatics Association: JAMIA*, *18*(5), 544–551. doi:10.1136/amiajnl-2011-000464 PMID:21846786

Niemann-Lenz, J., Bruns, S., Hefner, D., Knop-Huelss, K., Possler, D., & Reich, S. (2019). Crafting a Strategic Roadmap for Computational Methods in Communication Science: Learnings from the CCS 2018 Conference in Hanover | Commentary. *International Journal of Communication*, *13*, 3885–3893.

Oliveira, S. F., Furlinger, K., & Kranzlmuller, D. (2012). Trends in Computation, Communication and Storage and the Consequences for Data-intensive Science. *2012 IEEE 14th International Conference on High Performance Computing and Communication & 2012 IEEE 9th International Conference on Embedded Software and Systems*, 572–579. 10.1109/HPCC.2012.83

Peng, T.-Q., Liang, H., & Zhu, J. J. H. (2019). Introducing computational social science for Asia-Pacific communication research. *Asian Journal of Communication*, *29*(3), 205–216. doi:10.1080/01292986.2019.1602911

Rains, S. A. (2020). Big Data, Computational Social Science, and Health Communication: A Review and Agenda for Advancing Theory. *Health Communication*, *35*(1), 26–34. doi:10.1080/10410236.2018.1536955 PMID:30351198

Salganik, M. J. (2017). *Bit by bit: Social research in the digital age*. Princeton University Press.

Samuel, A. L. (1959). Some Studies in Machine Learning Using the Game of Checkers. *IBM Journal of Research and Development*, *3*(3), 210–229. doi:10.1147/rd.33.0210

Shah, D. V., Cappella, J. N., & Neuman, W. R. (2015). Big Data, Digital Media, and Computational Social Science: Possibilities and Perils. *The Annals of the American Academy of Political and Social Science*, *659*(1), 6–13. doi:10.1177/0002716215572084

(1971). Simulation model construction. InDutton, J. M., Starbuck, W. H., Dutton, J. M., & Briggs, W. G. (Eds.), *Computer Simulation of Human Behavior*. John Wiley.

Soffer, O., & Geifman, D. (2020). Comparing research topics in European and International Communication Association journals: Computational analysis. *The International Communication Gazette*, *0*(0), 1–13. doi:10.1177/1748048520928334

Törnberg, P., & Törnberg, A. (2018). The limits of computation: A philosophical critique of contemporary Big Data research. *Big Data & Society*, *5*(2). doi:10.1177/2053951718811843

van Atteveldt, W., Margolin, D., Shen, C., Trilling, D., & Weber, R. (2019). A Roadmap for Computational Communication Research. *Computer Communication Review*, *1*(1), 1–11. doi:10.5117/CCR2019.1.001.VANA van Atteveldt, W., & Peng, T.-Q. (2018). When Communication Meets Computation: Opportunities, Challenges, and Pitfalls in Computational Communication Science. *Communication Methods and Measures*, *12*(2–3), 81–92. doi:10.1080/19312458.2018.1458084

van der Hulst, R. C. (2009). Introduction to Social Network Analysis (SNA) as an investigative tool. *Trends in Organized Crime*, *12*(2), 101–121. doi:10.100712117-008-9057-6

Wasserman, S., & Faust, K. (1994). *Social Network Analysis: Methods and Applications*. Cambridge University Press. doi:10.1017/CBO9780511815478

Weaver, W. (1948). Science and complexity. *American Scientist*, *36*(4), 536–544. PMID:18882675

Windsor, L. C. (2020). Advancing Interdisciplinary Work in Computational Communication Science. *Political Communication*, 1–10. doi:10.1080/10584609.2020.1765915

ADDITIONAL READING

Kim, J., & Ng, Y. M. M. (2021, May 12). Teaching Computational Social Science for All. doi:10.31235/osf.io/pf7n6osf.io/pf7n6

KEY TERMS AND DEFINITIONS

Analytical Approach: A research method uses an appropriate process to break a problem down into the elements necessary to solve it.

Big Data: It refers to datasets that are large, complex, and more than main memory, internal and external disk that it is difficult or impossible to process using traditional methods.

Computation: It is the repeated transmission of information through space (communication) and time (storage), guided by an algorithmic procedure.

Computational Social Science: An interdisciplinary field in which computational tools and techniques are applied to advance social science research.

Data: It is a unit of information that describes a single quality or quantity of an object or phenomenon.

Empirical Approach: It is a research method based on observation and measurement of phenomena, as directly experienced by the researcher.

Theoretical Approach: A set of statements or principles devised to explain a group of facts or phenomena can be used to make predictions.

Chapter 2
Incorporating Computational Social Science in Political Science

Başak Taraktaş
https://orcid.org/0000-0001-5479-4801
Boğaziçi University, Turkey

ABSTRACT

This chapter discusses the challenges and opportunities of incorporating computational social science (CSS) into political science. Using an original dataset of quantitative methods courses offered at the top-40 schools, this study shows that CSS courses are currently underrepresented, but their number is likely to augment because of the competition among schools. Yet, this trend is likely to stay confined to North American and Western European schools. Also, collaboration in CSS requires reconciling research priorities in engineering and physics (prediction) and in political science (explanation). Regarding research, big data does not mitigate concerns about causation and representativeness. But simulations allow studying rare phenomena and phenomena for which experiments are not appropriate. By running thousands of experiments at various combinations of explanatory variables, simulations explore counterfactuals, assess the explanatory power of competing theories, and make forecasts.

DOI: 10.4018/978-1-7998-8553-5.ch002

INTRODUCTION

This chapter discusses the challenges and opportunities of incorporating computational social science (CSS) into the study of political phenomena. The application of computational techniques on big data has revolutionized biology and physics; but, such progress has been of limited scope in social sciences (Lazer et al., 2009). One reason is CSS was initially reserved for physicists and computer scientists or those who, following a major in physics, engineering, or mathematics, have converted into social sciences. The rise of born-and-raised social scientists with specialization in CSS is a fairly recent phenomenon (Salganik 2018). By implication, most published works in CSS are penned by physicists and computer scientists, or by a collaborative team of physicists and computer scientists, which include social scientists. Against this backdrop, teaching and conducting research in CSS present various challenges, which this study groups into three categories: training, collaboration, and research.

It will be argued that CSS presents significant opportunities to advance political science research. However, learning methods and coding posit a steep learning curve, which may deter many enthusiasts unless departments incorporate into their curricula compulsory coding and advanced methods classes to lay the foundation necessary for students to learn these skills. Without such a foundation, political scientists are likely to remain underrepresented in CSS. Currently, still, a handful of institutions offer CSS courses. Many CSS enthusiasts, who are unaffiliated with these institutions, have to learn computational techniques on their own either by following online courses or taking courses from other departments. An implication of this caveat manifests itself in multidisciplinary collaboration. Since successful multidisciplinary collaboration requires bridging principles of different disciplines and establishing a common language. Political scientists must have a certain familiarity with how computational techniques work for fruitful collaboration, which, in turn, necessitates methodological investments. Provided that such investment is made, there are significant benefits from each discipline bringing their expertise onto the table. Regarding research, big data can advance our knowledge of political phenomena if scholars adopt robust research designs and combine big datasets, which are not necessarily representative of the population, with traditional research methods, such as surveys (Salganik, 2018). Finally, while many associate CSS with the use of big data, simulation studies present significant opportunities to study rare historical social phenomena (e.g., revolutions) or phenomena, which cannot be studied using experiments.

TRAINING

Back in the early-2010s, when I was a graduate student at UPenn eager to learn network analysis and coding, no social science department offered such courses. I had to go audit courses at the engineering departments and follow various training to acquire necessary skills. When I entered the job market around 2016, the number of CSS jobs did not surpass two or three. By 2021, the number of courses and job opportunities has increased. However, this increase is clustered in North American and European universities.

I investigated the number and kind of quantitative methods courses that are offered in political science departments of the top 40 American and European universities according to Times' Higher Education (World University Rankings, 2021). I examined the graduate curricula in 2021 and coded the number of courses on introductory and advanced statistics, game theory, network analysis, agent-based modeling, and data science (e.g., big data, machine learning). The findings are represented in Figures 1 and 2.

Figure 1.

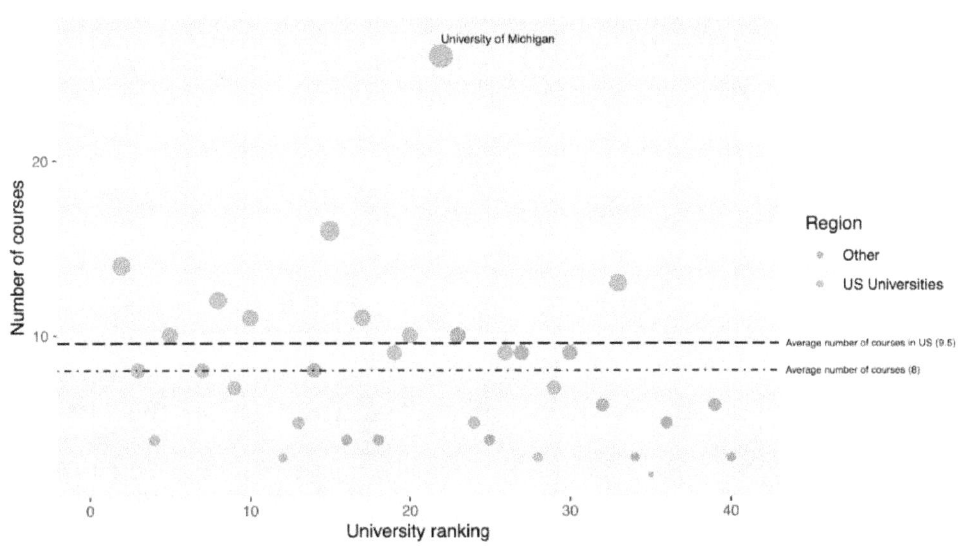

According to Figure, the average number of quantitative methods courses in the top-40 institutions is 8, which is below the average in American universities. This finding points to a striking gap between American and non-American universities. The former is keener on offering thorough methodological training to their students. The University of Michigan appears as an outlier, having 26 different quantitative courses in statistics alone. Another striking pattern is that schools within top-20 have more methods courses than those in top-30 and 40, which suggests that competition among schools incentivizes top schools to incorporate more methods courses into their curricula.

Next, I inquired into the breakdown of methods courses by methodological area, which Figure 2 below summarizes. According to the data, the schools in the top 40 introductory statistics mostly offer introductory statistics classes. Yet, the number of advanced statistics courses is fewer. Fewer still are the numbers of courses in data science and game theory —the median being 1. On the other hand, the top-40 schools do not necessarily have courses on agent-based modeling, network analysis, and coding except a few outliers. Hence, CSS courses are underrepresented even at top-40 schools. Moreover, the few courses that are offered concern data science, whereas network analysis and agent-based modeling conspicuously lag. In other words, there is an uneven development across areas of CSS. It is worth noting that the situation is worse in schools with a lower ranking, many of which are in the Global South. The underrepresentation of CSS courses in curricula presents a distinct challenge for CSS instructors or would-be computational social scientists who are working to find courses in these institutions.

Figure 2.

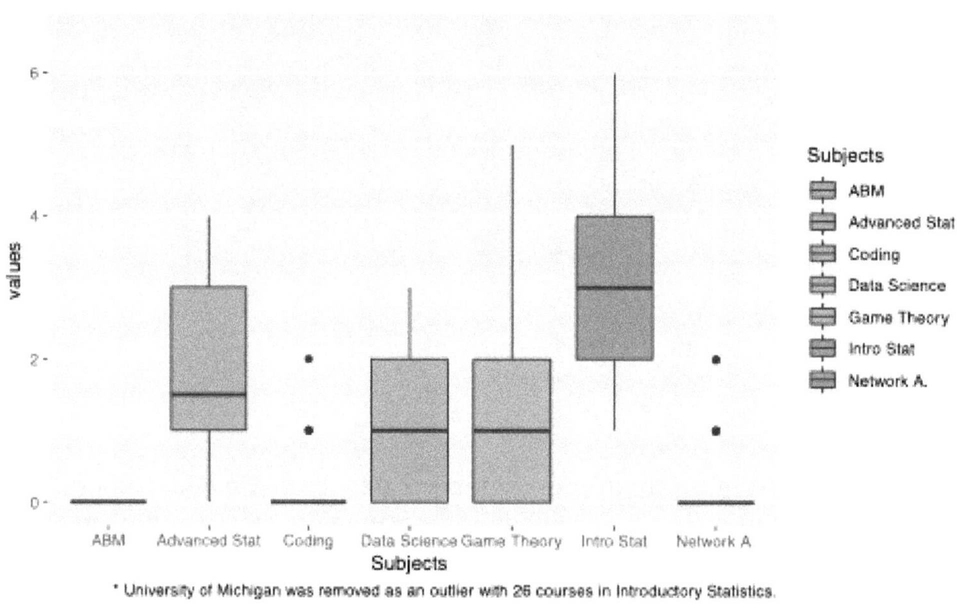

Due to the limited number of quantitative methods and coding classes in curricula, students interested in specializing in CSS are underequipped and are daunted by the steep learning curve that comes with having to learn both coding and methods. Taking courses from engineering or economics departments is an option. But many feel discouraged by having to compete with undergraduates who are natives of these fields and the eventuality of receiving a subpar grade by the end of the term. One solution is to introduce compulsory coding and methods courses to curricula. Yet, this solution is impractical if departments lack the faculty to teach these courses or have only a few. In the latter scenario, the few faculty to teach these courses have way more students than they can realistically handle. Therefore, in the short run, CSS enthusiasts are left with the following classes from other departments or online CSS courses.

Online courses seem a feasible option considering that platforms, such as Coursera or the Datacamp, offer good-quality training. The Coursera and Datacamp offer specialization tracks, which bundle must-have courses in the field of interest. The Datacamp requires membership, which, comes at a steep cost to those in Global South who do not make a living in USD. On the Coursera, audits are free, while certification and specialization tracks require a fee, which can be waived for a limited number of cases. Against this backdrop, if one cannot get financial assistance, auditing classes for free seems to be the best option. Yet, auditing is partially effective, since it does not involve any hands-on application or project assignments, which, however, is the most challenging part of CSS. Auditing large online courses can prove beneficial if one is disciplined and dedicated enough (Barak et al., 2016). However, research shows that a common problem in online teaching is the rapidly decreasing motivation (Jordan, 2014; Kauffman, 2015). Therefore, a classroom setting still is the best way to go about learning, whether it is an online course or a course at an institution offering a graduate degree.

A related alternative is methods or coding tutorials on the Internet. These tutorials are of limited help unless readers complement them with readings on methodological principles. Readers should bear in mind that tutorials on methods are introductory, and sample codes assist those with poorer coding skills, but one must still know the method. A short read on, say, decision trees, is not enough to run decision tree models. To obtain meaningful results, one must make sure that the method and the dataset are adequate to answer the research question. Moreover, because one is expected to justify the model selection and compare among performances of different models, one must know alternative machine learning techniques as well, such as random forests or support vector machines. Selecting and evaluating models, therefore, require knowing more than one model. To adequately complete these readings, one also needs a solid statistical background. Otherwise, one risks running poor-quality analyses using a method, whose surface one barely scratches and drawing spurious and/or misleading inferences. In effect, anyone who has some familiarity with modeling knows that methods produce results, but results are not necessarily meaningful (King, 1986). One must have a solid theory to test and know how the modeling technique works so that one does not attempt to model, say, a categorical response variable with linear regression instead of logistic regression. CSS enthusiasts must also be watchful about code templates found on the Internet. While some provide useful guidance, one must still make sure that the dataset that one is using is cleaned and lends itself to be studied with that code template. Also, one must make sure that the template contains a section on robustness checks. In short, there is no free lunch in CSS.

From an institutional perspective, a short-term solution to the paucity of quantitative methods courses in curricula is to ask faculty from engineering departments to offer compulsory courses on coding or data analysis. This strategy can prove effective if the needs of the department are properly communicated to the engineering faculty and political science students. Political science majors must understand the benefits of learning, say, coding from another department's faculty to their professional development, while the engineering faculty must be informed that they do not need to get as technical they would have with engineering students and instead provide simpler explanations about coding or mathematics.

In the medium run, the number of CSS courses offered at the top-40 schools is likely to incline as a result of the competitiveness among American and European research universities and the proliferation of grants by the NSF, the Russell Sage Foundation, and the European Commission, among others, offered to CSS research. While competition is likely to drive up the number of CSS jobs and courses in Western Europe and North American schools, other universities are likely to lag. One can surmise that unevenness will deepen the existing inequality in scientific production between North American and Western European universities and others, but this discussion is beyond the scope of this paper.

COLLABORATION

Multidisciplinary collaboration is exciting but also challenging in various respects. One major problem is to establish a common language between disciplines, which have different understandings as to what constitutes an interesting research question and argument. Engineers and physicists seek to find generalizable laws and make accurate predictions (Creager et al., 2007). In contrast, social scientists are primarily interested in explaining phenomena (Goertz & Mahoney, 2012; Mahoney, 2010), knowing under what conditions some phenomenon has come about, and what processes have played a part to draw lessons for similar phenomena. Also, it is hard to find generalizable laws in social sciences due to historicity, contextual contingencies, and intricacies of individuals' decision-making.

That said, some branches of political science are more likely to collaborate with physicists and engineers than others. Data-oriented studies in political science focus on effects of causes and examine large cases, whereas process-oriented studies, which seek to explain causes of effects on smaller samples considering contextual and historical contingencies, conduct single case studies or paired comparisons (Brady & Collier, 2010; Goertz & Mahoney, 2012). Given their interest in examining the effects of causes on large datasets, data-oriented scholars are better suited to collaborate with physicists and engineers; in effect, examples of such collaboration are many (Caldarelli et al., 2014; Crosas et al., 2015; Grimmer & King, 2011). Within process-oriented studies, those that follow a realist ontology—arguing that the world exists independently of our perceptions, theories, and ideas (Sil & Katzenstein, 2010)— may work with physicists and engineers. In contrast, those who follow a constructivist ontology—arguing that there is no such thing as scientific objectivity because reality is socially constructed and is not independent of our perceptions, theories, and ideas— are highly unlikely, since this premise contradicts the objectivity assumption in physics and engineering. Thus, the boundaries of interdisciplinary collaboration are drawn with respect to the compatibility of research paradigms.

Since the prevalence of big data and computational techniques, CSS research has proven effective in forecasting collective behavior and estimating the opinion of large groups of people (Cacciatore, 2021; González-Bailón & Paltoglou, 2015; W. Mason et al., 2014). However, some works are highly descriptive and offer little insight into the underlying mechanisms (Burscher et al., 2016; Ceron et al., 2015), which leaves unsatisfied social scientists, who are keen on mechanistic explanations (Goertz & Mahoney, 2012; Hedström & Ylikoski, 2010). The latter would rather be interested in learning about the implications of findings on the major questions of the field, such as (Justwan et al., 2018) study, which discusses satisfaction with democracy in relation to the finding that republicans and democrats lived in echo chambers before the 2016 presidential elections. This, however, might be less interesting to physicists or engineers. Therefore, forming consensus on what constitutes a meaningful research question, and a robust argument may be harder than presumed.

Another difficulty lies in developing a robust research design. Researchers from each discipline must be somewhat familiar with the techniques and approaches of the other field(s). Political scientists cannot simply expect engineers or physicists to collect and analyze data and present results for them to interpret. Similarly, engineers and physicists cannot unconcern themselves with social theory. In a fruitful collaboration, parties together must decide on an adequate model considering inherent properties of the subject matter (e.g., a multiparty electoral system is different than a majoritarian one and cannot be modeled in the same way) and develop relevant indicators and measurement scales. This can be challenging in two ways. First, it requires investment in the other field(s). Second, the subject matter must be well-conceptualized before being mapped on to some indicator. Although this challenge is not unique to interdisciplinary research, it becomes an even more important problem in CSS, because the availability of big data may trick researchers into thinking that traditional methodological principles are in desuetude. For instance, Kitts and Quintane criticize some social media studies, which run network models on digital data without properly conceptualizing what null ties signify (Kitts & Quintane, 2021). Their critique goes as follows: students of social media often conceptualize digital contact list —e.g., friendship on Facebook— as social ties and take certain transmissions —e.g., sending pictures or messages to a selected subset of friends— as indicators of the strength of the relationship —e.g., the strength of friendship. Yet, one could draw spurious inferences, because non-realized ties may embody both the lack of closeness among Facebook connections as well as closeness (Kitts & Quintane, 2021). For instance, one may not be messaging a close friend on Facebook, because one is texting or using or Whatsapp. But, one may also not be messaging some friend connection on Facebook because one considers the latter as an acquaintance.

This problem is not unique to the study of digital data with network analysis. In simulation studies, a critical step is to map concepts in sociopolitical life onto model features. Suppose we want to model the spread of misinformation using a susceptible-infected-recovered (SIR) model. Certain processes are similar: information spreads through contact; the more frequent the contact, the faster the diffusion; and racial or religious biases may inhibit transmission during contact as immunity does. On the other hand, in the case of infectious diseases, one receives a certain amount of viral load and becomes infected once one's system is overwhelmed. This threshold depends on one's genes, health, nutrition, among other things (Unckless et al., 2015). One could question whether believing in some piece of information is subject to a certain threshold the way infection is. Even if we were to answer affirmatively to the latter question, we would still need to specify what threshold consists of. Theoretically, the threshold varies by various factors, including the charisma and/or persuasiveness of the interlocutor (Appel & Richter, 2007), whether the information is delivered by a trustworthy someone (López & Sicilia, 2014; Wolf et al., 2012), the gullibility of the receiver of the information (Forgas & Baumeister, 2019), the wording of the piece of information (Greenhill et al., 2014; Thorson, 2016), the mental state of the receiver (Hughes et al., 2011; Rosnay et al., 2004), when information is delivered (R. J. Mason et al., 2020; Stalnaker, 2009), as well as prior beliefs of the receiver (Koehler, 1993; Morris, 1995). Researchers should be very specific in defining these parameters. In this process, scholars inescapably make strong assumptions as to the nature of information spread as in individuals believe some information if they are sufficiently exposed to it, or they believe some information but only repeat it after some systematic and sustained exposure to it by different sources (Garrett, 2009). In either case, one makes premises as to the putative equivalence between information spread and the diffusion of infectious diseases, which demand theoretical and empirical validation. As discussed earlier, this validation process requires social scientists to learn about the spread of infectious diseases, and the engineers, epidemiologists, and physicists to learn about processes of information procession and dissemination.

RESEARCH

Many associate CSS with data science. However, as King puts it, “big data by itself is not revolutionary” (King, 2017). In effect, the use of big data does not alleviate methodological concerns in political science. The less well-known aspect of CSS, simulation techniques, on the other hand, have the potential to make substantive contributions. This section discusses the challenges and opportunities that CSS brings up in relation to the broader methodological debates in the field.

Since the rise of behavioralism in the 1930s, political scientists have been preoccupied with how to establish causality and have sought ways to improve their methodologies. Influenced by the behavioralist idea that social phenomena can be studied in the same way as natural phenomena, political scientists developed an interest in explaining social phenomena using hypothesis testing (Bond, 2007). Accordingly, developing accurate measurements of political phenomena to make predictions and generate nomothetical (generalizable) explanations became primary concerns. Within this context, statistical techniques gained popularity as they allowed testing hypotheses, estimating uncertainties, and making predictions. In the 1990s, King, Keohane, and Verba, advanced a set of controversial claims, which rekindled methodological debates and divided political scientists. The latter argued that the study of political phenomena must follow the principles of statistical analysis to be more systematic and falsifiable, emphasizing, in particular, the unit homogeneity assumption, not selecting on the dependent variable, and developing generalizable theories (King et al., 1994).

This position has come under attack by qualitative researchers. One group of scholars stressed that social phenomena are shaped and constrained by history and context; therefore, findings can at best be of limited generalizability (Goertz & Mahoney, 2012; Pierson, 2004). From this perspective, it is not possible to develop an overarching theory of, say, a democratization process that explains experiences of Western, Latin American, and Asian societies at the same, because of the idiosyncrasy of historical and contextual conditions and the diversity of actors and resource availability across cases (Bunce, 2000). In addition, because time and space have causal effects on political phenomena, the unit homogeneity assumption, which underlies regression techniques, is untenable in many cases. For instance, although the United States, France, Austria, and Sweden are all cases of industrialized democracies that have been practicing collective bargaining, we cannot just assume that the Swedish, Austrian, French, and American institutions are comparable (apples to apples). In reality, conflicts around collective bargaining bear different meanings in these contexts and yield different outcomes, which makes these cases incomparable (apples to oranges) (Locke & Thelen, 1995). This school further retaliated by contending that large-N studies capture association instead of causation and emphasized the necessity to study processes and causal mechanisms (Falleti & Lynch, 2009; Hedström & Ylikoski, 2010). The qualitative scholars who espoused the constructivist ontology posed an even sharper critique targeting the very premise of objectivity in science. Objectivity does not exist, the latter argued, because the truth is socially constructed (Turco & Zuckerman, 2017). Scientists being embedded in their environments, their theories are value-laden, which have their roots in experiences, ideas, and beliefs. By the 2000s, mainstream political science had turned towards middle-range theories. Most social scientists have embraced multi-method research to complement the shortcomings of one method with the strengths of another (Goertz & Mahoney, 2012; Mahoney, 2010; Sil & Katzenstein, 2010).

Now, with the availability of big data, the old ambition of developing nomothetic explanations seems to have rekindled. Although many associate big data with large samples, big data is not necessarily representative of the population (Salganik, 2018). To give an example from social media studies, where big data research has thrived, several researchers have examined polarization using Twitter data (Conover et al., 2011; Gruzd & Roy, 2014; Hong & Kim, 2016). Yet, because these datasets predominantly feature users from Western societies, findings do not generalize to other contexts. For one, Twitter use is geographically patterned; 39% of Twitter connections lie in metropolitan regions (Takhteyev et al., 2012). Similarly, Internet use is higher in states, where the economy has higher levels of privatization and competition in the telecommunications sector (Guillen & Suarez, 2005). Moreover, even though social media connects users from various parts of the world, domestic political institutions remain the decisive factor that shapes polarization dynamics in societies (Urman, 2020). For states, where social media use is modest, classical survey design techniques might still yield more accurate results on polarization. Thus, because big data is not necessarily representative of the population, despite the availability of millions of observations, the major problems of the field, namely, causality and the scope of generalizability, do not go away.

In effect, the study of big data may leave partially satisfied those who are interested in explaining social phenomena, if big data research does not go beyond description and prediction. In this respect, one solution Salganik offers is to combine computational techniques—e.g., machine learning, topic modeling, or sentiment analysis— with existing methods —e.g., survey experiments or interviews for the latter are well-suited to answer "why" questions (Salganik, 2018). A perfect example is the (Burke & Kraut, 2016) study, where scholars combine survey techniques and Facebook logs (Salganik, 2018). Thus, once more, multi-method research alleviates methodological concerns. Another obvious requirement is a solid theoretical background to guide the research since the analysis of big data requires informed theoretical lenses to develop meaningful indicators and measurements and contextual knowledge to interpret findings —otherwise, one might derive spurious and sometimes contradictory inferences (Julious & Mullee, 1994; Wagner, 1982).

In the remainder of this section, I elaborate on another (somewhat less acclaimed) dimension of CSS, simulation techniques—e.g., agent-based modeling (ABMs) or network simulations, and discuss the five distinct aspects of simulations, which can substantively alleviate certain methodological concerns and advance our knowledge in the field.

First, simulations are appropriate for studying phenomena, for which experiments (i.e., natural or quasi-experiments) are ill-suited —e.g., civil war, and/or those that have rare occurrences in real life —e.g., revolutions (Gilbert, 1993). Both discrete and sequential political phenomena can be modeled using simulations—an example of discrete phenomenon would be revolutions (Moro, 2016), while an example of sequential phenomenon would be new product development and innovation (Garcia, 2005). The modeling process resembles that in statistics or game theory; it begins with an abstraction of the phenomenon or behavior to simulate (Gilbert, 1993). As in game theory, the challenge is to have a robust theory of how some phenomenon or behavior occurs. Without a thorough understanding of the explananda, the model becomes a simplified and bastardized version of the reality and risks yielding spurious results (Gilbert, 1993). To revisit the example of information spread, one can only develop a susceptible-infected-recovered (SIR) model of information spread if one can establish an equivalence between the way individuals process and repeat some information and the way metabolism interacts with viruses. Otherwise, the model would be meaningless.

Another strength of simulations is their ability to test multiple (even competing) theories. Going back to the example of information spread à la SIR, one can start with the simple scenario that some individual passes on some information to another, who, upon processing it, decides whether to repeat it to another person. Next, one can entertain the more complex scenario, in which that individuals are more likely to believe the information coming from a trustworthy someone. By adding the trustworthiness parameter to the model, one tests the hypothesis that the trustworthiness of the deliverer of the information matters. One can randomly assign some trustworthiness score to individuals at the onset of the model to ensure unbiasedness—a nonrandom distribution of this parameter is also possible provided there are theoretical and empirical justifications. One can additionally test the claim that individuals are more likely to believe information if it comes from someone in their social network by adding a network into the model. One can modify the structure of the network to explore the hypothesis that network structure affects information spread. Overall, just like in an experimental setting, one can run simulations for the baseline case, and compare them to simulations of more complicated scenarios. This presents a significant advantage over observational studies, in which respondents are not randomly assigned to groups, and over experiments with random assignments, whose caveat is the small sample size (Morton & Williams, 2008).

In addition, simulation studies run thousands or millions of experiments by varying parameters of interest within a theoretically validated range. For instance, one can explore how the level of compliance with lockdown measures in society affects infection rate by varying the level of compliance among low, medium, or high —which corresponds to a particular value range— and draw inferences by examining counterfactuals (Braun et al., 2020). The ability to analyze counterfactuals comes particularly handy for the study of rare events, such as revolutions, for which there do not necessarily exist a sufficient number of observations for all combinations of parameters —e.g., low, medium, and high levels of resources available to rebel organizations and low, medium, and high levels of state capacity. Notice that when studying rare events, qualitative scholars tend to make certain assumptions about the necessity and sufficiency of the factors of interest to draw inferences, e.g., necessary and sufficient, not necessary but sufficient, or INUS (an insufficient but non-redundant component of a combination of conditions that is unnecessary but sufficient for an outcome) (Mahoney & Barrenechea, 2019). Some of these assumptions (e.g., necessary and sufficient) generate very strong claims, which are hard to validate especially if the outcome variable is a historical case. Simulations explore counterfactuals by exploring a wide parameter space and avoid making strong assumptions. Moreover, experiments generate large datasets of outputs, which lend themselves to statistical analysis (Wilensky & Rand, 2015). Thereby, simulations alleviate concerns about causality by exploring counterfactuals and generating large samples of outputs.

Another strength of simulation studies is their predictive power. When models include theoretically informed variables, simulations enable doing forecasts. For instance, (Lustick et al., 2004) test competing theories of secessionism across several experiments and pinpoint the most likely scenarios, whereby their results allow establishing which theories have superior predictive power. In a simpler model, Schelling explores the conditions under which neighborhood segregation happens and advances the astonishing finding that people need not be racist for neighborhoods to become segregated; even weak preferences for the alike suffice to produce segregation (Schelling, 1971). Alternatively, scholars may feed empirical data into a more complex model, which is a closer representation of the reality, to do real-life forecasting (Lustick, 2010). Whether one goes with a simpler or more complex model has to do with one's methodological ambitions. Abstract models produce more generalizable findings that do not necessarily incarnate a particular political system or society, whereas more complex models produce more specific results but have poorer external validity. Either way, simulations offer significant opportunities to do forecasting and testing the predictive power of competing theories.

Yet, what I consider to be the biggest strength of ABMs is the ability to explain macro-level outcomes from microlevel actions (Conte & Gilbert, 1995). In ABMs, each agent behaves according to a simple set of rules (e.g., whether to stay in the current neighborhood or move to another if the number of those alike descends beyond some preferred level (Schelling, 1971)). When all agents interact and make decisions at the same time, local interactions produce very complex outcomes, which we would not be able to predict even if we had perfect knowledge and understanding of the phenomenon of interest (Darley, 1994). This is an intrinsic property of complex adaptive systems. Complex adaptive systems are complex in that the whole depends on its components and components affect the whole but the behavior of the system cannot be predicted just by looking at the behavior of its components. Such systems are adaptive because components adjust themselves with respect to each other's behavior and changes in the environment, whereby order spontaneously emerges (aka self-organization) (Miller & Page, 2007). In Schelling's study of neighborhood segregation, for instance, agents stay in the current neighborhood if there are a sufficient number of residents like them and move otherwise, provides, since one additional occupant is sufficient to alter the neighborhood composition. Changes in the neighborhood composition drive out those who are underrepresented, while the latter's migration, in turn, changes the composition of the destination neighborhood. Hence, agents choose between two alternatives, but their interactions generate neighborhood segregation patterns, which cannot be predicted by the behavior of single agents (Schelling, 1971). ABMs are very appropriate for studying social phenomena, which are inherently complex and adaptive. Take the case of small protests that suddenly shift to large-scale events, e.g., the 2013 Gezi Protests (Taraktaş & Över, 2017). Protests often start within a small group of militants. Yet, seeing the protesting crowd enlarge, bystanders become increasingly likely to join in the crowd despite initial reluctance to protest. What is complex in this process is that the marginal effect of each additional protester is not linear; once a critical mass forms, everyone joins in (Aytaç & Stokes, 2018; Kuran, 1991). ABMs are well-suited to capture such complexity (Elkink, 2011; Hu et al., 2015).

CONCLUSION

This study has discussed the opportunities and challenges of incorporating CSS into political science research. I stressed that CSS has a steep learning cost, which may deter many enthusiasts at the training level. However, these costs can be alleviated if departments include more methods classes into their curricula. One significant finding was that the current number of CSS courses in curricula is insufficient —though it has improved over the last decade, the competition among the top schools is likely to drive this number up. However, this trend applies to the top 40 schools; institutions of the Global South are likely to lag in this race. At the collaboration level, the most significant challenge of CSS research is to reach an agreement on what constitutes an interesting research question and a robust research design due to the misalignment in the ontological and epistemological positions of different fields. Therefore, theorizing and developing appropriate indicators and measurement scales may become even more challenging than in non-interdisciplinary works. Interdisciplinary works can be successful if all parties educate themselves about methods and theories of the other field(s).

At the research level, I argued that big data is not the panacea for longstanding methodological concerns in the field, specifically, causation and the scope of generalizability. The major caveat is that, despite offering millions of observations, big data is not necessarily representative of the population. Therefore, combining big data with traditional techniques or designing the study in a way to alleviate concerns about representativeness is necessary to draw meaningful inferences. On the other hand, simulation techniques —agent-based models, in particular— can make significant contributions to the field. First and foremost, simulations are appropriate for studying rarely occurring phenomena, such as revolutions, and those for which experimentation is impossible, e.g., civil wars. For such phenomena, an additional difficulty is to establish counterfactuals. Simulations address both issues. By varying parameters within the desired value range, they explore all possible outcomes within a vast parameter space. They thus analyze various counterfactuals for which there may not be a sufficient number of observations in real life. In so doing, they also run thousands of experiments. The resulting large samples enable researchers to apply statistical analysis and make predictions.

ACKNOWLEDGMENT

I would like to thank Egemen Buyukkaya for his invaluable assistance to this research.

This research was supported by the Marie Skłodowska-Curie Fellowship H2020-MSCA-IF-2020 (grant number: 101028566).

REFERENCES

Appel, M., & Richter, T. (2007). Persuasive Effects of Fictional Narratives Increase Over Time. *Media Psychology*, *10*(1), 113–134. doi:10.1080/15213260701301194

Aytaç, S. E., & Stokes, S. C. (2018). *Why Bother? Rethinking Participation in Elections and Protests* (1st ed.). Cambridge University Press. doi:10.1017/9781108690416

Barak, M., Watted, A., & Haick, H. (2016). Motivation to learn in massive open online courses: Examining aspects of language and social engagement. *Computers & Education*, *94*, 49–60. doi:10.1016/j.compedu.2015.11.010

Bond, J. R. (2007). The Scientification of the Study of Politics: Some Observations on the Behavioral Evolution in Political Science. *The Journal of Politics*, *69*(4), 897–907. doi:10.1111/j.1468-2508.2007.00597.x

Brady, H., & Collier, D. (2010). *Rethinking Social Inquiry: Diverse Tools, Shared Standards* (2nd ed.). Rowman & Littlefield Publishers.

Braun, B., Taraktaş, B., Beckage, B., & Molofsky, J. (2020). Simulating phase transitions and control measures for network epidemics caused by infections with presymptomatic, asymptomatic, and symptomatic stages. *PLoS One*, *15*(9), e0238412. doi:10.1371/journal.pone.0238412 PMID:32911518

Bunce, V. (2000). Comparative Democratization Big and Bounded Generalizations. *Comparative Political Studies*, *33*(6–7), 703–734. doi:10.1177/001041400003300602

Burke, M., & Kraut, R. E. (2016). The Relationship Between Facebook Use and Well-Being Depends on Communication Type and Tie Strength: Facebook and well-being. *Journal of Computer-Mediated Communication*, *21*(4), 265–281. doi:10.1111/jcc4.12162

Burscher, B., Vliegenthart, R., & de Vreese, C. H. (2016). Frames Beyond Words: Applying Cluster and Sentiment Analysis to News Coverage of the Nuclear Power Issue. *Social Science Computer Review*, *34*(5), 530–545. doi:10.1177/0894439315596385

Cacciatore, M. A. (2021). Misinformation and public opinion of science and health: Approaches, findings, and future directions. *Proceedings of the National Academy of Sciences of the United States of America*, *118*(15), e1912437117. doi:10.1073/pnas.1912437117 PMID:33837143

Caldarelli, G., Chessa, A., Pammolli, F., Pompa, G., Puliga, M., Riccaboni, M., & Riotta, G. (2014). A Multi-Level Geographical Study of Italian Political Elections from Twitter Data. *PLoS One*, *9*(5), e95809. doi:10.1371/journal.pone.0095809 PMID:24802857

Ceron, A., Curini, L., & Iacus, S. M. (2015). Using Sentiment Analysis to Monitor Electoral Campaigns: Method Matters—Evidence From the United States and Italy. *Social Science Computer Review*, *33*(1), 3–20. doi:10.1177/0894439314521983

Conover, M. D., Ratkiewicz, J., Francisco, M., Goncalves, B., Flammini, A., & Menczer, F. (2011). Political Polarization on Twitter. *Proceedings of the Fifth International AAAI Conference on Weblogs and Social Media.*

Conte, R., & Gilbert, N. (1995). *Artificial Societies.* Routledge. https://www.doabooks.org/doab?func=fulltext&rid=38833

Creager, A. N. H., Lunbeck, E., & Wise, M. N. (Eds.). (2007). *Science without laws: Model systems, cases, exemplary narratives*. Duke University Press. doi:10.1215/9780822390244

Crosas, M., King, G., Honaker, J., & Sweeney, L. (2015). Automating Open Science for Big Data. *The Annals of the American Academy of Political and Social Science*, *659*(1), 260–273. doi:10.1177/0002716215570847

Darley, V. (1994). Emergent phenomena and complexity. *Artificial Life*, 411–416.

Elkink, J. A. (2011). The International Diffusion of Democracy. *Comparative Political Studies*, *44*(12), 1651–1674. doi:10.1177/0010414011407474

Falleti, T. G., & Lynch, J. F. (2009). Context and Causal Mechanisms in Political Analysis. *Comparative Political Studies*, *42*(9), 1143–1166. doi:10.1177/0010414009331724

Forgas, J. P., & Baumeister, R. F. (2019). *The social psychology of gullibility: Fake news, conspiracy theories, and irrational beliefs*. Academic Press.

Garcia, R. (2005). Uses of Agent-Based Modeling in Innovation/New Product Development Research. *Journal of Product Innovation Management, 22*(5), 380–398. doi:10.1111/j.1540-5885.2005.00136.x

Garrett, R. K. (2009). Politically Motivated Reinforcement Seeking: Reframing the Selective Exposure Debate. *Journal of Communication, 59*(4), 676–699. doi:10.1111/j.1460-2466.2009.01452.x

Gilbert, N. (1993). Computer simulation of social processes. *Social Research Update*, 6.

Goertz, G., & Mahoney, J. (2012). *A tale of two cultures: Qualitative and quantitative research in the social sciences*. Princeton University Press. doi:10.23943/princeton/9780691149707.001.0001

González-Bailón, S., & Paltoglou, G. (2015). Signals of Public Opinion in Online Communication: A Comparison of Methods and Data Sources. *The Annals of the American Academy of Political and Social Science, 659*(1), 95–107. doi:10.1177/0002716215569192

Greenhill, M., Leviston, Z., Leonard, R., & Walker, I. (2014). Assessing climate change beliefs: Response effects of question wording and response alternatives. *Public Understanding of Science (Bristol, England), 23*(8), 947–965. doi:10.1177/0963662513480117 PMID:23825288

Grimmer, J., & King, G. (2011). General purpose computer-assisted clustering and conceptualization. *Proceedings of the National Academy of Sciences of the United States of America, 108*(7), 2643–2650. doi:10.1073/pnas.1018067108 PMID:21292983

Gruzd, A., & Roy, J. (2014). Investigating Political Polarization on Twitter: A Canadian Perspective: Investigating Political Polarization on Twitter. *Policy and Internet, 6*(1), 28–45. doi:10.1002/1944-2866.POI354

Guillen, M. F., & Suarez, S. L. (2005). Explaining the Global Digital Divide: Economic, Political and Sociological Drivers of Cross-National Internet Use. *Social Forces, 84*(2), 681–708. doi:10.1353of.2006.0015

Hedström, P., & Ylikoski, P. (2010). Causal Mechanisms in the Social Sciences. *Annual Review of Sociology, 36*(1), 49–67. doi:10.1146/annurev.soc.012809.102632

Hong, S., & Kim, S. H. (2016). Political polarization on twitter: Implications for the use of social media in digital governments. *Government Information Quarterly*, *33*(4), 777–782. doi:10.1016/j.giq.2016.04.007

Hu, H., Lin, J., & Cui, W. (2015). Intervention Strategies and the Diffusion of Collective Behavior. *Journal of Artificial Societies and Social Simulation*, *18*(3), 16. doi:10.18564/jasss.2872

Hughes, C., Ensor, R., & Marks, A. (2011). Individual differences in false belief understanding are stable from 3 to 6 years of age and predict children's mental state talk with school friends. *Journal of Experimental Child Psychology*, *108*(1), 96–112. doi:10.1016/j.jecp.2010.07.012 PMID:20846667

Jordan, K. (2014). Initial trends in enrolment and completion of massive open online courses. *The International Review of Research in Open and Distributed Learning*, *15*(1). Advance online publication. doi:10.19173/irrodl.v15i1.1651

Julious, S. A., & Mullee, M. A. (1994). Confounding and Simpson's paradox. *BMJ (Clinical Research Ed.)*, *309*(6967), 1480–1481. doi:10.1136/bmj.309.6967.1480 PMID:7804052

Justwan, F., Baumgaertner, B., Carlisle, J. E., Clark, A. K., & Clark, M. (2018). Social media echo chambers and satisfaction with democracy among Democrats and Republicans in the aftermath of the 2016 US elections. *Journal of Elections, Public Opinion, and Parties*, *28*(4), 424–442. doi:10.1080/17457289.2018.1434784 PMID:31231432

Kauffman, H. (2015). A review of predictive factors of student success in and satisfaction with online learning. *Research in Learning Technology*, *23*. Advance online publication. doi:10.3402/rlt.v23.26507

King, G. (1986). How Not to Lie with Statistics: Avoiding Common Mistakes in Quantitative Political Science. *American Journal of Political Science*, *30*(3), 666. doi:10.2307/2111095

King, G. (2017, January 4). *Big Data is Not About the Data!* https://gking.harvard.edu/presentations/big-data-not-about-data-16

King, G., Keohane, R. O., & Verba, S. (1994). *Designing Social Inquiry: Scientific Inference in Qualitative Research*. Princeton University Press. doi:10.1515/9781400821211

Kitts, J. A., & Quintane, E. (2021). Rethinking Social Networks in the Era of Computational Social Science. In R. Light & J. Moody (Eds.), *The Oxford Handbook of Social Networks* (pp. 70–97). Oxford University Press. doi:10.1093/oxfordhb/9780190251765.013.24

Koehler, J. J. (1993). The Influence of Prior Beliefs on Scientific Judgments of Evidence Quality. *Organizational Behavior and Human Decision Processes*, *56*(1), 28–55. doi:10.1006/obhd.1993.1044

Kuran, T. (1991). Now Out of Never: The Element of Surprise in the East European Revolution of 1989. *World Politics*, *44*(1), 7–48. doi:10.2307/2010422

Lazer, D., Pentland, A., Adamic, L., Aral, S., Barabási, A.-L., Brewer, D., Christakis, N., Contractor, N., Fowler, J., Gutmann, M., Jabara, T., King, G., Macy, M., Roy, D., & Van Alstyne, M. (2009). Computational Social Science. *Science*, *323*(5915), 721–723. doi:10.1126cience.1167742 PMID:19197046

Locke, R. M., & Thelen, K. (1995). Apples and Oranges Revisited: Contextualized Comparisons and the Study of Comparative Labor Politics. *Politics & Society*, *23*(3), 337–367. doi:10.1177/0032329295023003004

López, M., & Sicilia, M. (2014). eWOM as Source of Influence: The Impact of Participation in eWOM and Perceived Source Trustworthiness on Decision Making. *Journal of Interactive Advertising*, *14*(2), 86–97. doi:10.1080/15252019.2014.944288

Lustick, I. S. (2010). Secession of the Center: A Virtual Probe of the Prospects for Punjabi Secessionism in Pakistan and the Secession of Punjabistan. *Journal of Artificial Societies and Social Simulation*, *14*(1), 7. doi:10.18564/jasss.1696

Lustick, I. S., Miodownik, D., & Eidelson, R. J. (2004). Secessionism in Multicultural States: Does Sharing Power Prevent or Encourage It? *American Political Science Review*, (2), 209–229. doi:10.1017/S0003055404001108

Mahoney, J. (2010). After KKV: The New Methodology of Qualitative Research. *World Politics*, *62*(1), 120–147. doi:10.1017/S0043887109990220

Mahoney, J., & Barrenechea, R. (2019). The logic of counterfactual analysis in case-study explanation. *The British Journal of Sociology*, *70*(1), 306–338. doi:10.1111/1468-4446.12340 PMID:29265335

Mason, R. J., Farrow, D., & Hattie, J. A. C. (2020). Sports Coaches' Knowledge and Beliefs About the Provision, Reception, and Evaluation of Verbal Feedback. *Frontiers in Psychology*, *11*, 571552. doi:10.3389/fpsyg.2020.571552 PMID:33041941

Mason, W., Vaughan, J. W., & Wallach, H. (2014). Computational social science and social computing. *Machine Learning*, *95*(3), 257–260. doi:10.100710994-013-5426-8

Miller, J. H., & Page, S. E. (2007). *Complex adaptive systems*. Princeton University Press.

Moro, A. (2016). Understanding the Dynamics of Violent Political Revolutions in an Agent-Based Framework. *PLoS One*, *11*(4), e0154175. doi:10.1371/journal.pone.0154175 PMID:27104855

Morris, S. (1995). The Common Prior Assumption in Economic Theory. *Economics and Philosophy*, *11*(02), 227–253. doi:10.1017/S0266267100003382

Morton, R. B., & Williams, K. C. (2008). Experimentation in Political Science. In J. Box-Steffensmeier, H. E. Brady, & D. Collier (Eds.), *The Oxford handbook of political methodology* (pp. 339–357). Oxford University Press.

Pierson, P. (2004). *Politics in Time: History, Institutions, and Social Analysis* (1st ed.). Princeton University Press. doi:10.1515/9781400841080

Rosnay, M., Pons, F., Harris, P. L., & Morrell, J. M. B. (2004). A lag between understanding false belief and emotion attribution in young children: Relationships with linguistic ability and mothers' mental-state language. *British Journal of Developmental Psychology*, *22*(2), 197–218. doi:10.1348/026151004323044573

Salganik, M. J. (2018). *Bit by bit: Social research in the digital age*. Princeton University Press.

Schelling, T. C. (1971). Dynamic models of segregation. *The Journal of Mathematical Sociology*, *1*(2), 143–186. doi:10.1080/0022250X.1971.9989794

Sil, R., & Katzenstein, P. J. (2010). *Beyond Paradigms: Analytic Eclecticism in the Study of World Politics (Political Analysis*. Palgrave Macmillan.
Stalnaker, R. (2009). Iterated Belief Revision. *Erkenntnis*, *70*(2), 189–209. doi:10.100710670-008-9147-5

Takhteyev, Y., Gruzd, A., & Wellman, B. (2012). Geography of Twitter networks. *Social Networks*, *34*(1), 73–81. doi:10.1016/j.socnet.2011.05.006

Taraktaş, B., & Över, D. (2017). When does repression trigger mass protest? The 2013 Gezi protests. *Research in Social Movements, Conflicts and Change*, *41*, 207-241.

Thorson, E. (2016). Belief Echoes: The Persistent Effects of Corrected Misinformation. *Political Communication*, *33*(3), 460–480. doi:10.1080/10584609.2015.1102187

Turco, C. J., & Zuckerman, E. W. (2017). Verstehen for Sociology: Comment on Watts. *American Journal of Sociology*, *122*(4), 1272–1291. doi:10.1086/690762

Unckless, R. L., Rottschaefer, S. M., & Lazzaro, B. P. (2015). The Complex Contributions of Genetics and Nutrition to Immunity in Drosophila melanogaster. *PLOS Genetics*, *11*(3), e1005030. doi:10.1371/journal.pgen.1005030 PMID:25764027

Urman, A. (2020). Context matters: Political polarization on Twitter from a comparative perspective. *Media Culture & Society*, *42*(6), 857–879. doi:10.1177/0163443719876541

Wagner, C. H. (1982). Simpson's Paradox in Real Life. *The American Statistician*, *36*(1), 46–48. doi:10.1080/00031305.1982.10482778

Wilensky, U., & Rand, W. (2015). *An introduction to agent-based modeling: Modeling natural, social, and engineered complex systems with NetLogo*. The MIT Press.

Wolf, A. G., Rieger, S., & Knauff, M. (2012). The effects of source trustworthiness and inference type on human belief revision. *Thinking & Reasoning*, *18*(4), 417–440. doi:10.1080/13546783.2012.677757

World University Rankings. (2021). World University Rankings 2021. *Times Higher Education*. Retrieved from https://www.timeshighereducation.com/world-university-rankings/2021/world-ranking#!/page/0/length/25/sort_by/rank/sort_order/asc/cols/stats

Chapter 3
Opinion Mining in Sociopolitical Research

Israel Barrutia Barreto
Innova Scientific, Peru

Renzo Antonio Seminario Córdova
https://orcid.org/0000-0001-6992-5990
Innova Scientific, Peru

Mirella Rosa Gavidia Canaquiri
National Amazonian University of Madre de Dios, Peru

Victor Raul Ruiz Nunura
Jorge Basadre Grohman Higher Technological Institute, Peru

ABSTRACT

The objective of this study was to explore the potential of the opinion mining methodology in sociopolitical research, its techniques, and applications from the field of reflexivity. It is a non-experimental and exploratory study. It concludes that advances in the field of artificial intelligence have provided the sociopolitical sciences with tools that make it possible to approach the dominant trends of opinion in society during specific junctures where decision-making and/or the positioning of an idea, public policy, or social project can be measured in real-time, with broad demographic scopes that can be segmented, bringing the researcher closer to the subject of study with minimum levels of bias. Opinion mining research continues to be dominated by electoral and marketing topics; however, there are potentialities in the research of public policies, social programs, democracy, and governance that are still waiting for the application of opinion mining as a sociopolitical research methodology.

DOI: 10.4018/978-1-7998-8553-5.ch003

INTRODUCTION

The foundations of sciences have experienced drastic transformations connected to advances in various disciplines. The rupture with the positivist traditional knowledge strengthened in the linearity and segmentation in the discovery process and knowledge accumulation was expressed in Kuhn's postulates (1962), who proposed a revolutionary approach within the epistemology, which affirmed that supposed scientific establish links interrelated among various areas of the same discipline that find common referents, enabling to advance in quantum leaps, where each research is mainstreamed for the progress of the rests. In this context, epistemologists distinguish three big paradigms flows: Positivist, Critical theory, and Constructivism. In the Social Sciences field, these three paradigms transit by the epistemic challenge of the relationship between the knowing subject and the object of study, in a set with the methodology that enables the opening of layers that cover the object essence.

Within the positivist paradigm, the dominant is the observation and the measure applying quantitative, empiric, and rational approaches based on the application of technological tools that enable the discovery of object essence. In consequence, positivism is based on the checking of the hypothesis applying statistical methods that validate the obtained results. This perspective was extensive until the sciences of the social, which only could acquire the category of "science" when used statistical methods to the quantification of social events. As a result, the social researcher was excluded from the observation of processes and the variables' manipulation that gave quantifiable results as a requirement to the cataloging of scientific knowledge of the obtained results. In this context, the social scientist should demonstrate the absolute principle of the knowledge created by a discovered, described, and analyzed dominant reality that potentially can be expressed in universal laws.

From the ontological perspective, positivism establishes a clear distinction between the researcher and the object as an unavoidable mechanism to reduce the bias, which in the social field constituted a weakness, due to limiting the development of qualitative research. Subsequently, the postpositivist current made flexible the concept of the "apprehension of reality" as a unique condition to generate scientific knowledge. Postpositivists indicated that the apprehension of reality by science is only partially feasible since the dynamism of processes and the observer's subjective role disturbs the variables involved and, therefore, the obtained results. During interactive processes the reality is perceptible by the observer, where subject-object are influenced by the counterpart, in consequence, the reflexive exercise of the researcher affects the perception of results, so the theoretical foundation and the exercise of the fallacy of hypothesis enables an approach to the reality that support mixed studies, always under the predominance of the quantity approach, under three modalities: (i) exploratory, (ii) descriptive and (iii) correlational. The first one includes the approach to the phenomenon, the second the characterization and the third establishes relationships among variables.

The critical theory paradigm is based on the materialist dialectic perspective, where theories are confronted in processes that express the society dynamic, deriving in the synthesized expression of postulates in confrontation. The critical theory searches for the recognition of the dialogical relationship subject-object in processes of research, where the researcher can potentially perform active roles exercising reflexivity and participating in processes that induce change in the environment. The method applied in this theory is based on the research-action structured in three stages: (i) observation, (ii) reflection, and (iii) action. The observation phase includes the thematic delimitation and the data collection. In the second stage, the researcher thinks and contrasts the theoretical and methodological background with the collected information, interpreting processes that will guide toward the construction of the results. The action phase includes the intervention of the researcher within the social process in the study, with the finality to reach significant changes.

The constructivist paradigm emerges under the idea that knowledge is constructed as a consequence of social interaction (Berger & Luckman, 2003). The fundamental contribution of this paradigm is the postulated that affirms the generation of meanings is the result of the cultural substratum; in consequence, the social reality is perceived as diverse, multidimensional, that enables the construction of news realities from the subject-object interaction. Furthermore, it applies the hermeneutic method and the based theories, to construct knowledge under the qualitative approach, considering that cultural constructs are expressed in signs whose polysemic meanings demand the constructions of meanings that express the subjectivity of contents created by social groups. Constructivism is the dominant paradigm in the virtual era since promotes collaborative work oriented to the knowledge construction derived of the symbolic interactionism from metaheuristic, holistic and inclusive perspectives (Nambisan, *et al.*, 2017), openly resorting and without complex to technological advances (ICT) and the Artificial Intelligence (AI) as methodologies and tools that enable unusual reach to fields of social research. (Dick, 2019; Hariri *et al.,* 2019).

In this new stage of the civilizing process, where virtual technologies mainstream to the societies complexing the discursive construction, the sociopolitical researcher faces the challenge of moving from the segmentation of the science toward the transdisciplinary performance that enables the collection of information and content interpretation that flows into the network spaces (Martínez *et al.*, 2019; Meneses, 2018). From the hypercomplex approach, the constructivism finds in AI applications, tools of speeches' deconstruction and reconstruction, starting from the compilation of vast quantities of information; until the decoding, that reveals hidden meanings, overshadowed by the informative concomitance and the diversity: in this field, the objective of this chapter is to explore and describe the methodology of the Opinion Mining in Sociopolitical Research in diversity context.

BACKGROUND

The learning transfer among domains is essential to the opinion data mining, meanwhile, the opinion mining in social networks tries the reach extension from a repository to the inclusion of two or more. Initially, the opinion mining classifies contents in base to the positive or negative polarity; however, in domains, the polarity is not expressed as a concept, category, or word tribute, therefore demanding the construction of n-grams or dictionaries transferable among domains (Sonia, 2020).

Hajmohammadi *et al.* (2015) proposed a solution that includes the overcoming of linguistic barriers that are not connected to systems of automatic translation, that become distortions in the opinion mining as a consequence of dissimilar linguistic structures. The research of the mentioned authors proposed the use of unlabeled and labeled data based on semi-supervised learning, founded on graphics, which enable the incorporation of unlabeled data of the target language during the algorithm model. Subsequently, Khan *et al.* (2016) used SentiWordNet, which constitutes a lexical tool that provides support to applications oriented to the opinion mining constructed from the synsets automatically recorded according to polarity and neutrality levels, derived of algorithms of automatic record wordnet, which include aleatorily tasks after the semi-supervised learning.

Other researches have addressed the issue while the called "normalization", which includes the filtering of input data improving substantially the algorithm efficiency. This method has the imprint of requiring arduous filtering processes. The allocation methodology of "weight" to words enables the learning transfer among domains, using as references the distribution of probability (Buatoom *et al.*, 2020; Zheng *et al.*, 2015). Another application based on graphics of similarity among domains trains at the algorithm in the function of metrics derived from similarities calculating the weight of each word, which substantially minimized the classification errors (Moreo *et al.*, 2019).

Currently, the methodology that shows better results in the field of Opinion mining is the techniques of Naïve Bayes, based on conditional probabilities derived from the Bayesians inferences (Zervoudakis *et al.*, 2018). The technique ingenuity refers to the supposition of independence among attributes, even though it is known the interdependence among this. The advantage of the technique is that it allows the algorithm to execute classification tasks in presence of high bias and low variance (Giannoulis *et al.*, 2019). In linguistic matters, it enables to decrease deviations connected to ambiguous language. Xu (2019) applied the user profile modeling inset with the activity history, with the objective that the algorithm achieves to classify and categorize the "reliability" of the user. The procedure consists of the design of a targeted graphic, where each node expresses inherent characteristics to the user and the edges deploy the cause-effect relationship. In a second phase, it worked about the latent compounds using expectation-maximization algorithms, considering hidden variables.

Xusheng *et al.* (2018) established a Deep Learning framework for integration of inherent characteristics in a domain using two neural network schemes: (i) LSTM, which uses data sequences of complete voice and video in two metrics: which incorporate inherent characteristics at the domain and which incorporate metrics connected to functions of dictionary and verbal expressions; and (ii) convolutional neural network-based in probabilistic and inference. The use of open-source opinion of lexicons constitutes a base tool that enables the transfer between domains, still when the word differs in feelings expression. The open-source lexicons demand the permanent updating of the polarity of words, deriving in the cleansing applying approaches of semi-supervised learning.

MAIN FOCUS OF THE CHAPTER

Diversity and Artificial Intelligence

Sociocultural diversity comes from attributes' multiplicity that distinguishes a subject or to a social group. Categories such as ethnicity, nationality, language, class, beliefs system, theological foundations, age, genre, trade, etc., constitute attributes that the sociopolitical researcher requires filtering to delimit its study (Weber *et al.*, 2018). The relational demography of Tsui *et al.* (1992) indicated that social groups experience simultaneous processes of self-categorization —how are perceived—; identification —sociocultural secondment— and rooting of principles —values governing its performance—. From the self-categorization perspective, the subjects and social groups self-perceived affirming to the social group and establishing distinctions to the "others'', who are perceived as different, which not necessarily becomes in the exclusion (Pañellas, 2020; Sola, 2018). The identification refers to the recognition of attributes that enable the subject or group to recognize it as belonging to a society or specific social segment (Guanipa & Angulo, 2020). The principles correspond to the set of values shared intergenerationally or constructed as a product of life experiences (Flores, 2020).

Processes of self-categorization, identification and rooting of principles distinguish to social groups and the subjects, individualizing its development in all fields of life, without this constitutes an impediment to the multidirectional flow of cultural products be hampered, except for extreme cases where political, social or another nature junctural prevented from doing so. Therefore, how to delimitate attributes of a population or a sample in the development of social research, without facing the risk of bias? Traditionally, social science established limits to attributes such as genre, age, class, and location; nevertheless, when it refers to the construction and deconstruction of speech in social groups composed of thousands of individuals, traditional methods are insufficient. This is when Artificial Intelligence provides innovative methodologies (Daud & Himelboim, 2018; Paterson & Mc Donagh, 2018; Peng, 2018).

Artificial intelligence corresponds to the technology that enables the autonomous exercise of data interpretation from a specific and exogenous source by a system with the ability of learning and adapting, overcoming obstacles and learning of them (Jaakkola *et al.*, 2019). Since the 1970s of the 20th century, artificial intelligence has experienced exponential developments in algorithm designs, reaching the called machine learning or Deep Learning, which is based on the algorithm designs with a capacity to learn progressively during the interaction processes with the environment, in which identifies patterns, executing specific tasks that include identification, clustering, classification, prediction or regression (Barrios *et al.*, 2020; Domingos, 2019; Brundage *et al.*, 2018; Tsihrintzis & Jain, 2020).

The external sources of higher growth on which the AI works are called *Big Data* (Antons & Breidbach, 2017; George *et al.*, 2016). Big Data includes repositories of virtual data characterized by the called Five V's: volume, value, velocity, variety, and veracity, this corresponds to the characterizing of data as huge, valued, and commercialized actives in the market, of incessant production and exponential growth, characterized by diversity and reliability related to the source. Virtual repositories' quality of great capacity becomes of traffic information characterized by the exponential growth of data in the two last decades, including platforms and services as Twitter, Facebook, Google, Netflix, among others that do not dispose of the capacity to explore the potentiality of collected data in their Big Data. For this reason, there exists a marked trend towards the openness of public repositories, where researchers and academics get verifiable information that produces knowledge of the social to levels without precedents (Tokui *et al.*, 2019; Corvalán, 2018; Dolata, 2017; Wong *et al.*, 2016). Available information in Big Data requires procedures that enable the researcher's approach to the information that responds to posed questions, structuring data using metaheuristics procedures (Khan *et al.*, 2018). These procedures have given origin to multiple methodologies that converge in the design of a systematic process that orient the development of the mining activities.

The initial phase includes the so-called prior knowledge, where are defined the inherent categories to the problem of the study derived as the knowledge as a result of the researcher's experience. These categories constitute references that will enable the search delimitation (Antons *et al.*, 2018). In addition to this, the researcher should dispose of specific information about the repository in which will execute the mining process, with the finality of identifying potential fallacies that allow filtering patterns culling of irrelevant and invalid data (Pauwels & Mannay, 2019; Boulier, 2016). The control phase depends on the prior knowledge rigor where were defined the attributes that the algorithm should identify, oriented toward the output attributes generation that, after undergoing cleansing processes, they show the inherent characteristics to data that include structure, distribution, frequency, atypical nature, and interrelation (George *et al.*, 2016).

The cleansing involves the treatment of data using standardization procedures, discard of repeated data, isolation or processing of atypical data, and replacement of data lost. As a result of this phase, the algorithm is configured to the metaheuristic exercise, where it will identify patterns derived from the connection among the attributes. (Kobayashi *et al.*, 2017). In social sciences and humanistic field, the most recurrent techniques are (i) frequency determination of categories or words contained in dictionaries constructed by previous research or by the dictionary designed by the researcher in the function of the objectives that follow the study (Pennebaker *et al.*, 2015); and (ii) content analysis, which has two variants called supervised and unsupervised. The first of these is based on default categories by the researcher with the finality of limit the algorithm execution, addressing the search using the metadata labeled (Pauwels & Mannay, 2019); on the other hand, the unsupervised content analysis allows liberality in the algorithm execution that works in the function of clustering using the automatic word or categories association (Antons & Breidbach, 2017).

Subsequently, the definitive algorithm is modeled in which it will execute the metaheuristic process according to the researcher's specifications, instructing the algorithm to execute specific tasks according to the designed algorithm modality. In learning modality tasks that include classification, regression or prediction are executed. While the descriptive modality applies to cases where no previous control exists, this applies to association and clustering tasks. Finally, the detection modality corresponds to the identification of atypical values. Whether modeling, the algorithm proceeds the execution from where the output information or incremental knowledge comes (Antons *et al.*, 2018).

Opinion Data Mining

The disruption of the social research introduced by repositories Big Social Data and the AI is based on the rupture with mediation because the old audience messages' receivers of mass media acquired active roles, meanwhile, the availability of IoT devices approached to the common of people toward the discursive universe that feed social networks and different apps of the web, where users perform the active and collaborative role as content creators (Marozzo & Bessi, 2018; El Alaoui, 2018; Jeyapriya & Selvi, 2015). Users of the IoT technology were transformed in multipliers of information among their pairs, forming segments where the self-reference includes a first step to the identification with cybercommunities, from of which extends an intricate network of contacts that exponentially growth with indefinite impact levels that follow hierarchical patterns and of unpredictable reaches (Sharma & Shekhar, 2020; Wang *et al.*, 2021).

The positioning comes not only from the "virality" that the content reaches, but also from the temporal transcendence and the discursive chains that derive in the generation of public truthful and no manipulated opinion. Furthermore, the literature refers that message virality or influencer's followers not come in the univocity in front of a theme, whereas giving "like'' or resend the message does not express necessarily the secondment of users to general opinions of the called *influencers* (Himelboim & Golan, 2019, Rashidi *et al.*, 2017). The influencer is positioned in the function of the followers' number reaching high "hub", medium or low levels, according to the level of impact measured by the obtaining of "like'' or "resends", establishing temporary and binding parasocial interactions (Daniel *et al.*, 2018; Rasmussen, 2018; Díaz, 2017; De Veirman *et al.*, 2017). Temporality is connected to the influencer's capacity to preserve and increase the follower number, while the connection refers to a commitment based on the trust of followers (Himelboim & Golam, 2019). The capacity to induce conduct among the followers is based on the positioning of the influencer's brand (Díaz, 2017).

In the sociopolitical field, the influencer corresponds to the denominated opinion leaders, who through followers' networks, induce toward the positioning of ideas and the promotion of actions. The political influencer finds in social networks fields of action that expands of its speeches and proposes; nevertheless, unlike the influencer dedicated to the marketing of its image or of its sponsors, the political influencer has no evidenced levels of impact capable to modify political agendas. The study of Fernández, Hernández, and Sanz (2018) revealed the content of messages created in the social network Twitter in Spain during the elections to European Parliament of 2014 –still when more than 50% of the studied messages correspond to political messages–, they did not express ideologies, and also within the range of the non-political influencer hubs the dominant was the non-ideological messages. However, the mentioned study did identify dominant contents in the function of the most recurrent categories according to the liberty, equality, justice, diversity, and tolerance grams. In this same order, studies of Garimella *et al.* (2018) found the following of users to influencers is connected to the ideological affinity, which in political would limit the influence on like-minded followers and not to those doubtful or opposite segments (Dubois & Blank, 2017).

Nevertheless, this does not discredit the study of opinions expressed in social networks, still when it is in chains to followers' segments of one or more influencers, applying appropriate techniques that minimize the bias (Mebane *et al.*, 2017; Witten, 2017). Opinion mining was positioned as an analytical technique from the research of Nasukawa and Yi (2003), who established a range for the analysis of emotions expressed by people within a virtual environment using polarization. This proposal is based on the cataloging of opinions under the positive, negative or neutral category, related to texts' content created in the network. The availability of IoT devices approached the common of people toward the discursive universe that feeds social networks and many webs applications when users perform active and collaborative roles as content creators, which could position it as part of the public agendas. The positioning comes not only from the virality that from the content, but also of the temporal transcendence and the chaining discursive that derive in the generation of truthful and non-manipulated "public opinion". Platforms such as Twitter, Facebook, WhatsApp, Vkontakte, Instagram, WeChat, Snapchat, constitute important communication networks where millions of terabytes' contents are generated that are susceptible of mining to clarify tendencies in matters of public opinion about specific themes (Ureña, 2019).

Opinion data mining enables the diagnosis in real time of people's perception in the function of social, economic, political, cultural proposals and of any nature that involves the implementation of public policy. To identify patterns in opinions referring to critical themes, the decision-maker has the possibility of reshaping the proposal in the function of positive attributes, increasing the acceptance potentialities when addressing the initiative modification in function of segments of the most adverse population. According to levels, opinion mining works over: a) documents, where the opinion emerges of general considerations about a theme in which the documental text expresses a polarized opinion; b) phrases, that correspond at the application of classification algorithms that admit three options: positive, neutral and negative; and c) attributes that work over categories, words, and concepts identifying, classifying and recognizing connections.

The most common applications of opinion mining have been used in the commercial and marketing area, obtaining feedback on the user of products and services, testing the demand, competency, and satisfaction of the client without intermediaries. The feedback became extensible to all areas of social life, forming a powerful tool for business and government decision-making, where users are transformed into testers of products, services, and current and future government plans.

Iterative Opinion Mining

The iterative opinion mining consists of the content analysis created by users in different platforms of social networks applying neural networks. These come from statistical models based on hidden layers that establish a connection between the input information and the output information, this using a process of algorithm training (Belcastro *et al.*, 2019). This training process occurs in a matrix where data that subsequently emerge in the "output" are processed (Buduma & Locascio, 2017). Data transit by stages from the entrance, until that, emerge training data; constituting a process that derives in the results convergence of the attributes' classification expressed in a matrix, where potential errors substantially decrease (Han *et al.*, 2021; Kiran & Naik, 2021) the hidden layers correspond to complex nonlinear matrix operations, characterized by the capacity of dynamic and iterative transformation of the initial matrix (input) referenced in weighted coefficient values, that subsequently generate optimum results (Buduma & Locascio, 2017).

The neural networks are known for the allegory of their processes with the black box of Easton (Porcelli, 2020). Input data are submitted to processes of transfiguration that derive in the abstract representation of themselves. The process is sequential and the calculation of coefficients occurs in the following hidden layers, all of this as a result of the multiple iteration and transformations obtained from matrix calculations. In that way, the neural networks include several tiers or nodes where they execute calculations in base to the correspondent data at this layer and when performing mathematical operations in the next node, the new input constitutes the weighted value derived from the previous layer including the bias expressed as 1 or 0. The training corresponds to the result of the process of linear and progressive adjustment of nodes that, once obtained the real value and the error estimation, enable the coefficient updating of precedent layers (Buduma & Locascio, 2017).

The methodology application of neural networks about the available contents in the Big Data of social networks provides at the researcher classified or predictive information in function of the issue delimitation, with the singularity of the scope is exponentially higher than those of a survey, considering that classifies and validates results (Sonia, 2020). The iterative opinion mining is based on the use of dictionaries and neural networks to extract the textual or symbolic contents (Deshmukh & Tripathy, 2018). Nevertheless, it confronts the same weaknesses of the general opinion mining, due to algorithms designed for the mining of a domain are not necessarily adequate to labels assigned to the other domains. This derived in the called transfer learning, which corresponds to classifiers:

1. Inductive Transfer Learning, which includes cases where data of the objective domain are not labeled (Belcastro *et al.*, 2020). This potentially can include two assumptions:
    a. Availability of labeled data in the source domain. It applies the same methodology of Multitask Learning. The most used approach corresponds to Pytorch-FastAI, which starts the definition of data and the initial modeling using Pytorch, subsequently FastAI proceeds at the model adjustment.

       The multitask approach is oriented toward the simultaneity of tasks in an only model, in that way it allows for expansion of the scope until tasks related to training signs. This applies to cases where multiple variables have different numbers of possible output. The objective is that the model learns to weigh the bias, such as classification tasks as regression.

b. Low or no availability of labeled data in the source domain. In consequence, it applies the modality of machine learning, that mediate among the supervision and the no supervision, whereas the algorithm uses as a referent the structured data, without the demand that all data are labeled; and generate predictions from the generation of test data, which corresponds at the inductive learning. In another order, transductive learning is found, that is trained from labeled data, distinguishing it from the inductive which works generalizing available data until unlabeled data. The order of the described methods differs in the induction predicts based on evidence, while the transduction predicts from the training phase to generalize labels to all data.

2. Transductive Transfer Learning applies in cases where the intended objective and the data sought are used in the previous Big Data. The difference is that it corresponds to a new domain where data is not labeled. Furthermore, the advantage is that, from the original domain, all input data are labeled (Belcastro *et al.*, 2020). Present two possible modalities.
    a. Difference between characteristic spaces of domains.
    b. The similarity between characteristic spaces of domains, distinguishing distribution of marginal probability, demands adapting between domains.
3. Unsupervised Transfer Learning, which corresponds to cases where there exists a relation between executed tasks in the original domain and labeled data exist in both Big Data. Furthermore, it applies the methodology of unsupervised learning.

In three cases are required the solution of transfer problems, which is connected with qualities of transfer data, that present three variants: (i) specific allocation of weights to instances cataloged as hierarchical within of the objective domain; (ii) representation of distinctive characteristic between both domains that, once identified, are considered as pop-up domain, subsequently, an algorithm oriented toward this domain is modeled; and (iii) parametric transference, which is based on the transfer that includes relationships between data from the original domain toward the secondary domain.

Projects and Researches

The research in the sociopolitical field was reform by the technology of Neural Networks (NN), where the necessary development of competencies in the use of the software by the political and social research has been compensated for the development of programs that enable the technology applications in transdisciplinary exercise. The progressive development of open-source code framed the road toward the NN technology implementations to respond to demands in data diversity that can vary in format and length, deriving in different projects, of which three are the ones that stand out.

Caffe corresponds to a NN approach based on flexibility, velocity, modulation and expression. Caffe singularity is expressed in the adaptability to multiple architectures of Deep Learning, mainly in the images, voice and multimedia processing in lower temporalities that fluctuate between one and four milli-seconds (Jia *et al.*, 2014). The most recent developments of Caffe are connected to Recurrent NN. This modality can establish cycles among layers and neurons content in them, as a result, has demonstrated efficiency in alternative processes to the "input" and "output", which are released at the researcher from primary structuration, allowing the algorithm to learn in base to available data. The obstacle that confronts is the difference in learning velocity among neurons near the input and neurons near the output; while the solution is associated with data normalization. Caffe has compatibility with Long Short-Term Memory (LSTM) networks oriented toward the machine reading of contents, with the versatility of that, with the versatility that can be repeatedly applicable, thus solving differentiated memory problems among the neurons of each layer. Currently, Caffe merged with PyTorch (Caffe, 2021).

PyTorch, similar to Caffe, is within development tools under the Facebook domain and constitutes a library of machine learning developed under open-source. Furthermore, it has the peculiarity of having a wide range of packages in data sciences affiliated with the Python system. The user can design and combine methods of Deep learning and express graphically the productivity using nodes and edges, where the calculation bidirectionally stores moving forward and backward to calculate weights of contents, applying the Define-by-Run approach. In-text matter, corresponding to weights of n-grams, qualitatively is higher than other libraries as a consequence of the interaction among components of the TochServe model, one of the last tools presented by PyTorch with file and metric functions. In visualization, data cleansing is very efficient, enabling the researcher to access quickly to the results; in addition, its application is simple (Pytorch, 2021).

Chainer, in contrast with Caffe and PyTorch, works with guidance to the object and depending on it defines models, where parameters of neural networks are defined in classes, which are combined creating a progression. As a result, the model is expressed as trees and subtrees of which is feasible to collect information. In addition to this, Chainer decreases the demand for memory by combining algorithms of advanced and back-programming calculation, implementing reprogramming only in cases of necessity. Furthermore, Chainer has been implemented in the development of linguistic models to recurrent neural networks models, ergonomic estimation, reinforcement learning, self-encryptions, variations and deep learning in general (Tokui *et al.*, 2019).

To sociopolitical level, the available applications in Opinion Mining matter have been used in search of minimizing the bias using the contents weight that achieves expressing polarity or neutrality in front of a cultural or political product automatically in populations that have not been explored to micro, macro and in reduced temporalities levels. The three previously mentioned tools constitute samples of technology potentialities of the opinion mining, where the researcher can execute identification and classification tasks of users and receivers of public policy and sociologic phenomena opinions, establishing metrics about the social polarity and intensity that enable improving the interaction among institutions and citizens.

In function of topics, the opinion mining enables fragment contents concerning specific themes, where the general population or the segment population to which it is addressed to express qualities and deficiencies of a sociopolitical action that affects it and on which it may affect using the opinion exercise. For those responsible for public policy and social programs design, including an approach to social polarities that, once identified, enable the approach of them intending to improve governability levels.

Developments such as Caffe and PyTorch, which work in the Facebook platform, constitute powerful tools of mining, capable of learning about the syntaxis and the recurrence of contents that determine the weight of them as classifiers, qualifiers and predictors of mass behavior. In this order, within the academic field, Anton *et al.* (2018) explored potentialities of text mining guided to the extraction of rhetorical signals in scientific articles that generated 172 237 quotes during 35 years, finding the subject's attributes –novelty, approach and structure– and the rhetorical attributes –exclusivity, inclusivity, certainty and temporary– are connected with the knowledge consumption and impact level of the scientific production and its social applications.

Progress in reprogramming matters is encouraging to overcome gaps derived from linguistic idioms, orthographical errors, word contractions and the indiscriminate use of fuzzy concepts; nevertheless, applications to the sociopolitical level have been diversified, mainly in the electoral field and public policy. Bovet *et al.* (2016) applied techniques of data mining about Twitter, intending to infer the opinion of social networks' users related to the elections of the US in 2016. The research covered 73 million contents in Twitter between the months of June and September of 2016, finding the obtained results applying the technique of opinion mining showed an r = 0,9 of precision, which concluded that this methodology enables to predict tendencies with high margins of accuracy.

On the other hand, Aswini (2019) exposes the achievements of the BPJ party in India, implementing opinion mining. The research found that Indian political parties apply opinion mining for the adequacy of contents of their campaigns according to the aspirations and interests of voters, which was evident in the national elections of 2014 and 2019. The most significant is the opinion mining has enabled the segmentation of voters' groups, orchestrating to political parties with tools of content design that include specificities own of the elector or electors' group segmented by social structure, lineage, geographic location and prevalent demands.

In the same order, the research of Bilal *et al.* (2019) studied the impact of social networks on sociopolitical dynamic, finding that opinion mining and diverse approaches implemented during its execution –supervised and unsupervised learning– have demonstrated efficiency in the predictability, being Twitter the most used social network to the opinion mining by the researchers and designers of election campaigns. Authors indicate limitations found in mining matter in an only domain and the linguistic fluctuations in countries Malaysia, Pakistan and India, where the presence of various dialects affects the efficiency of algorithms as a consequence of semantic fluctuations, therefore is essential the leak of data and the accuracy in categories during the elimination of the problem and the shaping of the prior knowledge, in such a way that the incremental knowledge be reliable. For the same countries, Jaidka *et al.* (2019) were subjected to assessment of the volumetric approaches to the opinion mining in Twitter, finding that these are efficient in India and Pakistan cases, while to Malaysia language and syntaxis confluence do not allow the application of this approaches type, in consequence, proposed the concomitance of approaches in opinion mining were to converge volume and polarization.

Belcastro *et al.* (2020) applied iterative opinion mining using neural networks (IOM-NN), intending to identify the polarization in the contents of social networks. The methodology was based on machine learning, showing as output the incremental knowledge from neural networks. The information corresponds to a set of unstructured data including emojis and hashtags, on which they have applied classification rules that subsequently were applied at the set of available data in the repository for the dates covered in the study. The results showed high levels of precision in the estimation of an election polarization.

RECOMMENDATIONS

Opinion mining constitutes an area that demands the development of competencies in the design of sociopolitical research implementing new models of research connected to artificial intelligence. In consequence, the transdisciplinary exercise by researchers of sociopolitical constitutes an urgent task. The opinion mining has potentialities still not explored with extensive repercussions in the field of the consolidation of democratic governability and citizen participation. Therefore, it is essential to include in resumes of the political and sociological professions the methodology derived from Artificial Intelligence.

FUTURE INSTRUCTIONS OF RESEARCH

The open gaps and the new lines of research in sociopolitical matter necessarily should incorporate the following themes:

1. Opinion mining and citizen participation.
2. Opinion mining is oriented to the design of the public policy.
3. Opinion mining in the design of national, regional and local budgets.
4. Opinion mining is oriented to the citizen demands.
5. Opinion mining in the design of citizen security plans.

CONCLUSION

Progress in the field of Artificial Intelligence has given to the sociopolitical sciences of tools that enable the approaching to tendencies of dominant opinion in the society during specific junctures, where decisions making or the positioning of a public political or social project idea be susceptible of real-time measurement, with a broad demographic scope that can be segmented, bringing the researcher closer to the study subject with a low level of bias. This does not mean that techniques of mining opinions still suffer from weaknesses inherent to the processing of structured and unstructured data, whereas the researcher requires solid knowledge about the theme that enables the construction of referents that underpin the prior knowledge. Categories that constitute the researcher dictionary require exhaustive cleansing, in such a way that the research shows results with low levels of bias, which express the sociopolitical reality intended to know. Opinion mining researches continue dominating elections and marketing themes, nevertheless, exist potentialities in the research of public policy, social programs, democracy and governance that are still waiting for the implementation of Opinion mining as a methodology of sociopolitical research.

REFERENCES

Antons, D., & Breidbach, C. (2017). Big Data, Big Insights? Advancing Service Innovation and Design with Machine Learning. *Journal of Service Research*, *21*(1), 17–39. doi:10.1177/1094670517738373

Antons, D., Joshi, A., & Salge, T. (2018). Content, Contribution and Knowledge Consumption: Uncovering Hidden Topic Structure and Rhetorical Signals in Scientific Texts. *Journal of Management*, *45*(7), 3035–3076. doi:10.1177/0149206318774619

Aswini, V. (2019). Big Data Analytics and Transformation of Election Campaign in India. *Proceedings of the 2nd International Conference on Information Systems & Management Science (ISMS) 2019*. 10.2139srn.3511428

Barrios, H., Díaz, V., & Guerra, Y. (2020). Subjetividades e inteligencia artificial: Desafíos para 'lo humano'. *Veritas (Valparaíso)*, *47*(47), 81–107. doi:10.4067/S0718-92732020000300081

Belcastro, L., Cantini, R., Marozzo, F., Talia, D., & Trunfio, P. (2020). Learning Political Polarization on Social Media Using Neural Networks. *IEEE Access: Practical Innovations, Open Solutions*, *8*, 47177–4718. doi:10.1109/ACCESS.2020.2978950

Berger, P., & Luckmann, T. (2003). *La construcción social de la realidad.* Amorrortu-Murguía.

Bilal, M., Gani, A., Marjani, M., & Malik, N. (2019). Predicting elections: Social media data and techniques. *International Conference on Engineering and Emerging Technologies (ICEET)*, 1-6. 10.1109/CEET1.2019.8711854

Boulier, D. (2016). *Un classement qui fait un tri correct dans les offres d'opinion mining et de social monitoring*. Hypoteses. https://bit.ly/3kf1LdA

Bovet, A., Morone, F., & Makse, H. (2016). Validation of Twitter opinion trends with national polling aggregates: Hillary Clinton vs Donald Trump. *Scientific Reports*, *8*(1), 8673. doi:10.103841598-018-26951-y PMID:29875364

Brundage, M., Avin, S., Clark, J., Toner, H., Eckersley, P., Garfinkel, B., Dafoe, A., Scharre, P., Zeitzoff, T., Filar, B., . . . Amodei, D. (2018). *The malicious use of artificial intelligence: Forecasting, prevention, and mitigation.* Technical report, Future of Humanity Institute, University of Oxford. https://bit.ly/3wA3E6T

Buatoom, U., Kongprawechnon, W., & Theeramunkong, T. (2020). Document Clustering Using K-Means with Term Weighting as Similarity-Based Constraints. *Symmetry*, *12*(6), 967. doi:10.3390ym12060967

Buduma, N., & Locascio, N. (2017). *Fundamentals of Deep Learning: Designing Next-Generation Machine Intelligence Algorithms* (1st ed.). O'Reilly Media, Inc.

Caffe. (2021). *Caffe*. https://bit.ly/3yPH2km

Corvalán, J. (2018). Inteligencia artificial: retos, desafíos y oportunidades - Prometea: la primera inteligencia artificial de Latinoamérica al servicio de la Justicia. *Revista de Investigações Constitucionais*, *5*(1), 295–316. doi:10.5380/rinc.v5i1.55334

Daniel, E., Crawford, E., & Westerman, D. (2018). The Influence of Social Media Influencers: Understanding Online Vaping Communities and Parasocial Interaction through the Lens of Taylor's Six-Segment Strategy Wheel. *Journal of Interactive Advertising*, *18*(2), 96–109. doi:10.1080/15252019.2018.148 8637

Daud, I., & Himelboim, I. (2018). A Social Networks Approach to Online Social Movement: Social Mediators and Mediated Content in #FreeAJStaff Twitter Network. *Social Media + Society*, *4*(1), 1–14. 10.1177%2F2056305118760807

De Veirman, M., Cauberghe, V., & Hudders, L. (2017). Marketing through Instagram influencers: The impact of several followers and product divergence on brand attitude. *International Journal of Advertising*, *36*(5), 798–828. do i:10.1080/02650487.2017.1348035

Deshmukh, J., & Tripathy, A. (2018). Entropy-based classifier for cross-domain opinion mining. *Applied Computing and Informatics*, *14*(1), 55–64. doi:10.1016/j.aci.2017.03.001

Díaz, L. (2017). *Soy marca: quiero trabajar con influencers. Influencer Marketing*. PROFIT. https://bit.ly/3yQzuOC

Dick, S. (2019). Artificial Intelligence. *Harvard Data Science Review*, *1*(1). Advance online publication. doi:10.1162/99608f92.92fe150c

Dolata, U. (2017). Apple, Amazon, Google, Facebook, Microsoft: Market concentration-competition-innovation strategies. *Research Contributions to Organizational Sociology & Innovation Studies, SOI Discussion Papers,* (1). https://bit.ly/2VtLGGp

Domingos, P. (2019). *The master algorithm: How the Quest for the Ultimate Machine will Remake our World*. Basic Books.

Dubois, E., & Blank, G. (2017). The echo chamber is overstated: The moderating effect of political interest and diverse media. *Information Communication and Society*, *21*(5), 729–745. doi:10.1080/1369118X.2018.1428656

El Alaoui, I., Gahi, Y., Messoussi, Y., Chaabi, Y., Todoskoff, A., & Kobi, A. (2018). A novel adaptable approach for sentiment analysis on big social data. *Journal of Big Data*, *5*(1), 12. doi:10.118640537-018-0120-0

Fernández, J., Hernández, V. & Sanz, P. (2018). Influencers, marca personal e ideología política en Twitter. *Cuadernos.Info. Comunicación y medios en Iberoamérica*, *42*, 19-37. doi:10.7764/cdi.42.1348

Flores, M. (2020). Empatía y respeto entre otros valores: Análisis de experiencias docentes de colaboración con organizaciones sociales. *Revista Digital de Investigación en Docencia Universitaria*, *14*(1), e1195. doi:10.19083/ridu.2020.1195

Garimella, K., Morales, G., Gionis, A., & Mathioudakis, M. (2018). Political discourse on social media: Echo chambers, gatekeepers, and the Price of bipartisanship. *Proceedings of the 2018 World Wide Web Conference*, 913-922. 10.1145/3178876.3186139

George, G., Hass, M., & Pentland, A. (2014). Big Data and Management: From the Editors. *Academy of Management Journal*, *57*(2), 321–326. https://bit.ly/3wwO5Nz. doi:10.5465/amj.2014.4002

Giannoulis, G., Krithara, A., Karatsalos, C., & Paliouras, G. (2014). Splice Site Recognition Using Transfer Learning. In A. Likas, K. Blekas, & D. Kalles (Eds.), Lecture Notes in Computer Science: Vol. 8445. Artificial Intelligence: Methods and Applications. SETN 2014. Springer.

Guanipa, L., & Angulo, M. (2020). La identidad social en la educación: Hacia una participación ciudadana. *Desde el Sur, 12*(1), 155–166. doi:10.21142/DES-1201-2020-0010

Hajmohammadi, M., Ibrahim, R., & Selamat, A. (2015). Graph-based semi-supervised learning for cross-lingual sentiment classification. In N. Guyen, B. Trawiński, & R. Kosala (Eds.), Lecture Notes in Computer Science: Vol. 9011. *Intelligent Information and Database Systems. ACIIDS 2015* (pp. 97–106). doi:10.1007/978-3-319-15702-3_10

Han, G., Bohan, L., Wenbin, X., Yuxin, Z., Donghai, G., Weitong, Ch. & Ken C. (2021). CSIP: Enhanced Link Prediction with Context of Social Influence Propagation. *Big Data Research,* (24), 100217. doi:10.1016/j.bdr.2021.100217

Hariri, R., Fredericks, E., & Bowers, K. (2019). Uncertainty in big data analytics: Survey, opportunities, and challenges. *Journal of Big Data, 6*(44), 44. Advance online publication. doi:10.118640537-019-0206-3

Himelboim, I., & Golan, G. (2019). A Social Networks Approach to Viral Advertising: The Role of Primary, Contextual, and Low Influencers. *Social Media + Society, 5*(3). Advance online publication. doi:10.1177/2056305119847516

Jaakkola, H., Henno, J., Makela, J., & Thalheim, B. (2019). Artificial Intelligence Yesterday, Today & Tomorrow. *42nd International Convention on Information and Communication Technology, Electronics and Microelectronics (MIPRO).* 10.23919/MIPRO.2019.8756913

Jaidka, K., Ahmed, S., Skoric, M., & Hilbert, M. (2019). Predicting elections from social media: A three-country three-method comparative study. *Asian Journal of Communication, 29*(3), 252–273. doi:10.1080/01292986.2018.1453849

Jeyapriya, A., & Selvi, K. (2015). Extracting aspects and mining opinions in product reviews using supervised learning algorithm. *2nd International Conference on Electronics and Communication Systems (ICECS)*, 548–552. 10.1109/ECS.2015.7124967

Jia, Y., Shelhamer, E., Donahue, J., Karayev, S., Long, J., Girshick, R., Guadarrama, S., & Darrell, T. (2014). Caffe: Convolutional Architecture for Fast Feature Embedding. *arXiv:1408.5093*. https://bit.ly/2VpFUFK doi:10.1145/2647868.2654889

Khan, F., Qamar, U., & Bashir, S. (2016). S WIMS: Semi-supervised subjective feature weighting and intelligent model selection for sentiment analysis. *Knowledge-Based Systems*, *100*(15), 97–111. doi:10.1016/j.knosys.2016.02.011

Khan, N., Alsaqer, M., Shah, H., Badsha, G., Abbasi, A., & Salehian, S. (2018) The 10 Vs, issues & challenges of big data. *Proceedings of the 2018 International Conference on Big Data and Education*, 52-56. 10.1145/3206157.3206166

Kiran, R., & Naik, D. (2021). Novel sensitivity method for evaluating the first derivative of the feed-forward neural network outputs. *Journal of Big Data*, *8*(1), 88. doi:10.118640537-021-00480-4

Kobayashi, V., Mol, S., Berkers, H., Kismihók, G., & Den Hartog, D. (2017). Text Classification for Organizational Researchers: A Tutorial. *Organizational Research Methods*, *21*(3), 766–799. doi:10.1177/1094428117719322 PMID:29881249

Kuhn, T. (1962). *The structure of scientific revolutions*. Chicago University.

Marozzo, F., & Bessi, A. (2018). Analyzing polarization of social media users and news sites during political campaigns. *Social Network Analysis and Mining*, *8*(1), 1. doi:10.100713278-017-0479-5

Martínez-Plumed, F., Contreras-Ochado, L., Ferri, C., Hernández-Orallo, J., Kull, M., Lachiche, N., & Flach, P. A. (2019). CRISP-DM Twenty Years Later: From Data Mining Processes to Data Science Trajectories. *Transactions on Knowledge & Data Engineering*, *33*(1), 3048–3061. doi:10.1109/TKDE.2019.2962680

Mebane, W., Pineda, A., Woods, L., Klaver, J., Wu, P., & Miller, B. (2017). *Using Twitter to Observe Election Incidents in the United States*. Midwest Political Science Association. https://bit.ly/2T4YQsB

Meneses, M. (2018). Grandes datos, grandes desafíos para las ciencias sociales. *Revista Mexicana de Sociologia*, *80*(2), 415–444. https://bit.ly/3wAoPFZ

Moreo, A., Esuli, A., & Sebastiani, F. (2019). Learning to Weight for Text Classification. *IEEE Transactions on Knowledge and Data Engineering*, *32*(2), 302–316. doi:10.1109/TKDE.2018.2883446

Nambisan, S., Lyytinen, K., Majchrzak, A., & Song, M. (2017). Digital innovation management: Reinventing innovation management research in a digital world. *MIS Quartely*, *41*(1), 223–238. doi:10.25300/MISQ/2017/41:1.03

Nasukawa, T., & Yi, J. (2003). Sentiment analysis: Capturing favorability using natural language processing. *2nd International Conference on Knowledge Capture*, 70-77. 10.1145/945645.945658

Pañellas, D. (2020). Grupos e identidades sociales en cambio. *Novedades en Población*, *16*(31), 64–84. https://bit.ly/3egvdvI

Paterson, M., & Mc Donagh, M. (2018). Data Protection in an era of Big Data: The challenges posed by big personal data. *Monash University Law Review. Monash University. Faculty of Law*, *44*(1), 1–31. https://bit.ly/3i6YKcG

Pauwels, L., & Mannay, D. (2019). *The SAGE handbook of visual research methods*. University of Antwerp.

Peng, Y. (2018). Same Candidates, Different Faces: Uncovering Media Bias in Visual Portrayals of Presidential Candidates with Computer Vision. *Journal of Communication*, *68*(5), 920–941. doi:10.1093/joc/jqy041

Pennebaker, J., Boyd, R., Jordan, K., & Blackburn. (2015). *The Development and Psychometric Properties of LIWC2015*. University of Texas at Austin. https://bit.ly/3hH9UG5

Porcelli, A. M. (2020). La inteligencia artificial y la robótica: sus dilemas sociales, éticos y jurídicos. *Derecho global. Estudios sobre derecho y justicia*, *6*(16), 49-105. doi:10.32870/dgedj.v6i16.286

PyTorch. (2021). *From Research to Production*. https://pytorch.org/

Rashidi, T., Abbasi, A., Maghrebi, M., Hasan, S., & Waller, T. (2017). Exploring the capacity of social media data for modelling travel behaviour: Opportunities and challenges. *Transportation Research Part C, Emerging Technologies*, *75*, 197–211. doi:10.1016/j.trc.2016.12.008

Rasmussen, L. (2018). Parasocial Interaction in the Digital Age: An Examination of Relationship Building and the Effectiveness of YouTube Celebrities. *Social Media + Society*, *7*, 280–294. https://bit.ly/3hyPLBN

Sharma, A., & Shekhar, H. (2020). Intelligent Learning based Opinion Mining Model for Governmental Decision Making. *Procedia Computer Science*, *173*, 216–224. doi:10.1016/j.procs.2020.06.026

Sola, S. (2018). Los sentidos e interpretaciones del yo: Un análisis multidimensional. *Dixit*, (29), 20-33. https://bit.ly/2VrLrvt

Sonia, V. (2020). Opinion Mining Techniques and Its Applications: A Review. In *Proceedings of First International Conference on Computing, Communications, and Cyber-Security* (pp. 549-559). Springer. 10.1007/978-981-15-3369-3_41

Tokui, S., Okuta, R., Akiba, T., Niitani, Y., Ogawa, T., Saito, S., Suzuki, S., Uenishi, K., Vogel, B., & Vincent, H. (2019). Chainer: A Deep Learning Framework for Accelerat- ing the Research Cycle. *25th ACM SIGKDD Conference on Knowledge Discovery and Data Mining*. 10.1145/3292500.3330756

Tsihrintzis, G., & Jain, L. (2020). *Machine learning paradigms: Advances in Deep Learning-based technological applications*. Springer. doi:10.1007/978-3-030-49724-8

Tsui, A., Egan, T., & O'Reilly, Ch. (1992). Being Different: Relational Demography and Organizational Attachment. *Administrative Science Quarterly*, *37*(4), 549–579. https://bit.ly/3eecilk. doi:10.2307/2393472

Ureña, R. (2019). Autoridad algorítmica: ¿cómo empezar a pensar la protección de los derechos humanos en la era del "big data"? *Louisiana Law Review*, *2*(2), 99–124. doi:10.29263/lar02.2019.05

Wang, L., Wang, S., Yuan, Z., & Peng, L. (2021). Analyzing potential tourist behavior using PCA and modified affinity propagation clustering based on Baidu index: Taking Beijing city as an example. *Data Science and Management*, *2*, 12–19. doi:10.1016/j.dsm.2021.05.001

Weber, T., Sadri, G., & Gentry, W. (2018). Examining diversity beliefs and leader performance across cultures. *Cross Cultural & Strategic Management*, *25*(3), 382–400. doi:10.1108/CCSM-11-2016-0200

Witten, I., Frank, E., Hall, M., & Pal, C. (2017). *Data Mining: Practical Machine Learning Tools and Techniques*. Morgan Kaufmann.

Wong, F., Tan, C., Sen, S., & Chiang, M. (2016). Quantifying political leaning from tweets retweets and retweeters. *IEEE Transactions on Knowledge and Data Engineering*, *28*(8), 2158–2172. doi:10.1109/TKDE.2016.2553667

Xu, S. (2018). Naïve Bayesian Bayes classifiers for text classification. *Journal of Information Science*, *44*(1), 48–59. doi:10.1177/0165551516677946

Xusheng, L., Chengcheng, F., Ran, Z., Duo, Z., Tingting, H., & Xingpeng, J. (2018). A hybrid deep learning framework for bacterial named entity recognition with domain features. *BMC Bioinformatics*, *20*(S16), 1–9. doi:10.118612859-019-3071-3 PMID:31787075

Zervoudakis, S., Marakakis, E., Kondylakis, H., & Goumas, S. (2018). OpinionMine: A Bayesian-based framework for opinion mining using Twitter Data. *Machine Learning with Applications*, *3*, 100018. doi:10.1016/j.mlwa.2020.100018

Zheng, C., Liu, & Wong, H. (2015). Iterative term weighting for short text data. *IEEE International Conference on Systems, Man, and Cybernetics*, 1687-1692. 10.1109/SMC.2015.297

ADDITIONAL READING

Alamoodi, A., Zaidan, B., Zaidan, A., Albahri, O., Mohammed, K., Malik, R., Almahdi, E., Chyad, M., Tareq, Z., Albahri, A., Hameed, H., & Alaa, M. (2020). Sentiment Analysis and Its Applications in Fighting COVID-19 and Infectious Diseases. A Systematic Review. *Expert Systems with Applications*, *167*, 114155. doi:10.1016/j.eswa.2020.114155 PMID:33139966

Ali, M. (2021). Arabic sentiment analysis about online learning to mitigate covid-19. *Journal of Intelligent Systems*, *30*(1), 524–540. doi:10.1515/jisys-2020-0115

Blankers, M., van der Gouwe, D., & van Laar, M. (2019). 4-Fluoramphetamine in the Netherlands: Text-mining and sentiment analysis of internet forums. *The International Journal on Drug Policy*, *64*, 34–39. doi:10.1016/j.drugpo.2018.11.016 PMID:30551004

Chaturvedi, I., Cambria, E., Welsch, R., & Herrera, F. (2018). Distinguishing between facts and opinions for sentiment analysis: Survey and challenges. *Information Fusion*, *44*, 65–77. doi:10.1016/j.inffus.2017.12.006

Da'u, A., Salim, N., Rabiu, I., & Osman, A. (2020). Weighted aspect-based opinion mining using deep learning for recommender system. *Expert Systems with Applications*, *140*, 112871. doi:10.1016/j.eswa.2019.112871

Gupta, N., & Agrawal, R. (2020). Application and techniques of opinion mining. In S. Bhattacharyya, V. Snásel, D. Gupta, & A. Khanna (Eds.), *Hybrid Computational Intelligence* (pp. 1–23). Academic Press. doi:10.1016/B978-0-12-818699-2.00001-9

Lee, M., Lee, T., Lee, S., Jang, J., & Kim, E. (2020). Machine Learning-Based Data Mining Method for Sentiment Analysis of the Sewol Ferry Disaster's Effect on Social Stress. *Frontiers in Psychiatry*, *11*, 505–673. doi:10.3389/fpsyt.2020.505673 PMID:33424646

KEY TERMS AND DEFINITIONS

Information Traffic: Quantity of information circulating on the internet calculated in seconds.

Public Opinion: Thoughts and ideas expression of the subjects' community, who are connected by the community of interests around a theme.

Self-Categorization: Self-reference of the individual, who recognizes distinctive attributes.

Social Diversity: It refers to the multiplicity of social, cultural, productive, linguistic, organizational, among other characteristics of expressions that distinguish the societies and the subjects.

Sociopolitical: Social sciences that include Sociology and Political fields.

Text Mining: Search for words in Big Data repositories using algorithms designed for them.

Weighting: Estimation or calculation of expected results.

Chapter 4
Breaking Social Network Analysis in Organizational and Interpersonal Communication

Caroline Kiarie
University of KwaZulu-Natal, South Africa

Nicola J. Jones
University of KwaZulu-Natal, South Africa

ABSTRACT

Often we hear that human beings are social creatures who interact with one another. In organizations, employees communicate with one another using both formal and informal networks, but top management are unable to observe and manage these networks. This chapter addresses how social network analysis theory and computational social science can be combined to visualize and map out the relationship structures. The chapter seeks to address how the theory, which is commonly associated with mathematics and sociology disciplines can be used in communication since the research is hardly visible. It breaks down some aspects of the theory and describes another two theories that have developed from it. Finally, for illustration, the chapter applied R Studio software to compute the social structures within a media organization and help realize the benefit of theory in knowledge sharing and employee synergy.

DOI: 10.4018/978-1-7998-8553-5.ch004

INTRODUCTION

Often we hear that human beings are social creatures who interact with one another. In organizations, managers have taken notice of how employees are interacting and collaborating using informal networks (Chan & Liebowitz, 2006). The reality as acknowledged by Cross and Prusak (2002) is that top management consider these informal networks to be unobservable and unmanageable since they cannot track them. This makes it difficult to analyze the strength and weaknesses of these networks. However, scholars such as Jacob Moreno (1937), Mark Granovetter (1973), John Scott (1992), Ronald Burt (1992) and Stanley Wasserman and Katherine Faust (1994) have computed these networks into relationship structures and analyzed them using Social Network Analysis (SNA). This was after repeated failure and the realization that it was not plausible to study human society without studying the social structure (Moreno, 1937). Castells (2010) points out that a global network society describes the new ways human beings communicate in a networked society. This chapter will look into how SNA can be used by organizations in order to understand the employees' interpersonal communication. It will show the relevance of SNA both as a theory and methodology/framework to researcher and its advancement in organizational communication.

BACKGROUND

Social Network Analysis theory focuses on how individuals build relationships among interacting units (Wasserman & Faust, 1994). The theory observes a network structure where individuals, referred to as actors or nodes, are linked to other actors within the structure. Borgatti and Halgin (2011) define a network as a set of actors with ties that link them together. These links can either provide opportunities or constraints for information flow. SNA studies the communication between the actors in the social structure in terms of ties, edges, connections, brokerage, centrality and bridges. The ties may depict communication frequencies, friendships, information flow, relationships or even kinship ties. Scott (1992) viewed the social structures as units of analysis for investigating the relational aspects. The social ties form a structural pattern referred to as a network, and each actor occupies a certain social position (Borgatti & Halgin, 2011). The theory stands apart from other social sciences theories because it focuses on the social context rather than individual actors (Fredericks & Durland, 2005) in other words, the relationship and patterns between the actors, and not the individual actor as a stand-alone. Actors can be individuals, groups, or organizations that form the unit of analysis.

At the organizational level, SNA can reveal the organizational settings, information sharing, relationships and opinion leaders (Cross & Parker, 2004). Network analysis can also reveal informal communication networks that can be compared to the formal communication networks in an organization. In organizations, employees' form interpersonal relationship ties and communicate with each other using both formal and informal networks. This chapter addresses how Social Network Analysis theory and computational social science can be combined to visualise and map out the relationships structures.

SOCIAL NETWORK ANALYSIS

Social network analysis is a relational approach that studies how social structures affect behaviors based on formed relationships. Though SNA origins are in the mathematical field, other disciplines such as sociology, computer sciences and communication have adapted the theory to further explain and analyze relationships and ties. The identification and the analysis of the relationship structures within groups have been the subject of inquiry since the early 1930s (Fredericks & Durland, 2005).

One of the main contributors through his seminal work was Jacob Moreno in 1934, who examined how an individual's actions are affected based on his or her social relationships. To show these relationships, Moreno invented a sociogram that measures interpersonal relationships in small groups of two (dyads) or three (triads) individuals where the individuals are represented by points (nodes) and the relationships represented by lines connecting to various individuals' points (Fredericks & Durland, 2005; Wasserman & Faust, 1994). The lines would therefore show the flow of information or influence between the different nodes in the structure. Moreno envisioned a sociogram for the entire New York City population (Cross, Borgatti, & Parker, 2002). Moreno (1937) postulated that interrelations, whether in small groups of sex, age, communities or institutions, influence the world situation in some manner. This influence can be studied and tested using sociograms and sociometrics. Moreno added that the knowledge from the social structure contributed to a rational social action and better knowledge of each individual within the structure, thus warranting the study of interpersonal communication structures in the workplace.

Social Network Analysis theory assists in finding out how social networks bring people together. In an instance where two people have a common friend, then it is likely that they will all become friends or interact in future (Easley & Kleinberg, 2012). According to Fredericks and Durland (2005), Dorwin Cartwright and Frank Harary built on Moreno's work in the 1950s by using lines to depict either a positive or a negative value, reflecting the direction of the relationship or influence. Arrowheads were used to show the direction or flow of the relationship. Fredericks and Durland (2005) add that network analysis looks at interaction between the actors at multiple levels of analysis: 1) the structure as a whole, 2) the subsets formed with the group structure, and 3) the nodes or individuals who comprise the network.

Figure 1. Simple visual representation of SNA sociogram (Source: Figure constructed by author)

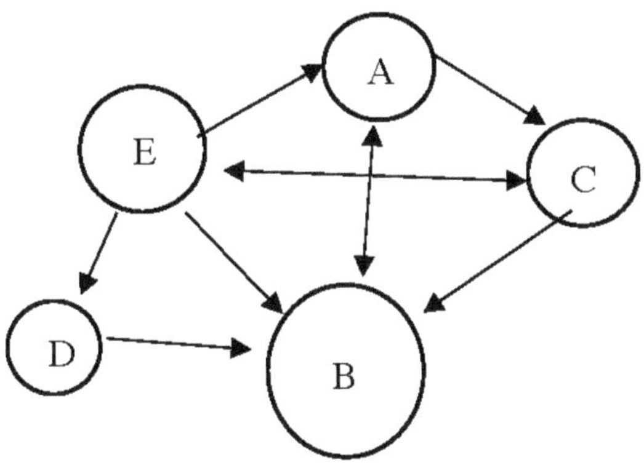

Figure 1 is an illustration of a simplified SNA depicting the social structure and the relationships within a network. The circles represent different individuals or actors or nodes. The size of the nodes may vary based on their position or contribution to the network structure. For instance, in Figure 1, B has the biggest node to show that B has the most incoming ties. The lines depict links or ties that can represent the communication flow and connections among the individuals. The arrows show the direction of the relationships. For example, A is a friend to C, while E is a friend to A. C does not consider A to be a friend since the arrow is one directional but E and C consider each other to be friends as the arrows are pointing both directions.

Studies completed by Lloyd Warner and Paul Lunt in 1941 on small urban communities in New England were carried out by the researchers through the formulation of complex algorithms and the creation of sociograms by hand which proved to be time consuming and tedious (Wasserman & Faust, 1994). Later in the 1970s, researchers started using computer- based software such as SOCK by Alba and Gutman (1972), SONET by Foster and Seidman (1978), MAGE by Richardson (2000), UNICET by Borgatti, Everett and Freeman (2002) and NetMiner by Cyram (2003). Many more software and packages exist and some even open source such as Gephi by Bastian, Heymann and Jacomy (2009) and RStudio (2020) that can be used for network analysis.

In reference to approach, SNA theory has been viewed both as a theory and as a methodological or as a framework that acts as a guide to network analysis. Fredericks and Durland (2005, p.19) express this by saying, "there is debate as to whether SNA is a theoretical field unto itself or merely a collection of methodologies that can be used in the study of social relations". However, Fredericks and Durland (2005, p.20) persist that the SNA context which includes social capital and support, communication flow, friendships networks, and exchange networks are the crucial elements which provide the theoretical framework from which evaluation questions and measures are formulated, adding that, "the context of a structure (the conceptual and theoretical framework of an evaluation design), crossed with empirical structures (levels of analysis), forms a matrix (levels of analysis crossed with contextual framework) for sorting the variety of research agendas that have been explored or are possible to explore and provide a framework for developing evaluation questions" are critical. This shows that context is important in SNA, for it provides the theoretical framework, research questions or hypothesis testing and objectives that align to the theory. To expound on the debate, SNA has been applied as a framework to which other theories have been linked, such as strong and weak ties theory and structural holes theory (Hatala, 2006). The sections below gives a brief overview of both theories in order to establish their connection to SNA and their relevance in communication.

Strong and Weak Ties Theory

Strong and weak ties (SWT) theory by Mark Granovetter in 1973 focuses on the strength of friendship networks ties between individuals and categories the relational ties as either strong or weak (Granovetter, 1973). SWT theory highlights the closeness between individuals. Strong ties comprise of actors who are of close (homophilous) knits, exhibit high levels of intimacy, and self-disclosure and reciprocal services, while weak ties are those actors of irregular interactions, acquaintances and little emotional connection (Hatala, 2006). SWT theory analyses the characteristics and the strength of ties between the actors (Hatala, 2006; Kozinets, 2010). Furthermore, Granovetter (1973) alludes that the degree of overlap between two individuals' friendship networks varies based on the strength of the ties, adding that the strength of an interpersonal tie is based on the amount of time, emotional intensity, intimacy and reciprocity. When two ties are strong, then their social worlds tend to overlap too (Borgatti & Halgin, 2011).

Granovetter initially explored the ties in his research that aimed to find out how recently hired employees learned about their new jobs. The findings indicated that individuals (employees) learned through their acquaintances (Easley & Kleinberg, 2012). In other words, they learned from weak ties. This is explained by Easley and Kleinberg (2012) using triadic edges and triadic closure in a social network scenario (see Figure 2 below) whereby two individuals (B and C) who are strangers to each other but have a common friend (A). A is a strong tie to B and C. The strong tie is indicated in Figure 2a using a continuous line. Note that initially, as highlighted in Figure 2a, B and C are not friends since there is no line. This concept is referred to as triadic edge, whereby we have three individuals, but not all are friends thus an incomplete triangle. After a period of time, the likelihood of A introducing B and C and becoming friends increases. Once they interact, there is transitivity, they become acquaintances and then we have a triadic closure in the social network as indicated by the broken line between B and C in Figure 2b. B and C form a weak tie.

Figure 2. Simple visual representation of strong and weak Ties (Source: Figure constructed by author)
2a. Triadic edge: strong ties -A & C, A & B
2b. Triadic closure-weak tie between C & B

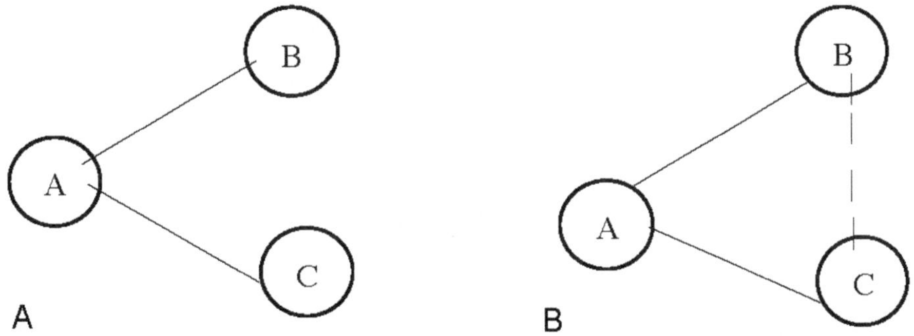

Applying the illustration on Figure 2 of triadic edge and triadic closure to Granovetter's research on SWT, let us assume B is looking for employment, A and B are strong ties since they are relatives, while A and C are strong ties since they went to the same university and shared a room. Strong ties tend to have the same information since they are homophilous. Therefore, in this situation, A will not assist B in providing him with employment but is likely to connect him to C who knows of current openings. B is most likely to get employed using the information received from C. As Borgatti and Halgin (2011) note, C is a source of novel information to B. In conclusion A's role (strong tie) was to connect B and C (weak ties). B learned about the new job from C, however without A's connection B would have not learned about the job. The network progressed from triadic edge to triadic closure. Triadic closure in social network structures is likely to happen due to three reasons: opportunity, trust and incentive, as explained by Easley and Kleinberg (2012, p.50) below:

One reason why B and C are more likely to become friends, when they have a common friend A, is simply based on the opportunity for B and C to meet: if A spends time with both B and C, then there is an increased chance that they will end up knowing each other and potentially becoming friends. A second, related reason is that in the process of forming a friendship, the fact that each of B and C is friends with A (provided they are mutually aware of this) gives them a basis for trusting each other that an arbitrary pair of unconnected people might lack. A third reason is based on the incentive A may have to bring B and C together: if A is friends with B and C, then it becomes a source of latent stress in these relationships if B and C are not friends with each other.

In an interpersonal communication setting, SWT theory influences who an individual meets, the kind of information communicated, the flow of information and bridges between relations. In an organization, employees in a certain department will have strong ties with their colleagues of the same department, while they will have weak ties with employees from different departments. In situations where an employee in one department has to interact with employees from a different department, they form a weak tie and increase their social capital. When the employee goes back to their initial department, they are likely to communicate the information received from the weak tie. Therefore, the theory encourages more weak ties to form social capital and implies people with more weak ties are more successful, while people with more strong ties may have a strong local cohesion but weak global cohesion (Borgatti & Halgin, 2011). Cross, Borgatti, and Parker (2002) noted that whether it is at an individual, team or organizational level, effective informal networks lead to a growth in social capital, which has implications for performance. Social media also acts as the channel that can be used for information flow. The employees (nodes) link with other employees within the department and also outside the department. The link can also extend to employees from different organizations, linking and bridging each other either by strong or weak ties.

Structural Holes Theory

Structural holes theory by Ronald Burt (1992) is another theory from SNA that analyses "the cloud of nodes surrounding a given node, along with all the ties among them", thus ego networks and bridging of ties by the actors (Borgatti & Halgin, 2011, p.1171). It compares one node's strengths and redundancy. Noyes (n.d) adds that structural holes predicts a company's connection or absence of certain connections which shapes the amount of information the company obtains. The structural holes are viewed as openings between nodes that share no relationship (Fredericks & Durland, 2005). However, with time, a node comes into the structure and bridges the gap between the social structures. Structural holes theory, in essence, takes advantage of social capital (the node that bridges the gap) because of their position in the social structure (Burt, 2004). Burt sees structural holes as the gaps created by people within one group in connection to another group. In that people within the same network will only concentrate on activities within their network, thus creating holes in any information flow to other networks. Meaning, people within the same social structure will have common information flowing amongst them, while people connected to several social structures will benefit from the diversity of information, opinions and behaviors from the different structures (Burt, 2004). This is illustrated in Figure 3 below.

Figure 3 illustrates information flow in a network structure. Visually this network structure has three subgroups. A, E, F, B belong to the same subgroup therefore have common information. However, B is also connected to D and C subgroups therefore benefits from novel information. B is considered the ego or the connector between the different subgroups. B is spanning the structural holes that exist amongst the three structures, thus acting as the brokerage.

Some of the advantages of brokerage in an organization include amplifier of information, source of power and control over regulating information. As observed by Burt (2004), social capital brokerage are the people who bridge the structural holes and have a diversity of information and experiences compared to people who are within a homogeneity group. Burt adds to the advantages by saying that the egos are positioned to detect and develop opportunities since they arbitrate information by translating and providing this information across different social structures. The ego has a pool of networks and is likely to receive non-redundant information (Borgatti & Halgin, 2011). For instance, in an organization where there is miscommunication between different departments, the employee (ego) who brokerages the information between departments, can step in and clear the misunderstanding. This makes them important to learning, influence and creativity in an interpersonal communication setting since they are in a position to influence other employees based on the information they pass on their social networking platforms.

Figure 3. Simple visual representation of Structural Hole (Source: Cornell X. 2014, INFO2040X mod1 Kleinberg structural holes v1)

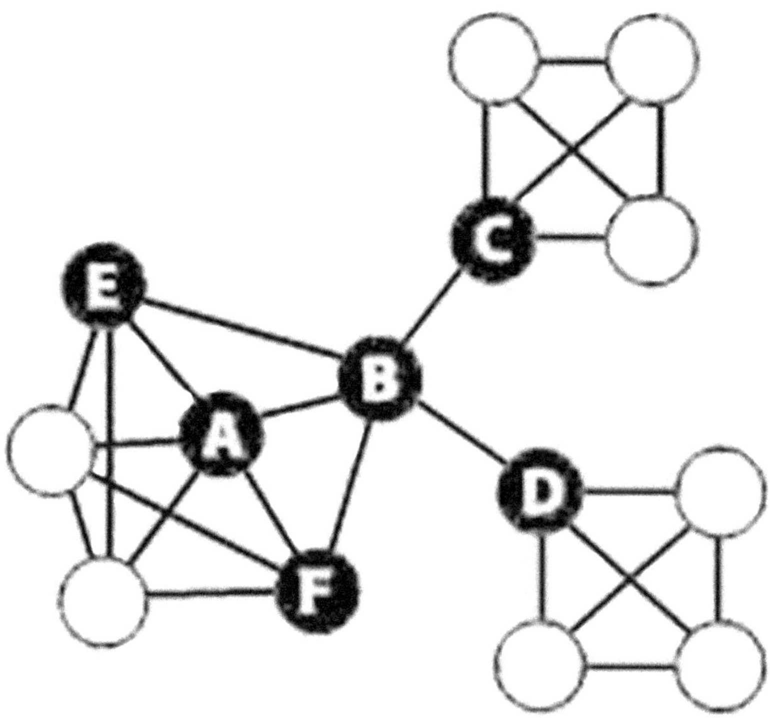

Social capital is an element that influences social structure in that, "who you know often has a great deal to do with what you come to know" (Cross, Borgatti, & Parker, 2002, p.25). SNA assists with mapping out the relationships in order to analyze the flow and assess the collaborations (Cross, Parker, & Sasson, 2003). This is done by mapping out the ties among employees in an organization and SNA theory helps in identifying the ties, relationships, holes, strengths and the weaknesses of the network ties. In their studies, Cross and Prusak (2002) contributed to the levels of analysis and identified four key players in the networks as central connectors, boundary spanners, information brokers and peripheral specialists. Central connectors have the most ties and links in the network, boundary spanners link different networks together, information brokers communicate with all the different networks while peripheral specialists provide expertise in the networks. Network ties which are generally considered invisible become visible through the SNA, therefore providing decision makers with information to improve performance, collaboration and increase influence in organizations (Cross, Parker, & Sasson, 2003).

Organizational Communication Studies on Social Network Analysis

While conducting network analysis, scholars have advanced frameworks, graphs and diagrams to show how the network structures are established and the effects they have on the actors. Cross, Borgatti, and Parker's (2002) study focused on making invisible networks visible in organizations for the purposes of strategic collaboration. They identified informal networks as a source for collaboration and knowledge sharing as employees relied heavily on their relationship networks to solve problems. They conducted several studies with 40 informal networks from 23 different organizations. The objectives of each study were to first, establish scenarios using SNA and second, develop the insights of the scenarios into analysis so that practitioners could benefit from the findings. Cross, Borgatti, and Parker (2002) went about these objectives by formulating a process for analyzing networks in an organization. The first step was to ensure they selected the right group, then they composed the right questions before designing the survey, collected the data, analyzed it and finally interpreted the results for the practitioners. After discussions with the practitioners and management, the organizations went ahead to implement, and another survey was conducted nine months later. For example, in one of their studies on making the invisible networks visible in a consulting firm, the initial findings on information sharing were represented in the pictorial figure below depicting the SNA for two departments.

Figure 4. Pre-intervention information sharing within an expert consulting group (Source: Cross, Borgatti, & Parker, 2002)

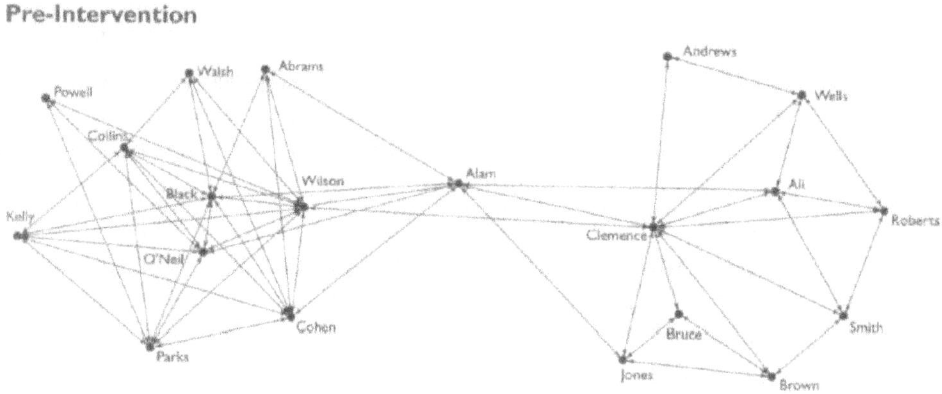

Figure 4 shows how employees in two departments (Strategy workforce and technical workforce) are linked to one another in the initial survey (Pre-Intervention). The figure shows two distinct subgroups. Each department had their network but with little information sharing within and between the two departments. For example, if Alam (at the centre of the figure) who acts as a brokerage ego was fired, then information sharing would almost be non-existent. Each subgroup is homophilous in nature as they share the same information but Alam has a diversity of information as he benefits from both groups in information sharing.

After the results from the survey were shared with the organization, measures were taken such as joint staffing of employees from the different departments on internal projects and joint sale goals (Cross, Borgatti, & Parker, 2002). This ensured information and knowledge was shared between the departments. Nine months later, Cross, Borgatti, and Parker (2002) conducted another survey (Post-Intervention) and findings indicated a more integrated structure as shown in the figure below.

Figure 5 depicts the SNA of the two departments post intervention. It reveals a well-integrated information sharing scenario between technical and strategy departments. This shows only one group as compared to the Figure 4 which had two subgroups.

Figure 5. Post-Intervention information sharing within an expert consulting group (Source: Cross, Borgatti & Parker, 2002)

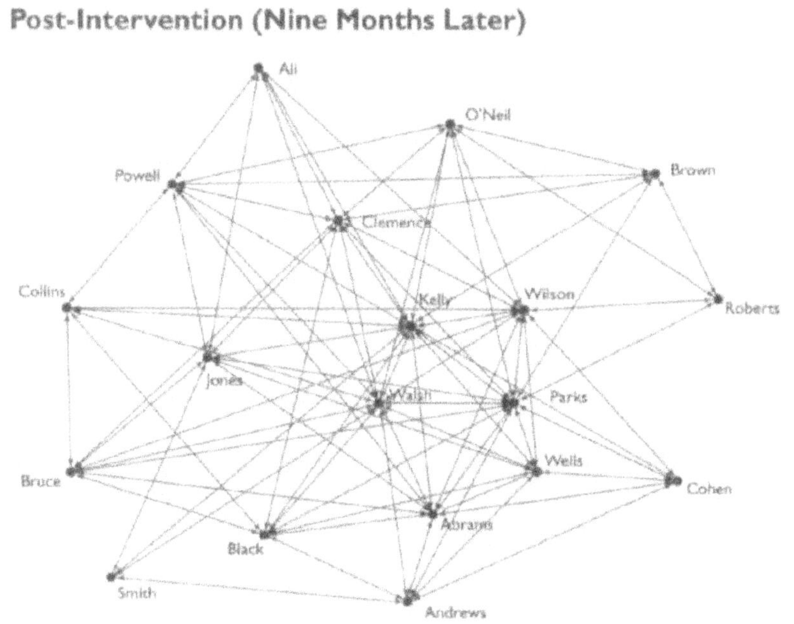

In a similar survey to study the collaboration across merged divisions conducted by Cross, Borgatti, and Parker (2002) of 126 executives across eight divisions, the initial analysis figures indicated minimal collaboration in most divisions. The participants cited the reasons for minimal collaboration as lack of knowledge on what the other divisions did and cultural barriers that restricted information seeking and sharing.

In a Foundation organization, Chan and Liebowitz (2006) applied the Cross, Borgatti, and Parker (2002) process and acknowledged that formal structures do not reflect the actual flow of knowledge in organizations, therefore giving credit to informal structures that are used for collaboration by employees. The objective of the case study was to bring out the importance and effectiveness of SNA application in knowledge mapping. Knowledge mapping assists in identifying knowledge sources, flows and relationships by making actors visible to the organizations (Liebowitz, 1999). To achieve the objective, a knowledge audit was first done by sending out a survey to all 85 employees, but was later narrowed to 25 employees, and follow up interviews were conducted to determine the flow of information within the foundation (Chan & Liebowitz, 2006). The survey collected data on knowledge sharing in the following areas:

general advice, management advice, leadership advice, institutional knowledge, technical knowledge and subject matter expertise. The data was computed using a SNA software and analyzed. The findings tabulated how knowledge was shared within the departments and also across the different departments using several pictorial diagrams. The network analysis was able to pin point each individual to determine the central connector and sub-structures in the organization. Freeman, White, and Romney (1989) highlight that analysis technique focuses on the patterns of human interaction, how they tie into a larger web of social connections, and how this has the ability to map issues that would not be otherwise easily visible.

The above studies show that both formal and informal networks exist in organizations. Information and knowledge sharing takes place within the structures. Establishing, mapping and analyzing the patterns and social structures are paramount for management to understand the flow of information and the key connectors.

Contrary to the findings on Chan and Liebowitz (2006) and Cross, Borgatti, and Parker (2002) not all individuals in the structure are willing to share information. This was the case in an experimental study by Bonacich (1990) on communication dilemmas. Bonacich conducted two laboratory experiments and the results indicated individuals hoarding information especially in a competitive environment. He adds that in organizations, employees can either decide to collaborate and cooperate by sharing information or they may decide to withhold information from other people in the network. In the experiment, communication dilemmas exist because the individuals have an incentive to withhold information, even though the withholding may delay the achievement of their network goals (Bonacich, 1990). Trust and understanding are also important elements within the networks and must be built since they play a major role in information sharing and collaboration (Chan & Liebowitz, 2006; Krebs, 2004). Though they did not expound on their research, Cross, Borgatti, and Parker (2002) touch on communication dilemma by noting that at times it may be difficult to get employees to integrate and share their perspectives because they feel overburdened by direct ties and therefore they tend to hoard information. Similarly, Krebs (1998) asserts that for a network to be efficient, the centrality in the network needs to have more indirect ties than direct ties in order to achieve a wide network reach.

Mutoh, Imura, Kato, Matsui, and Inuzuka (2016) conducted a study on how friendship networks based on SNA are formed by university students. They adopted Hiramatsu's model as an agent-based friendship network model but later modified and collected the data using 56 students' class log over a period of eight years and questionnaires. The Hiramatsu model assumes a cost benefit analysis is done before one becomes friends with another. One calculates the cost incurred for forming the friendship and decides if it is beneficial. The findings showed that two people who have the same friend tend to become friends with each other's cluster, therefore students make friendship decisions based on their current friendship network and not necessarily based on the Hiramatsu model of cost benefit analysis.

The reality of organizational networks is important when analyzing the social structures. It helps managers to know the key people in networks and their role within the social network. Kilduff, Crossland, Tsai, and Krackhardt (2008) mapped and analyzed perceived friendships verses the actual friendships among 116 perceived networks in four organizations. Kilduff et al. (2008) used small world principles to map out the friendships in an organization. The principles are based on perceived networks, where one arranges the people in the network into clusters, then connect the clusters with short paths. Individual cognitive schemas are utilized to interpret the perceived social networks and patterns. The challenge with cognitive schema is they are based on individuals' memories which may not be accurate (Kilduff et al., 2008). The findings of the study showed that perceived friendships are not actual friendships as indicated in the degree of small worldedness. The short paths in perceived friendships were actually longer when compared to actual friendships, where, due to increased isolation from one, more time and effort is needed to link with one another. Therefore, what employees may believe to be a cluster, connectedness or brokerage is likely not to be the case in reality. Even though social cognition and individual perceptions are important in shaping an organization's reputation, functioning and culture, managers need to be careful not to depend on perceived friendships, since it may be misleading compared to the actual friendships. As Chan and Liebowitz (2006) warn, an in-depth analysis of SNA is needed to determine what is real.

Adamic, Buyukkokten, and Adar (2003) conducted a similar study using small world principles and Club Nexus (a community-based website at Stanford University) with the aims of analysing real-world social networks and characterizing the connections. The social network of 2,469 users depicted 10,119 links between the users. Adamic, Buyukkokten, and Adar (2003) observed a small world effect depicted by short paths between any two users. The findings indicated a negative correlation, meaning when dissimilar people interact, they shorten the distance between any two users.

Analysis and Discussions of the Informal Social Networks in the Workplace

Quantitative data was collected from the employees' network using ego centered perspective, which means that respondents were first identified to form a list of focal actors or egos (Chan & Liebowitz, 2006). The focal actors, who were six managers from different departments in the organization, were requested to randomly select three employees from their departments to fill in the questionnaire. In total the sample size was N=25. The questionnaire was distributed to the respondents. In the questionnaire, the respondents were requested to fill in four employees from whom and how frequently they go to for advice on private life, work related, leadership, institutional knowledge and for collaboration.

From the returned questionnaires, N=25, the respondents' names and filled in names were then coded based on the individuals and departments before entering the data into R Studio software where sociograms were drawn. The sociograms were mapped using small circles which are called nodes to identify all the employees in the network. Different colours were also used to identify the different departments. Lines indicated the links between the nodes (employees) while the arrows show the direction of the relationships. The analysis in this study focused on the department sociograms as the individual sociograms are too detailed for this study.

Since the data was collected using ego centric networks, only ego network size and ego network composition were measured. In ego network size, the degree of the actors, which is the number of direct ties an actor is linked to in the network structure is measured (Chan & Liebowitz, 2006). The more links an actor has, the more central they are and more powerful they can be in the structure. This basically means that the central actor has many ties and does not have to rely on one actor to transmit information. Ego network composition measures homophily and heterophily which help determine whether an ego is connected to people similar to themselves or different people in terms of the department, and also if the ego is accessing a diverse group of people (Halgins, 2012). Homophily according to Paul F. Lazarsfeld and Robert K. Merton (Rogers & Bhowmik, 1970) is when similar people interact with one another often, that they tend to have similar information and knowledge with each other. Dyads and triads will also be identified from the sociograms in order to analyse which set is most connected or most isolated from the network structure. The sociograms are presented and discussed below. The first sociogram, Figure 6, was on private life advice which is not work related. However, the data was collected in order to compare if employees seek advice from the same set of employees as for private life issues.

Figure 6. Private life sociogram based on departments

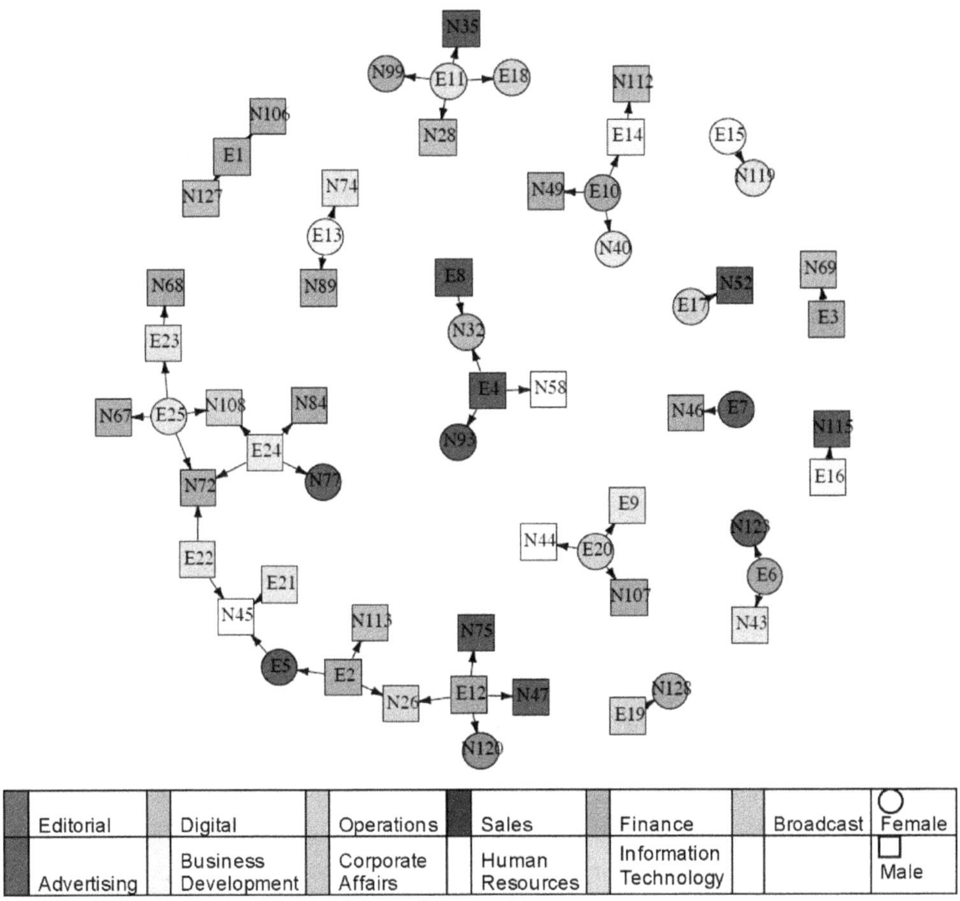

Each color represents different departments as shown in the key. Circles represent female while squares represent male. In Figure 6, the egocentric sociogram outlines the 25 egos (E1 to E25) who identified 48 alters in their private life network. There are 14 separate networks formed meaning there is no outright opinion leader or employee that other actors go consult on their private matters. There are five ego-alters (E5, E9, E14, E18 and E23) meaning that five ego respondents were also identified as people other ego respondents go to for advice. Also, in the sociogram, there are six dyads which are basic level connections between two actors, while there were three triadic edge subsets composed of three actors in each. There is also a likelihood that the triadic edges would become triadic closure where the three nodes would be connected to become friends (Easley & Kleinberg, 2010). In terms of ego network size, degree is used to measure the number of connections. In the private life egocentric sociogram N45 and N72 have three indegree connections, meaning most alters go to them for private life advice.

Looking at the ego network composition of the sociogram in relation to strong and weak ties theory by Mark Granovetter (1973) that extends on SNA, where strong ties comprise actors who are of close (homophilous) knits, one can deduce that this sociogram exhibits high levels of intimacy, self-disclosure and reciprocal services based on the dyads and triads subsets. Moving to the slightly larger subsets in the sociogram, it was noted that the respondents rarely discuss private life with co-workers in their departments, who are mostly not interconnected with other employees. The sociogram also shows that the Editorial department (maroon nodes) formed most of the network. Only two employees were identified from the Digital department. Factoring that the data was based on whom employees consult on private life matters, the small subsets were expected.

This sociogram will be compared with the work related sociogram to determine if the networks will also comprise of small subsets.

Each color represents a different department. There were 25 egos who identified 70 alters. The sociogram shows one big network with four dyads and one triad that can be classified as vulnerable populations. These means that do not consult on work related information from employees in the big sociogram. The sociogram also categorizes six employees as ego-alters. These were: E7, E18, E19, E21, E23, and E25.

The work-related ego network size which measures degrees shows that E18 and E25 have six in and out degree connections. Both E18 and N108 have four indegree connections reflecting that most employees consult them on work related information. E18 and N108 would be considered opinion leaders or influencers (Cross & Parker, 2002). Further analysis on the ego network composition show that N108 has homophily connections since all the connections are from the same (Operations) department even though N108 is from a different (Broadcast) department. E18 has heterogeneity connections as the alters are all from different departments. E18 would therefore be considered an influencer as well as a broker. When an influencer is connected to alters from different department, they also act as brokers as they are able to network and spread information or knowledge to employees from several departments. Strong ties tend to have the same information, according to Borgatti and Halgin (2011), since they are homophilous and their social world also tends to overlap as depicted by N108 who has four connections but all from the same department. The work related sociogram also shows that the network comprised of employees from eleven different departments. However, each of the departments is clustered in one place in the sociogram. This means that employees mainly go to fellow employees in the same department for work related advice, thus homophilous networks where the information shared is redundant since the network comprises of employees within the same department who will not have a diversity of information.

Figure 7. Work related sociogram based on departments

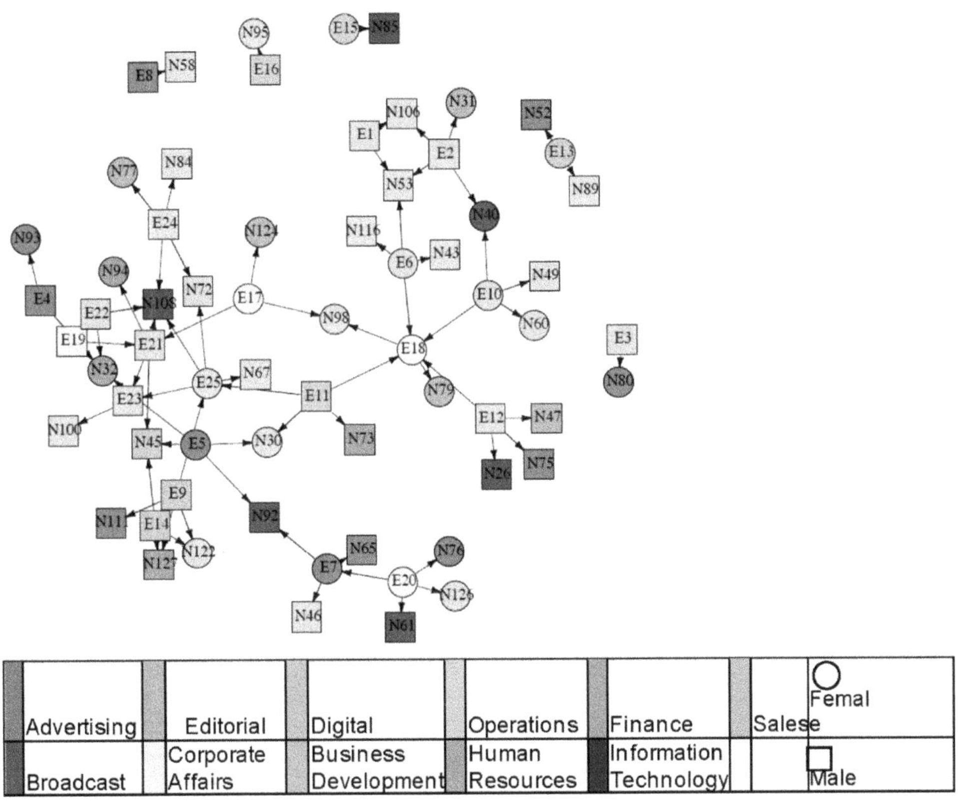

Compared to the private life sociogram in Figure 6, the work related sociogram had only four dyads compared to six and there were one triad compared to three in the private life sociogram. The identified alters in the work related sociogram were 70 different alters compared to 48 from the private life sociogram. This shows that the work related sociogram has more networks and are broader compared to the private life network, and employees choose to seek advice from smaller links for private life issues compared to work related matters.

In Figure 8, the leadership network was mapped out based on the names indicated by the respondents.

Figure 8. Leadership advise sociogram based on departments

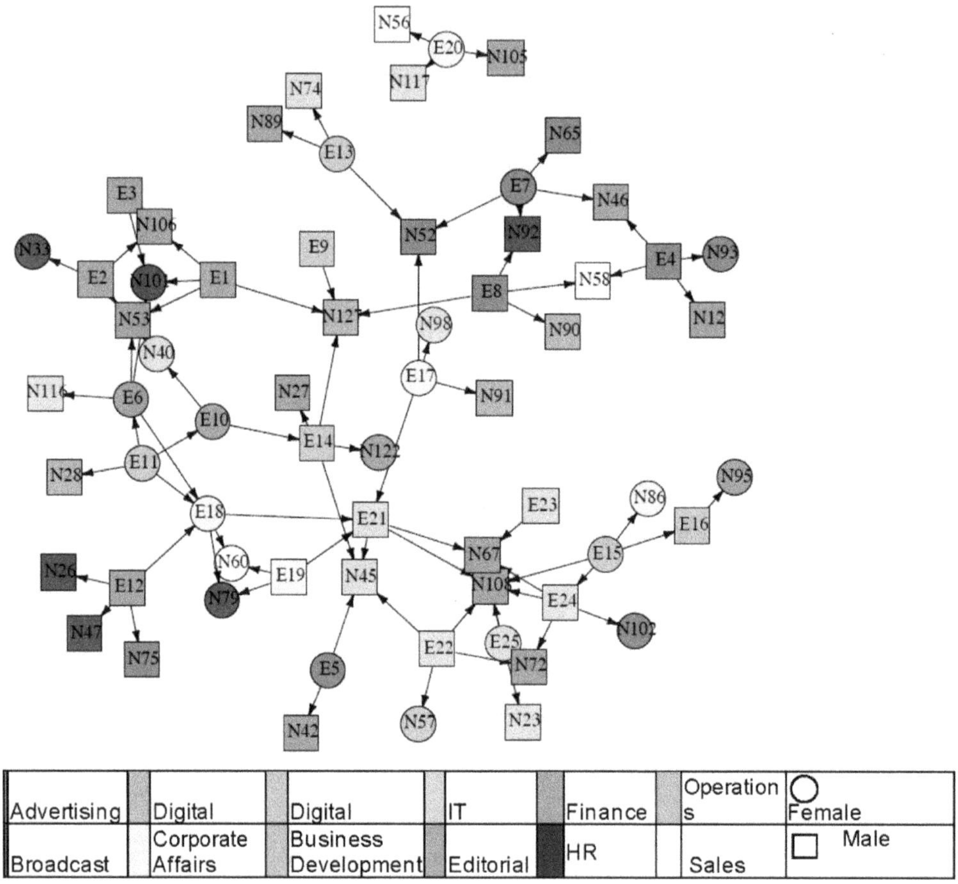

Each color represents a different department. The sociogram included 25 egos who identified 80 alters. The sociogram categorizes nine respondents as ego-alters, meaning that nine respondents (egos) were also identified as employees that other respondents go to (alters) for leadership advice. In the sociogram, all degree measures show that both E18 and E21 have six connections. Alter N108 has five homophily indegree connections meaning N108 can be an opinion leader or an influencer. Again, strong ties are homophily, therefore they have similar information. Most importantly E21 is considered a cutpoint or broker. A cutpoint is a connector who acts also as a broker by bridging the ties in the network (Borgatti & Halgin, 2011). The removal of the cutpoint would result in unconnected paths in the network. One of the benefits of being a broker is that they have access to a diversity of information from the different structures and can be used to share information too. In structural hole theory by Ronald Burt (1992) which is an extension of SNA, a broker can clear misunderstandings, amplify information and therefore also act as an influencer (Burt, 2004). Effective informal networks lead to a growth in social capital, which has positive implications for employees' performance, as employees are able to collaborate and share work related information.

The next sociogram is based on institutional knowledge. The respondents were asked to fill in the employees they consult on organizational knowledge. Figure 9 is a visual representation of the network based on the employees identified the respondents.

Each color represents a different department. There were 25 egos who identified 81 alters. Nearly all cases were connected with the exception of two dyads which are classified as vulnerable groups. The sociogram has 11 respondents as ego-alters.

There are six employees who have five connection each. N45 and N108 each have four indegree measures and their ego network compositions are heterogeneity in nature meaning their connections are from different departments. In the institutional knowledge sociogram there is no outright opinion leader or influencer as employees go to different people for institutional knowledge.

The final sociogram, Figure 10 was a network structure on the collaboration network the respondents identified.

Each color represents a different department. The sociogram included 25 egos who identified 84 alters with largely two informal groups. This sociogram had the most alters compared to the other sociograms in the study. The sociogram has 15 ego-alters. N108 is an influencer in this sociogram with four ego connectors. The collaboration sociogram has one big sociogram with one clique and one triad. This shows that respondents interact and collaborate a lot at work. This builds on information and knowledge shared, or better collaboration within the organization, and thus better performance and employee effectiveness.

Figure 9. Institutional knowledge advise sociogram based on departments

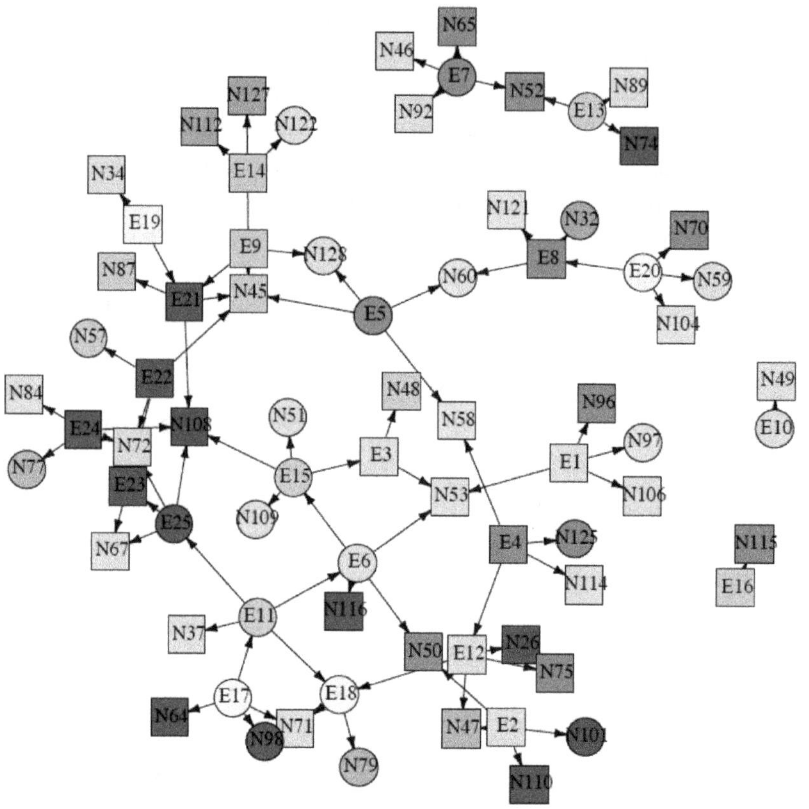

Advertising	Editorial	Digital	Sales	Finance	Female
Broadcast	Corporate Affairs	Business Development	HR	Operations	Male

RESULTS AND DISCUSSIONS

In ego network size, the degree of the actors, which is the number of direct ties an actor is linked to in the network structure is measured (Chan & Liebowitz, 2006). The more links an actor has, the more central they are and more powerful they can be in the structure. Ego network composition measures homophily and heterophily which help determine whether an ego is connected to people similar to themselves or different people in terms of the department, and also if the ego is accessing a diverse group of people (Halgins & Borgatti, 2012). Homophily according to Paul F. Lazarsfeld and Robert K. Merton (Rogers & Bhowmik, 1970) is when similar people interact with one another often, that they tend to have similar information and knowledge with each other. Dyads and triads will also be identified from the sociograms in order to analyse which set is most connected or most isolated from the network structure.

Figure 10. Collaboration sociogram based on departments

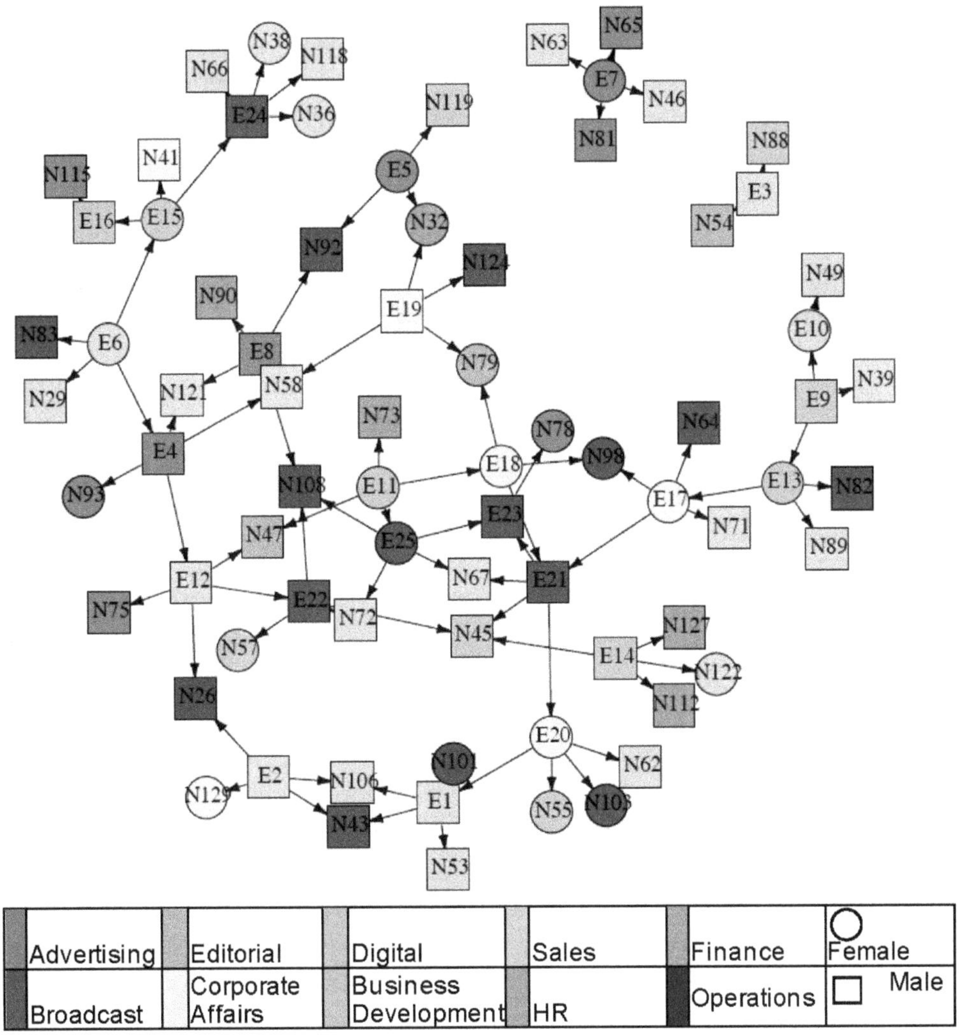

The five sociograms show how employees use their interpersonal communication informal structure to influence the flow of information. The information shared can be used to influence employees' interpersonal communication in the workplace. Castells (2010) observed the technological paradigm as a global network society where information was produced and communicated to manage human lives. The global society is being experienced in the workplace as informal networks are being formed and the actors influencing interpersonal communication.

By mapping out informal communication networks using SNA, the networks reveal the most influential, opinion leaders, brokers and gatekeepers employees. Informal networks in organizations need to be acknowledged (Chan & Liebowitz, 2006) and these networks exist based on employee's friends and colleagues. Knowledge management (Chan & Liebowitz, 2006) can also be applied using SNA informal networks where employees' positions such as influencers and brokers are determined and effectively used for information flow. By using structural hole theory by Ronald Burt (1992) to identify the gaps in the networks, employees and organizations can bridge the holes and create competitive advantage to influence interpersonal communication (Burt, 2017).

The sociogram networks also show how to effectively utilize employees' ties in the informal networks to share knowledge and information, and how the information can influence other employees in the organization. Using SNA, the analysis encourages more weak ties to form social capital and implies that people with more weak ties are more successful, as people with more strong ties may have a strong local cohesion but weak global cohesion (Borgatti & Halgin, 2011). The spread of knowledge especially from different departments creates a variety of information (Behrendt, Richter & Trier, 2014). The networks formed and information shared can be utilized by management to support decision making and collaborations. With technological advancement and social networking sites, González-Bailón, Borge-Holthoefer and Moreno (2013) suggests that online networks are efficient as one can be able to reach a larger group of people. This can be an area where management can explore by using both consumer based social networking sites as well as enterprise based sites.

However, it should be noted that the type of communication can influence employees in the network positively or negatively as warned by Lim, Cortina, and Magley (2008). Management should use work related sociograms for a spread of information that is relevant to the organization's objective, and not used to instigate employees or used for non-work related information. Leadership sociograms can be used to pinpoint the influencer and brokers as they are trusted by other actors. Institutional knowledge influencers can be trained on different aspects of the organizations as they are relied on for knowledge.

the reason why online networks are so efficient is because they have a very centralized structure that allows reaching a high number of people with short chains of diffusion

CONCLUSION

By mapping out the networks, organizations can be able to see visually the employees' networks and analyse the influence that relational ties have on interpersonal communication and employees' effectiveness in the workplace. Through SNA, networks can be mapped that identify the key employees and determine the type of influence they can have on their colleagues. SNA is mostly associated with other disciplines rather than with social sciences (Schlauch, Obradovic, & Dengel, 2012). However, the analysis can be applied in human communication to predict behaviour. Therefore, future studies can be done to test the different positions such as influencers and brokers to confirm the influence they have on the flow of information and their influence in the workplace.

With the realisation that informal networks are formed, organizations need to do comprehensive mapping to outline the networks and how information is transmitted. By effecting SNA as a methodology and technique, network analysis focuses on how individuals build relationships among interacting units (Wasserman & Faust, 1994). The analysis observes a network structure where individuals referred to as actors (egos and alters) or nodes are linked to other actors within the structure. These links can either provide opportunities or constraints for information flow. The networks formed would assist in exploring the influences of interpersonal communication in the workplace by examining the informal networks in the workplace and information sharing among employees. The results are usually presented using sociograms as they are visual presentations of the findings based on the individuals or actors represent. The structural patterns in the network show the position each actor occupies and their influence in the network. By mapping out informal intra-organizations (individuals, departments or levels) and inter-organizations (different companies) communication networks using SNA, the networks reveal the most influential, opinion leaders, brokers and gatekeepers employees.

SUMMARY

The above studies show that when applying SNA, the researcher has to factor and study the current structures first. This helps in analyzing how actors and structures interact with each other. How the structures are formed is important to determine whether they are formal or informal networks. As the networks evolve over time, it is important to establish how they influence interaction, communication and information flow, especially in an organizational setting. As pointed out in Cross, Borgatti, and Parker studies, the networks are important as managers can pin point the ties and actors' roles, and therefore be able to influence information flow. At the same time, studies such as Bonanich's (1990) show that competition can lead to communication dilemma, therefore the information does not flow within the networks. Perception versus reality in network studies is also paramount, since what is perceived as friendship and short paths may not necessarily be the reality as observed by Adamic, Buyukkokten, and Adar (2003).

Strong and weak ties theory by Mark Granovetter (1973) and structural hole theory by Ronald Burt (1992) are examples of theories that have been formulated from SNA. It is also important to note whether the removal of any node or person in the network will lead to low connectivity or reduce the knowledge movement within an organization (Schlauch, Obradovic, & Dengel, 2012). By using structural hole theory by Ronald Burt (1992) an organization can identify the gaps in the networks and can bridge the holes and create competitive advantage to influence interpersonal communication (Burt, 2017). The sociogram networks also show how to effectively utilize employees' ties in the informal networks to share knowledge and information, and how the information can influence other employees in the organization. Using SNA, the analysis encourages more weak ties to form social capital and implies that people with more weak ties are more successful, as people with more strong ties may have a strong local cohesion but weak global cohesion (Borgatti & Halgin, 2011). The spread of knowledge especially from different departments creates a variety of information (Behrendt, Richter & Trier, 2014). The networks formed and information shared can be utilized by management to support decision making and collaborations.

SNA as a theory and methodology was also used to map out informal networks in the workplace. Information was collected from employees to find out to whom they consult on different issues while in the workplace. Areas such as private life matters, work related matters, leadership advice, institutional knowledge and collaboration were covered and the sociograms mapped out. Using visual presentation of egos and alters, the networks were discussed based on the data collected. The private life sociogram showed small subsets as employees chose small networks, while the other sociograms were relatively large, even though employees still interacted more with employees from the same departments. A few influencers and brokers were identified in the sociograms as they would be relevant in information sharing and knowledge management.

Finally as stated in the introduction, informal networks in the workplace cannot be ignored. SNA theory can be used to show the key employees that other employees go to for different work-related issues. As recommended by Chan and Liebowitz (2006) and also by this study, organizations need to map out their informal networks in order to analyse the flow of information and knowledge management. The strength of the different ties would be identified as well as any structural holes that exist. Once an audit has been done and a sociogram drawn, organizations can come up with ways to encourage connections within the departments based on these initial findings. Thereafter, another analysis can be done to investigate whether there was improvement in knowledge management and information sharing, as this would have a positive influence on employees' interpersonal communication. If an organization is using enterprise social networking sites (ESNSs), then the mapping can be used to analyse the interconnected systems, the alliances and the reliance of SNSs to obtain and share information.

ACKNOWLEDGMENT

This research was supported by the National Institute for the Humanities and Social Sciences- Council for the Development of Social Research in Africa (Project Number: APS16/1014) towards this research is hereby acknowledged. Opinions expressed and conclusions arrived at are those of the author and not necessarily to be attributed to the NIHSS-CODESRIA.

REFERENCES

Adamic, A.L.A., Buyukkokten, O., & Adar, E. (2003). *A social network caught in the web*. Retrieved January 15, 2018 from https://journals.uic.edu/ojs/index.php/fm/article/view/1057/977

Alba, R. D., & Gutmann, M. P. (1972). SOCK: A sociometric analysis system. *ACM SIGSOC Bulletin*, *3*(3), 11–12. doi:10.1145/1103251.1103252

Bastian, M., Heymann, S., & Jacomy, M. (2009). Gephi: An open source software for exploring and manipulating networks. In *International AAAI Conference on Weblogs and Social Media*. Association for the Advancement of Artificial Intelligence.

Behrendt, S., Richter, A., & Trier, M. (2014). Mixed methods analysis of enterprise social networks. *Computer Networks*, *75*, 560–577. doi:10.1016/j.comnet.2014.08.025

Bonacich, P. (1990). Communication dilemmas in social networks: An experimental study. *American Sociological Review*, *55*(3), 448–459. doi:10.2307/2095768

Borgatti, S. P., Everett, M. G., & Freeman, L. C. (2002). Ucinet for Windows: Software for social network analysis. Analytic Technologies, 6.

Borgatti, S. P., & Halgin, D. S. (2011). On network theory. *Organization Science*, *22*(5), 1168–1181. doi:10.1287/orsc.1100.0641

Burt, R. (1992). *Structural holes*. doi:10.4159/9780674029095

Burt, R. S. (2004). Structural holes and good ideas. *American Journal of Sociology*, *110*(2), 349–399. doi:10.1086/421787

Burt, R. S. (2017). Structural holes versus network closure as social capital. In Social capital: Theory and research. Routledge. doi:10.4324/9781315129457-2

Castells, M. (2010). *The information age: Economy, society, and culture*. Wiley-Blackwell.

Chan, K., & Liebowitz, J. (2006). The synergy of social network analysis and knowledge mapping: A case study. *International Journal of Management and Decision Making*, *7*(1), 19–35. doi:10.1504/IJMDM.2006.008169

Cornell, X. (2014). *INFO2040X mod1 kleinberg structural holes v1* (video file). Retrieved on January 17, 2018 from https://www.youtube.com/watch?v=GaQLRCaLQG4

Cross, R., Borgatti, S. P., & Parker, A. (2002). Making invisible work visible: Using social network analysis to support strategic collaboration. *California Management Review*, *44*(2), 25–46. doi:10.2307/41166121

Cross, R., Parker, A., & Sasson, L. (Eds.). (2003). *Networks in the knowledge economy*. Oxford University Press. doi:10.1093/oso/9780195159509.001.0001

Cross, R., & Prusak, L. (2002). *The people who make organizations go–or stop*. Networks in the Knowledge Economy.

Cross, R. L., Cross, R. L., & Parker, A. (2004). *The hidden power of social networks: Understanding how work really gets done in organizations*. Harvard Business Press.

Cyram. (2003). *NetMiner II*. Ver.2.4.0 [computer software]. Cyram Co., Ltd.

Easley, D., & Kleinberg, J. (2012). Networks, crowds, and markets: Reasoning about a highly connected world. *Significance*, *9*, 43–44.

Fredericks, K. A., & Durland, M. M. (2005). The historical evolution and basic concepts of social network analysis. *New Directions for Evaluation*, *2005*(107), 15–23. doi:10.1002/ev.158

Freeman, L. C., White, D. R., & Romney, A. K. (1989). *Research Methods in Social Network Analysis*. George Mason University Press.

González-Bailón, S., Borge-Holthoefer, J., & Moreno, Y. (2013). Broadcasters and hidden influentials in online protest diffusion. *The American Behavioral Scientist*, *57*(7), 943–965. doi:10.1177/0002764213479371

Granovetter, M. S. (1973). The strength of weak ties. *American Journal of Sociology*, *78*(6), 1360–1380. doi:10.1086/225469

Hatala, J. P. (2006). Social network analysis in human resource development: A new methodology. *Human Resource Development Review*, *5*(1), 45–71. doi:10.1177/1534484305284318

Kilduff, M., Crossland, C., Tsai, W., & Krackhardt, D. (2008). Organizational network perceptions versus reality: A small world after all? *Organizational Behavior and Human Decision Processes*, *107*(1), 15–28. doi:10.1016/j.obhdp.2007.12.003

Kozinets, R. V. (2010). *Netnography: Doing ethnographic research online*. Sage publications.

Krebs, V. E. (1998). *Knowledge networks: mapping and measuring knowledge creation and reuse*. White Paper. Available at: www. orgnet. com/IHRIM. html

Krebs, V. E. (2004). *Managing the connected organization*. www. orgnet. com

Liebowitz, J. (Ed.). (1999). *Knowledge management handbook*. CRC Press.

Lim, S., Cortina, L. M., & Magley, V. J. (2008). Personal and workgroup incivility: Impact on work and health outcomes. *The Journal of Applied Psychology*, *93*(1), 95–107. doi:10.1037/0021-9010.93.1.95 PMID:18211138

Moreno, J. L. (1937). Sociometry in relation to other social sciences. *Sociometry*, *1*(1/2), 206–219. doi:10.2307/2785266

Mutoh, A., Imura, Y., Kato, R., Matsui, T., & Inuzuka, N. (2016). A model of friendship networks based on social network analysis. *Artificial Life and Robotics*, *21*(2), 165–170. doi:10.100710015-016-0275-8

Noyes, E. (n.d.). *Structural Hole Theory: The Relationship between Corporate Ties and Corporate Innovation.* Retrieved on September 02, 2016 from https://www.bu.edu/tech/support/research/visualization/gallery/structhole/

Richardson, D. C. (2000). *MAGE, Computer Software*. Duke University.

RStudio Team. (2019). *RStudio: Integrated Development for R*. RStudio. https://www.rstudio.com/

Schlauch, W., Obradovic, D., & Dengel, A. (2012, September). Organizational Social Network Analysis–Case Study in a Research Facility. In *35th German Conference on Artificial Intelligence* (p. 78). Academic Press.

Scott, J. (1992). *Social Network Analysis*. Sage.

Seidman, S. B., & Foster, B. L. (1979). Sonet-1: Social network analysis and modeling system. *Social Networks*, *2*(1), 85–90. doi:10.1016/0378-8733(79)90013-3

Wasserman, S. & Faust, K. (1994). *Social network analysis: Methods and applications* (Vol. 8). Cambridge University Press.

KEY TERMS AND DEFINITIONS

Employee Communication: The process of conveying information from one employee to another.

Informal Networks: Social structures that incorporate aspects of communication that are used by employees to interact with one another in an organizations.

Interpersonal Communication: Communication by one employee to one or more employee in an organization.

Networks: Employee's social structures.

Social Networks Analysis: Theory or methodology that show employees' social ties within an organization.

Ties: Connections formed by employees in an organization. These ties form social structures or networks in organizations.

Chapter 5
Applying Machine Learning to Online Data?
Beware! Computational Social Science Requires Care

Ulya Bayram
https://orcid.org/0000-0002-8150-4053
Çanakkale Onsekiz Mart University, Turkey

ABSTRACT

The immense impact of social media on contemporary cultural evolution is undeniable, consequently declaring them an essential data source for computational social science studies. Alongside the advancements in natural language processing and machine learning disciplines, computational social science researchers continuously adapt new techniques to the data collected from social media. Although these developments are imperative for studying the sociological transformations in many communities, there are some inconspicuous problems on the horizon. This chapter addresses issues that may arise from the use of social media data, like biased models. It also discusses various obstacles associated with machine learning methods while also providing possible solutions and recommendations to overcome these struggles from an interdisciplinary perspective. In the long term, this chapter will guide computational social science researchers in their future studies, from things to be aware of with data collection to assembling an accurate experimental design.

DOI: 10.4018/978-1-7998-8553-5.ch005

INTRODUCTION

In the current digital age, online data availability is exponentially growing. Consequently, the interest in computational social science (CSS) research is rising, which spans many disciplines (social psychology, anthropology, economics, political science, sociology, and various levels of analysis) (Oboler, Welsh, & Cruz, 2012). Studies conducted on past and recent Congressional records of many countries including the United States (Bayram, Pestian, Santel, & Minai, 2019; Diermeier, Godbout, Yu, & Kaufmann, 2012; Gentzkow, Shapiro, & Taddy, 2016; Iyyer, Enns, Boyd-Graber, & Resnik, 2014; Jensen et al., 2012; Lauderdale & Herzog, 2016; Thomas, Pang, & Lee, 2006; Yu, Kaufmann, & Diermeier, 2008), political records from the British Parliament (Peterson & Spirling, 2018), and the Irish Dail debates (Lauderdale & Herzog, 2016), are among the plethora of studies that became possible thanks to the online availability of these collections. Similarly, old and new newspaper articles (Burley et al., 2020; Neresini, 2017), speeches of political figures including those from the past centuries (Jackson, Watts, List, Drabble, & Lindquist, 2021; Savoy, 2010), digital books (Brooke, Hammond, & Hirst, 2015), and many other textual online data have been the main focus of CSS research. While all these online data sources bring rich contributions to the broad range of CSS research areas, there is one domain that requires special attention: social media data.

Data collected from social media platforms facilitate many possibilities such as answering serious social science-related questions, finding insights into both individual-level and anthropological phenomena (Harford, 2014; Lazer et al., 2009; Olteanu, Castillo, Diaz, & Kiciman, 2019). There is also a growing consensus that data collected from these domains can provide more than simple observations (Olteanu et al., 2019); social media domains are amongst the most valuable data sources for CSS research areas. The wide-range public usage of social media domains, the absence of data use restrictions, the simplicity of data acquisition through application programming interfaces (APIs), and the valuable content of the data made them attractive for researchers. These social media and social network platforms (e.g. Twitter, Facebook, Reddit, Wikipedia, other forums) can easily capture the evolution of sociological norms and rapid changes culturally and globally. For example, recent movements such as "Me Too" and "Black Lives Matter" could not expand globally without these platforms. This fact makes these platforms one of the principal sources of information for CSS research on such events. Recent studies utilize social media data to evaluate the effects of crises like the mass killings in the United States (Burley et al., 2020).

The large availability of data drove CSS researchers towards using natural language processing (NLP), machine learning, and deep learning methods. They follow the NLP and machine learning literature to determine which techniques would be beneficial for their studies. Additionally, their openness to collaborate with professionals from different domains prompted the CSS studies to become more interdisciplinary. Studies they conduct utilizing NLP, machine learning, or deep learning techniques report new findings that were previously unattainable due to lack of proper automated tools. While all these developments on computational methods and online data availability are very advantageous for the future of CSS research, certain aspects of utilizing them demand more care and attention because there are significant problems inconspicuously haunting the studies. Data collected from social media may contain racist, sexist, or otherwise abusive language. These collections may also include samples with misinformation about the subject of interest and may create biased models. Also, machine learning methods are susceptible to predicaments like overfitting, underfitting, unsuitable method selection, and costly parameter tuning. Likewise, improper experiment designs could affect the generalizability of the findings, which would invalidate the reported results. Meanwhile, the black-box nature of machine learning and deep learning models causes a lack of interpretability regarding how or on which basis the results were obtained from these methods, making it difficult to justify the findings.

This chapter focuses on problems related to using online data and machine learning methods in CSS research from an interdisciplinary perspective. Each of the four main sections explains a range of problems related to a subject through examples to raise awareness towards constructing better studies. The following sections also propose recommendations and resolutions on how to overcome some of these obstacles. This chapter aims to inform a wide range of audiences that aspire to conduct CSS research utilizing online data and machine learning methods; while also intends to serve as a guide for future studies.

BACKGROUND

Since social media domains become a part of everyday life and the common subject of many CSS studies, researchers began to raise concerns. Among these concerns is how the use of social media in CSS should be constrained legally and ethically to protect society (Oboler et al., 2012). CSS studies on areas like social anthropology and political science can have significant negative impacts, such as the subversion of democracy, profiling of individuals or groups for the development of better manipulation or even brainwashing techniques (Oboler et al., 2012). It is known that during the last few presidential elections in the United States, social media data was actively utilized to shape the course of elections (Bessi & Ferrara, 2016; Issenberg, 2013; Sen, Flock, &Wagner, 2020). In that perspective, the power of conducting CSS studies on online data is unequivocal. Therefore not committing any measurement errors is of utmost importance for a functioning democracy as it is vital for scholars (Sen et al., 2020). There is a great responsibility on the part of CSS researchers for making sure their models and results are correct.

In addition to the ethical concerns, there are several pitfalls related to using data acquired from online platforms such as social media (Olteanu et al., 2019). For instance, the existence of big data may not always be a blessing. In some cases, problems can be solved with a subsection of the big data, and using more than enough can make the estimations worse (Harford, 2014). Besides the data size, there is a notorious phenomenon called "bias," which is a word very generously uttered by studies without a clear definition (Blodgett, Barocas, Daume III, & Wallach, 2020). Algorithms are not known for being ethically neutral regardless of the circumstances (Tsamados et al., 2021). They are not magical; they are prone to learning noise or bad samples from the data. Also, there are inherent problems related to the algorithms/machine learning methods as well. All these issues can produce different types of biases. For example, various studies show that algorithmic advertisements regarding opportunities for higher-paying jobs in science and technology fields are advertised to men more often than those advertised to women (Datta, Tschantz, & Datta, 2015; Lambrecht & Tucker, 2019). It is only one class of studies demonstrating that machine learning methods can become biased towards gender. Another example shows that the prediction algorithms used in the United States health care systems enable white patients to receive measurably better care than black patients (Obermeyer, Powers, Vogeli, & Mullainathan, 2019). It is another demonstration of how serious the real-life consequences of a biased algorithm can be. The existence of bias in machine learning methods in CSS is dangerous and has to be eliminated. Olteanu et al. (2019) provide a detailed insight on different types of biases (population bias, behavioral bias, content bias, linking bias, temporal bias, and redundancy) with corresponding definitions and possible methods to overcome them.

Although studies acknowledge the existence and importance of various kinds of biases, only a few studies propose techniques for measuring or alleviating them (Blodgett et al., 2020). Nonetheless, using these techniques may not be enough to guarantee a problem-free CSS research. The study of Jacobs and Wallach (2021) shows that even when the systems are designed to be unbiased, the fairness measures used can also be harmful due to the assumptions made during the design. They state that making assumptions can introduce potential mismatches between the theoretical understanding of the measured subject and the actual model constructed to perform the measurement. There are many other challenges regarding the social media data, such as labeling, feature extraction, feature elimination, class imbalance, among others. However, CSS research is not only threatened by data-related problems. Besides these issues, there are also other difficulties associated with using machine learning algorithms. Studies like L. Zhou, Pan, Wang, and Vasilakos (2017) and Domingos (2012) summarize some of these difficulties. There are challenges like overfitting, underfitting, scalability, incorrect feature selection implementations, selecting the wrong objective functions, among many others. Meantime, the popular deep learning methods also have specific drawbacks (Miotto, Wang, Wang, Jiang, & Dudley, 2018). In addition to the computational complexity, they can suffer from issues like a lack of interpretability, i.e. their black-box nature. This causes a requirement for a level of expertise in machine learning as not every method is suitable for every data type, size, or subject under analysis (L. Zhou et al., 2017). CSS researchers are from various backgrounds and the field is interdisciplinary, but not all researchers can be experts at machine learning.

As these background studies show, conducting CSS studies using online data and machine learning methods is a sensitive quest. Using algorithmic methods and interpreting the findings demand attention, knowledge and caution, all proportional to the subject-sensitivity. A computer scientist conducting CSS research without proper data sensitivity knowledge on the research subject may fail to be careful or fail to interpret the results accurately. Similarly, a political scientist conducting a CSS research study using machine learning might select methods based on their popularity rather than their suitability to the research subject, or might fail to build an optimal model and reach the wrong conclusions. This chapter is to guide these researchers in realizing some of these issues briefly and effectively. Those who seek more information regarding specific obstacles related to data or machine learning can refer to the Additional Reading section.

WORKING WITH ONLINE DATA

The wide-range availability of online data has increased the interest in NLP research. Consequently, various CSS research areas became attractive for researchers from distinct fields. Especially the emergence of social media platforms where individuals can freely express their thoughts and opinions shaped the current state of CSS research interest. Researchers collect data from these platforms for purposes like studying the recent social movements like "Me Too" and "Black Lives Matter," for modeling the information flow concerning the evolution and the effects of conspiracy theories like "QAnon," or the aftereffects of some critical events like "US Capitol riots of 2021." They employ standard NLP techniques on these rich data collections and implement the fundamental pre-processing methods before training the algorithmic models. To label the data, they commonly look for pre-selected keywords related to the subject or the hashtags to avoid manual labeling costs (Grace, Halse, Aurite, Montarnal, & Tapia, 2019). Alternatively, some studies use crowd-sourcing to label the data (Chang, Amershi, & Kamar, 2017). Next, they train selected machine learning models with an assortment of these labeled data and conduct their analyses, classifications, or predictions based on their hypotheses and goals. However, all these operations have several associated costs. Among them, the data alone can vitiate a CSS study.

The challenge of using social media data begins with the data collection step. Properly collecting samples that include data from various demographics and groups uniformly and fairly is very important for CSS research (Olteanu et al., 2019). Also, data collected from social media domains contain many typos and errors, which may induce problematic results (Olteanu et al., 2019). Further, the existence of sarcasm or spam within the samples can go unrecognized by the data collection algorithms, and their presence would harm the machine learning results. The vast volumes of collected tweets, for example, will contain samples that are sarcastically mocking the movements or ideologies under analysis, as these mockers could use similar keywords or hashtags as the supporters. CSS researchers who are unaware of these possibilities will include measurements from these bad samples and report incorrect results. Also, there could be data in the collections intentionally containing misinformation to subvert or taint the movements or ideologies. Studies show how "fake news" emerges, especially during the elections (Allcott & Gentzkow, 2017; Wu, Morstatter, Carley, & Liu, 2019). Likewise, the existence of abusive language or curse words in data might result in incorrect measurements about the analyzed problem. Machine learning methods that are trained to perform a CSS study, unless specifically fine-tuned to do otherwise, cannot detect the existence of misinformation or sarcasm. Thus, all these "bad samples" present within the data collection procured from the social media domains might bias the studies (Bender, Gebru, McMillan-Major, & Shmitchell, 2021).

As mentioned in the previous section, the word bias is commonly encountered in the literature. There are many different types of biases. The study of Olteanu et al. (2019) provides a detailed survey of possible biases with proper definitions and explanations. Because of the high number of bias types, how a model becomes biased is a complex problem to detect. However, creating a model containing bias is very easy. A data collection may appear to be balanced, but the samples might induce a biased algorithmic outcome. A study demonstrates this possibility through a real-life example: machine learning models proposed for use in the judicial system in the United States return racially inequitable decisions because the training data has latent patterns correlated with race (Rice, Rhodes, & Nteta, 2019). The examples in the previous section related to gender and healthcare are also critical examples regarding the biased models. These examples are the types of biases caused by the data. Meantime, there are many other possible ways to produce bias in models. Regardless of the type of bias present, none of the classification outcomes proclaimed by these biased models would be reliable (Bender et al., 2021). However, detecting and eliminating the possible sources of bias is not an easy task. While it is crucial to manually inspect a small subset of the data collection to grasp the contents, it is unattainable to manually investigate every sample in a dataset containing thousands or even millions of samples. A feasible approach for detection and elimination of bias is through analysis and data elimination.

Researchers have focused on possible ways to detect and reduce the likely roots of problems in data collections. These ways can be divided into two based on their complexity. Some of these methods used in text related tasks can be summarized as follows:

- Some simple methods
    - Removing typos
    - Checking language
    - Detecting semantics
    - Using ontologies
    - Plotting distributions
    - Using experts during labeling

- Some complex methods
    - Using power-law distributions
    - Following auto-text generation literature

Simple methods include tools available in NLP literature for detecting typos, language, and semantics within the data. Removing typos would eliminate many uninformative samples that could harm the models. Similarly, identifying which language do the texts contain is essential for social media datasets. Because domains like Twitter comprise posts in many languages and the tweets containing multiple languages can have the same hashtags or keywords used for labeling, and their existence may cause failure during the experiments. Meanwhile, checking the semantics can help eliminate texts containing indirectly expressed opinions such as sarcasm. Also, ontologies like Linguistic Inquiry and Word Count (Pennebaker, Francis, & Booth, 2001) can be used for removing the texts falling under undesired categories. Alternatively, the study of Olteanu et al. (2019) proposes comparing the samples in the data collection with reference samples from other sources. To handle these comparisons, techniques developed for textual data matching operations could be of help. Meantime, researchers can plot distributions over statistics such as demographics (if available) for creating balanced datasets. They also can reach out to experts to eliminate labeling-related biases.

Compared to the simple methods, there are alternative methods for detecting and eliminating data related problems. However, employing them would require adding another layer of a computational process to the CSS research. For example, to remove samples containing hateful comments, a researcher would need to implement one of the methods in the hatefulness-detection literature (Fortuna & Nunes, 2018). Similarly, studies like X. Zhou and Zafarani (2020) that automatically detect the existence of "fake news" and misinformation can be used to eliminate bad samples from the data collections. Yet, there are some challenges regarding bad sample detection that are waiting to be resolved in the future (Blodgett et al., 2020). Also, the addition of another layer of computation to detect and eliminate unwanted samples comes with the cost of increasing the computational complexity of research. Therefore, social scientists should consider the sensitivity of their research subject before deciding whether increasing the level of complexity is worth the effort.

Problems in a CSS research that may emerge due to online data are not limited to these. Another potential problem is the assumption that the texts are created by humans. There are many language models like Long short-term memory (LSTM) (Sherstinsky, 2020), Bidirectional Encoder Representations from Transformers (BERT) (Devlin, Chang, Lee, & Toutanova, 2019), generative pre-training (GPT) (Radford, Narasimhan, Salimans, & Sutskever, 2018), among others. They are analyzed and improved frequently to auto-generate better and more believable texts (Otter, Medina, & Kalita, 2020). In the past, evaluating whether the data follows a power-law distribution would be beneficial to determine whether the data was human-generated (Clauset, Shalizi, & Newman, 2009). However, the recent developments in NLP and machine learning disciplines are changing the level of difficulty. A model called GPT-3 shows strong capabilities in convincing readers as to whether the generated texts were actually from a human (Hao, 2020). These models are trained over big data and learn which words are more likely to follow each other through complex mathematical methods and then generate texts automatically on a given subject (Devlin et al., 2019). They are likely to affect the future of NLP research on online data. Hence, the CSS researchers will also have to deal with these computer-generated texts besides other problems. Researchers need to be aware of such developments in the literature.

WORKING WITH MACHINE LEARNING METHODS

Machine learning is part of the artificial intelligence field where methods learn patterns present within the given labeled or unlabeled dataset, based on the algorithmic structure of the selected model. These methods can roughly be divided into three based on the learning process they contain: supervised, unsupervised, and semi-supervised. Supervised methods require labeled training sets for learning the optimal ways of separating the data into classes based on the labels. Meanwhile, the unsupervised techniques do not require any labeled sets. Instead, they utilize different processes to find the optimal ways to separate the data without label-related knowledge. Alternatively, the semi-supervised learning methods use a mixture of a few labeled and many unlabeled data. These learning processes are a collaboration of representation, evaluation, and optimization (Domingos, 2012). A sub-field of machine learning research, known as deep learning, can also be explained through these general descriptions. However, deep learning also has its specific differences. These methods contain multiple layers of neural networks with complex mathematical processes. This section focuses on some problems the CSS researchers who are not experts in machine learning may encounter and need to be aware of, followed by related recommendations and solutions:

- The importance of feature elimination/selection
- Assumptions made by machine learning algorithms
- Selecting a method based on biased opinion
- Deep learning burdens
- Experience and knowledge required for properly tuning the methods
- High expectations from machine learning methods

Most machine learning methods require data to be transformed into a feature space through certain mathematical operations. In working with textual data, one of the choices is using n-grams. They are the word frequencies for unigrams (n=1), concurrent word pair frequencies for bigrams (n=2). These unigram and bigram features together showed success in the past (Bayram et al., 2019). Thanks to the developments in NLP literature, there are other options like the word embeddings (Mikolov, Sutskever, Chen, Corrado, & Dean, 2013). For a successful machine learning application, it is necessary to use features that can capture the patterns relevant to the data and to the main aim. The most appropriate solution for this is to search the literature to determine the most preferred/recommended for the studied subject. However, extracting the correct set of features is not enough to promise a successful machine learning application for a CSS study. Before using them for learning processes, it is also necessary to perform elimination after feature extraction (Domingos, 2012). The presence of a large number of uninformative features can introduce a burden over the learning process. It can also cause problems like learning noise and damaging the generalizability of the model. For avoiding these, it is possible to eliminate features using statistical methods such as the Kolmogorov-Smirnov test or Principal Component Analysis, where the feature variances are computed. However, creating a golden feature set cannot promise a problem-free machine learning application.

The use of machine learning methods possesses various possible inherent issues independent from the feature elimination. One of these issues is how every method makes certain assumptions about the data beyond the existing knowledge, which is the central goal (Domingos, 2012). For example, the naive Bayes classifier that uses the Bayes theorem makes an assumption of independence between the features given the class. On that note, whether this assumption holds for the actual data used to train this classifier is not considered. Similarly, linear classifiers always have the assumption that the data is linearly separable, which may not be true. Some data collections might have complex patterns that would thrive with non-linear models instead of linear ones. Nevertheless, without experimenting with both linear and non-linear models, it is nearly impossible to determine. Thus there is no guarantee that any of these inherent assumptions of the selected algorithms will be accurate for every dataset and every classification problem. A way to handle any predicaments that may emerge from these assumptions is to experiment with different types of methods. Another concern regarding the use of machine learning is method selection. It is a known phenomenon that the method selection typically reflects the past experience of a researcher, which is justifiable since it is easier than learning and experimenting with a new model. However, this method selection bias can create more problems like using methods that are not suitable for the study. There could be methods more fitting for the type of data, size of the collection, or the subject of interest, and relying on the knowledge a researcher already possesses might result in incorrect results. Thus, researchers need to be deliberate and reasonable when making their choices to overcome this issue. Perhaps the most straightforward solution could be to conduct a literature search over possible methods used for the studied problem and stating the arguments for method selections before initiating the implementations.

The mentioned problems are also valid for the subfield of machine learning called deep learning. There is an undeniable bias towards preferring deep learning methods over more manageable methods because of their popularity. While deep learning methods have proven to be successful on various difficult data problems, thus rightfully deserving this popularity, a drawback is that they expect plenty of training for returning acceptable results (Otter et al., 2020), which may not be possible in some problem domains. Yet, they cannot guarantee success in every problem and data domain. They come with the burden of computational complexity. In other words, they require additional computational resources for providing adequate performance. However, not every CSS researcher can access expensive servers to run these complicated learning algorithms over large data collections. Researchers should consider using deep learning methods when it is necessary to bring the computational complexity to the studied subject. They should initially experiment with simple, well-tuned machine learning methods, and pursue deep learning methods only when the simple ones do not return satisfactory results. In fact, any study from any research filed that uses a deep learning method should also report results from the well-tuned simple machine learning methods. That is a good way of rationalizing the necessity for complexity.

Machine learning and deep learning methods require some level of knowledge from the users regarding parameter tuning and objective function selection. An objective function is a proxy to the true goal, which is to generalize the learned model over previously unseen data (Domingos, 2012). Methods can return completely conflicting results if different objective functions are selected (Olteanu et al., 2019). Therefore, it is of utmost importance to perform the tunings and function selections cautiously. The needed knowledge is available if the researchers are willing to seek them. For example, to handle the parameter tuning properly, literature shows that sometimes finding a local optimum by a randomized search can be more efficient than finding a global optimum through a greedy search (Bergstra & Bengio, 2012). Thus, researchers need to refer to the literature when facing such choices during their implementations instead of willfully selecting parameters or objective functions. Finally, the most effective recommendation is to be aware that machine learning models are not magical; they cannot produce something out of anything (Domingos, 2012). These methods are limited by the information and patterns present in the data. Consequently, researchers should have realistic expectations when working with machine learning methods and should be prepared to handle failures.

EVALUATION AND GENERALIZATION

The fundamental goal of machine learning is to generalize the evaluations beyond the examples present in the labeled set (Domingos, 2012). Any CSS research that uses machine intelligence algorithms also has the same goal: to make general claims about the world based on what is observed from the data evaluations. However, obtaining results from one collection and accepting the observations as the golden truth about the studied social science phenomenon can induce various problems. Because the researcher could be using the incorrect metrics for the evaluations, and the observations could be proportionally problematic. Similarly, the dataset could be problematical, thus causing faulty generalizations. A few of such problems are explained in this section:

- Selecting the correct evaluation metrics
- Relying on the generalization results

Following the implementation of a machine learning method, the next step is to evaluate the results, which is not easy. Selecting the correct evaluation metric might affect a research study takeaways (Olteanu et al., 2019). There are many metrics to evaluate the success of a machine learning model, including accuracy, precision, recall, the area under the ROC curve, among others. Before selecting metrics to evaluate the results of a CSS study, researchers need to consider a few factors. One of these factors is the class imbalance in the data collection. An example of imbalanced data collection could be forum posts containing many positive views about a political party, where the research goal is to detect the few negative opinions. There are methods to handle training set class imbalance problems at the data level (e.g. reducing the number of positive view posts from the collection), algorithm level (e.g. using machine learning methods that can handle learning imbalanced data), or hybrids that combine the both (Krawczyk, 2016). When the test set has class imbalance, the evaluation metric selection becomes important. Meanwhile, the existence of class imbalance on test sets also requires attention. For example, the accuracy metric is not appropriate for imbalanced test sets since its equation (the number of correct detections divided by all) is not fit well to represent the classes with small number of samples compared to the other classes. In such cases, a researcher can use balanced accuracy metrics (Brodersen et al., 2010). In addition to class imbalance, the meaning of the evaluation metric alone can be important depending on the subject of interest. For instance, the recall metric might be more suitable when detecting the positive class data in health-care related domains.

Another error a CSS researcher may face towards the end of a study is to have too much faith in the results and to make global generalizations about the world based on the observed outcomes. However, machine intelligence results are only as good as the data and the algorithm. Therefore, the trained models that return the evaluation scores or the analyzed outcomes should also be studied to ensure whether the results are interpretable. The study of Ribeiro, Singh, and Guestrin (2016) shows an example where a deep learning model that returns high classification scores actually learned to detect husky images based on the existence of snow in the background instead of learning any features related to specifying the shape or properties of the animal. This problem would not be discovered if the researchers did not analyze the learned features. In that case the model would be applied to real-world classification tasks and could return incorrect results. Another study demonstrates that pre-trained deep learning methods that return top scores on ImageNet competition actually have been overfitting (Recht et al., 2019). They demonstrate that when slightly harder generalization experiments are introduced using the same or similar data, the reported high scores drop by 3-15%. Problems like overfitting can cause observing high results, which is due to memorizing the training data to the point of eventually damaging the ability to generalize to other data (Domingos, 2012). It is fundamental not to rely on within-dataset scores alone. Studies like Sen et al. (2020) are good examples regarding the importance of performing generalization experiments. The generalization evaluation is also known as measuring the external validity of the outcomes found through within-dataset evaluations (Olteanu et al., 2019). One of the goals of the NLP studies is constructing and training methods that can be re-used (Sen et al., 2020). When the CSS research areas are considered, the value of this generalizability principle becomes more significant because the found outcomes should hold for other data collections obtained from the same or different sources. Otherwise, the complete foundation of the CSS research would fall apart, and the validity of claims and the credibility of researchers would become dubious. Researchers should not prefer some methods over others based on their reported results in the literature as the study of Recht et al. (2019) demonstrates how the generalization experiments are useful to detect the faulty models.

In addition to the generalization experiments, comparing the evaluation and generalization results of different methods is necessary for the credibility of the findings. For example, some experiments show simple methods can over-perform the complex ones on various data collections (Bayram et al., 2019; Bayram & Benhiba, 2021). In a similar case where data favors simple methods over the complex ones, if the researchers only experiment with the popular complex methods and report their results, they might come to wrong conclusions about the subject of interest due to low performance they observe. Thus including a range of methods with different complexities is also essential for a machine learning study. However, it is important to note that the method comparisons should be conducted fairly. For example, a researcher who favors a method over the others might tune the favored method well, while not conducting any necessary parameter search or fine tuning on the other compared methods. Such an experiment would return results favoring the favored method, but the reliability of the study and its claims would be questionable. Conducting a good CSS research requires a lot of caution and attention so the reported evaluation and generalization results would be correct, trustworthy, and can aid the future research studies.

INTERPRETING THE RESULTS

The vitality of interpreting the evaluation results in CSS earns it a separate section in this chapter. Correctly interpreting the results is at the core of social science. Therefore it is essential for a researcher to be aware of some potential issues when interpreting the findings obtained from the trained models. Some of the elements to consider when interpreting the results of a CSS study:

- Not mixing correlations with causations
- The black-box property of machine learning methods
- Ethics/need for an expert opinion

One of the most common pitfalls in research is mixing the correlation with causation (Domingos, 2012). Especially in CSS studies, it is easy to make this mistake when interpreting the findings. Machine learning methods are powerful. Especially the power of deep learning technology enables researchers to automatically detect complex patterns present within the large data collections. However, the expectation should be limited to finding the patterns present within the data, and not to lean towards causative interpretations. Because, in principle, machine learning only learns patterns algorithmically found to be correlated to the goal, but it does not or cannot learn all the variables that exist in the real-world (Leetaru, 2019). For example, a hypothetical study could be detecting a positive correlation between the male gender and a high number of research publications after analyzing the author genders in a journal. Thus, interpreting this correlation with the causation of "male authors are better at publishing than the authors of other genders," or even as "male academics are more successful than the others" would be profoundly problematic and false. There could be other factors behind the correlation results such as the training data or the used model having a gender bias. In another example, a CSS researcher conducting a machine-learning study to detect anti-vaxxers from online posts might find a correlation between anti-vaxxers and where they live, e.g. majority of the anti-vaxxers are found to be living in the coastal areas. Therefore, when interpreting the results, the researcher should refrain from making remarks such as "living in the coastal areas causes individuals to oppose to vaccines." Instead, the CSS researcher should look deeper into the data, which might show that the majority of the posts are collected from coastal area residents, or there could be other latent problems in the data.

Another matter to be aware of when interpreting the machine learning results is the black-box property of the models. Some machine learning libraries provide tools to analyze the trained models by ranking the features based on their effectiveness during the training process. Simple, linear classifiers commonly provide such techniques to detect the top features. However, in complex machine learning and deep learning methods, interpreting the decision-making mechanism behind a result is no longer straightforward. Especially those researchers that lack proper education or training on machine learning theory might find it arduous to understand the underlying structure that returns the obtained results. Thanks to the growing research interest in deep learning, new methods are being developed to overcome the back-box property of these complex methods (Montavon, Samek, & Muller, 2018). A study conducted by Google researchers attempts to go through the deep learning process backwards and returns visually appealing images they call "how machines dream" (Mordvintsev, Olah, & Tyka, 2015). While the researchers unveil the structures of these trained complex models, they are still difficult to interpret for those who lack theoretical training in the field. Researchers should consider the importance of interpreting the results by taking the underlying structure of their models into account because the models are responsible for the obtained results. Otherwise, their interpretations might lack proper reasoning and may mislead other researchers.

Perhaps one of the most important issues related to the use of machine learning methods in CSS problems is the possibility of obtaining biased models, where bias in this sentence refers to ethical issues. In the previous sections, how the use of machine learning models in the justice system could cause a bias towards race was mentioned. A study by Angwin et al. (2016) expands the racial bias in judicial system algorithms in great detail with real-life examples. They find that the scores returned by the system were remarkably unreliable in forecasting future violent crime. Additionally, the formula was found to be falsely flagging black defendants as future criminals very frequently, almost twice the rate as the white defendants. Meantime, white defendants were mislabeled with low future crime risk scores more often than the black defendants. Two individuals with different race who commit the same crime receive different future crime prediction scores, which is highly unfair. Another study by Buolamwini and Gebru (2018) studies algorithms that classify gender from the face images and report that three commercial gender classification systems perform significantly worse on the images of individuals with darker skin tones. These studies show that the machine learning algorithms used in CSS problems are far from being perfect for many reasons. While there is a research focus on finding ways to improve the fairness of these algorithms, CSS researchers should be aware of the possibility of obtaining unfair results. The ethical side of research is important. Any interpretation of the results obtained from an unfair model could be harmful in many aspects. A solution could be to consult social scientists (Olteanu et al., 2019). A social scientist could perform an independent statistical analysis over the data and the machine learning results to validate their fairness, could provide different interpretations, and could eliminate the ethical concerns. Also, consulting the experts would be useful when the studies are conducted by interdisciplinary researchers, because the lack of social science knowledge may cause incorrect interpretations of the findings as well.

FUTURE RESEARCH DIRECTIONS

The growth of social media evokes more attention to CSS research, thus causing the field to become progressively more interdisciplinary. Thanks to all this attention CSS receives, the latest developments in NLP and machine learning research domains are getting executed by the interdisciplinary researchers over various CSS problems. They inform the public with their new and significant findings, causing conspicuous changes in everyday life through studies covering critical domains such as political science and health care. With more CSS studies conducted, the society becomes more conscious of the ongoing problems reported by these studies, thus hopefully enforcing a change towards the positive in everyday life. For example, those who read the previously mentioned CSS studies reporting how machine learning is actively operated on social media during the elections might become more aware of the content they see, thus might become more resistant to potential manipulations. Meanwhile, studies like Bender et al. (2021) inform the researchers and the public about problems like race or gender bias in machine learning. Thanks to the increasing awareness, the future may behold better tools to detect and eliminate these biases.

There are also negative consequences to the advancements in NLP and machine learning disciplines regarding the future of CSS research. While these advancements are making it possible to develop better automated language models (e.g. GTP-3), these language models can be used for malicious purposes. For example, the language auto-generator models can be used on social media to change public opinion regarding politics, alter election outcomes, easily manipulate large crowds, and ultimately cause adverse events in the future like the US Capitol riots of 2021, which was also due to the spread of manipulative information. These generative models can even be utilized to further ignite the ongoing riots through trolling activities and generate more chaos. Thus these language models can become an immense threat to the future of society. Moreover, texts created by these models can escape detection tools due to their complex nature. While these models are very recent and are yet to become widely available, CSS researchers need to be aware of this potential threat.

With the wide-range availability of machine learning courses, CSS researchers who do not have a deep computational background are learning more information than the basics of the models. Also, the developers are working on constructing open-source tools to help researchers efficiently access and use the new techniques that are better at handling the problems explained in the previous sections. Meanwhile, studies such as this chapter and those present in the Additional Reading section are helpful in further apprising the researchers regarding the value of awareness. Overall, in the light of these developments and problems, the future of CSS research has a great potential to unveil more unknowns regarding society as a whole. The central core of future CSS research should be to endure all these obstacles and persevere through them. The significance of the CSS research problems makes them indispensable.

CONCLUSION

The impact of social media on contemporary cultural evolution is undeniable. This impact led many computational social scientists to dedicate their efforts to capturing these evolutions over data collected from social media using natural language processing and machine learning methods. However, in these efforts, they struggle with various problems. Among these problems, there are many issues related to working with social media data. Data from online sources are prone to containing typos, possessing words from different languages, comprising texts with irony and sarcasm, and may include texts generated by machines. There are also problems inherent to the machine learning methods. These methods can learn bias from data or the extracted features, while researchers can select incorrect methods or parameters without proper knowledge. Also, researchers can employ complex learning methods in their computational social science studies like the deep learning methods solely based on their popularity in the recent literature. Choosing these complex methods over the simpler alternatives without a justifiable decision-making process may increase the computational burden immensely while failing to return correct results. Furthermore, researchers can select incorrect evaluation metrics, which may disturb the accuracy of the reported results. The computational social science researchers may also neglect to perform generalization experiments on different collections and might be reporting results from methods that are suffering from overfitting. This chapter addresses a range of these issues. Under each section, it proposes recommendations on how to avoid, detect, and handle these issues. Yet, the problems computational social science researchers might encounter are uncountable. When starting a new study, the researchers are taking a great responsibility in terms of awareness towards these issues and readiness for handling them. The future computational social science research will become a lot different than the current version. Methods will become more advanced, while newer and more troubling problems emerge. Until then, this chapter will guide the computational social science researchers in constructing better studies and it will prepare them for the inevitable future difficulties.

ACKNOWLEDGMENT

This research received no specific grant from any funding agency in the public, commercial, or not-for-profit sectors.

REFERENCES

Allcott, H., & Gentzkow, M. (2017). Social Media and Fake News in the 2016 Election. *The Journal of Economic Perspectives*, *31*(2), 211–236. doi:10.1257/jep.31.2.211

Angwin, J., Larson, J., Mattu, S., & Kirchner, L. (2016). *Machine Bias*. Propublica. https://www.propublica.org/article/machine-bias-risk-assessments-in-criminal-sentencing

Bayram, U., & Benhiba, L. (2021). Determining a Person's Suicide Risk by Voting on the Short-Term History of Tweets for the CLPsych 2021 Shared Task. In *Proceedings of the Seventh Workshop on Computational Linguistics and Clinical Psychology: Improving Access* (pp. 81-86). 10.18653/v1/2021.clpsych-1.8

Bayram, U., Pestian, J., Santel, D., & Minai, A. A. (2019). What's in a Word? Detecting Partisan Affiliation From Word Use In Congressional Speeches. In *2019 International Joint Conference on Neural Networks (IJCNN)* (pp. 1-8). 10.1109/IJCNN.2019.8851739

Bender, E. M., Gebru, T., McMillan-Major, A., & Shmitchell, S. (2021). On the Dangers of Stochastic Parrots: Can Language Models Be Too Big? In *Proceedings of the 2021 ACM Conference on Fairness, Accountability, and Transparency* (pp. 610-623). 10.1145/3442188.3445922

Bergstra, J., & Bengio, Y. (2012). Random Search for Hyper-Parameter Optimization. *Journal of Machine Learning Research*, *13*(2).

Bessi, A., & Ferrara, E. (2016). Social Bots Distort the 2016 US Presidential Election Online Discussion. *First Monday*, *21*, 11–17.

Blodgett, S. L., Barocas, S., Daume, H. III, & Wallach, H. (2020). Language (Technology) Is Power: A Critical Survey of "Bias" in NLP. In *Proceedings of the 58th Annual Meeting of the Association for Computational Linguistics* (pp. 5454–5476). 10.18653/v1/2020.acl-main.485

Brodersen, K. H., Ong, C. S., Stephan, K. E., & Buhmann, J. M. (2010). The Balanced Accuracy and Its Posterior Distribution. In *Proceedings of the IEEE 20th International Conference on Pattern Recognition* (pp. 3121-3124). 10.1109/ICPR.2010.764

Brooke, J., Hammond, A., & Hirst, G. (2015). Gutentag: An NLP-Driven Tool for Digital Humanities Research in the Project Gutenberg Corpus. In *Proceedings of the Fourth Workshop on Computational Linguistics for Literature* (pp. 42-47). 10.3115/v1/W15-0705

Buolamwini, J., & Gebru, T. (2018). Gender Shades: Intersectional Accuracy Disparities in Commercial Gender Classification. In *Proceedings of the 2018 ACM Conference on Fairness, Accountability and Transparency* (pp. 77-91). ACM.

Burley, T., Humble, L., Sleeper, C., Sticha, A., Chesler, A., Regan, P., Verdeja, E., & Brenner, P. (2020). NLP Work Flows for Computational Social Science: Understanding Triggers of State-Led Mass Killings. In Practice and Experience in Advanced Research Computing (pp. 152-159). Academic Press.

Chang, J. C., Amershi, S., & Kamar, E. (2017). Revolt: Collaborative Crowdsourcing for Labeling Machine Learning Datasets. In *Proceedings of the 2017 CHI Conference on Human Factors in Computing Systems* (pp. 2334-2346). 10.1145/3025453.3026044

Clauset, A., Shalizi, C. R., & Newman, M. E. (2009). Power-Law Distributions in Empirical Data. *SIAM Review, 51*(4), 661–703. doi:10.1137/070710111

Datta, A., Tschantz, M. C., & Datta, A. (2015). *Automated Experiments on Ad Privacy Settings: A Tale of Opacity, Choice, and Discrimination. Proceedings on Privacy Enhancing Technologies*. doi:10.1515/popets-2015-0007

Devlin, J., Chang, M.-W., Lee, K., & Toutanova, K. (2019). BERT: Pre-Training of Deep Bidirectional Transformers for Language Understanding. In *Proceedings of the 2019 Conference of the North American Chapter of the Association for Computational Linguistics: Human Language Technologies* (vol. 1, pp. 4171-4186). Academic Press.

Diermeier, D., Godbout, J.-F., Yu, B., & Kaufmann, S. (2012). Language and Ideology in Congress. *British Journal of Political Science*, *42*(1), 31–55. doi:10.1017/S0007123411000160

Domingos, P. (2012). A Few Useful Things to Know About Machine Learning. *Communications of the ACM*, *55*(10), 78–87. doi:10.1145/2347736.2347755

Fortuna, P., & Nunes, S. (2018). A Survey on Automatic Detection of Hate Speech in Text. *ACM Computing Surveys*, *51*(4), 1–30. doi:10.1145/3232676

Gentzkow, M., Shapiro, J. M., & Taddy, M. (2016). *Measuring Polarization in High-Dimensional Data: Method and Application to Congressional Speech*. National Bureau of Economic Research.

Grace, R., Halse, S., Aurite, W., Montarnal, A., & Tapia, A. (2019). Expanding Awareness: Comparing Location, Keyword, and Network Filtering Methods to Collect Hyperlocal Social Media Data. In *Proceedings of the 52nd Hawaii International Conference on System Sciences* (pp. 2699-2708). 10.24251/HICSS.2019.325

Hao, K. (2020). *A College Kid's Fake, AI-Generated Blog Fooled Tens of Thousands. This Is How He Made It.* https://www.technologyreview.com/2020/08/14/1006780/ai-gpt-3-fake-blog-reached-top-of-hacker-news/

Harford, T. (2014). Big Data: A Big Mistake? *Significance*, *11*(5), 14–19. doi:10.1111/j.1740-9713.2014.00778.x

Issenberg, S. (2013). How President Obama's Campaign Used Big Data to Rally Individual Voters. *Technology Review*, *116*(1), 38–49.

Iyyer, M., Enns, P., Boyd-Graber, J., & Resnik, P. (2014). Political Ideology Detection Using Recursive Neural Networks. In *Proceedings of the 52nd Annual Meeting of the Association for Computational Linguistics* (vol. 1, pp. 1113-1122). 10.3115/v1/P14-1105

Jackson, J., Watts, J., List, J.-M., Drabble, R., & Lindquist, K. (2021). From Text to Thought: How Analyzing Language Can Advance Psychological Science. *Perspectives on Psychological Science*. Advance online publication. doi:10.1177/17456916211004899 PMID:34606730

Jacobs, A. Z., & Wallach, H. (2021). Measurement and Fairness. In *Proceedings of the 2021 ACM Conference on Fairness, Accountability, and Transparency* (pp. 375-385). 10.1145/3442188.3445901

Jensen, J., Naidu, S., Kaplan, E., Wilse-Samson, L., Gergen, D., Zuckerman, M., & Spirling, A. (2012). Political Polarization and the Dynamics of Political Language: Evidence From 130 Years of Partisan Speech. *Brookings Papers on Economic Activity*, *2012*(1), 1–81. doi:10.1353/eca.2012.0017

Krawczyk, B. (2016). Learning From Imbalanced Data: Open Challenges and Future Directions. *Progress in Artificial Intelligence*, *5*(4), 221–232. doi:10.100713748-016-0094-0

Lambrecht, A., & Tucker, C. (2019). Algorithmic Bias? An Empirical Study of Apparent Gender-Based Discrimination in the Display of STEM Career Ads. *Management Science*, *65*(7), 2966–2981. doi:10.1287/mnsc.2018.3093

Lauderdale, B. E., & Herzog, A. (2016). Measuring Political Positions From Legislative Speech. *Political Analysis*, *24*(3), 374–394. doi:10.1093/pan/mpw017

Lazer, D., Pentland, A., Adamic, L., Aral, S., Barabasi, A.-L., Brewer, D., Christakis, N., Contractor, N., Fowler, J., Gutmann, M., Jebara, T., King, G., Macy, M., Roy, D., & Van Alstyne, M. (2009). Computational Social Science. *Science*, *323*(5915), 721–723. doi:10.1126cience.1167742 PMID:19197046

Leetaru, K. (2019). A Reminder That Machine Learning Is About Correlations Not Causation. *Forbes*. https://www.forbes.com/sites/kalevleetaru/2019/01/15/a-reminder-that-machine-learning-is-about-correlations-not-causation/?sh=2f44af576161

Mikolov, T., Sutskever, I., Chen, K., Corrado, G. S., & Dean, J. (2013). Distributed Representations of Words and Phrases and Their Compositionality. In Advances in Neural Information Processing Systems (pp. 3111-3119). Academic Press.

Miotto, R., Wang, F., Wang, S., Jiang, X., & Dudley, J. T. (2018). Deep Learning for Healthcare: Review, Opportunities and Challenges. *Briefings in Bioinformatics*, *19*(6), 1236–1246. doi:10.1093/bib/bbx044 PMID:28481991

Montavon, G., Samek, W., & Muller, K.-R. (2018). Methods for Interpreting and Understanding Deep Neural Networks. *Digital Signal Processing*, *73*, 1–15. doi:10.1016/j.dsp.2017.10.011

Mordvintsev, A., Olah, C., & Tyka, M. (2015). *Inceptionism: Going Deeper Into Neural Networks*. https://ai.googleblog.com/2015/06/inceptionism-going-deeper-into-neural.html

Neresini, F. (2017). Old media and new opportunities for a computational social science on PCST. *Journal of Science Communication*, *16*(2), C03. doi:10.22323/2.16020303

Obermeyer, Z., Powers, B., Vogeli, C., & Mullainathan, S. (2019). Dissecting Racial Bias in an Algorithm Used to Manage the Health of Populations. *Science*, *366*(6464), 447–453. doi:10.1126cience.aax2342 PMID:31649194

Oboler, A., Welsh, K., & Cruz, L. (2012). The Danger of Big Data: Social Media as Computational Social Science. *First Monday*, *17*(7).

Olteanu, A., Castillo, C., Diaz, F., & Kiciman, E. (2019). Social Data: Biases, Methodological Pitfalls, and Ethical Boundaries. *Frontiers in Big Data*, *2*, 13. doi:10.3389/fdata.2019.00013 PMID:33693336

Otter, D. W., Medina, J. R., & Kalita, J. K. (2020). A Survey of the Usages of Deep Learning for Natural Language Processing. *IEEE Transactions on Neural Networks and Learning Systems*, *32*(2), 604–624. doi:10.1109/TNNLS.2020.2979670 PMID:32324570

Pennebaker, J. W., Francis, M. E., & Booth, R. J. (2001). Linguistic Inquiry and Word Count: LIWC 2001. Lawrence Erlbaum Associates.

Peterson, A., & Spirling, A. (2018). Classification Accuracy as a Substantive Quantity of Interest: Measuring polarization in Westminster systems. *Political Analysis*, *26*(1), 120–128. doi:10.1017/pan.2017.39

Radford, A., Narasimhan, K., Salimans, T., & Sutskever, I. (2018). *Improving Language Understanding by Generative Pre-Training. Technical Report.* OpenAI.

Recht, B., Roelofs, R., Schmidt, L., & Shankar, V. (2019). Do ImageNet Classifiers Generalize to ImageNet? In *International Conference on Machine Learning* (pp. 5389-5400). Academic Press.

Ribeiro, M. T., Singh, S., & Guestrin, C. (2016). "Why Should I Trust You?" Explaining The Predictions of Any Classifier. In *Proceedings of the 22nd ACM SIGKDD International Conference on Knowledge Discovery and Data Mining* (pp. 1135-1144). 10.1145/2939672.2939778

Rice, D., Rhodes, J. H., & Nteta, T. (2019). Racial Bias in Legal Language. *Research & Politics*, *6*(2), 2053168019848930. doi:10.1177/2053168019848930

Savoy, J. (2010). Lexical Analysis of Us Political Speeches. *Journal of Quantitative Linguistics*, *17*(2), 123–141. doi:10.1080/09296171003643205

Sen, I., Flock, F., & Wagner, C. (2020). On the Reliability and Validity of Detecting Approval of Political Actors in Tweets. In *Proceedings of the 2020 Conference on Empirical Methods in Natural Language Processing (EMNLP)* (pp. 1413-1426). 10.18653/v1/2020.emnlp-main.110

Sherstinsky, A. (2020). Fundamentals of Recurrent Neural Network (RNN) and Long Short-Term Memory (LSTM) Network. *Physica D. Nonlinear Phenomena*, *404*, 132306. doi:10.1016/j.physd.2019.132306

Thomas, M., Pang, B., & Lee, L. (2006). Get Out the Vote: Determining Support or Opposition From Congressional Floor-Debate Transcripts. In *Proceedings of the 2006 Conference on Empirical Methods in Natural Language Processing* (pp. 327-335). 10.3115/1610075.1610122

Tsamados, A., Aggarwal, N., Cowls, J., Morley, J., Roberts, H., Taddeo, M., & Floridi, L. (2021). The Ethics of Algorithms: Key Problems and Solutions. *AI & Society*, 1–16.

Wu, L., Morstatter, F., Carley, K. M., & Liu, H. (2019). Misinformation in Social Media: Definition, Manipulation, and Detection. *SIGKDD Explorations*, *21*(2), 80–90. doi:10.1145/3373464.3373475

Yu, B., Kaufmann, S., & Diermeier, D. (2008). Classifying Party Affiliation From Political Speech. *Journal of Information Technology & Politics*, *5*(1), 33–48. doi:10.1080/19331680802149608

Zhou, L., Pan, S., Wang, J., & Vasilakos, A. V. (2017). Machine Learning on Big Data: Opportunities and Challenges. *Neurocomputing*, *237*, 350–361. doi:10.1016/j.neucom.2017.01.026

Zhou, X., & Zafarani, R. (2020). A Survey of Fake News: Fundamental Theories, Detection Methods, and Opportunities. *ACM Computing Surveys*, *53*(5), 1–40. doi:10.1145/3395046

ADDITIONAL READING

Buolamwini, J., & Gebru, T. (2018). Gender Shades: Intersectional Accuracy Disparities in Commercial Gender Classification. In *Conference on Fairness, Accountability and Transparency* (pp. 77-91).

Dressel, J., & Farid, H. (2018). The Accuracy, Fairness, and Limits of Predicting Recidivism. *Science Advances*, *4*(1), eaao5580. doi:10.1126ciadv.aao5580 PMID:29376122

Molina, M., & Garip, F. (2019). Machine Learning for Sociology. *Annual Review of Sociology*, *45*(1), 27–45. doi:10.1146/annurev-soc-073117-041106

Nakkiran, P., Kaplun, G., Bansal, Y., Yang, T., Barak, B., & Sutskever, I. (2020). Deep Double Descent: *Where Bigger Models and More Data Hurt. In International Conference on Learning Representations (ICLR).*

Stilgoe, J. (2018). Machine Learning, Social Learning and the Governance of Self-Driving Cars. *Social Studies of Science*, *48*(1), 25–56. doi:10.1177/0306312717741687 PMID:29160165

KEY TERMS AND DEFINITIONS

Bias: Prejudice towards or against a person, a group, or a class. In a machine learning context, there are various types of biases. Each bias can affect a model differently.

Deep Learning: A subfield of machine learning that works with artificial neural networks containing many hidden layers and complex structures.

Interdisciplinary Research: It is a type of research that employs knowledge, data, techniques, and theories from multiple disciplines. The main goal is to analyze or solve a specific problem of interest using the strengths of these different disciplines.

Language Generation: It is the process of automatically generating texts from models containing artificial intelligence. The goal of this process is to auto-generate texts that appear to be created by humans.

Machine Learning: A subfield of artificial intelligence where models can learn patterns from the data in a supervised or unsupervised fashion and tune themselves during the learning process.

Noise: In the context of machine learning, noise corresponds to the type of data or features that do not contain meaningful patterns related to the problem of interest and have a possibility of disrupting and harming the learning process.

Overfitting: Corresponds to the event when a machine learning model memorizes the training set data instead of learning the patterns present within it for accurate generalization. When a model overfits data, the model can return high within-dataset performance while it fails to generalize to other data.

Tuning: The set of operations within machine learning algorithms to improve the performance of classification and prediction. Some of the tuning procedures happen during the learning process, while it is also possible to tune a model after the initial run of the training process.

Underfitting: Corresponds to the event when a machine learning model does not learn the patterns present within the training set properly for reasons such as incorrect parameter selection or a small number of epochs for the case of neural networks. A machine learning that suffers from underfitting would fail to return acceptable results from the within-dataset experiments and the generalization experiments.

Chapter 6
Generating Big Data in (Micro)Economics

Yigit Aydogan
https://orcid.org/0000-0002-1823-0352
Kirklareli University, Turkey

ABSTRACT

One can expect the economics profession to gravitate towards microeconomics after the big data revolution is completed. The term big data refers to unconventionally large data streams from many sources to a bunch of (not necessarily known) recipients. Relying on aggregate relations by disregarding underlying dynamics is a suboptimal when the micro data is available. Via an international organization, all costs could be decreased, and gains could be increased with global optimization of the big data just like the International Space Station (ISS). Big data is a completely new way of practice, and it must develop its own ethical standards. A few economies such as Turkey can be pioneers in terms of big data utilization in economic research if necessary technical, practical, and legal steps are taken.

INTRODUCTION

The term *Big Data* refers to unconventionally large data *streams* from many sources, to a bunch of (not necessarily known) recipients. It might be better for the term to be defined as a co-existence of *data streams* rather than a *data set* because of the trouble with its storage and handling as a whole due to its dynamic nature and enormous size. A *set* of data is ontologically a comprehendible static data frame which promises a possibility of mastering.

DOI: 10.4018/978-1-7998-8553-5.ch006

However, Big Data is closer to be defined as *entropy of social universe*, unrelated to social entropy concept in sociological theory, and is likely to be remained as abstract and unamenable for a considerable future. It is not viable to categorize the Big Data for limited uses. For that reason, a pinch of Big Data can arguably be appropriate for economic, sociologic or any other kind of disciplinary research demanding high level expertise even for humble quests. It serves as a unified scientific outlet which reaches beyond interdisciplinary efforts. The fundamental aim of this chapter is then to provide a mere perspective for early use of the aforementioned general concept of Big Data in economics until *a unified science* arrive to tackle it.

Economics has been a theoretical profession with *never enough* ties to the empirics for a long time. The line between speculation and prediction depends on the perceived soundness of the empirical model. Data oriented economic research papers are cursed with such reliability issues because their claims are of general interest. While there are only a handful of people cares about the actual specifications of the highly-popular *CERN experiments*, millions get involved when a paper on the inflation dynamics or consumer choice gets distributed. This popularity levies a burden on economists to match the evidence with more lucid models relying on improved data availability. However, one can say that most economists increasingly respond to this interest with enigmatic methods and vague claims to maintain methodological solidity.

Contemporary economists have largely recognized the importance of their works' empirical grounds. When it comes to empirical studies with big data, the gap between main branches of the field such as macroeconomics and microeconomics became vague in favor of the micro. Economic research has been traditionally labeled by the scale/aggregation level of the activity. As the precision and the availability of the data increases, all branches in the literature are methodologically forced to converge towards the lowest level -or higher frequency- of interactions. Among others, microeconomics has been a more data-oriented practice in the field of economics which usually considers agent behavior. Relying on aggregate relations by disregarding underlying dynamics is a suboptimal modeling when the micro data is available. Therefore, introducing Big Data shall favor microeconomics above others as a methodological basis to a more unified economic research. Similarly, Currie et al. (2020) reports that applied microeconomics papers' weight have increased from 55% to 75% in high quality general interest journals recently.

Time stamps in economic modeling can traditionally be classified as *ex-ante* and *ex-post*, but the economy is a real-time phenomenon. Unlike contemporary information sciences related to computerized environments, gathering and handling high quality and large data sets which have use for economists is a hard task to manage. For this reason, the literature of economics has been evolving around macro data usage with limited representations, which goes hand in hand with hard and limiting assumptions to provide tractable modeling for colleagues.

Data sources and toolkit of economists have significantly increased during the last decades. These came along with interdisciplinary researchers *e.g.* physicists or biologists, who manage to apply data analysis techniques when there are plausible similarity of the tasks at hand. While *emergence* of the *complexity economics* is offering new perspectives, there have been a wide range of branches occurred such as *econophysics* and/or *econobiology* in order to benefit from the progress of other fields.

Economics has become an increasingly applied scientific endeavor. It is a natural by-product of a new world which is governed by unlimited data. Big data in economic research is a newly forming practice. Einav and Levin (2014) compose a great survey with focus on possible difficulties on the data collection and links to the existing literature. Moreover, Varian (2014) suggests that newly developed data analysis techniques such as deep learning, neural network or decision trees might have great use for traditional economics. Big data is becoming popular in finance and other related disciplines that has been spanned by the economics originally. Therefore, one must admit that economic theory must embrace the impact of big data by definition. The paper at hand aims to provide an insight to the problem by surveying the contemporary framework and exampling preliminary data orientation of microeconomics.

BACKGROUND

Contemporary economic research has strong ties with econometric analysis. Due to the availability of multi-dimensional and high-quality data sources, researchers feel the indispensable need of relying on applied methods. Econometric models is the first and most used set of tools to extract information from data. A typical economics graduate is equipped with adequate skills to use a handful of them. It can be said that econometrics has become an *industry standard* in *manufacturing economists* during the last few decades all around the world. It served well to all parties in the profession: econometrics have promoted the occupation in public opinion and provided a momentum in a way that economists are now presenting quantifiable interpretations of the economy, making understandable predictions and standing up to defend their claims in popular interdisciplinary statistical framework.

However, econometrics more than often requires strict assumptions to provide statistical significance. Each method has a specific type of data and relationship between variables to work properly that generally gets overlooked. Quality papers constitute wisely selected models and consider the importance of tests on data such as unit root or multicollinearity. Even so, sampling from a population is a tricky task, let alone modeling relationships. It is generally unlikely or unfeasible to generate a truly randomized sample (Qin, 2017). It must not be shocking to anyone to read that *p-value reporting* is an overrated method of data analysis (Carver, 1993). Loss of information due to conventional modeling is an unfortunate mistake when the data is of high-quality. The questioning of the representativeness of the representative agent and restrictive econometric tools have brought new methods to the field. Recently, agent-based modeling (ABM) benefits from heterogeneity of agents and incorporate simulation methods to overcome those restrictions (for a comprehensive handbook see Tesfatsion & Judd, 2006).

Loss of meaning when using aggregated data has been called for in many cases. The literature attempts to combine micro and macro perspectives in many occasions. One can refer to the strand on *microfoundations of macroeconomics* as the first tackling of the challenge. However, the debates on the *Walrasian* implications of macroeconomics is highly criticized (starting from as early as Weintraub, 1977). General Equilibrium models constitute elegant yet somehow trivial outcomes. Certain improved versions are available concerning bounded rationality of agents and aggregation of behavior (Branch & McGough, 2018).

The second attempt to the problem can be called *macrofoundations of microeconomics* or *bottom-up macroeconomics* where the economy is modeled as an outcome of the actions of interacting agents (Epstein & Axtell, 1996; Delli Gatti et al., 2008; De Grauwe, 2010; Delli Gatti et al., 2011; Turrell, 2016). Bottom-up macroeconomics is especially promising with the introduction of Big Data. In order to understand economic dynamics and replicate stylized facts, agent-based simulations step forward and they rely on a similar of input as promised by Big Data transformation. As an alternative, the *granular hyphothesis* links the shocks that individual firms face with the aggregate fluctuations, particularly of GDP (Gabaix, 2011). All stated strands in the literature will likely nourish when the Big Data becomes widely accessible.

Li-ping (2013) provides an introduction to the embracing Big Data in economics. It was stated that the phenomenon proposes shifts in econometrics, statistics and field work of economics. Beyond the conventional applications, Big Data is likely to have impact on experimental economics, complexity economics, theoretical economics, and the links of the field with natural and social sciences. Taylor et al. (2014) provides perspectives on Big Data's impact on economics by interviewing the researchers. They put forward how the new type of data is being used, replacing which practices, improving economic modeling and assessing the expected contribution regarding econometric methodology. They also assert that close ties with corporations is essential in order to access Big Data in economics or business. Poppe et al. (2015) and Coble et al. (2018) provides insight on the expected impact of Big Data on farming technologies, along with challenges and opportunities regarding the embracing of this new method. Collins (2016) brings the health economics at the verge of a revolution by stating that it should enable disease and location specific economic analyses with inclusion of personal data such as life style or real-time data from Internet of Things (IoT) devices.

Harding & Hash (2018) warns about two issues that are also addressed with solutions in this paper: the first one is that unintentional selection bias is a concern if the data source is a specific collector even if the data is "big". And the second warning is about the current limited number of private Big Data companies which might threaten the researcher freedom in case of partnering with them in order to get hands on the data.

Following the recent practices in information theory and computational methods, there are many tools to be implemented for economics similar to those suggested by Varian (2014). Handling big data consisting millions of agents with thousands of variables in different computerized environments is a technical necessity which requires high level analytical thinking, reaching beyond the common experience with Microsoft Excel®, or Stata® of economists. Creating a simulation environment with this data to answer economic questions is a much more complex problem. For this reason, usage of these data and models are mainly done in cooperative workgroups, relying on interdisciplinary researchers' application talents. Despite these ready-to-use help, selecting and training versatile economists who can stand along in such tasks is a must for improving the perspectives. Only this way such new approaches reach beyond being a mere validation-or rejection- tool for available economic theories and provide benchmarks for building up new horizons in economic thinking. History of economic research had a similar "catching up time" from the first implementation of econometrics. This time with early efforts, the adaptation can be faster.

TRANSFORMATION OF (EMPIRICAL) ECONOMICS OR ECONOMICS OF EMPIRICISM

The words *rational* and *empirical* has become less and less meaningful in the field of economics as the economists move from well-educated theoretical to more applied sciences backgrounds. Comparing rationalism with empiricism is not a task to be accomplished in a section, let along hermeneutics' or relativism's claims on the philosophy of economics. Nor that is relevant for the subject matter (refer to McCloskey (1998) and Wright (2003) for a detailed review on the evaded discussions). Decades, even centuries of arguing piled up on different schools of thought. One can brutally summarize the aforementioned literature to a struggle of observation and description: Can we observe the economy? Even if we do, can we fully process or understand it? The answer to this question might be changing in the near future.

Complexity and Evolutionary Economics

Needs for rehabilitation in the field of economics goes way back to the nineteenth century, almost since the day zero of the profession. The main criticism was not being away from evolutionary approach at all, but not even acknowledging its absence. Focusing on data analyses with claims of being *realistic* does not self-prove the realism of economics (Veblen, 1898). Veblen (1898) also states that if one wishes to analyze the continuity of economic development, one must study the *motor forces of the process of economic development*. The sole glimpse of evolutionary economics was put forth by Marshall (1961) positing in the preface "the Mecca of the economist lies in economic biology rather than in economic dynamics", but such methodology had not been followed neither in his work nor his followers' (Hodgson, 1993).

The economy is to be considered as a *complex system*, building on the fact that it comprises many subjects such as consumers, firms, governments and these *agents* operate through their local connections on whichever scale they might be. Although mostly physicists have been looking for general rules for complex systems earlier, complexity can find its roots just after invention of computers. In the 1940s, there are ideas already stating that computers and living organisms have much in common (Mitchell, 2009). Within the battle of physicists whose work reside between relativity and quantum mechanics, *statistical physics* is a fair playground for economic purposes (Farmer & Lux, 2008). Decades after Marshall and Veblen statistical physics had been built up its toolkit has been incorporated in economics via physicist- economists (reviewed thoroughly in Farmer, Shubik & Smith (2005)) and found great acceptance building up the methodology for the *new* economics (Kırer & Eren, 2015). After the foundation of the Santa Fe Institute in 1984, the Complexity Economics has gained its momentum.

The most common way of data analysis has been detecting stylized facts, mainly power laws. Looking for power laws might seem contra-evolutionary to the eye (Veblen, 1898), but the scope of this work is far from legitimizing the possible commonality of power law feature of the firm-size distribution as a work of teleological perspective would be. Instead, proving common ordering for a developing economy would provide evidence against the discussions that the capitalist system might be dying. If the firm behavior keeps its primitive settings, meaning that market processes which reflect on these keep their macro or collective behavior, one can conclude that the system may still be functioning with health in its playground.

What is the Expected Impact of Big Data in Economics?

Empirical economics has been increasingly popular and the researchers which enjoy the power of data to back up their assertions and step aside the conflict above. However, empirics in economics will never be that simple after the introduction of Big Data. How can one observe economic agents better? How can one model agents when there is always a better observation method? The fundamentals of advanced modeling reside in several philosophers' remnants (mainly Plato & Descartes, Aristotle & Locke and finally Hume) even if not mentioned in any empirical work. Should we treat the economic behavior *innate* in all? Can we build up an economy from *tabula rasa*? Origins of the economic behavior should (and will) be the main goal for the empirical studies in the near future after Big Data.

Introduction of Big Data to economics might yield a total invasion of the field in no time. Morrison (2016) calls Big Data a "game changer for businesses". If conventionally gathered data is informative on a subject matter, Big Data is an ultra-high-definition motion picture of it. Research on economic dynamics follow a rather straightforward pattern. Consider an economist who wants to analyze consumer behavior in a town or about a certain type of product. The regular starting effort would be to set the grounds of the endeavor. It can be a theoretical micro- paper with some data from any kind of sources about some product, perhaps with luck, comes along with a little information about the buyers, too. Alternatively, it can depend on data from a survey. These types of observations are equivalent to reading from marble inscriptions while ignoring (hypothetical) video surveillance system records in order to learn about economic behavior of the residents of Ephesus during 300 BC. In short, Big Data is the ultimate tool to assess the consumer behavior (Stoicescu, 2016).

Figure 1. Emergence, policy reaction to the economic phenomena and impact of the big data

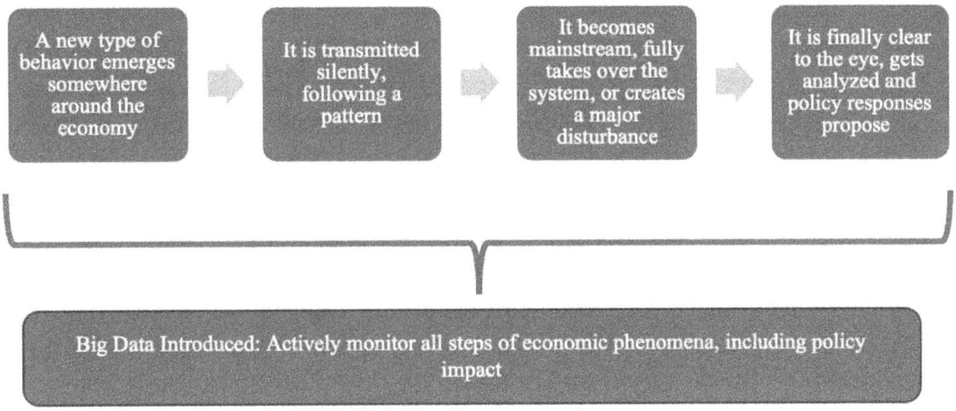

Social or Para-Economic Data

Society is built up with more than economic transactions. Economic outcomes more than often originate from non-economic relations or decisions. Distribution of economic means and all practical encounters among social counterparts generate data which has not yet been fully theorized (see Ramos, 2020 for a detailed review). For example, it was shown in Kurien (1994) that the larger ethnicity of the individual has strong effects on the use and benefits of migrant remittances which are important phenomena for local economies like India and Turkey. This kind of para-economic data can be associated with quantifiable economic activity with Big Data.

There is more to the para-economic data than socioeconomic characteristics coinciding with economic activity. Technological advances have made possible to track and monitor almost all actions in our daily life. Some of them are measured for economic research in lab environments such as behavioral economics or neuroeconomics. Most of the experiments try to understand actual responses of individuals against certain problems or choices. With IoT, researchers do not need to conduct *soft* experiments in lab environments in order to capture behavioral patterns. Surely, a brain scan during a choice cannot be replaced with remotely collected Big Data. However, if one can record each and every choice of almost all consumers then perhaps neuroeconomics studies can focus more specific issues. Besides, IoT devices improve each day. For example, if appropriate integration is done with privacy permissions, a consumer's hearth rate, blood oxygen levels, blood pressure and eye movement can be captured during online shopping-or during any activity- via his/her mobile phone and smartwatch. Security cameras equipped with AI can categorize and collect shoppers' physical responses against specific ads or labels. There is no need to ask people in surveys what they would do if they were offered some options when you can already know the actual responses in life. There is no limit for economic utilization of all kinds of Big Data. Gathering billions of people's data would mean a lot for economic research.

The Big Data as known today mostly relies on tracking people over social media. It requires sophisticated data mining techniques with highly skilled researchers and only technology giants like Amazon, Apple, Google and Facebook can benefit from it. The main discussions are therefore dwell around privacy concerns and how to let or prevent private companies benefiting from personal data whether it is voluntary or not. As explained above, social media interactions is a drop in the Big Data Ocean.

SOLUTIONS AND RECOMMENDATIONS

The challenge posed by the introduction of the Big Data to economics is troublesome. There are both theoretical and practical issues to be addressed as a starting point. Economic theory is not ready, nor close, to a comprehensive portraying the propositions of the Big Data in explaining economic behavior at any level. A sound theory of Big Data Economics must incorporate interdisciplinary participation due to the necessity of advanced technological and mathematical methods besides the economic thought. When it comes to the model building, it will not be possible to treat data management and data handling apart from the Big Data Economics. Therefore, there must be large research centers, *e.g.* universities dedicated to Big Data, comprising academics from diverse backgrounds. There is an online and non-academic data-science oriented example of Big Data university build by IBM, aimed at providing much needed skilled employees to the sector (IBM, n.d.). Beyond this initiative, a Big Data university would serve as an effective organization in order to scholarly work could be done swiftly. IBM can reach throughout the world in order to provide data science certificates without any boundaries, just to increase the supply of the available specialists. On the other hand, academics are subject to many obstacles when creating work groups and networks. A hub of Big Data researchers organized as a university in any country would serve as a major lab for the theoretical efforts and let the initiating state lead the future.

The field is in a better position regarding the practical problems related to the introduction of the Big Data to economics. There is a strong analytical research lines in economics and many researchers have already started to publish papers based on the utilization of simple versions of the Big Data as mentioned in the literature review of this paper. However, the methods that has been widely used in economic analysis are not adequate to work with Big Data (Varian, 2014). Especially econometric methods that rely on hypothesis testing and statistical significance are not relevant when there is a complete set with millions of data points. Forming a theoretically sound model and detecting a relationship between variables is not to be statistically questionable when the utilized data covers the complete population. Therefore, a new analytical approach has to be commonly taught to the researchers. The adoption of econometrics in the field during the near history took several decades before it has become an industry standard. So, one might expect that at least a few decades shall pass before Big Data research in economics becomes widespread. It must be noted that the mentioned countdown shall start after an implicit convention occurs among the developed academics and a collective action emerges.

One of the main issues with Big Data is its limited availability to researchers. As stated by Taylor et al. (2014), their interviewed professors also claim having hierarchical advantages over others is essential for accessing the Big Data. This is a problem of private and/or sectional/fragmental data sets which can be constituted as pioneering investments. Due to the profitability challenges of individual efforts gathering and sharing big data, they are remaining mainly private. The ultimate age of Big Data would start when there is a global streaming of all available data. When many parties (both public and private) chip in to a common goal, and most likely with support of academic institutions like Big Data University, access to the data would be much easier or at least there would be formal ways apart from "networking". It can be stated that Big Data is short on supply today, so the so-called price is much higher in order to benefit from it. When the world adopts to a common gateway, it will be abundant and the associated price would be much lower.

The viability of the Big Data in economic research depends on its versatility and manageability. As Varian (2014) states, practicality diminishes as the number of data points increase from hundreds to billions. There must be advanced automated ways for data manipulation in order to benefit from the Big Data. There are numerous tools, both company specific and open-source which are cited in there. Extracting information from raw data is a must before the researchers get their hands on it. A simpler counterpart and one of the most popular tools in economic research is generating indices using different types of data. The concept of enveloping available data into meaningful layers span from Human Development Index to Consumer Price Index. Although such efforts provide easy-to-follow frameworks for policymakers, traditionally they suffer from considerable lags. With Big Data and nowcasting, lags are to be destroyed.

Sensitive and aggressive deep learning and neural network analysis tools which goes beyond-but combined with- the banking/financial data might generate great superiority both in terms time and power of knowledge. Different frequencies of several data entries might be of higher value. Employment entries of higher or lower frequencies, invoices of consumer goods, car license plate movements between cities, ATM or credit card transactions of certain types are only a fraction of time sensitive data to be of different value at some intervals for policy-making. Additionally, relations between data points might be varying at different frequencies. For future research, this *fractal* nature of data can be examined in depth. One can create *meso* data layers to summarize regional and/or sectoral data Moreover, there is an urgent need for sorting the national data sources in a specific catalogue which can be transformed into a big data environment in a manageable environment.

Nowcasting is a new way of the data management that has been one of the main breakthroughs of the Big Data. It is possible to monitor the data as it is being generated. It allows economic variables to be handled as they appear. As an example, a private company gathers and analyses wide range of macroeconomic variables to make short-term predictions as an extremely basic level (Now-Casting, n.d.). The monetization opportunities over the Big Data has been the origin of the earliest efforts. Almost all of the banks around the world with a dedicated research team has been trying to benefit from the use of Big Data they gather from their customers over real-time business transactions (Deutsche Bank, 2014). For example, a Spanish origin commercial bank, BBVA, has a Big Data Research division which humbly provide consumption indices on several countries they operate in (BBVA Research, n.d.). The need for much more sophisticated horizons in higher-frequency data sets and advanced analytical tools which were mentioned above is important. To example the power of even limited models of economic simulations, Delli Gatti et al. (2011) proposes an ABM which is founded on the emergent phenomena in complexity economics to replicate stylized facts such as firm size or growth distribution. With more complete data sets and adequate theoretical approaches, economic research and forecasting can be taken to another level of precision. Whether financial, macro or micro, the output of such modeling might span all economic questions.

Contemporary Issues on Big Data in Economics

Taking part in the Big Data Era requires advanced technological infrastructure and capital. Since the machinery can be purchased from elsewhere, it mainly comes to the finances. Associated costs with building and maintaining giant data centers can be divided into three: The first one is the initial investment of the computers and related machinery. Big Data centers often utilize multiple plants with millions of computers (Varian, 2014). The second one is the operating costs of the data centers. The plants are very high maintenance and heat management is a major CO2 emission source (Soltanshahi et al., 2019). The literature on optimizing the location of a data center in order to decrease costs and also increase performance is abundant. It is beneficial for the investors to place the data center in cooler climates to save on cooling costs and associated CO2 emissions (Daraghmeh & Wang, 2017). Moreover, there are advanced applications on integrating data centers as renewable energy *producers* due to their excess heat (Huang et al., 2020). The third input for data center management is the human capital. It cannot be overlooked since data centers are estimated to be needing 300,000 more skilled workers by the 2025 in nearly 230 job types (Judge, 2021). All these issues can be worked on in an intergovernmental organization.

The need for large amounts of skilled workers in data centers is the key for intergovernmental cooperation motives. Jobs in information technologies sector usually require specific computing or hardware knowledge rather than presenting shiny college degrees. Moreover, developed countries usually lack spare working age people for newly forming industries, and luckily, less developed economies can provide many of them. Training programs and coinciding optimal locations of data centers with needed skilled workers require sincere international efforts. Combining the needs and offerings is a viable goal for an intergovernmental organization.

Through an international organization, all costs could be decreased and gains could be increased with global optimization of the Big Data just like the International Space Station (ISS). The nations with space programs have created a successful partnership in order to optimize on space research with the ISS. It is stated as "the largest peaceful cooperative program human beings have ever conceived and implemented" (Sadeh, 2013). There are only 15 countries and their 5 space agencies backing the ISS program due to its high technological requirements (NASA, 2020). On the other hand, almost all countries other than low-income ones have large investments in data centers even if they do not produce necessary equipment.

Currently, the US is by far the world leader with 2,670 data centers, the UK is in the second place with 452 data centers and Germany is in the third place with 443 (Alsop, 2021). The gap between the leader and the followers indicates that the age of data yields its natural monopolies. The technological leaders with more capital tend to and equipped with enough power to protect their interest over the rest of us. There is a UN led initiative about providing better internet infrastructure to promote equal opportunities for low-income countries but it is only a matter of access. Foster et al. (2021) reports that digital literacy efforts is being ramped up in Africa. Combining with the lack of any data centers or national corporations in the sector, it means that low-income countries will contribute to Big Data of developed world, without any control or rights. It puts further importance on global agreements on digital rights.

Where to Start?

Big Data has already been revolutionizing the field of microeconomics (Nguyen & Wait, 2015). A few economies such as Turkey can be pioneers in terms of Big Data utilization in economic research if necessary technical, practical and legal steps are taken. To start with, one may aggregate the available data at hand by complying with the data security and privacy legislations in place (Jain et al., 2016). The solid foundation of e-government applications in Turkey makes it plausible to merge all personal and institutional data on common grounds of economic research. Personal IDs can be mapped with other aspects of the economy such as firm IDs. Even this simple matching of persons with firms would create billions of resourceful data points.

Table 1. A brief sample of labels in use for economic research which can be linked over a common database

Consumer	Home-owner	Employer	Renter	Member
Shopper	Landlord	Lender	Student	User
Employee	Household	Borrower	Alumni	Agent

Table 1 examples the general labeling of economic agents in models. Many of them naturally co-exist within a person: John Doe can be a consumer, employer, borrower and a lender at the same time. In conventional modeling, intersections of such titles cannot be addressed. However, a common data set with actual IDs would define all agents at the same time. For example, one can assess the choices of consumers depending on their actual financing positions and also their employment status. Credit cards, bank statements and social security registers are digitally compatible but not connected yet. This type of real-life data would revolutionize the economic research when available.

Regarding the firm side, the most enriched dataset currently available in Turkey is the Enterprise Information System maintained by the Ministry of Industry and Technology. After the generation of more complex and multi-layered data, it should be possible to intervene in economic problems at earlier stages. For example, inflation is aimed/fight against by CBRT, expected by all, calculated by the TURKSTAT, and then realized by many parties. Moreover, if an agency can combine real-time expectations with realizations over big data, it would be possible to direct the legislative power or incentives more efficiently.

Firms' interactions with consumers can also be mapped precisely, too. A single purchase generates a multi-dimensional data colliding the profile of shopper and subjected goods and services. Consumption bundles and real budget constraints would yield precious data for utility analysis. Behavioral and game theoretical research might be boosted with such high-definition data. Many of the economic research would not be based on small sample surveys, but to be built upon Big Data.

Economic policy finds its value when it is able to affect the expectations of economic agents. Without big data and live streaming of indicators, policy-makers have to bet against psychological behavioral patterns based on ex-ante calculations and surveys, which may turn fragile if communications not done properly. Although the policy-makers generally have informational advantages against the market players, instant monitoring of indicators would also create a time gap. However, if one could observe "all" economic activity with complex data analysis tools, timing of strategies would be ahead of the market.

Research Ethics and Concerns About Big Data

Big Data is a completely new way of practice and it must develop its own ethical standards. It comprises high-definition personal information. Even if the data is gathered with consent, people might not be aware the degree of the information collected or shared with others. Whether the desired personal information is censored for use, it might be reverse-engineered with special efforts (Richards & King, 2014). Therefore, a general perspective when collecting digital information other than a simple consent might be needed.

The most active and important concern over Big Data is the data privacy against misuse. For example, online chat application Whatsapp® claims that text messages are private and do not get analyzed, but several information is shared with other parties such as location (Ovide, 2021). Generally, advertisers benefit from recent locations and search interests to promote more relevant banners to the consumers. There is an endless debate on the *propertization* of personal information (for an introduction, see Schwartz, 2003). The legislations on personal information protection needs international consensus since the data cannot be contained geographically once it is online. Whether the official announcements try to convince people that their sensitive personal information is safe, digital age has taught people that nothing digital can be a hundred percent safe. For this reason, governments try to protect civil rights as they can. However, it is urged in this paper that international agreements on Big Data protection is needed since it is more of a global problem and possible outlaws require international intervention. A common legislation or at least a "statement of digital rights" would provide path for international joint work groups.

FUTURE RESEARCH DIRECTIONS

Data center management is the ultimate challenge before the Big Data era begins. There are millions of computers that are dedicated around the world and countless public and private data centers are active. Being a profitable and competitive business, those data centers are not under any mutual agreements. If the ultimate goal is reaching a Big Data utilization spanning all aspects of life, then at some point there should be a collective behavior among all parties. Besides, the energy consumption of these plants is extremely high and a real issue for environmental concerns. Data centers around the world are estimated to account for more than 1% of total power consumption and expected to be sharply increased by 2025 (Nadjahi et al., 2018). So, the benefits and potential dangers of global Big Data adaptation is an international issue and recently United Nations Committee of Experts on Big Data and Data Science for Official Statistics (UN-CEBD) was formed (United Nations, n.d.). Although the Committee is at a preliminary state, multinational efforts on maintaining data centers and cross compatibility of data should be a goal for all countries. This way the future might yield better managed data centers and ensure swift agreements among nations regarding the data security.

Channeling live and accurate data into a work pool is no easy work. First of all, it requires digitalization for almost all parties in the economy. The importance of interdisciplinary efforts becomes evident at every step. Thousands of different regions and the electronics already invested in require a common gateway to consolidate the diverse economic data, let alone the *para-economic* data.

One of the most crucial fallacies today is defining the Big Data as a branch under the computer science. Human efforts are evidently less than being adequate for maintaining and examining such data streams. So, Big Data is handled with specialized computerized environments and with help of contemporary humble Artificial Intelligence (AI) units. Extending the sovereignty of AI is critical to cope with the data. The term *digital world* should not refer to our planet with digitized tools of humans, but a parallel *digital universe* consists of electronics. Big Data spans both physical world's and digital universe's data streams. It can be exampled with Internet of Things (IoT) which currently digitize our daily life but their potential rather unlimited. The real essence of Big Data is not to be grasped until *everything* is measured. Therefore, the possibility of full utilization of Big Data resides on advances in all disciplines with the help of AI.

The fight against the claims of logical positivists might come to life with destroying them and opposers, both. Unlocking the full power of Big Data in the near future, values, morality, ethics might be subject to be observed and handled analytically. This might be the most intriguing part of assessing the impact of the Big Data.

CONCLUSION

As mentioned earlier, Big Data might revolutionize the field of economics in a foreseeable future. Any phenomena will be open to analysis with its underlying mechanisms. When the day of full Big Data transformation comes, there would be no need for any aggregations or representative/instrumental data. Therefore, one can expect the economics profession to gravitate towards microeconomics.

The data might seem to be abundant already, yet its value is determined by the manipulation technologies at work. So, it can be said that the actual cost of benefiting from Big Data is not due to the data itself or even storing it in advanced and expensive data centers. But the real burden originates from kneading the raw data just to make it practical. The complex structure of Big Data will be maintained and summarized for researchers by the AI.

It was previously stated that working with private companies might threaten independence of the researchers. Proposed Big Data University and internationally co-funded Big Data centers might be a solution to this problem. Moreover, even with Big Data, the data can be biased if the supplier collects from limited sources. In order to overcome the selection bias, Big Data from different areas, sectors or societies should be bundled together, or at least should be compatible. It puts importance on international cooperation on the collecting and using Big Data. If global organizations like the UN, World Bank or OECD could manage to mediate on international regulations on sharing and utilizing local data, many of the problems could be solved much easier.

ACKNOWLEDGMENT

This research received no specific grant from any funding agency in the public, commercial, or not-for-profit sectors.

REFERENCES

Alsop, T. (2021, April 29). *Number of data centers worldwide 2021, by country*. Retrieved from https://www.statista.com/statistics/1228433/data-centers-worldwide-by-country/

BBVA Research. (n.d.). https://www.bbvaresearch.com/en/special-section/charts/

Branch, W. A., & McGough, B. (2018). Heterogeneous expectations and micro-foundations in macroeconomics. In *Handbook of computational economics* (Vol. 4, pp. 3–62). Elsevier.

Carver, R. P. (1993). The case against statistical significance testing, revisited. *Journal of Experimental Education*, *61*(4), 287–292. doi:10.1080/00220973.1993.10806591

Coble, K. H., Mishra, A. K., Ferrell, S., & Griffin, T. (2018). Big data in agriculture: A challenge for the future. *Applied Economic Perspectives and Policy*, *40*(1), 79–96. doi:10.1093/aepp/ppx056

Collins, B. (2016). Big data and health economics: Strengths, weaknesses, opportunities and threats. *PharmacoEconomics*, *34*(2), 101–106. doi:10.100740273-015-0306-7 PMID:26093888

Currie, J., Kleven, H., & Zwiers, E. (2020, May). Technology and big data are changing economics: Mining text to track methods. *AEA Papers and Proceedings. American Economic Association*, *110*, 42–48. doi:10.1257/pandp.20201058

Daraghmeh, H. M., & Wang, C. C. (2017). A review of current status of free cooling in datacenters. *Applied Thermal Engineering*, *114*, 1224–1239. doi:10.1016/j.applthermaleng.2016.10.093

De Grauwe, P. (2010). Top-down versus bottom-up macroeconomics. *CESifo Economic Studies*, *56*(4), 465–497. doi:10.1093/cesifo/ifq014

Delli Gatti, D., Desiderio, S., Gaffeo, E., Cirillo, P., & Gallegati, M. (2011). *Macroeconomics from the Bottom-up*. Springer. doi:10.1007/978-88-470-1971-3

Delli Gatti, D., Gaffeo, E., Gallegati, M., Giulioni, G., & Palestrini, A. (2008). *Emergent macroeconomics: an agent-based approach to business fluctuations*. Springer Science & Business Media.

Deutsche Bank. (2014). *Big Data: How it can become a differentiator*. https://cib.db.com/docs_new/GTB_Big_Data_Whitepaper_(DB0324)_v2.pdf

Einav, L., & Levin, J. (2014). Economics in the Age of Big Data. *Science*, *346*(6210), 1243089. Advance online publication. doi:10.1126cience.1243089 PMID:25378629

Epstein, J. M., & Axtell, R. (1996). *Growing artificial societies: social science from the bottom up*. Brookings Institution Press. doi:10.7551/mitpress/3374.001.0001

Farmer, J. D., & Lux, T. (2008). Applications of statistical physics in economics and finance. *Journal of Economic Dynamics & Control*, *32*(1), 6. doi:10.1016/j.jedc.2007.01.019

Farmer, J. D., Shubik, M., & Smith, E. (2005). Is economics the next physical science? *Physics Today*, *58*(9), 37–42. doi:10.1063/1.2117821

Foster, V., Comini, N., & Srinivasan, S. (2021, May 6). *Improving data infrastructure helps ensure equitable access for poor people in poor countries*. Retrieved from https://blogs.worldbank.org/opendata/improving-data-infrastructure-helps-ensure-equitable-access-poor-people-poor-countries

Gabaix, X. (2011). The granular origins of aggregate fluctuations. *Econometrica, 79*(3), 733–772. doi:10.3982/ECTA8769

Harding, M., & Hersh, J. (2018). Big Data in Economics. *IZA World of Labor: Evidence-Based Policy Making, 451*. Advance online publication. doi:10.15185/izawol.451

Hodgson, G. M. (1993). The Mecca of Alfred Marshall. *Economic Journal (London), 103*(417), 406–415. doi:10.2307/2234779

Huang, P., Copertaro, B., Zhang, X., Shen, J., Löfgren, I., Rönnelid, M., Fahlen, J., Andersson, D., & Svanfeldt, M. (2020). A review of data centers as prosumers in district energy systems: Renewable energy integration and waste heat reuse for district heating. *Applied Energy, 258*, 114109. doi:10.1016/j.apenergy.2019.114109

IBM. (n.d.). *Cognitive Class*. https://cognitiveclass.ai

Jain, P., Gyanchandani, M., & Khare, N. (2016). Big data privacy: A technological perspective and review. *Journal of Big Data, 3*(1), 25. Advance online publication. doi:10.118640537-016-0059-y

Judge, P. (2021, January 28). *Data centers need to find 300,000 more staff by 2025*. Retrieved from https://www.datacenterdynamics.com/en/news/data-centers-need-find-300000-more-staff-2025/

Kırer, H., & Eren, E. (2015). İktisat-Fizik İlişkisine Tarihsel Bakış. *Ekonomi-tek- International Economic Journal, 4*(2), 25–60.

Kurien, P. A. (1994). Non-economic bases of economic behaviour: The consumption, investment and exchange patterns of three emigrant communities in Kerala, India. *Development and Change, 25*(4), 757–783. doi:10.1111/j.1467-7660.1994.tb00535.x

Li-ping, Y. U. (2013). Big Data and Big Data Economics. *China Soft Science, 7*, 177–183.

Marshall, A. (1961). *The Principles of Economics* (9th ed.). Macmillan.

McCloskey, D. N. (1998). *The Rhetoric of Economics*. University of Wisconsin Press.

Mitchell, M. (2009). *Complexity: A guided tour*. Oxford University Press.

Morrison, A. (2016, February 23). *Attention governments: Big Data is a game changer for businesses*. Retrieved from https://blogs.worldbank.org/opendata/attention-governments-big-data-game-changer-businesses

Nadjahi, C., Louahlia, H., & Lemasson, S. (2018). A review of thermal management and innovative cooling strategies for data center. *Sustainable Computing: Informatics and Systems*, *19*, 14–28. doi:10.1016/j.suscom.2018.05.002

NASA. (2020, October 15). *International Cooperation*. Retrieved from https://www.nasa.gov/mission_pages/station/cooperation/index.html

Nguyen, B., & Wait, A. (2015). *Essentials of Microeconomics*. Routledge. doi:10.4324/9781315690339

Now-Casting. (n.d.). www.now-casting.com

Ovide, S. (2021, January 13). The Truth About Your WhatsApp Data. *The New York Times*. Retrieved from https://www.nytimes.com/2021/01/13/technology/whatsapp-data.html

Poppe, K., Wolfert, J., Verdouw, C. N., & Renwick, A. (2015). A European perspective on the economics of big data. *Farm Policy Journal*, *12*(1), 11–19.

Qin, J. (2017). *Biased sampling, over-identified parameter problems and beyond*. Springer. doi:10.1007/978-981-10-4856-2

Ramos, A. G. (2020). 9. Para-economy: Paradigm and Multicentric Allocative Model. In The New Sciences Organizations (pp. 153-165). University of Toronto Press.

Richards, N. M., & King, J. H. (2014). Big data ethics. *Wake Forest Law Review*, *49*, 393.

Sadeh, E. (2013). Cooperation in Orbit: The Evolution of the International Space Station Program. *World Politics Review*. Retrieved from https://www.worldpoliticsreview.com/articles/12803/cooperation-in-orbit-the-evolution-of-the-international-space-station-program

Schwartz, P. M. (2003). Property, privacy, and personal data. *Harvard Law Review*, *117*(7), 2056. doi:10.2307/4093335

Soltanshahi, M., Asemi, R., & Shafiei, N. (2019). Energy-aware virtual machines allocation by krill herd algorithm in cloud data centers. *Heliyon*, *5*(7), e02066. doi:10.1016/j.heliyon.2019.e02066 PMID:31372538

Stoicescu, C. (2016). Big Data, the perfect instrument to study today's consumer behavior. *Database Systems Journal*, *6*, 28–42.

Taylor, L., Schroeder, R., & Meyer, E. (2014). Emerging practices and perspectives on Big Data analysis in economics: Bigger and better or more of the same? *Big Data & Society*, *1*(2), 2053951714536877. doi:10.1177/2053951714536877

Tesfatsion, L., & Judd, K. L. (Eds.). (2006). *Handbook of computational economics: agent-based computational economics*. Elsevier.

Turrell, A. (2016). Agent-based models: understanding the economy from the bottom up. *Bank of England Quarterly Bulletin*, Q4.

United Nations. (n.d.). *United Nations Committee of Experts on Big Data and Data Science for Official Statistics* [UN-CEBD]. https://unstats.un.org/bigdata/

Varian, H. R. (2014). Big Data: New Tricks for Econometrics. *The Journal of Economic Perspectives*, *28*(2), 3–28. doi:10.1257/jep.28.2.3

Veblen, T. (1898). Why is economics not an evolutionary science? *The Quarterly Journal of Economics*, *12*(4), 373–397. doi:10.2307/1882952

Wright, J. (2003). *The ethics of economic rationalism*. UNSW Press.

ADDITIONAL READING

Banks, J., & Blundell, R. (2019). Empirical Microeconomics in Changing Times: A Reflection on 50 Years of IFS Research. *Fiscal Studies*, *40*(4), 451–484. doi:10.1111/1475-5890.12210

Bentley, R. A., O'Brien, M. J., & Brock, W. A. (2014). Mapping collective behavior in the big-data era. *Behavioral and Brain Sciences*, *37*(1), 63–76. doi:10.1017/S0140525X13000289 PMID:24572217

Bok, B., Caratelli, D., Giannone, D., Sbordone, A. M., & Tambalotti, A. (2018). Macroeconomic nowcasting and forecasting with big data. *Annual Review of Economics*, *10*(1), 615–643. doi:10.1146/annurev-economics-080217-053214

Buono, D., Kapetanios, G., Marcellino, M., Mazzi, G., & Papailias, F. (2018). Big data econometrics: Now casting and early estimates. *Milan, Bocconi University, Baffi-Carefin centre working paper, 82*.

Chang, C. L., McAleer, M., & Wong, W. K. (2018). Big data, computational science, economics, finance, marketing, management, and psychology: Connections. *Journal of Risk and Financial Management*, *11*(1), 15. doi:10.3390/jrfm11010015

D'Orazio, P. (2017). Big data and complexity: Is macroeconomics heading toward a new paradigm? *Journal of Economic Methodology*, *24*(4), 410–429. doi:10.1080/1350178X.2017.1362151

Giannone, D., Lenza, M., & Primiceri, G. E. (2021). *Economic predictions with big data: The illusion of sparsity* (No. 2542). ECB Working Paper.

Hassani, H., & Silva, E. S. (2015). Forecasting with big data: A review. *Annals of Data Science*, *2*(1), 5–19. doi:10.100740745-015-0029-9

Loebbecke, C., & Picot, A. (2015). Reflections on societal and business model transformation arising from digitization and big data analytics: A research agenda. *The Journal of Strategic Information Systems*, *24*(3), 149–157. doi:10.1016/j.jsis.2015.08.002

López-Robles, J. R., Rodríguez-Salvador, M., Gamboa-Rosales, N. K., Ramirez-Rosales, S., & Cobo, M. J. (2019). The last five years of Big Data Research in Economics, Econometrics and Finance: Identification and conceptual analysis. *Procedia Computer Science*, *162*, 729–736. doi:10.1016/j.procs.2019.12.044

Mohanty, H. (2015). Big data: An introduction. In *Big Data* (pp. 1–28). Springer. doi:10.1007/978-81-322-2494-5_1

Raghavan, P. (2014). It's time to scale the science in the social sciences. *Big Data & Society*, *1*(1). Advance online publication. doi:10.1177/2053951714532240

Shapiro, J. M. (2017, November). Is Big Data a Big Deal for Applied Microeconomics? In *Advances in Economics and Econometrics:* Volume 2*: Eleventh World Congress* (Vol. 59, p. 35). Cambridge University Press. 10.1017/9781108227223.002

Titiunik, R. (2015). Can big data solve the fundamental problem of causal inference? *PS, Political Science & Politics*, *48*(1), 75–79. doi:10.1017/S1049096514001772

Weinandy, T. J. (2021). Applied Microeconomics and Business Intelligence in the Digital Age. *Dissertations*. 3694. https://scholarworks.wmich.edu/dissertations/3694

Yoo, Y. (2015). It is not about size: A further thought on big data. *Journal of Information Technology*, *30*(1), 63–65. doi:10.1057/jit.2014.30

Zwitter, A. (2014). Big data ethics. *Big Data & Society*, *1*(2). Advance online publication. doi:10.1177/2053951714559253

KEY TERMS AND DEFINITIONS

Big Data: Unconventionally large data *streams* from many sources to a bunch of (not necessarily known) recipients.

Complexity Economics: Research area in economics that depicts the most of the economic phenomena as emergent, claiming that the whole is being more than the sum of its parts; meaning that there are different interactions among agents at different levels which in turn generate case specific outcomes.

Econobiology: Interdisciplinary academic research area combining the methods and subjects from economics and biology, such as evolutionary approaches to dynamics of economic phenomena.

Econophysics: Interdisciplinary academic research area combining the methods and subjects from economics and physics, such as applying statistical physics' methods to microeconomic data.

Ephesus: A giant ancient city located in Western Anatolia, Turkey, which was inhabited from 6000 BC to the fifteenth century.

Internet of Things: Digital data transmitting devices that are attached to any kind of goods, generating data about their use or the state of the user.

Para-Economic Data: Data on anything that are related but not directly subject to economic nature such as ethnicity, marital status, or as stated in this paper, data from daily life collected through Internet of Things.

Chapter 7
The Virtual Persona Triad:
From Self-Presentation to Social Media Mining

Ana Carolina Espírito Santo Lima
Mackenzie Presbyterian University, Brazil

Leandro Nunes de Castro
Mackenzie Presbyterian University, Brazil

ABSTRACT

Each person projects behavioral patterns through actions. Even in a virtual environment we express our way of seeing, feeling, and reacting to the world. The analysis of the data generated allows the identification of pattern behaviors associated with users. Therefore, it is possible to obtain a better understanding of the user, the image he/she decided to express, and how he/she behaves in social media, which we name here the virtual persona. Machine learning techniques make it possible to develop a framework that allows to infer psychological and behavioral aspects of the virtual persona. The goal of this chapter is to introduce the virtual persona concept as a mechanism to understand social media users. Emphasis is given to the self-presentation of virtual persona, the perception of physical persona over virtual persona, and the description of three computational frameworks to study virtual persona, what we call here the virtual persona triad.

INTRODUCTION

If the current pace of technological innovation is maintained, by 2025 most of the world's population, estimated at eight billion, will be online. The mass internet adoption is leading to one of the most exciting social, cultural,

DOI: 10.4018/978-1-7998-8553-5.ch007

and political transformations in history, and these effects are entirely global (Schmidt & Cohen, 2013). In this context, it is indispensable to have a better comprehension of the virtual society and how it can affect the real (physical) environment. There is an urgent need for a better understanding of the interconnected society complexity, as well as the capacity to apply such knowledge to formulate policies to solve problems (Lovari & Valentini, 2020).

Within social media, one can usually fill in a *profile* with a description of him/herself, choose some *groups* or *networks* to participate, and *interact* in various forms (e.g. by generating content, posting photos or videos, liking, etc.) with users and groups. So, it is possible to analyze the user behavior in two levels: *individual*, based on user decisions; and *collective*, based on group decisions. There is a growing opportunity to apply computational techniques to these behavioral patterns. It is possible to identify influencers, detect implicit or hidden groups, predict the sentiment of users, develop more personalized recommendation systems, understand the evolution of networks and the changes in the relationship between entities, protect users' privacy and safety, create more efficient collaborative groups, build and strengthen trust among users or between entities, or even predict social crises, political preferences and natural disasters (Gundecha & Liu, 2012).

The range of applications is extensive due to the combination of user understanding and different areas of knowledge, such as psychology, sociology, anthropology, data science, statistics, language processing, games, collaborative learning, economics, political science, marketing, human-computer interaction, engineering, and computer science. However, data from social media are unstructured or semi-structured, imposing a constant challenge for the development of research tools. In this context, *data mining* techniques can overcome the challenges posed by social data through sophisticated methods of data pre-processing and analysis (Safari, Rahmani, & Alizadeh, 2019; Rathore, Kar, & Ilavarasan, 2017).

In this chapter, the term *social media mining* is used to refer to the scope of techniques focused on mapping and analyzing data from various web services aimed at sharing and creating content by the user (Lima A. C., 2016). The goal is to structure a position on social media mining and explore its applicability in the study of the main psychological factors of users. This gives rise to what is defined here as the *virtual persona*, what role they take on the internet, and the construction they make of themselves. (Lima A. C., 2016). It is proposed that three sets of characteristics contribute to the understanding of the virtual persona: sentiment; personality; and temperament, which together form the *virtual persona triad*. Based on this concept, this chapter presents a set of frameworks that aim to help understand the virtual persona triad.

THE VIRTUAL PERSONA AS AN IMAGE OF THE SELF WITHIN SOCIAL MEDIA

There is a dichotomy in social media between *isolation* and *interaction*. Although hidden behind the devices, there is a predisposition of people to expose to and relate with other people. As social beings we have a fundamental necessity to connect with others. Social media intensify such behavior, as we are constantly exposed to photos, videos, messages and feedbacks about our actions, such as likes, shares and comments. Associated with this, self-referential thoughts also stimulate our nervous system, feeding our desire to communicate (Meshi, Tamir, & Heekeren, 2015).

When an individual interacts in a social sphere he paints before himself a *mask* of his identity, which becomes even more stressed to the extent that the individual needs to fill a profile, and his publications expose his writing style and vocabulary (Wiszniewski & Coyne, 2002). Carl Gustav Jung called this mask a *persona* (Jung, 2000). He pointed out that people conceive a mask before society in response to the demands of conventions and social traditions, and their own internal needs. The purpose of the mask is to cause a definite impression on others and often, though not necessarily, hide the true nature of the person. The persona is the public personality, those aspects that are presented to the world or that the public opinion imposes on the individual, in contrast to the private personality behind the social façade (Hall, Lindzey, & Campbell, 2000).

The goal here is to investigate and understand the specificities of each user, such as temperament, personality and emotional state (Lima, de Castro, & Corchado, 2015; Lima & de Castro, 2016). It is believed that the identification and connection of the elements exposed by a user, leads to the organization of the image that he wants to show and, thus, a posteriori, a parallel with some archetype can be made. A group of personas may indicate some archetypes.

The *virtual persona is defined as the image formed from how people present themselves and behave in social media, which involves their profile (description about themselves), their social identity (notion and feeling of belonging to certain social groups), and their behaviors (how they interact, what they like, share, post, watch, etc.).* Figure 1 summarizes the virtual persona concept and its main components.

Social media is defined here as an infrastructure to create and share content in a decentralized way, under the all-to-all, or many-to-many, participation logic, which uses the internet as a production and transmission channel. Essentially, there are three key components associated with the virtual persona: profile; connections (or social identity); and behavior (or interaction).

Figure 1. The virtual persona concept and its main components.

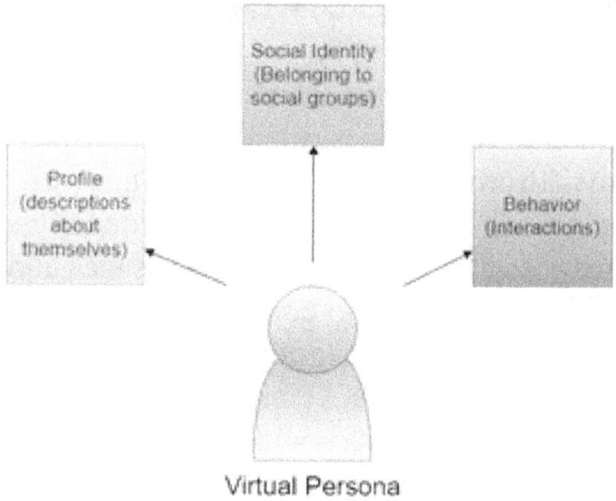

The virtual persona can reveal many things about oneself and stimulate insights and comparisons with the physical persona. The following section is dedicated to discussing how the interaction among virtual personas can affect the reality perception of one another. This kind of impact transcends the virtual world as this leads to comparisons with our physical persona, stimulating our reward system, our desire to share and making our feelings both positively and negatively affected.

VIRTUAL PERSONA SELF-PRESENTATION AND WELL BEING

This section presents different perspectives on the knowledge that can be extracted from studying the virtual persona. The goal here is to show that patterns within social media data can be analyzed and studied in different areas, such as Computer Science, Sociology, Anthropology and Psychology, leading to a better understanding of the virtual persona. The presentation starts with a discussion on the virtual personas' self-presentation and follows with the perception of physical personas over virtual personas.

On The Virtual Personas' Self-Presentation

For Jung, true individuality is in the unconscious, as opposed to the conscious ego (Jung, 2000). The persona would have nothing "real" and it would be a compromise between the individual and the environment in which he is inserted as a way of creating an accepted identity. Thus, even in the real world the individual could not be who he is (Farias & Monteiro, 2012). Baptista (2003) believes that users create a specificity of their identity, called "online self" (i.e., the virtual persona), which can be understood like a facet of a wider identity. Baker (2009) argued about a "blended identity" in which the physical persona and the virtual persona interact, so that one contributes with the development of the other (Bullingham & Vasconcelos, 2013).

Buss (2001) proposed that a person's identity is made up of a *public self* and a *private self*, where three important aspects make up the public self (*appearance*, *style* and *personality*); and three make up the private self (*thoughts*, *feelings* and *fantasies*). Three concepts of self can be identified (Higgins, 1987): *ideal*; *duty*; and *present*. The ideal contains the qualities that a person strives to possess, duty has the qualities one feels obliged to possess, and the present includes the qualities that one expresses to others at the moment (Bargh, McKenna, & Fitzsimons, 2002).

The internet provides an opportunity for self-presentation, so one can hope to try to express the aspects of the self that he has the strongest need to externalize of which it might not be easy to express to others (Bargh, McKenna, & Fitzsimons, 2002). This self-expression facilitation would happen due to anonymity, which enables expressions and behaviors in a different way than usual, done in the social sphere, for it would be free of expectations and constraints. In addition, in face-to-face interactions there is always the risk of negative exposure (Bargh, McKenna, & Fitzsimons, 2002).

Feelings of belonging and self-presentation are great motivators for social media use (Seidman, 2013). Social network sites allow users to fulfill belonging needs through communicating with and learning about others. Online activities that accomplish self-presentational goals include posting photographs, profile information, and wall content. It has been also argued that the frequent use of SNS reduce the engagement in reflective thinking, what came to be known as the *shallowing hypothesis* (Annisette & Lafreniere, 2017).

The Perception of Physical Personas Over Virtual Personas

Essentially, people use social media for three reasons: connect with others; search for information; and cause an impression on (or impact) others (Meshi, Tamir, & Heekeren, 2015; Stockdale & Coyne, 2020). This means that when a person decides to interact, he/she sees that on the other side there is another person who can fill some of their needs or perceive them in a specific way, and social media have several types of triggers in these directions. Our ability to think about the mental state of others with which we interact (mentalizing) gave us the power to infer their beliefs and intentions (Tamir & Ward, 2015).

Some early works on the relationship between social media use and its impacts on psychological distress and mental health dealt with the association between the time spent on these media and *jealousy* (Utz, Muscanell, & Khalid, 2015; Muise, Christofides, & Desmarais, 2009). It was identified that the exposure to information about a partner may potentially cause jealousy, creating a cycle in which jealousy increases and leads to a greater surveillance of the partner social media.

Furthermore, social network sites, like Facebook, Instagram, Snapchat, Tik-Tok and others, enable abundant opportunities for social comparisons. Several research works focus on understanding the use of social media in social comparison processes (Hawi & Samaha, 2016; Muqaddas, Soomro, & Ahmad, 2017; Hawi & Samaha, 2019). Most studies show that the more a person uses and exposes himself in social media, the lower is his *self-esteem*, independently of gender and culture. In general, by seeing social media profiles with positive content (e.g., health and fitness) was associated with worse self-esteem and self-assessments.

Envy is also one of the most common feelings that emerge out of social media use and interactions. The literature shows that the passive use of social media exacerbates feelings of envy and decrease life satisfaction (Krasnova, Widjaja, Buxmann, Wenninger, & Benbasat, 2015; Wallace, James, & Warkentin, 2017; Wu & Srite, 2021; Charoensukmongkol, 2018). Users often perceive social media as stressful environments where envy is a common feeling. In general, envy is triggered by contents about travel and leisure, social interactions, relationships and happiness. Such triggers also hold true for physical personas. Virtual personas' long-term passivity triggers upward social comparisons and hostile emotions. These studies explore the rising of self-presentation and narcissistic behaviors, a phenomenon referred to as *self-promotion spiral envy*, in which users react with even more self-promoting content to self-promoting others.

There are also studies about how the perception of happiness may be affected by the use of SNSs (Chou & Edge, 2012; Lup, Trub, & Rosenthal, 2015). They show that the more time spent in social media, the more we believe that others are happier than ourselves. Besides, these researches evidence that the more friends are added to our network without knowing them in person, the stronger is the feeling that others have a better life and are happier. On the other hand, the longer virtual personas interact with the physical personas of their friends, the less they agree that others have a better life and are happier. These works identified that to keep contact with known people did not result in negative feelings, such as resentment, envy and loneliness. By contrast, following unknown people may lead or reinforce negative feelings about themselves, mostly driven by a negative social comparison.

Finally, *narcissism* is a personality trait that involves self-promotion, vanity and the need of attention. There are currently several authors arguing that social networks provide narcissistic individuals with an ideal medium to display vanity, self-promotion, admiration demand, manipulation of their public images, and gaining approval and attention (Bergman, Fearrington, Davenport, & Bergman, 2011; Sorokowski, et al., 2015; Savci, Turan, Griffiths, & Ercengiz, 2019; Wang, et al., 2018). There are also works investigating the association between narcissism and self-esteem, suggesting that fragile self-esteem is related to a lack of selfies, probably due to a fear of negative feedback or no feedback at all (Barry, Doucette, Loflin, Rivera-Hudson, & Herrington, 2017; Biolcati & Passini, 2018). Although narcissists usually want large numbers of virtual friends, they do not want to engage in real physical relationships with the same intensity, as the latter requires a lot of emotional investments (Bergman, Fearrington, Davenport, & Bergman, 2011).

These works stress that social media interactions are such that virtual personas impact physical personas in different ways, sometimes causing envy, jealousy, social comparisons, a decrease in self-esteem, depression, narcissism, and various other negative feelings and mental disorders (Keles, McCrae, & Grealish, 2020). There are those who go beyond and explore the dark side of social media, detaching thematic stressors in them: managing inappropriate content, being tethered, lack of privacy and control, social comparisons and jealousy, and relationship tensions and conflicts (Fox & Moreland, 2015). These more negative feelings are usually counterbalanced when the physical personas know the virtual personas they follow or are connected with, because the former realize that the virtual personas build an ideal profile and social identity, showing behaviors that are not necessarily their daily ones.

ANALYTICAL FRAMEWORKS FOR THE VIRTUAL PERSONA TRIADE

The concepts and discussion presented previously shows the importance of understanding the virtual persona triad and this is now going to be made from a computational perspective emphasizing three different psychological models:

1. *Sentiment*: Although there are several theories about emotions (James, 1884; Cannon, 1927; Damasio, 2003; Darwin, Ekman, & Prodger., 1998; LeDoux, 1998), there is a consensus about their physiological nature that allows organisms to compose fast and effective treatments aimed at their survival. Emotion can be seen as a chemical response of the brain when faced with unordinary situations. When the brain in a normal state breaks the balance, this response is triggered. Emotion reflects a discrete response, for a limited time, to an internal or external event that entails synchronized characteristics, including subjective experience, expression, bodily response and tendency to actions. Ekman et al. (1982), after photographic analyzes of facial expressions observed in different cultures, proposed a model of six basic emotions: *anger*; *disgust*; *fear*; *happiness*; *surprise*; and *sadness*. Four of these emotions are negative, suggesting that humans may be more attentive to negative signals than positive ones, as negative signals may be dangerous and impel us to respond.
2. *Temperament*: Characterizes a set of mental tendencies related to the way in which one perceives, analyzes and makes decisions daily (Calegari & Gegmani, 2006). It represents the uniqueness and intensity of psychic affections and the dominant structure of mood and motivation in each individual (Volpi, 2004). Psychologist Keirsey proposed four types of temperament: *guardian*, *artisan*, *idealist*, and *rational*. The artisan obtains information in a sensory way and have an external orientation towards perception, focusing on works related to bodily and kinesthetic, spatial, musical and interpersonal intelligence. Guardians have a judgmental relationship with the outside world and are therefore careful, obey the laws, follow the rules and respect the rights of others. The idealists rely more on intuition than on the senses and prefer to make decisions based on human values and, finally, rational, although intuitive like the idealists, submit everything to reason (Calegari & Gegmani, 2006).
3. *Personality*: Many researchers believe that temperament is the basis from which personality develops (Ito & Guzzo, 2002; Volpi, 2004; Calegari & Gegmani, 2006). Personality results from genetically inherited elements (temperament) and those acquired from the environment. It is built during the stages of psycho-affective development from the set of temperamental elements that were inherited during pregnancy and elements acquired from the environment during the stages of development, thus forming the inner psychic world of a person (Volpi, 2004). Personality traits make the set of relatively stable characteristics that represent a certain behavior. The *Big Five Factors*, also known as the OCEAN model,

describes a structure for personality by dividing it into five dimensions (Hall, Lindzey, & Campbell, 2000), namely: Openness to experience; Conscientiousness; Extroversion; Agreeableness; and Neuroticism.

The virtual persona triad in its computational form will be presented in the following sequence: a Sentiment Analysis Framework (SAFRA), capable of identifying the polarity and emotional state of messages; a Temperament Classification Framework (TECLA), capable of identifying the user's temperament from the Myers and Briggs perspective or the four temperaments of David Keirsey; and a Personality Prediction Framework (PERSOMA), suitable for an analysis based on the behavior of users and groups of messages.

SAFRA: Sentiment Analysis Framework

Sentiment analysis is one of the most studied classification methods in social media. The most common version of this type of system is *polarity classification*, that is, the classification of messages into positive or negative (Yue, Chen, Li, Zuo, & Yin, 2019; Yadav & Vishwakarma, 2020). There are also works focusing on the classification of tweets based on Ekman's model of emotions (joy, anger, disgust, sadness, fear and surprise) (Balabantaray, Mohammad, & Sharma, 2012), and also following Plutchik's model (joy, sadness, anger, fear, confidence, disgust, surprise and anticipation) (Suttles & Ide, 2013).

The Sentiment Analysis Framework (SAFRA) corresponds to a sentiment analysis system that allows both the classification of polarity and emotional states (Lima, de Castro, & Corchado, 2015; Lima & de Castro, 2012). In both cases, the classification can be seen as follows: given a message $\mathbf{t}_i$ Î **T**, ∀*i*, where **T** is the corpora (set of all messages), $\mathbf{t}_i$ is associated with a class that belongs to the set $C = \{c_1, c_2, ..., c_k\}$ of classes, also called labels or categories. Through a learning method or algorithm, a classifier learns a function γ that maps each message into a class γ: T ® C (Manning, Raghavan, & Schütze, 2008).

The framework consists of the following modules: *data acquisition module*; *knowledge module* (also called *knowledge base* module); *contextual classification module*; *message pre-processing module*; *sentiment classification module*. Finally, the *evaluation module* is used only when there is the need to measure the results of the system (Figure 2).

Figure 2. SAFRA framework.

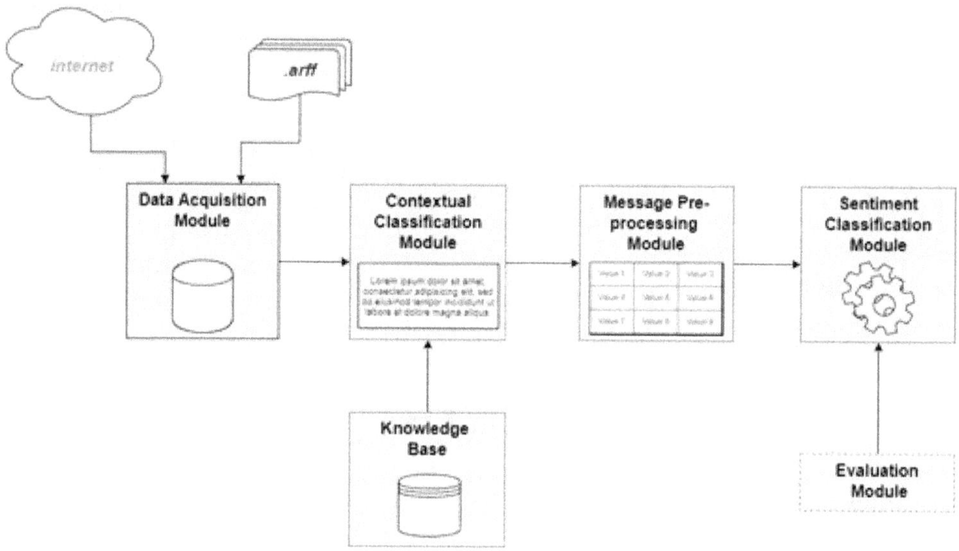

Data Acquisition Module

The data acquisition module obtains texts in two ways: files structured in the Weka model (.arff); or through a social media crawler developed to access social media services and retrieve messages according to search strings. In all subsequent processes, the handling of messages is done following the arff file model, therefore, when the messages are downloaded, they are structured in this format. The knowledge base defines what kind of sentiment analysis will be done, whether by polarity or emotional states.

Contextual Classification Module

The contextual classification module receives the messages from the data acquisition module and the knowledge base content and then performs the automatic classification of the messages. First, the occurrence of classifier elements (CE) is verified. Weights are assigned to the classifier elements to highlight the most representative terms among words and emoticons. Weights are obtained using the SentiStrength tool (Thelwall, Buckley, Paltoglou, & Cai, 2010). An example of the list of words and weights provided by SentiStrength is shown in Figure 3.

Figure 3: Example list of words associated with SentiStrength weights.

```
abdicate*    -2  General Inquirer Feb 2010
abhor*  -4  General Inquirer Feb 2010
abject  -2  General Inquirer Feb 2010
abnormal*    -2  General Inquirer Feb 2010
abolish*     -2  General Inquirer Feb 2010
```

If there is a predefined set of classification targets (CT), the system deals with the proximity between the CEs and the CT, as the closest CE will define the sentiment. This is done because in some cases the message has more than one entity and several classification elements. This module performs the following analyzes in the text:

- Survey all classifier elements present in the text.
- If classification targets are predefined, check for their existence in the text.
- Classification according to the closest classifier element.

The classification will depend on the representation model of the sentiment adopted. If it is a polarity analysis, then the CE can be positive (CE_+), negative (CE_-) or neutral (CE_#). In this case, these are the following possible classification scenarios:

- Message with CE_+: it is checked if the CE_+ is close to the CT, if so, the message is classified as positive.
- Message with CE_-: it is checked if the CE_- is close to the CT and, if so, the message is classified as negative.
- Message with CE_+ and CE_-: it is checked which element is closest to the classification target, with the smallest distance determining the message class.
- Message with CE_#: if the message contains only neutral classifier elements, then the message is labeled "neutral".

In the first three scenarios described, the occurrence of some negation word before the element is analyzed, such as, "no" or "never", then the message is classified in the opposite way. For the classification by emotional states, the CE is associated with a label, for example, following the Ekman model, the following classifying elements are obtained: CE_{anger}; $CE_{disgust}$; CE_{fear}; CE_{joy}; $CE_{sadness}$; $CE_{surprise}$ in addition to CE_#. The functioning of the contextual classifier follows the same principle as the polarity classification. The exception is in how to deal with negation words, as in general there is no explanation about the opposition between emotions, that is, what would result from their denial. All automatically classified messages compose the training set. If the message does not contain a classifier element, it will be classified in the emotion classification module.

Message Pre-Processing Module

The message pre-processing module creates a data matrix from the texts, that is, it transforms an unstructured document into a structured dataset. Some precautions were taken to reduce sparsity and improve the representation of the matrix, such as replacing emoticons with words, for example ":-)" for "happy", replacing any mention of the user with the word USERNAME, replacing links by the word URL, removing stopwords and applying stemming (Feldman & Sanger, 2007; Ignatow & Mihalcea, 2017; Witten, 2005). This module can structure the messages in the following ways: *n*-grams; LIWC; MRC Psycholinguistic Database (MRC); Stanford POSTagger; and Apache OpenNLP.

Sentiment Classification Module

The sentiment classification module is responsible for labeling the unclassified messages during the contextual process, that is, classifying the messages whose labels are unknown. This step uses the training set to build a classifier using machine learning techniques (de Castro & Ferrari, 2016). The classification was constructed in three different ways to understand the best configuration of a system for determining sentiment in short messages.

Evaluation Module

Finally, a module with an assessment methodology was implemented. The evaluation module has a system of random selection (sampling) of messages to obtain a sample from the dataset. From this sample, it is possible to classify it manually and evaluate the system's response. The measures provided by the polarity classification system are *accuracy*, *precision*, and *F-measure*.

TECLA: A Temperament Classification Framework

A temperament, or psychological type, classifier must identify, from an analysis of linguistic characteristics and behaviors related to web services, which set of characteristics that user most resembles. Assuming that there is a temperament taxonomy model, it outlines characteristics inherent to each type. For example, looking at Table 1, there is a set of characteristics for each of David Keirsey's four temperament types. Thus, when classifying a user as an artisan, it is stated that what he/she exposes tends to this set of characteristics, that is, to people more predisposed to act and speak in a more impulsive way.

Table 1. Comparison between people of Keirsey's four temperament types (Source: http://www.keirsey.com/4temps/overview_temperaments.asp).

Guardian	**Artisan**
Talk most of the time about their roles and responsibilities, about the care they take to obey the laws, follow rules and respect the rights of others.	Impulsive, they speak their minds and tend to do what works, which gives them quick and effective pleasure, even if they have to break rules.
Idealist	**Rational**
They want to act with a good conscience, always trying to reach their goals without compromising their personal code of ethics.	Talk about what new problems intrigue them and what new solutions they plan. Pragmatists, they act as efficiently as possible to achieve their goals, ignoring rules and conventions if necessary.

One of the computational proposals presented in this chapter is a framework for temperament analysis, offering the possibility of having a vision of the virtual persona based on the David Keirsey model (Lima & de Castro, 2016). For this purpose, the framework entitled Temperament Classification Framework (TECLA) was developed, also built in a modular way, aiming at greater independence between each step of the process (Claro, Lima, & de Castro, 2018; Claro, Lima, & de Castro, 2019; Lima & de Castro, 2019). This approach makes it possible to couple and test different techniques to each module. Even if a priori only the Keirsey classification is allowed, it is possible to expand the framework by inserting other taxonomies.

The classification process has the following modules (Figure 4): *data acquisition module*; *message pre-processing module*; *temperament classification module*; and an *evaluation module*.

Figure 4. The TECLA framework.

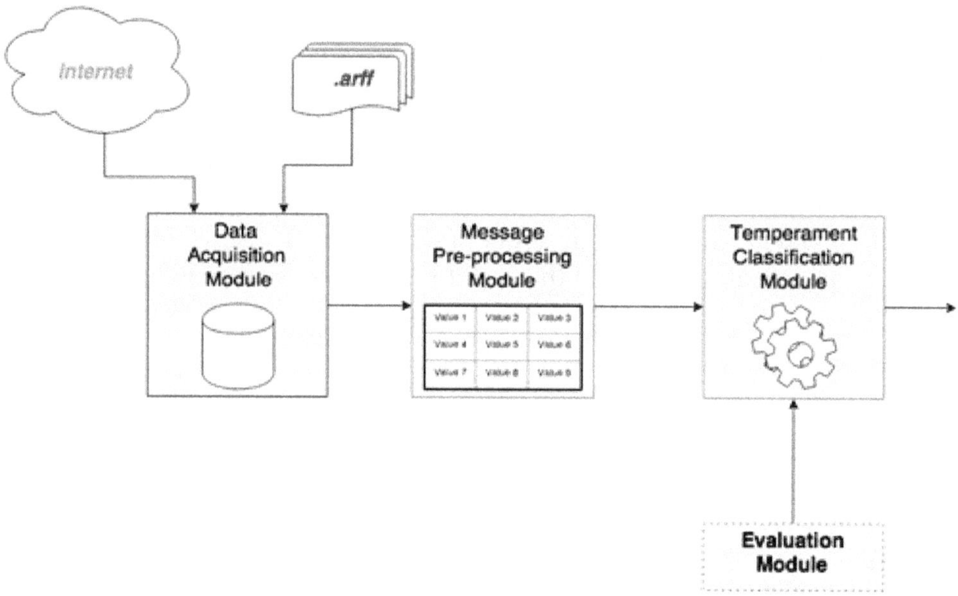

Data Acquisition Module

The first step in the process takes place in the data acquisition module, responsible for receiving information from the user whose temperament has to be classified. It is necessary to obtain usage information, such as number of messages, number of followers and followed (when using social media data), as well as a set of messages from the user. This information can be entered through a file or retrieved by the system crawler.

Message Pre-Processing Module

Then, the data is pre-processed in the message pre-processing module to create an array of objects by meta-attributes. This module is responsible for extracting meta-attributes from the corpus and for building a new database, called meta-base, from the extracted meta-attributes.

TECLA does not work directly with texts coming from messages, but uses information extracted from them, called meta-attributes. Such information can be divided into two categories: grammatical and behavioral. The behavioral category extracts information about social media usage and is specific to each media type; in the case of Twitter, the number of tweets, number of followed, followers, favorites, number of listings, and number of times the user was liked. The grammatical category considers information from LIWC, MRC, sTagger or oNLP, extracted from the user's message set, in the same way as done for SAFRA.

Temperament Classification Module

Finally, the temperament classification module infers a temperament from the characteristics (meta-attributes) extracted in the previous process. In principle this module can incorporate any type of classifier. For the classification based on the Keirsey model, a sequence of classifiers was constructed. One strategy to work with multiclass classifiers is the combination of the classifiers generated in binary sub-problems. With that, there is a decomposition of the problem into binary problems. Separating the problem into binary classifiers can reduce the computational complexity involved in solving the total problem, with simpler sub-tasks (Lorena & Carvalho, 2008).

PERSOMA: A Personality Classification Framework

The Personality Classification Framework (PERSOMA) is a personality prediction system for social media that consists of an algorithm-independent multi-label classifier and label-based transformation (Tsoumakas, Katakis, & Vlahavas, 2006; Lima & de Castro, 2014). A *multi-label* problem is one in which the objects in the database can belong to more than one class (label) simultaneously (Coelho, 2011; Moyano, Gibaja, Ciosb, & Ventura, 2018).

The algorithm-independent approach, used in PERSOMA, breaks the problem down into one or more single-label classification problems and disregards the possible correlation between the different labels. This decomposition can be either label-based or based on database instances (Carvalho & Freitas, 2009). After separation, a traditional classification algorithm can be applied (Cherman & Monard, 2009).

The label-based transformation technique, also known as *label powerset*, divides the multi-label problem *L* into *M* binary problems and therefore *M* classifiers are created, where *M* is the number of labels/classes in the database. For each classifier, a label is associated and training is done in order to solve the single label problem. The instance-based transformation technique converts the problem into one or more single-label problems according to the set of labels associated with each object. The main strategies used by this technique are (Carvalho & Freitas, 2009): elimination of multi-label cases; creation of new unique labels using existing multi-labels; and converting multi-label cases to single-label instances.

The algorithm-dependent approach involves modified single-label classifiers to deal with the multi-label problem. The advantage of this approach is that in many cases the modification improves the results in real world problems when compared to the algorithm-independent approach. Many techniques have been adapted to solve multi-label problems, such as decision trees, *Support Vector Machines* (SVM), *k*-nearest neighbors, association rules, evolutionary algorithms, swarm algorithms, and neural networks.

For this study involving personality analysis, each personality trait in the OCEAN model is assigned a binary classifier that indicates whether a certain person (user) has or has not that personality trait. The system allows two types of data analysis: 1) predicting users' personality traits; and 2) predicting personality traits in message groups. In the first case, messages are collected from a specific user and the traces are analyzed. In the second case, the idea is to allow a perspective about the general traits in a group of messages, for example, to understand the personality traits of people who talk about a certain brand or product. In this case, the categorized messages can be inserted into the system, or some type of clustering algorithm can be used to perform the categorization.

After this preliminary step, PERSOMA extracts a set of meta-attributes from the messages, instead of working directly with the text, and finally transforms the multi-label classification problem into binary problems and then applies a classification algorithm to predict personality. The PERSOMA execution sequence involves the following modules: *data acquisition module*; *data clustering module*; *message pre-processing module*; *data transformation module* and *classification module*; as shown in Figure 5. It also has an optional *evaluation* module.

Data Acquisition Module

As in the other frameworks, it is the stage of the process in which data can be collected or entered into the system. Similarly to TECLA, it is necessary to obtain usage information, such as number of messages, number of followers and followed, in addition to a set of messages from the user.

Data Clustering Module

This is an optional module where data captured or entered can be grouped. If the interest is to identify personality traits in groups of messages, the data clustering module is responsible for clustering the messages. This module should only be used if the goal is to identify trends in groups. The *K*-means,

Hierarchical Grouping, Expectation Maximization, Cobweb and FarthestFirst algorithms are part of this module in the experiments to be presented further.

Figure 5. The PERSOMA framework.

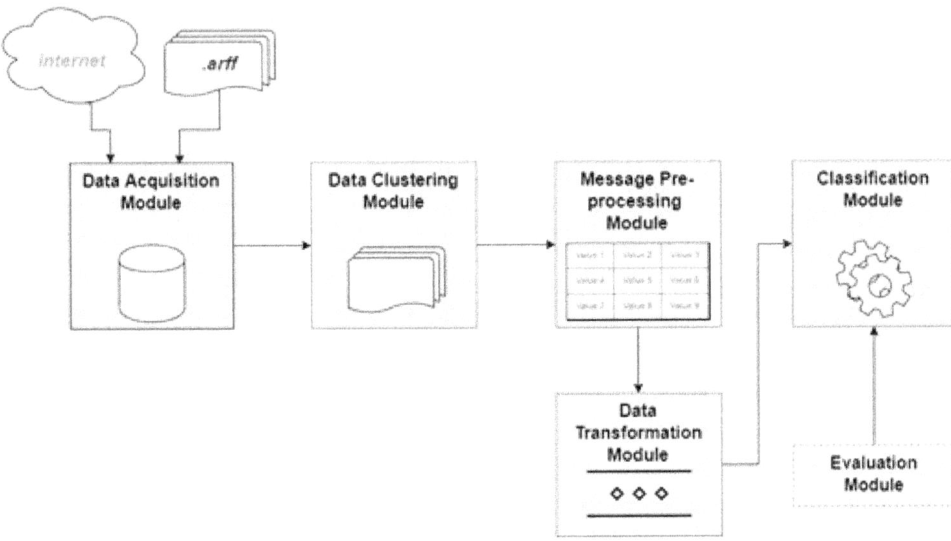

Message Pre-Processing Module

The message pre-processing module is responsible for extracting meta-attributes from the corpus and for building a new database, the “meta-base”, from the extracted meta-attributes. Such attributes are extracted from message sets. Thus, an object $o_i=\{t_1,t_2,\ldots,t_n\}$ is composed of the messages $t_1,\ldots,t_n$. In the classification process, the framework does not work directly with the messages, but uses information extracted from them. Such information can be divided into two categories: *grammatical* and *behavioral*. The grammatical category considers counting information, such as the number of words used and the number of punctuation marks used in the text (Mairesse, Walker, Mehl, & Moore, 2007). The behavioral category extracts information about the use of social media and is specific to each type of media (Adali & Golbeck, 2012).

Transformation Module

The transformation module is in charge of converting the multi-label problem into single-label binary problems. Each label corresponds to a personality trait in the OCEAN model in the binary problem; that is, each message group may or may not contain a personality trait. The object $\mathbf{o}_i$ in the meta-base is associated with a set of labels **Y**, **Y Í C**, where **C** is the set of labels for the problem. Consequently, a multi-label classifier Γ maps each object into a set of Y labels, Γ: O ®Y. This mapping can be done in two ways: through a problem-adapted classification algorithm (algorithm-dependent); or the problem can be divided into problems with a single label (independent of algorithm) (Tsoumakas, Katakis, & Vlahavas, 2006).

Figure 6 shows an example of how this transformation is done in PERSOMA. Let $\mathbf{o}_i$ be an object (individual) characterized by extraversion, conscientiousness and neuroticism. After the transformation, the object has five labels, referring to each trait, but with extroversion, conscientiousness and neuroticism marked as "1" and the other two traits, kindness and neuroticism, marked as "0". In the classification module, each classifier is responsible for determining whether the object has the personality trait or not.

Figure 6. The workings of the transformation module.

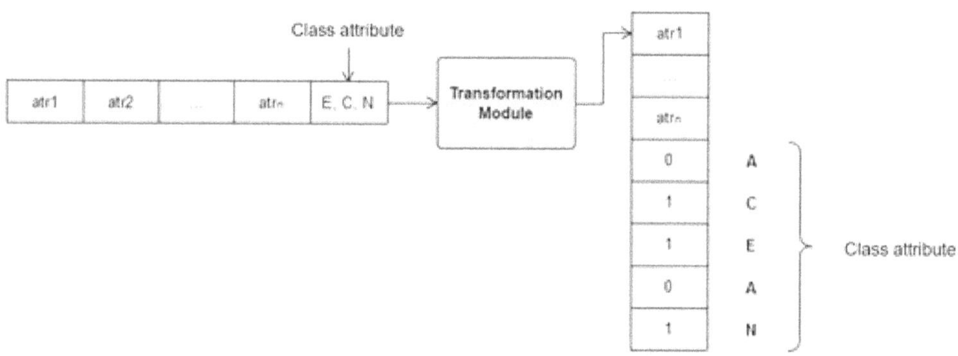

Classification Module

The classification module is responsible for determining whether or not there is a personality trait in the message set. This one receives a labeled meta-base, which is called a training meta-base or training set, already transformed into five binary problems, in addition to the unlabeled data, called a test set. Multi-label classification is done by five classification algorithms, each responsible for a single class. It should be noted that although five classifiers are used, the response of the classification module is a binary vector, where each position corresponds to a personality trait. The classifiers used in the experiments will be trained using semi-supervised learning, so the training set increases as new classifications are made, in the *semi-supervised transductive learning style* (Chapelle, Schölkopf, & Zien, 2006; Engelen & Hoos, 2020).

Semi-supervised learning is in between supervised and unsupervised learning, in the sense that labeled and unlabeled data are used to train the classifier. Thus, this approach uses the labeled data (training set) to continuously label the unlabeled data (test set) (Chapelle, Schölkopf, & Zien, 2006; Engelen & Hoos, 2020). This approach is recommended in scenarios where there is a small number of labeled data (training set) and a large number of unlabeled data, making manual sorting impractical. The idea of semi-supervision is to use labeled objects to obtain information about the problem and use this information to guide the learning process. This technique can be used for both sorting and grouping. In the case of classification, it consists of labeling some objects from the test set and then inserting them into the training set.

PERFORMANCE ASSESSMENT

This section describes the performance of each framework when applied to a number of problems aiming at answering the following questions:

- What is the sentiment that a certain user expresses when referring to an entity (brand, product, person, artist, politician, or any other element in social media)? Is this sentiment related to the polarity of the emotion or the user's emotional state?
- From what the user writes is it possible to infer his/her temperament?
- Is it possible to identify personality traits based on what the user writes and how he/she interacts?

SAFRA

SAFRA was evaluated for its ability to predict polarity and emotional states. In both cases, the following classifiers were tested in the emotion classification module: Naïve Bayes (NB); Support Vector Machines (SVM); decision tree (J48); and *k*-nearest neighbors (KNN). For the pre-processing module the following settings will be used: data represented using the standard TF-IDF method with *n*-grams; data represented by the MRC, LIWC, sTagger, and oNLP dictionary categories.

Polarity Analysis

The version of SAFRA for polarity analysis was called PAFRA (Polarity Analysis Framework) (Lima, de Castro, & Corchado, 2015). To assess the performance of PAFRA, five sets of Twitter data available in the literature were used: *Obama-McCain Debate* (OMD); *SentiStrenght Twitter Dataset* (SS-Twitter); *Sanders*; *SemEval2013*; and *Sentiment140*. Although the datasets have different labels, they all contain messages with positive and negative labels. Thus, only these messages were used for the evaluation, transforming the problem into a binary classification task.

The first experiment carried out was the test of the support (coverage) of the knowledge bases for the dataset. The average knowledge base support (i.e., {ε} È {ω} support) for the four databases was 67.30%. For the application, it is considered that the knowledge base must have a minimum support of 5%. As all datasets have a support much greater than this value, no manual labelling was needed. Then, the accuracy of the automatic classification algorithm was analysed using the labels available in the databases as a reference. Both results can be seen in Table 2.

Table 2. Datasets' support and accuracy of the automatic classification.

	Support			Accuracy		
Dataset	**Positive**	**Negative**	**Total**	**Positive**	**Negative**	**Total**
OMD	481 (38,60%)	765 (61,40%)	1246 (62,08%)	73,08%	67,06%	69,24%
Sanders	283 (45,72%)	336 (54,28%)	619 (61,78%)	87,83%	76,92%	82,04%
SS-Twitter	819 (53,46%)	713 (46,54%)	1532 (66,93%)	90,05%	75,80%	84,37%
SemEval	2068 (57,38%)	1536 (42,62%)	3604 (71,54%)	85,78%	76,51%	83,07%
Sentiment140	114 (42,86%)	152 (57,14%)	266 (74,09%)	88,97%	79,74%	84,23%

Observing the performance by dataset, it is noted that the OMD had the smallest support, with 62.08% of the data being able to be classified automatically due to the existence of a classifier element. Among those automatically classified messages, 69.24% were correct. Although the classification methodology influences the result, SAFRA leads to a standardization of classification, which is not achieved in manual classification.

After automatic classification, the data were separated into training and testing. The training set has the tweets classified automatically, while the test set has those that were not classified in this process. Table 3 shows the number of messages per class and the total for each of these sets.

Table 3. Tweet distributions per class.

	Training			Test		
	+	–	Total	+	–	Total
OMD	481	765	1246	303	458	761
Sanders	283	336	619	195	187	382
SS-Twitter	819	713	1532	444	313	757
SemEval	2068	1536	3604	1073	361	1434
Sentiment140	114	152	266	56	37	93

The results of the Naïve Bayes algorithm, SVM, J48, 1NN, 2NN and 3NN, Bagging, AdaBoost and Random Forest are presented in Figure 7 and the following discussion for all the different forms of representation of the possible documents in SAFRA. This figure shows the boxplot for the accuracy obtained by the algorithms for each representation. In this case, *k*-fold cross-validation was not used, as the training set will always be the one provided by the system's automatic classifier.

The measures chosen to determine the best result were accuracy and F-measure. As can be observed in Figure 7, the LIWC representation promoted an overall best accuracy of the classifiers. In summary, the best results for each dataset are listed below:

- OMD: classification via AdaBoost and 2-gram or 3-gram structuring obtained accuracy of 65.85% and F-measure of 50.76%.
- Sanders: classification via AdaBoost and structuring via LIWC obtained an accuracy of 69.92% and an F-measure of 72.99%.
- SS-Twitter: classification via Bagging and structuring via LIWC obtained accuracy of 71.91% and F-measure of 79.45%.
- SemEval: classification via AdaBoost and structuring via LIWC obtained an accuracy of 77.48% and F-measure of 84.16%.
- Sentiment140: classification via J48 and structuring via LIWC obtained accuracy of 77.36% and F-measure of 80.22%.

Figure 7. SAFRA classification accuracy for polarity analysis and the different representation schemes.

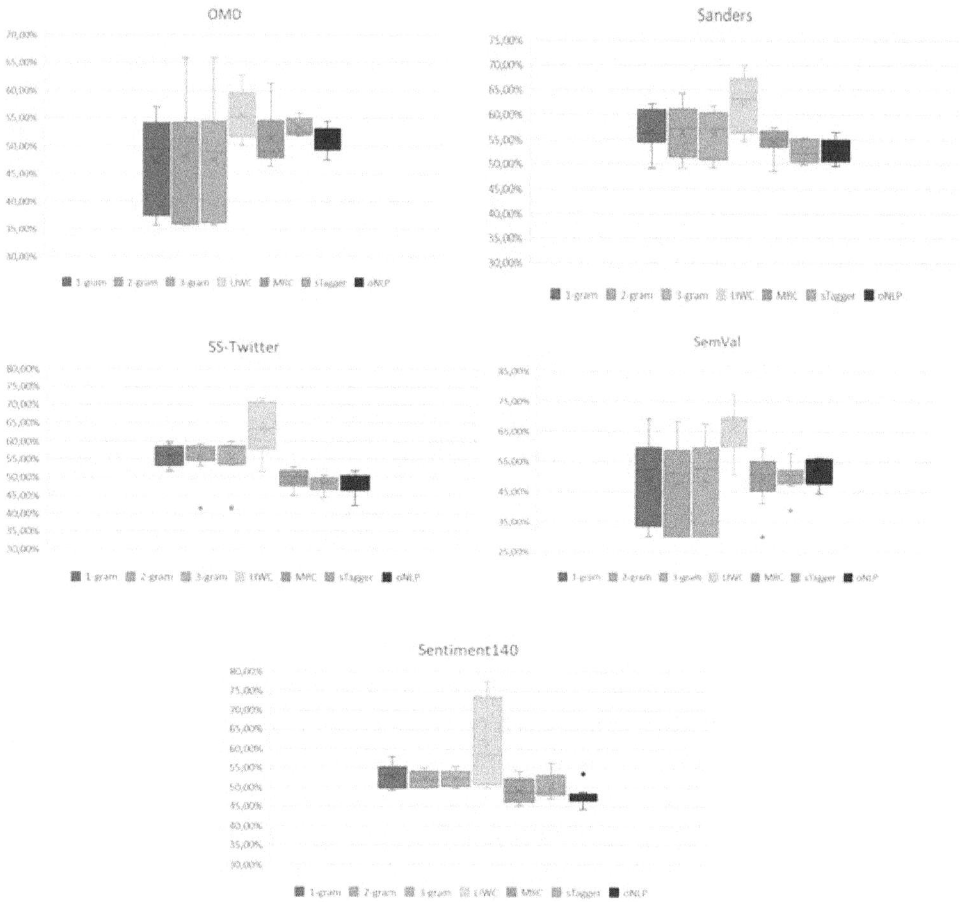

Emotional State Analysis

To contextualize the performance of classification by emotional states with the literature, the assessment was carried out from a sample of 28,598 tweets from the database provided by (Wang, Chen, Thirunarayan, & Sheth, 2012). The authors created a tweet dataset categorized into joy, sadness, anger, love, fear, thankfulness and surprise based on monitoring and capturing 131 different hashtags about emotions. They believed that sentiment is expressed in the hashtags. Thus, even if other words represent other emotions, the authors consider that the hashtag represents the main emotion that the user wanted to demonstrate. This is corroborated in (Hasan, Rundensteiner, &

Agu, 2014). The database was made available by the authors at http://knoesis.org/projects/emotion..

As the mapping by Wang et al. (2012) is closer to the Ekman model, we opted for this taxonomy. Thus, tweets labeled thankfulness in the research by Wang et al. (2012) were discarded, as this emotional category does not exist in Ekman's model. The love and joy categories were condensed into happiness. The original data also does not contain the category disgust and, therefore, tweets with hashtags with this word were considered. Table 4 summarizes the proportion of tweets for each emotional state. The disgust and surprise classes represent less than 2% of the data each, which could negatively impact the performance of the classifiers and, therefore, were removed from the experiments.

Table 4. Number of tweets for each emotional state.

Emotional State	Number of tweets	Relative Frequency
anger	6227	21,78%
disgust	**539**	**1,88%**
fear	1642	5,74%
happiness	12458	43,57%
sadness	7440	26,02%
surprise	**289**	**1,01%**
Total	28.595	100%

Table 5 presents the support of the knowledge base and the accuracy of each class according to the contextual classification system, as well as an example of words used as a classifier element. The sadness state has the largest support, with about 48.94% of tweets classified by the automatic system. However, only 19.00% of the fear category is classified by the automatic system. Overall, the mean base support was 33.34% and the mean accuracy of the contextual classification was 82.39%.

In the emotional states analysis, *k*-fold cross-validation was also not performed, as the training set was determined by the system's automatic classifier. The test procedure was performed with the *n*-gram, LIWC, MRC, OpenNLP and sTagger techniques, and the Naïve Bayes, SVM, J48, 1-NN, 2-NN, 3-NN, Bagging, AdaBoost and Random Forest classifiers, and evaluation through accuracy by class and F-measure.

Table 5. Support and accuracy analysis of the Wang data for emotional state classification.

Emotion	Classifying element examples	Total	Knowledge base support	Automatic classification accuracy
anger	*irritating, annoyed, frustrate, fury*	6227	22,48%	80,79%
fear	*fear, panic, fright, worry, scare*	1642	19,00%	58,97%
happiness	*affection, lovin, loving, fondness, excited, happy, elated, proud*	12458	42,92%	98,78%
sadness	*sorrow, unhappy, depressing, lonely*	7440	48,94%	91,02%

All classifications in which dictionaries (LIWC, MRC, OpenNLP and sTagger) were used to represent the text achieved 100% accuracy, as can be observed in Figure 8. On the other hand, although the result of the *n*-gram is satisfactory in the case of the anger emotional state, the result of the F-measure showed that the classifier tended towards one of the classes. It is concluded that for this classification the use of *n*-gram is not recommended.

In the classification via Naïve Bayes, the system obtained the best results from the structuring of texts by the MRC. For sTagger and OpenNLP the performance was over 98% for all classes. In the classification via SVM, the behavior was similar to the previous one, but with results reaching 100% accuracy and F-measure in all emotional states from the structuring of texts by LIWC, MRC, sTagger and oNLP. For J48 the performance was 100% for MRC, sTagger and oNLP. In the case of LIWC, the mean was 97.75% accuracy. However, the *n*-gram presented the worst results so far with no success for the fear, happiness and sadness classes. For KNN, the results with $k = 1$ were the lowest among the used classifiers. For the other cases ($k = 2$ and $k = 3$) the behavior was similar to the previous ones, with better performance in the representation of texts by dictionary. In the ensemble Bagging and AdaBoost techniques the accuracy and precision were 100% in all classes.

TECLA: Temperament Classification Framework

All tests were performed with *k*-fold cross-validation ($k = 5$) and 10 runs. It will be shown the results for the Keirsey model, that is, whether from the input data it is possible to identify an Artisan, Guardian, Idealist or Rational person. In all cases, the measure adopted for evaluation was the accuracy by class.

Figure 8. SAFRA accuracy per class for emotional state classification of the Wang et al (2012) data and the different representation schemes.

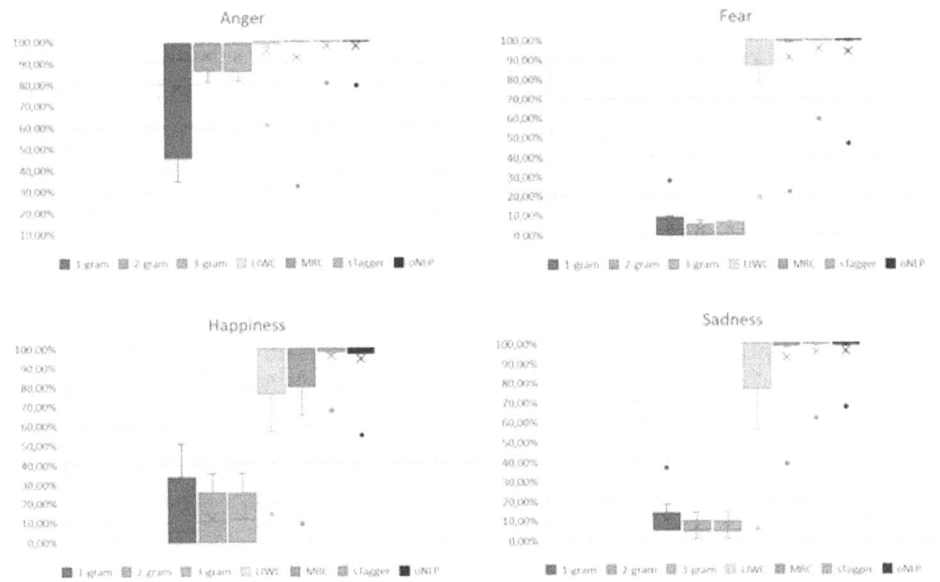

Figure 9 shows the test results for the Keirsey model considering each of the four temperament types: Artisan, Guardian, Idealist and Rational. The best performance for the Artisan and Guardian types presented an average accuracy of 89.04% ± 0.00% and 85.62% ± 0.00%, respectively. On the other hand, the Idealist and Rational classes presented a maximum average accuracy of 65.27% ± 0.44% and 59.93% ± 1.11%, respectively. Such values for Idealists and Rationals can be an outcome of unsuitable attributes to represent the behavior of both. That is, what differentiates Artisans and Guardians is the judgment/perception characteristic, while Idealists and Rationals differ by the feeling/thought pair.

For the representations via *n*-gram, the values of *n* were varied between 1 and 3. In this case, the performance was also greater than that of the Artisan and Guardian classes and less than that for Idealist and Rational. From the T-test with a 5% significance level, a similarity probability of 74.72% between 1-gram and 2-gram in the AdaBoost algorithm and 63.76% between 2-gram and 3-gram in Naïve Bayes is observed. In the others it was less than 50%.

For the MRC the dimensionality is lower than for LIWC, but in general the classifiers' performances were similar, except for the Idealist class where in J48 the accuracy was 63.84% ± 1.56%. Running the T-test with a 5% significance level in the results of both to assess the hypothesis of equality between the mean accuracy values, the probability of equality was greater than 90% for the Random Forest and around 85.31% for the results of the KNNs, Bagging and AdaBoost. This means that the hypothesis that the values between these techniques were equivalent cannot be discarded. The T-test indicated a similarity probability of 63.78% in J48, and 58.67% in Bagging. In the others, the probability was less than 50%. Observing the average result by class, oNLP has a slight advantage over the sTagger: 83.55% versus 82.54% for Artisan; 80.30% versus 79.99% for Guardian; 58.11% versus 56.81% for Idealist; and 53.34% versus 52.20% for Rational.

Analyzing only the attributes obtained by using Twitter, the average accuracy considering all classifiers was 82.28%, 75.71%, 61.74%, 55.43% for Artisan, Guardian, Idealist and Rational, respectively. Comparing with the other structures: 83.71%, 79.74%, 56.07%, 51.61 for LIWC; 84.06%, 78.53%, 59.87%, 53.84 for MRC; 83.55%, 80.30%, 58.11%, 53.34 for Open; 82.54%, 79.99%, 56.81%, 52.20 for sTagger. This demonstrates that in all cases the addition of a dictionary improved performance for the Artisan and Guardian classes but worsened for Idealist and Rational. The same behavior was observed with the *n*-gram technique: 86.23%, 79.06%, 56.24%, 54.11 for 1-gram; 84.34%, 79.17%, 56.64%, 51.93 for 2-gram; and 84.32%, 78.32%, 56.17%, 51.42 for 3-gram.

PERSOMA: Personality Classification Framework

To evaluate PERSOMA's performance, standard multi-label evaluation measures were used. The challenge in evaluating this system is the availability of a database in the literature for comparisons, mainly for Twitter. However, the widely used myPersonality base was found in the literature and was adopted to evaluate the framework: 9,917 Facebook status updates from 250 users, with Facebook network properties (such as network size, betweenness centrality, density and transitivity) tagged with personality traits (Celli, Pianesi, Stillwell, & Kosinski, 2013).

The analysis is performed syntactically with the help of the LIWC and the MRC. The result is a value in the range [1 (smallest), 7 (largest)]. For the experiments in this work, it was defined that a feature with a value lower than 3 implies its absence, while values equal to or higher than 3 imply the presence of this feature.

All tests for the base myPersonality were run with a *k*-fold cross-validation ($k = 5$) with 10 runs, with the algorithms Naïve Bayes, J48, SVM, KNN, in addition to the ensemble methods AdaBoosting, Bagging and RandomForest. The structure of the texts was also evaluated using LIWC, MRC, oNLP and sTagger, in addition to the *n*-gram technique. It should be noted that in all cases of representation of myPersonality, the network data provided by the database were also considered.

Figure 9. TECLA performance for the Keirsey model presenting the average and standard deviation for each type of representation model, each classifier and temperament.

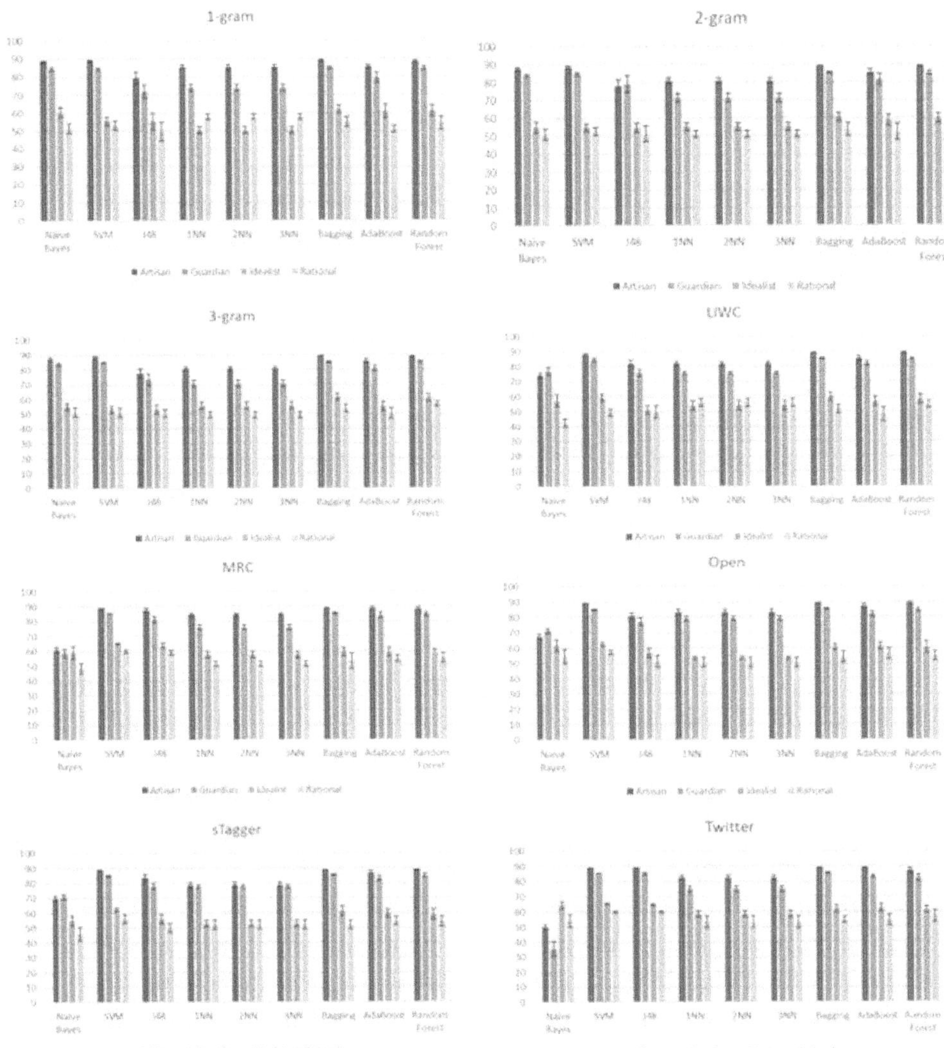

Figure 10 summarizes the average percentage and standard deviation of correct ratings for each of the personality traits in the myPersonality database. On average, the results did not exceed 70%, indicating that the attributes may not be ideal for the dataset. In the paper in which the myPersonality database is presented, the best result (measure F = 0.904) was achieved with the combination of attributes: demographic and social information, Part Of Speech, emotional values of words through the AFINN dictionary (Nielsen, 2011) and word intensity scale using the H4Lvd. Markovicj et al. (2013), also achieved a similar result using the same attributes in the database in question. Both these and new attributes or combinations of them can be considered in new versions of the system.

For this dataset, the PERSOMA achieved better results in the openness to experience trait with a maximum average accuracy of 70.52%±0.26 and F-measure of 82.67%±0.00 with the SVM algorithm and representation via oNLP. However, it was not able to discriminate the neuroticism trait with an accuracy level greater than 60.28%±1.79. In all representations, the lowest accuracy values were reached with the Naïve Bayes algorithm.

In the representations via *n*-gram, the results were equivalent for all techniques regarding the best classifier with a superior performance for the 2-gram. However, the values were not good enough for the MRC and the oNLP and sTagger representations. For the F-measure, the performance remained higher for the openness to experience trait. In this case, there was the worst performance of PERSOMA in the execution of KNN for the traits of openness to experience, conscientiousness, extraversion and agreeableness. In the first set of attributes, the LIWC associated with the network data provided with the myPersonality data, the accuracy by class did not exceed an average value of 68.60%±0.78. The F-measure indicates a better classification of the yes class in the trait of openness to experience. There was no change in both the accuracy and F-measure in the KNN variations (k =1, 2 and 3).

With the MRC, the performance in relation to accuracy improved in all traits, reaching the percentage of 70.40%±0.00 at the openness to experience. As for the F-measure, there was also an improvement with the best result for the openness to experience trait with 82.63%±0.00. For the oNLP and sTagger accuracies the performance was worse than that of the MRC, but again greater than the LIWC. This may indicate that the high dimensionality of LIWC in relation to other techniques interferes in the decision of the classification algorithm. Analyzing the F-measure, the behavior follows the same pattern with better results for the openness to experience trait, as can be seen for oNLP and sTagger.

Figure 10. PERSOMA accuracy for each personality trait and representation method for a k-fold cross-validation and the myPersonality data.

CONCLUSION

Social interaction through virtual means evolves in a fast pace. The different ways of interacting (digital tools, social media, smartphones, etc.) have redefined concepts such as identity, friendship, privacy, and liking. It changes the form, reality, mind and the ability to deal with each environment. "All technology gradually creates a whole new human environment", said McLuhan (1994, p. 10). If, on the one hand, the machine is seen as a barrier to proximity, on the other, it can be understood as another bridge bringing people together in a new way of coexistence.

Sharing content on the internet has a spontaneous essence and, therefore, there is the potential to convey the emotions, frustrations, anxieties, fears and joys of each user. All this makes the cyberspace a psychological space with opportunity to identity flexibility and anonymity, social status equivalence, overcoming spatial limits, stretching and condensing time, to access multiple relationships, to record one's experience, and to promote the disinhibition effect.

This chapter presented the virtual persona concept as a way to promote a less abstract view about social media users. Motivated by the sense of belonging and self-presentation one builds images of himself. Thus, each decision to share a multimedia content and consequently interact with others in the social media environment gives rise to a virtual persona, that is, an image formed from how we present ourselves and behave in social media. The virtual persona is the result of all the characteristics and behaviors we adopt in social media. Although we create a sort of mask, or we configure the things that we want to show, it is argued, based on the literature, that the physical personas are deeply affected by what one absorbs in the virtual world, sometimes producing an inverse effect. It was argued that, indeed, one can study and map psychological factors from virtual behaviors and, with that, understanding social media users means being able to measure behaviors. New computing technologies allow us to store massive amounts of data and process them almost in real time allowing us to have quick answers to the new problems faced by society in which the real and virtual are so intertwined.

Virtual personas express cognitive-affective processes through their profile, social identity and behaviors. Think about others' mental state as a form to engage successfully and thereby reinforce the need to connect with others (Tamir & Ward, 2015), thus, creating an identity is also an important part of the cognitive-affective processes (thoughts and feelings) about oneself (Mehdizadeh, 2010).

Furthermore, this chapter presented three inference systems: a Sentiment Analysis Framework (SAFRA); a Temperament Classification Framework (TECLA); and a Personality Classification Framework (PERSOMA). The purpose of the analyzes was to show the predictive capacity based on the combination of text analysis techniques, natural language processing and machine learning, and not necessarily a comparison between classification algorithms. The frameworks were designed to support different text structuring techniques and classification algorithms and, thus, offer a greater possibility of configuration in relation to a specific classification problem. The structuring in modules also made it possible to couple other techniques and expand the possibilities for configuring the tools.

The three frameworks make up tools for analyzing the profile of the virtual persona triad. SAFRA is more related to content-based analysis, as it does not depend on user monitoring but rather on an entity, but it can also be used to gauge a user's general sentiment by looking at his/her messages. This result could also be used as an attribute in other frameworks, but this issue has not yet been addressed. TECLA and PERSOMA, on the other hand, are related to behavior-based analysis. These are tools for identifying or mapping a profile. These systems hold promise as marketing tools for social media companies. These companies can classify users and provide them with specific advertising or promotion with high accuracy. Not only that, it is important to highlight the wide effort in the studies of David Keirsey (1998) to link his temperament model to professional aspects, relationships, conflicts and education. Thus, one also sees a great potential of the presented tools in the areas of recruitment and selection, since the use of social media profiles to identify potential collaborators or abusive behaviors is increasingly recurrent. The strong connection between temperament and professional profiles can facilitate the search for professionals who are more aligned with the companies' values and interests.

ACKNOWLEDGMENT

The authors would like to thank CNPq, Capes, Fapesp and MackPesquisa for the financial support.

REFERENCES

Adali, S., & Golbeck, J. (2012). Predicting Personality with Social Behavior. In *2012 IEEE/ACM International Conference on Advances in Social Networks Analysis and Mining (ASONAM)* (pp. 302 - 309). Istanbul: IEEE. 10.1109/ASONAM.2012.58

Annisette, L. E., & Lafreniere, K. D. (2017). Social media, texting, and personality: A test of the shallowing hypothesis. *Personality and Individual Differences*, *115*, 154–158. doi:10.1016/j.paid.2016.02.043

Baker, A. J. (2009). *Mick or Keith: blended identity of online rock fans*. Identity in the Information Society.

Balabantaray, R. C., Mohammad, M., & Sharma, N. (2012). Multi-class twitter emotion classification: A new approach. *International Journal of Applied Information Systems*, *4*(1), 48–53. doi:10.5120/ijais12-450651

Baptista, L. (2003). Framing and cognition. In Goffman's legacy. Rowman & Littlefield Publishers.

Bargh, J. A., McKenna, K. Y., & Fitzsimons, G. M. (2002). Can you see the real me? Activation and expression of the "true self" on the Internet. *The Journal of Social Issues*, *58*(1), 33–48. doi:10.1111/1540-4560.00247

Barry, C. T., Doucette, H., Loflin, D. C., Rivera-Hudson, N., & Herrington, L. L. (2017). "Let Me Take a Selfie": Associations Between Self-Photography, Narcissism, and Self-Esteem. *Psychology of Popular Media Culture*, *6*(1), 48–60. doi:10.1037/ppm0000089

Bergman, S. M., Fearrington, M. E., Davenport, S. W., & Bergman, J. Z. (2011). Millennials, narcissism, and social networking: What narcissists do on social networking sites and why. *Personality and Individual Differences*, *2011*(5), 706–711. doi:10.1016/j.paid.2010.12.022

Biolcati, R., & Passini, S. (2018). Narcissism and self-esteem: Different motivations for selfie posting behaviors. *Cogent Psychology, 2018*(5). doi:10.1080/23311908.2018.1437012

Bullingham, L., & Vasconcelos, A. C. (2013). 'The presentation of self in the online world': Goffman and the study of online identities. *Journal of Information Science*, *39*(1), 101–112. doi:10.1177/0165551512470051

Buss, A. (2001). *Psychological dimensions of the self*. Sage Publications.

Calegari, M. d., & Gegmani, O. H. (2006). *Temperamento e Carreira* (4th ed.). Summus.

Cannon, W. B. (1927). The James-Lange theory of emotions: A critical examination and an alternative theory. *The American Journal of Psychology*, *39*(1/4), 106–124. doi:10.2307/1415404 PMID:3322057

Carvalho, A. C., & Freitas, A. A. (2009). A Tutorial on Multi-Label Classification Techniques. *Studies in Computational Intelligence, 205*, 177–195.

Celli, F., Pianesi, F., Stillwell, D., & Kosinski, M. (2013). Workshop on Computational Personality Recognition (Shared Task). *Proceedings of WCPR13, in conjunction with ICWSM-13.*

Chapelle, O., Schölkopf, B., & Zien, A. (2006). Semi-Supervised Learning. In Adaptive Computation and Machine Learning. The MIT Press. doi:10.7551/mitpress/9780262033589.001.0001

Charoensukmongkol, P. (2018). The Impact of Social Media on Social Comparison and Envy in Teenagers: The Moderating Role of the Parent Comparing Children and In-group Competition among Friends. *Journal of Child and Family Studies, 2018*(27), 69–79. doi:10.100710826-017-0872-8

Cherman, E. A., & Monard, M. C. (2009). Um Estudo sobre Métodos de Classificação Multirrótulo. *Proceedings of do IV Congresso da Academia Trinacional de Ciências*, 1, 1-10.

Chou, H.-T. G., & Edge, N. (2012). They are happier and having better lives than I am": the impact of using Facebook on perceptions of others. Cyberpsychology, Behavior, and Social Networking, 15, 117-121.

Claro, C. F., Lima, A. C., & de Castro, L. N. (2018). Predicting Temperament using Keirsey's Model for Portuguese Twitter Data. In *Proceedings of the 10th International Conference on Agents and Artificial Intelligence* (vol. 1, pp. 250-256). 10.5220/0006700102500256

Claro, C. F., Lima, A. C., & de Castro, L. N. (2019). The Application of Keirsey's Temperament Model to Twitter Data in Portuguese. In Agents and Artificial Intelligence. ICAART 2018. Lecture Notes in Computer Science (Vol. 11352, pp. 408-421). doi:10.1007/978-3-030-05453-3_19

Coelho, T. A. (2011). Uma estratégia híbrida para o problema de classificação multirrótulo. Universidade Federal de Minas Gerais, Instituto de Ciências Exatas.

Damasio, A. (2003). *Looking for Spinoza: Joy, Sorrow, and the Feeling Brain.* Harvest.

Darwin, C., Ekman, P., & Prodger, P. (1998). *The expression of the emotions in man and animals.* Oxford University Press.

de Castro, L. N., & Ferrari, D. G. (2016). *Introduction to Data Mining: Basic Concepts, Algorithms, and Applications*. Saraiva.

Ekman, P., Friesen, W. V., & Ellsworth, P. (1982). What emotion categories or dimensions can observers judge from facial behavior? In *Emotion in the human face* (pp. 39–55). Cambridge University Press.

Engelen, J. E., & Hoos, H. H. (2020). A survey on semi-supervised learning. *Machine Learning*, *109*(2), 373–440. doi:10.100710994-019-05855-6

Farias, L., & Monteiro, T. (2012). A identidade adquirida nas redes sociais através do conceito de persona. *XIX Prêmio Expocom 2012 – Exposição da Pesquisa Experimental em Comunicação - Intercom - Sociedade Brasileira de Estudos Interdisciplinares da Comunicação*. http://www.intercom.org.br/papers/regionais/nordeste2012/resumos/R32-1497-1.pdf

Feldman, R., & Sanger, J. (2007). *The Text Mining Handbook Advanced Approaches in Analysing Unstructured Data*. Cambridge University Press.

Fox, J., & Moreland, J. J. (2015). The dark side of social networking sites: An exploration of the relational and psychological stressors associated with Facebook use and affordances. *Computers in Human Behavior*, *2015*(45), 168–176. doi:10.1016/j.chb.2014.11.083

Gundecha, P., & Liu, H. (2012). Introduction Mining Social Media: A Brief Introduction. *INFORMS TutORials in Operations Research*, 1-17.

Hall, C. S., Lindzey, G., & Campbell, J. B. (2000). *Teorias da Personalidade*. Artmed.

Hasan, M., Rundensteiner, E., & Agu, E. (2014). EMOTEX: Detecting Emotions in Twitter Messages. In *ASE Bigdata/Socialcom/Cybersecurity Conference*, (pp. 1-10). Stanford University.

Hawi, N., & Samaha, M. (2019). Identifying commonalities and differences in personality characteristics of Internet and social media addiction profiles: Traits, self-esteem, and self-construal. *Behaviour & Information Technology*, *38*(2), 110–119. doi:10.1080/0144929X.2018.1515984

Hawi, N. S., & Samaha, M. (2016). The Relations Among Social Media Addiction, Self-Esteem, and Life Satisfaction in University Students. *Social Science Computer Review*. Advance online publication. doi:10.1177/0894439316660340

Higgins, E. T. (1987). Self-discrepancy: A theory relating self and affect. *Psychological Review, 94*(3), 319–340. doi:10.1037/0033-295X.94.3.319 PMID:3615707

Ignatow, G., & Mihalcea, R. F. (2017). *An Introduction to Text Mining: Research Design, Data Collection, and Analysis*. Sage Publications.

Ito, P., & Guzzo, R. S. (2002). Diferenças individuais: Temperamento e personalidade; importância da teoria. *Estudos de Psicologia, 19*(1), 91–100. doi:10.1590/S0103-166X2002000100008

James, W. (1884). What is an emotion? *Mind, os-IX*(34), 188–205. doi:10.1093/mind/os-IX.34.188

Jung, C. G. (2000). Os arquétipos e o inconsciente coletivo (2nd ed.). Perrópolis: Vozes.

Keles, B., McCrae, N., & Grealish, A. (2020). A systematic review: The influence of social media on depression, anxiety and psychological distress in adolescents. *International Journal of Adolescence and Youth, 25*(01), 79–93. doi:10.1080/02673843.2019.1590851

Krasnova, H., Widjaja, T., Buxmann, P., Wenninger, H., & Benbasat, I. (2015). Why Following Friends Can Hurt You: An Exploratory Investigation of the Effects of Envy on Social Networking Sites among College-Age Users. *Information Systems Research, 16*(3), 585–605. doi:10.1287/isre.2015.0588

LeDoux, J. (1998). *The emotional brain: The mysterious underpinnings of emotional life*. Simon and Schuster.

Lima, A. C. (2016). *Social media mining as a tool for triad analysis of the virtual person* [Mineração de mídias sociais como ferramenta para a análise de tríade da persona virtual]. PhD Thesis.

Lima, A. C., & de Castro, L. N. (2012). Automatic sentiment analysis of Twitter messages. *Fourth International Conference on Computational Aspects of Social Networks (CASoN)*, 52-57. 10.1109/CASoN.2012.6412377

Lima, A. C., & de Castro, L. N. (2014). A multi-label, semi-supervised classification approach applied to personality prediction in social media. *Neural Networks, 58*, 122–130. doi:10.1016/j.neunet.2014.05.020 PMID:24969690

Lima, A. C., & de Castro, L. N. (2016). Predicting Temperament from Twitter Data. In *Advanced Applied Informatics (IIAI-AAI), 2016 5th IIAI International Congress on* (pp. 599-604). IEEE.

Lima, A. C., & de Castro, L. N. (2019). TECLA: A temperament and psychological type prediction framework from Twitter data. *PLoS One*, *14*(3), e0212844. Advance online publication. doi:10.1371/journal.pone.0212844 PMID:30861015

Lima, A. C., de Castro, L. N., & Corchado, J. M. (2015). A polarity analysis framework for Twitter messages. *Applied Mathematics and Computation*, *270*, 756–767. doi:10.1016/j.amc.2015.08.059

Lorena, A. C., & Carvalho, A. C. (2008). Estratégias para a combinaçao de classificadores binários em soluçoes multiclasses. *Revista de Informática Teórica e Aplicada*, *2*(15), 65–86. doi:10.22456/2175-2745.7016

Lovari, A., & Valentini, C. (2020). Public Sector Communication and Social Media: Opportunities and Limits of Current Policies, Activities, and Practices. The Handbook of Public Sector Communication. doi:10.1002/9781119263203.ch21

Lup, K., Trub, L., & Rosenthal, L. (2015). Instagram# Instasad? Exploring associations among Instagram use, depressive symptoms, negative social comparison, and strangers followed. *Cyberpsychology, Behavior, and Social Networking*, *18*(5), 247–252. doi:10.1089/cyber.2014.0560 PMID:25965859

Mairesse, F., Walker, M., Mehl, M. R., & Moore, R. K. (2007). Using Linguistic Cues for the Automatic Recognition of Personality in Conversation and Text. *Journal of Artificial Intelligence Research*, *30*, 457–500. doi:10.1613/jair.2349

Manning, C. D., Raghavan, P., & Schütze, H. (2008). *Introduction to Information Retrieval*. Cambridge University Press. doi:10.1017/CBO9780511809071

Markovikj, D., Gievska, S., Kosinski, M., & Stillwell, D. (2013). Mining facebook data for predictive personality modeling. *Proceedings of the 7th international AAAI conference on Weblogs and Social Media (ICWSM 2013)*, 1-4.

McLuhan, M., & Lapham, L. H. (1994). *Os meios de comunicação como extensões do homem*. The MIT Press.

Mehdizadeh, S. (2010). Self-presentation 2.0: Narcissism and self-esteem on Facebook. *Cyberpsychology, Behavior, and Social Networking*, *13*(4), 357–364. doi:10.1089/cyber.2009.0257 PMID:20712493

Meshi, D., Tamir, D. I., & Heekeren, H. R. (2015). The emerging neuroscience of social media. *Trends in Cognitive Sciences*, *19*(12), 771–782. doi:10.1016/j.tics.2015.09.004 PMID:26578288

Moyano, J. M., Gibaja, E. L., Ciosb, K. J., & Ventura, S. (2018). Review of ensembles of multi-label classifiers: Models, experimental study and prospects. *Information Fusion*, *44*, 33–45. doi:10.1016/j.inffus.2017.12.001

Muise, A., Christofides, E., & Desmarais, S. (2009). More information than you ever wanted: Does Facebook bring out the green-eyed monster of jealousy? *Cyberpsychology & Behavior*, *12*(4), 441–444. doi:10.1089/cpb.2008.0263 PMID:19366318

Muqaddas, J., Soomro, S. A., & Ahmad, N. (2017). Impact of Social Media on Self-Steem. *European Scientific Journal*, *13*(23), 329–341. doi:10.19044/esj.2017.v13n23p329

Nielsen, F. Å. (2011). *A new ANEW: Evaluation of a word list for sentiment analysis in microblogs.* arXiv preprint arXiv:1103.2903.

Rathore, A. K., Kar, A. K., & Ilavarasan, P. V. (2017). Social Media Analytics: Literature Review and Directions for Future Research. *Decision Analysis*, *14*(4), 229–249. doi:10.1287/deca.2017.0355

Safari, R. M., Rahmani, A. M., & Alizadeh, S. H. (2019). User behavior mining on social media: A systematic literature review. *Multimedia Tools and Applications*, *78*(23), 33747–33804. doi:10.100711042-019-08046-6

Savci, M., Turan, M. E., Griffiths, M. D., & Ercengiz, M. (2019). Histrionic Personality, Narcissistic Personality, and Problematic Social Media Use: Testing of a New Hypothetical Model. *International Journal of Mental Health and Addiction*. Advance online publication. doi:10.100711469-019-00139-5

Schmidt, E., & Cohen, J. (2013). *The New Digital Age*. Knopf.

Seidman, G. (2013). Self-presentation and belonging on Facebook: How personality influences. *Personality and Individual Differences*, *54*(3), 402–407. doi:10.1016/j.paid.2012.10.009

Sorokowski, P., Sorokowska, A., Oleszkiewicz, A., Frackowiak, T., Huk, A., & Pisanski, K. (2015). Selfie posting behaviors are associated with narcissism among men. *Personality and Individual Differences*, *85*, 123–127. doi:10.1016/j.paid.2015.05.004

Stockdale, L. A., & Coyne, S. M. (2020). Bored and online: Reasons for using social media, problematic social networking site use, and behavioral outcomes across the transition from adolescence to emerging adulthood. *Journal of Adolescence*, *79*, 173–183. doi:10.1016/j.adolescence.2020.01.010 PMID:31978836

Suttles, J., & Ide, N. (2013). *Distant Supervision for Emotion Classification with Discrete Binary Values*. Computational Linguistics and Intelligent Text Processing. doi:10.1007/978-3-642-37256-8_11

Tamir, D. I., & Ward, A. F. (2015). Old desires, new media. The Psychology of Desire, 432-455.

Thelwall, M., Buckley, K., Paltoglou, G., Cai, D., & Kappas, A. (2010). Sentiment strength detection for the social Web. *Journal of the American Society for Information Science and Technology*, *61*(12), 2544–2558. doi:10.1002/asi.21416

Tsoumakas, G., Katakis, I., & Vlahavas, I. (2006). A Review of Multi-Label Classification Methods. In *Proceedings of the 2nd ADBIS Workshop on Data Mining and Knowledge Discovery (ADMKD 2006)*, (pp. 99-109). Academic Press.

Utz, S., Muscanell, N., & Khalid, C. (2015). Snapchat Elicits More Jealousy than Facebook: A Comparison of Snapchat and Facebook Use. *Cyberpsychology, Behavior, and Social Networking*, *18*(3), 141–146. doi:10.1089/cyber.2014.0479 PMID:25667961

Volpi, J. H. (2004). *Particularidades sobre o temperamento, a personalidade e o caráter, segundo a psicologia corporal*. Centro Reichiano.

Wallace, L., James, T. L., & Warkentin, M. (2017). How do you feel about your friends? Understanding situational envy in online social networks. *Information & Management*, *54*(5), 669–682. doi:10.1016/j.im.2016.12.010

Wang, W., Chen, L., Thirunarayan, K., & Sheth, A. P. (2012). Harnessing twitter "big data" for automatic emotion identification. In *Privacy, Security, Risk and Trust (PASSAT), 2012 International Conference on and 2012 International Conference on Social Computing (SocialCom)* (pp. 587-592). IEEE.

Wang, Y., Xie, X., Wang, X., Wang, P., Nie, J., & Lei, L. (2018). Narcissism and selfie-posting behavior: The mediating role of body satisfaction and the moderating role of attitude toward selfie-posting behavior. *Current Psychology (New Brunswick, N.J.)*. Advance online publication. doi:10.100712144-018-9795-9

Wiszniewski, D., & Coyne, R. (2002). Mask and Identity: The Hermeneutics of Self-Construction in the Information. In Building Virtual Communities: Learning and Change in Cyberspace (Learning in Doing: Social, Cognitive and Computational Perspectives) (pp. 191-214). Cambridge University Press.

Witten, I. H. (2005). Text mining. In *Practical handbook of internet computing*. Chapman & Hall/CRC Press.

Wu, J., & Srite, M. (2021). Envy on social media: The good, the bad and the ugly. *International Journal of Information Management*, *56*, 16. doi:10.1016/j.ijinfomgt.2020.102255

Yadav, A., & Vishwakarma, D. K. (2020). Sentiment analysis using deep learning architectures: A review. *Artificial Intelligence Review*, *53*(6), 4335–4385. doi:10.100710462-019-09794-5

Yue, L., Chen, W., Li, X., Zuo, W., & Yin, M. (2019). A survey of sentiment analysis in social media. *Knowledge and Information Systems*, *60*(2), 617–663. doi:10.100710115-018-1236-4

Chapter 8
The Flow of Influence From Two-Step to Network Perspectives

Enes Abanoz
https://orcid.org/0000-0002-4250-1845
Ondokuz Mayıs University, Turkey

ABSTRACT

The two-step flow of communication by Paul Lazarsfeld and Elihu Katz is one of the curial theories in the communication science field. The theory focused on the mass media message flow in society and showed that message flowed from opinion leaders to other individuals. Although the study is a groundbreaking masterpiece in its time, significant developments in the mathematical models of contagion theory, simulation technique, empirical data, and digital technologies necessitate a revision of the theory. This chapter focuses on how computational methods can apply to the two-step flow of communication theory and how computational approaches can handle the less valued or non-evaluable dimensions.

INTRODUCTION

Computational methods facilitate the review of existing theories and the development of new ones by applying methods from different disciplines in studies in the fields of social sciences. This situation has triggered the tendency of researchers to review the theories that come to the fore in the scientific field and examine them from different dimensions. This trend has

DOI: 10.4018/978-1-7998-8553-5.ch008

also affected theories of great importance in the communication field, such as agenda-setting, the two-step flow of communication model, and the diffusion of innovations that were re-examined by computational methods. The studies on the two-step flow model of influence are one of the most important of this approach. The model was developed by Pual Lazarsfeld, Elihu Katz, and colleagues (E. Katz & Lazarsfeld, 1955; Lazarsfeld et al., 1968) in the 1940s and 1950s. The model formulated a breakthrough theory of public opinion formation under the growing effect of media on the decision-making process. According to the model, the decision-making process, which can range from political to personal subjects, may be influenced more by exposure to each other than the media.

It is not enough to explain the development of this trend by the mere introduction of computational methods into communication studies. The digitalization of communication processes, environments, and social ties, which form the basis of communication studies, is another crucial factor. Through digital networks, the realization of social life and communication, which is its natural extension, has created an infrastructure that allows the message to circulate rapidly around the world, shortened the social distance between individuals, and created digital traces that will enable detailed monitoring of all processes (González-Bailón, 2017). These network structures have mainly solved the inability to participate in analyzing the effect of the social environment on the individual, which is one of the central problematics of communication studies since they are the social living spaces of individuals. Thus, it has become possible to systematically and geographically monitor the processes that make it possible to mobilize many individuals to act in a certain way, such as the effect and spread of contagion, which can cause changes in the behavior and attitudes of individuals.

The effect of digital networks on social life and communication processes has made the phenomenon known as the small-world effect more visible and measurable. In general, the small-world effect is used to describe the effect of technological developments on distance and to explain this effect through the network structure (Boettcher et al., 2008; Hautz et al., 2016; Milgram, 1967; Travers & Milgram, 1969; Watts, 1999; Watts & Dodds, 2007). Individuals are connected by the network structure created by communication tools in this world. The number of connections and intermediaries that provide access from one individual to another is considerably small. The outcome of this situation, supported by the results of many studies carried out on different social media platforms, is that individuals can access each other through shortcuts within global network structures, and these ways can be determined to a large extent.

The general spread of knowledge and behavior from person to a person effectively forms collective behaviors such as epidemics, rumors, and social movements, which can be considered events in which an individual acts under the influence. In this process, some individuals act as diffusers and initiate or maintain the dissemination of content, thought, or action. Some individuals only act under the influence and assimilate this content, thought, or action. This sort of contagion could only be channeled by communication-a channel for influence that is strengthened every time new technologies arise (e.g., the telegraph, the Internet) (González-Bailón, 2017, p. 74).

This theory of contagion, its effects on society and the individual has been the focus of researchers interested in communication since the emergence of mass media. The study, one of the most important of these researches, directs communication research; It is a two-step flow of communication model developed by Pual Lazarsfeld, Elihu Katz, and colleagues. Although the study is a groundbreaking masterpiece in its time, significant developments in the mathematical models of contagion theory, simulation technique, empirical data, and digital technologies necessitate a revision of the theory. This chapter is based on examining and comparing two articles: 'The Two-Step Flow of Communication: An Up-To-Date Report on an Hypothesis' (E. Katz, 1957) and 'Influentials, Networks, and Public Opinion Formation' (Watts & Dodds, 2007). While the first study includes the evaluation of the two-step of communication model, the second study includes the addition of the simulation method, a computational social sciences method, to the study. The chapter will proceed by examining both papers and explaining what changes and results may occur as a result of this review, as a result of applying computational social science methods to communication studies.

THE TWO-STEP FLOW OF COMMUNICATION

Several subsequent studies have tested the two-step flow of communication based on the idea that it often flows from media to opinion leaders and from them to society. These studies have attempted to test the two-step flow of communication theory and look for the different solutions for the problems that emerged from the design and application of the theory. The paper of one of the founders of the theory is titled 'The Two-Step Flow of Communication: An Up-To-Date Report on an Hypothesis' (E. Katz, 1957). It mainly focused on some of these subsequent studies and evaluated them. Therefore, this section is mainly based on this paper.

The paper starts with defining and explaining people's decision-making process analysis. Some studies proposed the one-step flow of communication or the linear effect of media, such as a hypodermic model that considers media messages injected directly into the audience's brains (Bineham, 1988). According to Paul Lazarsfeld and colleagues (1968), the flow of thoughts, ideas, and perspectives via mass communication tools to the public may be less direct than was commonly supposed. According to them, the process may be worked that way; (1) the influence of the mass media first reaches 'opinion leaders,' and (2) they pass the thoughts, ideas, and perspectives which they have gotten from mass media to the individuals they influence. This hypothesis was called 'the two-step flow of communication' (E. Katz, 1957).

The theory sees the media audience as a mass where individuals interconnect each other like a network through a mass communication channel. In this network, the flow follows the path illustrated in Figure 1. As shown in the figure, some premise called opinion leaders had gotten the mass media content. Then the content, or at least its fundamental, is passed to other individuals who have a social connection with an opinion leader. These individuals value the opinion leader's thoughts, ideas, and perceptions. Thus, the flow happens.

The author focused on some papers that have attempted to examine the people's choice hypothesis and build upon it. Thus, the present state of the two-step flow hypothesis, the conformation of the model's outcomes, how it has been extended, contracted, and formulated can be examined (E. Katz, 1957). These studies are the Rovere study on interpersonal influence and communication behavior; the Decatur study on decision-making in marketing, fashions, public affairs; the Elmira study on the 1948 election campaign; the study on the diffusion of a new drug among doctors. The common denominator of these studies is a systematic attempt on research design by focusing on interpersonal relations to build a sort of *sociometric* survey.

The part of sociono*my*[1], which deals with the mathematical study of the psychological properties of populations, the experimental technique, and the results obtained by applying quantitative methods, is called sociometry (Moreno, 1934, p. 10). As a general rule, the results of sociometric testing are presented by means of a diagram or graph called a sociogram which has for its purpose the illustration of the structure of the group, with its subgroups, cliques, leaders, isolates, and rejectees (Forsyth & Katz, 1946, p. 341). The sociometric analysis shows that the chosen and actual relations often differ, and the position of an individual in any group structure cannot be fully understood without including his/her all group members (Holland & Leinhardt, 1970; L. Katz, 1947, 1953; Moreno, 1934). Hence, the sociometric approach can be considered the fundamental of network analysis, a computational social science method, and network analysis can be used to strengthen and extend the two-step flow of communication theory.

The outcomes of the studies, as mentioned earlier on the people's choice, can be categorized into three subjects: (1) *the impact of personal influence*; (2) *the flow of personal influence*; and (3) *the opinion leaders and the mass media* (E. Katz, 1957).

Figure 1. According to the two-step flow of communication model, the flow of influence from media to opinion leaders, and then to the public.

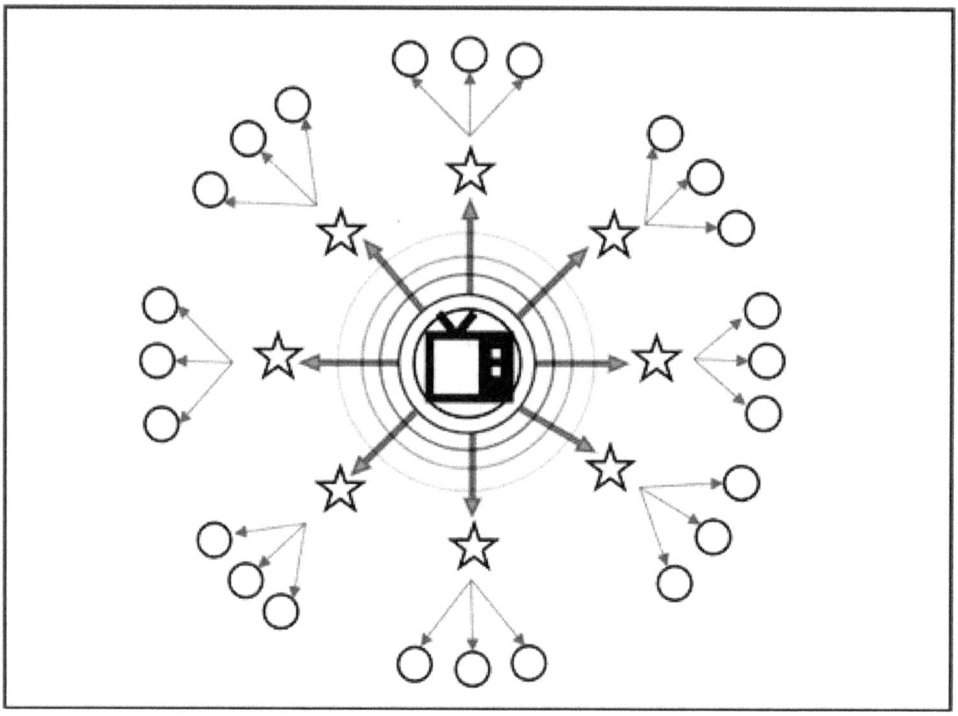

The Impact of Personal Influence

Since the individual lives in a community, interacting with other individuals is one of the basic requirements of the social structure. Kinship, friendship, and co-worker relations are examples of these interactions processes. In this interaction process, parties can influence each other, and norms such as thought, action, and behavior flow from the high-impact to the low-impact side. The necessity, the frequency, and the flow direction of interaction cause change of individual minds. Many studies have shown that this is more effective in the change in the thinking of an undecided individual than in the change in the thinking of a determined individual. Another factor in observing this situation is the tendency of individuals to show homophily. Another factor in observing this situation is that individuals tend to homophily - a concept in sociology that describes the tendency of individuals to relate and bond with similar others. As an outcome of homophily, the opinions in a group display homogeneity, which means that the group members will have similar or shared ideas, thoughts, and behavior due to interpersonal influence dynamics in the group. In studies under review, this situation was observed in the primary group structures, defined as groups where communication occurs person-to-person.

When the frequency of interactions with other individuals in daily lives is compared with the frequency of encountering the messages conveyed by the mass media, it is undeniable that personal messages will be more dominant than the messages of the mass media in influencing the individuals. The 1940 study (Lazarsfeld et al., 1968) showed that personal influence is more effective than mass media in voting decisions, especially for individuals who changed their minds during the campaign.

The study also showed that the non-purposiveness, flexibility, and trustworthiness could be some reasons for personal influence being more effective than mass media. The message of mass media has generally aimed to change ideas, sell products, or make desired behaviors in viewers. Contrary to this, personal messages sometimes can be non-purposiveness, and they can only arise as a natural part of the current process. This natural process may cause the individual to accept the message more quickly and be affected. The sender's role in a conversation can be easily changed between people, so this flexibility enhances the influence of the message for individuals rather than the message of mass media, where the sender's role is in a standing position. Personal contact with any person provides different cues such as body language, vocal cues, acts of other people towards that individual. They can improve the influence of a person over the influence of mass media.

The Flow of Personal Influence

After showing that personal influence is more effective than the mass media, the second important question about this phenomenon is whether some people were more important than others in the transmission of influence. When comparing individuals based on the transmitter and receiver roles in the flow of communication, the studies viewed showed that individuals who act as opinion leaders are more interested in the subject than other people in communities. The opinion leaders definition means that people who are active media users with collecting, interpret, and diffuse the meaning of media messages to less active media consumers.

The individuals who change their minds frequently mention that the influencer person can be found among family members, friends, co-workers, and members of one's social circles. Hence, it turned out that opinion leaders can be found on every level of society. In addition to this, people's reactions to media messages are mediated by interpersonal communication with members of their social environment, so that opinion leaders are very much like the people they influence in terms of social status, occupation, and interests. Therefore, it can be put forth that the distribution of opinion leaders is almost even in every class and occupation. This can also be interpreted in a way that opinion leaders were not concentrated in the upper strata of society but can be seen in almost equal proportions in every social group and strata of society (E. Katz, 1957).

The Opinion Leaders and the Mass Media

The mass media habits of opinion leaders and other individuals are another reason why communication flows to other individuals. Opinion leaders are considerably more exposed to the content of mass media such as radio, newspapers, and magazines when compared with the rest of the population. Hence, the opinion leaders have more information about the content, and they can think more deeply and transfer this information to their environment. The third aspect of the two-step flow of communication hypothesis states that opinion leaders are more exposed to the mass media than those they influence (E. Katz, 1957). This can be interpreted that ideas, thoughts, and behaviors often flow from mass media to opinion leaders who are more exposed to the content than the less active sections of the population who are less exposed to the content.

The Fundamental Rationales for the Computational Method Approach

The two-step flow of communication theory, also called opinion leaders or influential, has taken a central position in the literature and research methods of different fields such as sociology, communication, and marketing (Menzel & Katz, 1955; Rogers, 1983; Vernette, 2004; Weimann, 1991). The popularity and wide application of the theory make it one of the most critical formulations in the behavioral sciences, and it has become the dominant paradigm of media sociology (Watts & Dodds, 2007).

Although the theory has gotten more attention from different fields and is used in various research, the study's authors point out that a better method would have been based on investigating the interaction between advisers and advisees. The main problem in this approach is the extreme difficulty of getting the sample that has included all leader and follower interactions in the flow of communication between advisers and advisees. Many follow-up studies that mainly focused on the two-step flow had attempted to solve this problem, which was considered the most crucial problem in the approach. For example, Herbert Menzel and Elihu Katz (1955) used a sociometric approach to study the epidemiology of a new drug among the medical profession to overcome the sample problem. In this study, they asked each doctor the name of three colleagues separately he saw most often socially, talked most frequently, and looked for information and advice. Even though this approach reduced the impact of advisers and advisees' sample problem, it could not eliminate it entirely or to a large extent. This brings us to the first fundamental rationale why applying computational methods to the theory is necessary. Computational methods such as simulations and big data can provide the whole or nearly all sample so that researchers can analyze all interactions between the sides of the influence flow (see chapter 1 for more information).

The sociometric approach also provides the opportunity to map the interpersonal relations networks. This opportunity reveals two necessary factors for the diffusion of influence: attention to a specific item in the course of gaining acceptance, and a record of this diffusion over time (E. Katz, 1957). These factors make it possible that the individual's position in the interpersonal network can be used to understand social influence structure besides the own testimony of individuals. This brings us to the second fundamental rationale why applying computational methods to the theory is necessary. Computational methods mean applying the different methods from different fields such as computer science, mathematics, and physics. Social/semantic network analysis provides a new perspective where the flow of influence among individuals can see the whole picture. Therefore, computational methods should integrate into the two-step flow of communication to overcome the shortcomings identified by the authors of the theory.

NETWORK AND THE FLOW OF COMMUNICATION

The two-step flow of communication theory detailly explains the personal influence and opinion leader concepts mainly related to the flow of ideas, thoughts, and behaviors from some premise individuals to other individuals in the society. On the other side, it is unclear that the influences of the two-step flow how, or even if, affect the diffusion and social change process (Watts & Dodds, 2007). This process can be conveyed and analyzed in more detail and clarity by using a computational method that makes possible an approach and method expressed by the founders of the theory. Therefore, the simulation approach and network analysis can shed light on the influence of social change. As a result of this, this part mainly focused on the paper titled 'Influentials, Networks, and Public Opinion Formation` by Watts and Dodds (2007). The authors examined the 'influentials hypothesis' by using a series of computer simulations of interpersonal influence processes.

Before evaluating the approach and results of the article in more detail, it should be explained what the concept of computer simulation is. A computer simulation can be defined as "duplication of the essence of a system or activity, that is, the essential characteristic of the system" (Dutton et al., 1971, p. 122). Computer simulations play an essential role in science, and it has a long history that parallels the development of early digital computing. It is difficult sometimes to subject theories to systematic empirical tests because of legal as well as ethical constraints to experimentation with real systems, societies, and human populations (Jacobsen & Bronson, 1995). In addition to this, many systems are constantly changing and making exact replications of them almost impossible. However, the power of computer simulations with combining sample data from these systems provides a new method to overcome these problems. In this way, complex theories can be tested by using computer simulations with the juxtaposition of empirical data and mathematical models. Computer simulations provide the ability to study systems not yet tractable with analytical methods, and can fill the gap between theory and experiment (Heermann, 1990). The outcomes of computer simulation provide a data set produced by the model, which can be used for empirical adequacy for theory.

Computer simulations are enabled more flexibility in design experiments by giving the control power to hold, change, remove, or add over variables. Computer models are of value only if variables are carefully selected and based on analyses of intelligible aspects of realistic phenomena (Federico & Figliozzi, 1981, p. 517). Thus, computer simulations have built upon theory and can assist researchers with relationships among variables comprising a system based on the hypothesis.

There are many studies about the flow of influence in different systems and structures, and the sociometric approach has been used in most of them. The analysis in the sociometric approach tends to focus on an individual level rather than network properties. For studies that focus on the networks' properties, methods different from the sociometric approach should be used. This leads us to the computer simulation method used in computational social sciences. Computer simulation methods have been used to understand the large-scale networks' properties. Some of these empirical works have tended to analyze how and to what extent the network's properties affect the flow content, which can be an idea, disease, interaction, and word-of-mouth influence in a structure (Leskovec et al., 2007). The computer simulation approach provides the network properties used to determine the position actors occupy, such as the betweenness, transitivity, degree, and closeness; at the same time, network properties help to understand how connections between actors affect the entire network dynamics like diffusion of information (González-Bailón, 2017).

The position actors occupy in a network is vital because the position directly affects the ability of an actor to reach other actors. The actors in the reachable range of an actor determine the direction and strength of influence flow in the network according to the actor's related neighbor's ability to be impressive or affected. This network dynamic was the start point of Watts and Dodds' study (2007) that aimed to understand how network structure affects the flow of influence by revisiting the groundbreaking two-step flow of communication theory. The study showed that the flow of influence in the network might trigger some additional endogenous activations, depending on the model parameters and the properties of any actor's neighbors, which are chosen randomly. Thus, when a neighbor of the actor gets activated, this neighbor acts as a link in the chain, allowing the movement to spread and generating a sequence of activation, called a 'cascade' (Watts, 2002). This process repeated many times with regenerating the parameters such as population size, the structure of the network, and initial conditions. It was observed that the distribution of cascade sizes is associated with the change in these parameters.

The flow mechanism of influence in the network structure is shown in Figure 2. The flow of influence between actors has two sides which means that influence movement can go both ways. This structure is totally different from the two-step flow of communication theory, which evaluates the direction of influence movement from media to opinion leaders then to the public. Another difference is in the step numbers of the influence flow. In the network model, the influence flow can span multiple steps among actors according to their neighbors' ability to become affecting or affected. This process can have only two steps: from media to opinion leaders then to the public in the two-step flow of communication theory.

The study showed the micro-foundations of the influence process, which is who influences whom and how to require meticulous articulation in order for its validity to be meaningfully assessed. The authors pointed out that under most conditions, cascades succeed with a critical mass of easily influenced individuals influencing other easy-to-influence people, contrary to what the two-step flow of influence theory suggests a few highly influential individuals influencing everyone else (Watts & Dodds, 2007).

Figure 2. The flow of influence from media to the public according to the network model.

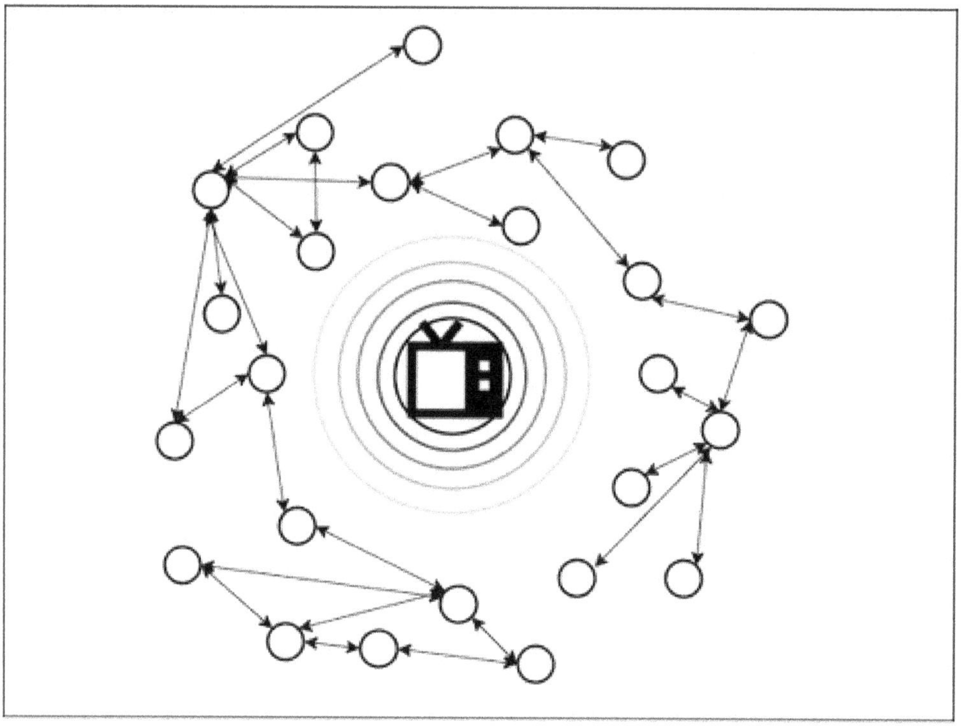

FUTURE RESEARCH DIRECTIONS

This study focuses on evaluating the two-step flow of communication theory, which is considered a groundbreaking work in communication research, by reconsidering it with computational social science methods. While this study shows how computational social science methods can be re-evaluated from existing theory and empirical approaches in communication studies, it also shows that these methods can be applied to other disciplines in general. From this point of view, it will be helpful for future studies to focus on the application examples of the computational social sciences approach in theoretical and empirical research, which stand out in different fields of science, or the results that can be obtained as a result of its application.

CONCLUSION

Computational social science methods can be used as a valuable tool in reconsidering, applying, testing, and eliminating possible technical and theoretical deficiencies, considering the individual and social level changes because of the digitalization of existing theories and approaches in the field of social sciences. In line with the point mentioned above, this section includes a review of two papers: the groundbreaking two-step flow of communication theory in the field of communication and its re-evaluation. The first article revealed that the messages conveyed by the mass media do not affect every individual at the same level. The effect occurs in a two-stage process from the mass media to the opinion leaders, which we can define as antecedents, and from there to the other individuals. The second article revealed that effect is spread by a critical mass of easily influenced individuals, influencing other easy-to-influence people in web-mediated communication tools, such as those implemented through blogs, social networking sites, online forums, and recommendation systems.

The study of Lazarsfeld & Katz (E. Katz, 1957) did not anticipate the importance of interpersonal relations in analyzing the data. However, the study of Watts and Dodds focused on this perspective, and using computational methods, they proved how the flow of influence among individuals could be changed (Watts & Dodds, 2007). This computational method approach also put forth essential factors such as the number of active sources, the structure of interpersonal connection, and the critical mass size that mediate the flow of influence. This process, an outcome of a computer simulation experiment, is called complex contagion (Centola & Macy, 2007), and suggests that the influence, which is one cause for becoming individual active, needs reinforcement from multiple sources (González-Bailón, 2017).

The computational social science methods help overcome essential limitations in the analysis of social sciences by enabling the advantages of digital technologies and moving the debate from abstractions and metaphors to concrete mechanisms that can be measured and tested (González-Bailón, 2017, p. 95). Herewith, researchers have started to approach old problems in a new way by collecting and simulating the related evidence and taking further steps for subjects stuck due to scarcity of evidence. The computational methods in social sciences have increased the testability of the theoretical and empirical assumptions. It has offered researchers the opportunity to revisit and evaluate old approaches in their field at a level that did not exist before from different perspectives.

REFERENCES

Bineham, J. L. (1988). A historical account of the hypodermic model in mass communication. *Communication Monographs*, *55*(3), 230–246. doi:10.1080/03637758809376169

Boettcher, S., Gonçalves, B., & Guclu, H. (2008). Hierarchical regular small-world networks. *Journal of Physics. A, Mathematical and Theoretical*, *41*(25), 252001. doi:10.1088/1751-8113/41/25/252001

Centola, D., & Macy, M. (2007). Complex contagions and the weakness of long ties. *American Journal of Sociology*, *113*(3), 702–734. doi:10.1086/521848

Federico, P.-A., & Figliozzi, P. W. (1981). Computer Simulation of Social Systems. *Sociological Methods & Research*, *9*(4), 513–533. doi:10.1177/004912418100900408

Forsyth, E., & Katz, L. (1946). A Matrix Approach to the Analysis of Sociometric Data: Preliminary Report. *Sociometry*, *9*(4), 340–347. doi:10.2307/2785498

González-Bailón, S. (2017). *Decoding the social world: Data science and the unintended consequences of communication*. MIT Press. doi:10.7551/mitpress/10271.001.0001

Hautz, W. E., Krummrey, G., Exadaktylos, A., & Hautz, S. C. (2016). Six degrees of separation: The small world of medical education. *Medical Education*, *50*(12), 1274–1279. doi:10.1111/medu.13102 PMID:27873413

Heermann, D. W. (1990). *Computer Simulation Methods in Theoretical Physics* (2nd ed.). Springer. doi:10.1007/978-3-642-75448-7

Holland, P. W., & Leinhardt, S. (1970). A Method for Detecting Structure in Sociometric Data. *American Journal of Sociology*, *3*(3), 492–513. doi:10.1086/224954

Jacobsen, C., & Bronson, R. (1995). Computer-simulations and empirical testing of sociological theory. *Sociological Methods & Research*, *23*(4), 479–506. doi:10.1177/0049124195023004004

Katz, E. (1957). The Two-Step Flow of Communication: An Up-To-Date Report on an Hypothesis. *Public Opinion Quarterly*, *21*(1), 61–78. doi:10.1086/266687

Katz, E., & Lazarsfeld, P. F. (1955). *Personal influence: The part played by people in the flow of mass communications*. Free Press.

Katz, L. (1947). On the Matric Analysis of Sociometric Data. *Sociometry*, *10*(3), 233–241. doi:10.2307/2785073

Katz, L. (1953). A new status index derived from sociometric analysis. *Psychometrika*, *18*(1), 39–43. doi:10.1007/BF02289026

Lazarsfeld, P. F., Berelson, B., & Gaudet, H. (1968). The People'S Choice: How the Voter Makes Up His Mind in a Presidential Campaign. In *The People's Choice*. Columbia University Press. doi:10.7312/laza93930

Leskovec, J., Adamic, L. A., & Huberman, B. A. (2007). The dynamics of viral marketing. *ACM Transactions on the Web*, *1*(1), 5. doi:10.1145/1232722.1232727

Menzel, H., & Katz, E. (1955). Social Relations and Innovation in the Medical Profession: The Epidemiology of a New Drug. *Public Opinion Quarterly*, *19*(4), 337. doi:10.1086/266584

Milgram, S. (1967). The Small-World Problem. *Psychology Today*, *1*(1), 61–67.

Moreno, J. L. (1934). *Who Shall Survive? A New Approach to the Problem of Human Interrelations*. Nervous and Mental Disease Publishing Company. doi:10.1037/10648-000

Rogers, E. M. (1983). *Diffusion of innovations* (3rd ed.). Free Press.

(1971). Simulation model construction. InDutton, J. M., Starbuck, W. H., Dutton, J. M., & Briggs, W. G. (Eds.), *Computer Simulation of Human Behavior*. John Wiley.

Travers, J., & Milgram, S. (1969). An Experimental Study of the Small World Problem. *Sociometry*, *32*(4), 425–443. doi:10.2307/2786545

Vernette, É. (2004). Targeting Women's Clothing Fashion Opinion Leaders in Media Planning: An Application for Magazines. *Journal of Advertising Research*, *44*(1), 90–107. doi:10.1017/S0021849904040061

Watts, D. J. (1999). Networks, Dynamics, and the Small-World Phenomenon. *American Journal of Sociology*, *105*(2), 493–527. doi:10.1086/210318

Watts, D. J. (2002). A simple model of global cascades on random networks. *Proceedings of the National Academy of Sciences of the United States of America*, *99*(9), 5766–5771. doi:10.1073/pnas.082090499 PMID:16578874

Watts, D. J., & Dodds, P. S. (2007). Influentials, Networks, and Public Opinion Formation. *The Journal of Consumer Research*, *34*(4), 441–458. doi:10.1086/518527

Weimann, G. (1991). The Influentials: Back to the Concept of Opinion Leaders? *Public Opinion Quarterly*, *55*(2), 267–279. doi:10.1086/269257

ADDITIONAL READING

González-Bailón, S. (2017). *Decoding the social world: Data science and the unintended consequences of communication*. MIT Press. doi:10.7551/mitpress/10271.001.0001

Watts, D. J. (2002). A simple model of global cascades on random networks. *Proceedings of the National Academy of Sciences of the United States of America*, *99*(9), 5766–5771. doi:10.1073/pnas.082090499 PMID:16578874

KEY TERMS AND DEFINITIONS

Computation: It is the repeated transmission of information through space (communication) and time (storage), guided by an algorithmic procedure.

Computational Social Science: An interdisciplinary field in which computational tools and techniques are applied to advance social science research.

Data: It is a unit of information that describes a single quality or quantity of an object or phenomenon.

Network Flow: It refers to the flow of influence between people through many steps and bi-directionally from the most influential to the most influenced.

Two-Step Flow: It refers to the flow of influence between people through only two steps and unidirectionally from the source to the intermediary then to the general.

ENDNOTE

1 Socionomy is a science concerned with the psychological properties of populations and the joint problems that these properties produce.

Conclusion

The expansion of digitalization and the associated technologies reflect a fundamental transformation in every aspect of society and the relations between all sides in it. The emergence of the enormous stream of digitalized data manifests a more profound paradigm change. It can be said that big social data, or big data about social phenomena, is already beginning to play a transformative role as a driver of growth in social knowledge (C. Cioffi-Revilla, 2021, p. 2). Thus, modern sciences, particularly social sciences, have been faced with new and diverse challenges that require the development of sophisticated techniques which provide new approaches beyond the classical methods. Computational methods have brought new directions in many academic disciplines, ranging from economics, biology, and politics to communication. Therefore, computational methods play an increasingly crucial role in scientific research.

Computational methods are an emerging area that offers vast and thrilling approaches and tools for research, such as information extraction from different digital data sets, network analysis, machine learning, and computer simulations. Computational methods require theories, models, simulations, and other scientific constructions in terms of that it is an empirical, social, and computational science. The empirical dimension of computational science is based on observation and measurement, which are needed for the laws that describe how phenomena occur. The social part of computational science has come from focusing on the subjects and theories in social sciences, explaining the mechanisms and processes in social sciences, and offering new approaches and methods that can be used to formulate new hypotheses for social phenomena. The computational extension of computational sciences arises from its dual nature in social sciences with usage as a theory and tool. This dual nature is enabled by computing and the use of computational paradigm, in theory, hypothesis, and analysis processes. The computing here means that programming languages such as R, Python, Stata, and MATLAB are directly used in the analyses process. The computational paradigm implies that the simulation, network analysis, and machine learning approaches have been used.

Conclusion

Until recently, most social sciences, in which quantitative approaches have been used, have been limited to the conventional statistical analysis of survey data. The survey-research model and its attendant analytical tools largely rely on the sampling of independent observations (Jarvis et al., 2021, p. 35). Adopting the questionnaire and the accompanying analytical approaches made it difficult to determine the social phenomena seen in the general population and expand through social networks with the data obtained at the individual level. With the developments in computational social science methods and the expansion of its applicability, this deficiency encountered in the detection and evaluation of social phenomena has been reduced. Computational methods have made it possible to obtain digital data on the platforms where social relations are realized, and social phenomena occur and re-establish the social relation network with a back-engineering approach. Thus, it has been possible to perform analyzes that will make it possible to reveal complex processes on these datasets.

Computational social science methods offer the opportunity to study the behavior of large interacting populations without the influence of an artificial field such as a laboratory and conduct traditional laboratory experiments online that are designed to study behavior among various participant groups under specified conditions (Centola, 2018; Salganik & Watts, 2009). This research design makes it possible to examine the social processes resulting from behavioral interdependence at the macro level. Contrary to the old experimental tradition, it evaluates the participants as separate social systems, each serving as a unit of analysis.

Over the last decade, digitization has led to an abundance of social science-relevant data from social media platforms, mobile apps, historical archives, the Internet of Things, and administrative registers. Typically, observational data from digital traces are not only wide – capturing, in the extreme, entire populations – but also deep in terms of granularity and the sheer number of variables available (Jarvis et al., 2021, p. 41). This large amount of online data has made it possible to develop appropriate tools and criteria for identifying, defining, analyzing, and evaluating new phenomena in the social relationship structure that has evolved and changed with digitalization. It also provides to examine the structural effects of the platforms where this social relationship structure takes place. Thus, the foundations were laid for faster and easier application of research methods used in computer and linguistics sciences such as machine learning, network analysis, sentiment analysis, subject modeling in large datasets in social sciences such as communication, geography, history, and economics. For example, with integrating the natural language processing method into communication studies, text analysis studies in different languages that focus on examining the relationships between words in studies in the communication field have begun to be encountered more frequently in the literature. Thus, researchers are equipped with new tools that they can use to examine common understandings of terms standard in a given population or to analyze individuals' beliefs, feelings, and tastes.

The paradigm guides inquiry and provides a valuable perspective to form a comprehensive worldview in the social sciences and scientific research. Therefore, the paradigm is an essential element in scientific approaches. The information processing paradigm—how social systems, society, and individuals process information—forms the basis of computational social science, and the information-processing paradigm points toward computing as a fundamental instrumental approach for modeling and understanding social complexity (C. A. Cioffi-Revilla, 2014, p. 3). A vital instrument that comes to the fore in this process is the revolutionary integration of computers into daily life, which is used both in the information-processing and the analysis of the information-processing. Thus, traces of the transformation created by computational methods have been observed in many social sciences.

SOCIAL COMPLEXITY AND SIMULATION

Methodological approaches, which will be evaluated under social complexity and social simulation headings, are at the forefront of computational social science methods and techniques. In order to maintain their existence and improve their quality of life, human societies have had to build and develop systems in challenging and often complex environments according to their abilities or capacities. These structures are defined as *complex systems* (Simon, 1996). Providing accessible and fast transportation, they can be of a concrete structure such as land, air, and sea routes and the rules that ensure their operation. Or they may be abstract, such as the bureaucratic system that creates the functioning and regulations of social life. Complex structures generally combine concrete and conceptual designs. As in the road example, the road itself and the transportation network are tangible, while the rules to be followed in the transportation process are intangible. Social life evolving in the digitized world is social complexity, and computational social science methods provide the appropriate tools and empirical framework for this process to be defined, studied, analyzed, explained, and made sense of it.

One of the most critical computational social science methods is simulation. Computer simulation can be used as a methodology to analyze and explain social complexity through computational modeling. Thus, a better understanding of social complexity as an emerging phenomenon related to social complexity, which cannot be obtained with other methodological approaches such as statistical, mathematical, or historiographic, can be achieved.

Social Complexity

The best scientific way to make sense of social complexity is to examine its causes based on proven principles backed by data. Computing and information processing plays an essential role in the current social structure and provides critical infrastructure to sustain and improve daily life.

Underneath people's urges to make decisions and behave, there is a mechanism defined as *bounded rationality* —making satisfactory choices rather than optimal, rather than striving to find all the information necessary to make a rational decision due to cognitive and temporal constraints (Simon, 1955). Many disciplines, especially behavioral social science, tend to understand human behavior by focusing on the bounded rationality model. In understanding this part of the social complexity structure, computational social science methods and digitalization make it possible to include more inputs in the evaluation process. In the process of determining, analyzing, and making sense of individual and social actions and behaviors; the difference that computational social science methods provide is the ability to follow not only the data about the individual and the community that emerged during the activation process but also the previously created and accessible digital footprints of them.

Simulation

Simulations have the ability to represent social systems in ways that other methodological approaches do not. A well-constructed simulation; provides powerful formalism in theorizing, experimenting, and making sense of social complexity. The simulation method makes it possible to apply the types of analysis that will answer many questions that social sciences focus on by constructing a computer model - a virtual structure - that represents the relevant aspects of the reality of the social system under consideration. The simulation model can make it possible to explore complex social systems and processes within and beyond statistical or mathematical models. The simulation method makes it possible to analyze many variables of social complexity, which is defined as high dimensionality, and the interaction between them. One of the general problems that arise in the process of examining social systems is that it is not possible to conduct experiments on these systems for many reasons, primarily practical and ethical. Since the simulation method is built on an artificial structure; It makes it possible to discover and test hypotheses with treatments related to the social system, control groups, and many different experimental designs.

CORE ISSUES: REPRESENTATION POWER AND PRIVACY

Digital data is at the center of computational social science methods, and therefore data should be considered an essential building block of this structure on its own. Digital data promises to avoid the sources of error that often come with survey designs, which consist of a series of questions and answers in the context of the designed interview. For this reason, it comes to the forefront for those working in the field of social sciences. The increasing involvement of human behaviors in digital environments causes the behaviors performed in these areas to be observed frequently with content (text data) and traces of action (metadata) digital observation formats (Engel & Dahlhaus, 2021).

The power of representation comes first among the problems that arise in this observation process. Due to the nature of big data, the high amount of existence naturally causes the researchers to assume that these data sets have high representative power. However, the large amount of data does not mean that the representative power is high. It is not about the amount of representative power of the data, but how much the data that constitutes the researched subject can reflect the holistic structure of the universe. For example, a study that wants to measure the tendencies of the public in the election process. When it focuses only on the digital data created on social networking platforms, it means that the data only represents the open-access content produced by individuals with the skills and technical means to access digital platforms. Naturally, the power of representation of this data is not as high as it is thought. Because it excludes users who do not use these platforms, do not have access to skills and opportunities, and do not allow access to content.

One of the ways to reduce or eliminate the representative power problem of the data is the use of mixed data. The power of the computational social science method makes it possible to use data designed for research (such as survey, observation) and data produced for commercial purposes (social media content, mobile phone traffic, etc.) (Salganik, 2017). In addition, it is another factor that it gives a new perspective to the methods and approaches used in the relevant science in which the research is designed. Thus, the problems arising from the representative power of the data can be minimized.

Another current problem in terms of computational social science methods is the privacy of the data producer. The issue of privacy is a fundamental problem in all scientific research approaches. In particular, the increasing sharing of digital data due to the expanding production of digital data in many fields, the fact that it is more accessible by researchers, the reliability of research methods, and academic sensitivities such as reproducibility bring the issue of privacy to the focus. For this reason, care is taken by both researchers and institutions.

Conclusion

A huge part of the digital data used in computational social science methods consists of data produced on social networks, social media, and applications created for commercial purposes. Mixed data usage methods make it possible to re-personalize the anonymized data used for research by back-engineering. For example, Jonathan Mayer and colleagues (Mayer et al., 2016) showed that it is possible to identify individuals in the dataset and access sensitive information about them by combining anonymized (i.e., no name and address information) call records with publicly available information. Therefore, the issue of privacy stands out as a problem that needs more attention in computational social science methods.

Enes Abanoz
Ondokuz Mayıs University, Turkey

REFERENCES

Centola, D. (2018). *How behavior spreads: The science of complex contagions*. Princeton University Press.

Cioffi-Revilla, C. (2021). The scope of computational social science. In U. Engel, A. Quan-Haase, S. X. Liu, & L. Lyberg (Eds.), Handbook of Computational Social Science (vol. 1, pp. 17–32). Routledge. doi:10.4324/9781003024583-3

Cioffi-Revilla, C. A. (2014). *Introduction to computational social science: Principles and applications*. Springer. doi:10.1007/978-1-4471-5661-1

Engel, U., & Dahlhaus, L. (2021). Data quality and privacy concerns in digital trace data. In U. Engel, A. Quan-Haase, S. X. Liu, & L. Lyberg (Eds.), Handbook of Computational Social Science (vol. 1, 1st ed., pp. 343–362). Routledge. doi:10.4324/9781003024583-23

Jarvis, B. F., Keuschnigg, M., & Hedström, P. (2021). Analytical sociology amidst a computational social science revolution. In U. Engel, A. Quan-Haase, S. X. Liu, & L. Lyberg (Eds.), Handbook of Computational Social Science (vol. 1, pp. 33–52). Routledge. doi:10.4324/9781003024583-4

Mayer, J., Mutchler, P., & Mitchell, J. C. (2016). Evaluating the privacy properties of telephone metadata. *Proceedings of the National Academy of Sciences of the United States of America*, *113*(20), 5536–5541. doi:10.1073/pnas.1508081113 PMID:27185922

Salganik, M. J. (2017). *Bit by bit: Social research in the digital age*. Princeton University Press.

Salganik, M. J., & Watts, D. J. (2009). Web-Based Experiments for the Study of Collective Social Dynamics in Cultural Markets. *Topics in Cognitive Science*, *1*(3), 439–468. doi:10.1111/j.1756-8765.2009.01030.x PMID:25164996

Simon, H. A. (1955). A Behavioral Model of Rational Choice. *The Quarterly Journal of Economics*, *69*(1), 99. doi:10.2307/1884852

Simon, H. A. (1996). *The sciences of the artificial*. MIT Press.

Glossary

Analytical Approach: A research method uses an appropriate process to break a problem down into the elements necessary to solve it.

Bias: Prejudice towards or against a person, a group, or a class. In a machine learning context, there are various types of biases. Each bias can affect a model differently.

Big Data: It refers to datasets that are large, complex, and more than main memory, internal and external disk that it is difficult or impossible to process using traditional methods.

Big Data: Unconventionally large data streams from many sources to a bunch of (not necessarily known) recipients.

Complexity Economics: Research area in economics that depicts the most of the economic phenomena as emergent, claiming that the whole is being more than the sum of its parts; meaning that there are different interactions among agents at different levels which in turn generate case specific outcomes.

Computation: It is the repeated transmission of information through space (communication) and time (storage), guided by an algorithmic procedure.

Computation: It is the repeated transmission of information through space (communication) and time (storage), guided by an algorithmic procedure.

Computational Social Science: An interdisciplinary field in which computational tools and techniques are applied to advance social science research.

Computational Social Science: An interdisciplinary field in which computational tools and techniques are applied to advance social science research.

Data: It is a unit of information that describes a single quality or quantity of an object or phenomenon.

Data: It is a unit of information that describes a single quality or quantity of an object or phenomenon.

Deep Learning: A subfield of machine learning that works with artificial neural networks containing many hidden layers and complex structures.

Econobiology: Interdisciplinary academic research area combining the methods and subjects from economics and biology, such as evolutionary approaches to dynamics of economic phenomena.

Econophysics: Interdisciplinary academic research area combining the methods and subjects from economics and physics, such as applying statistical physics' methods to microeconomic data.

Empirical Approach: It is a research method based on observation and measurement of phenomena, as directly experienced by the researcher.

Employee Communication: The process of conveying information from one employee to another.

Ephesus: A giant ancient city located in Western Anatolia, Turkey, which was inhabited from 6000 BC to the fifteenth century.

Informal Networks: Social structures that incorporate aspects of communication that are used by employees to interact with one another in an organizations.

Information Traffic: Quantity of information circulating on the internet calculated in seconds.

Interdisciplinary Research: It is a type of research that employs knowledge, data, techniques, and theories from multiple disciplines. The main goal is to analyze or solve a specific problem of interest using the strengths of these different disciplines.

Internet of Things: Digital data transmitting devices that are attached to any kind of goods, generating data about their use or the state of the user.

Interpersonal Communication: Communication by one employee to one or more employee in an organization.

Language Generation: It is the process of automatically generating texts from models containing artificial intelligence. The goal of this process is to auto-generate texts that appear to be created by humans.

Machine Learning: A subfield of artificial intelligence where models can learn patterns from the data in a supervised or unsupervised fashion and tune themselves during the learning process.

Network Flow: It refers to the flow of influence between people through many steps and bi-directionally from the most influential to the most influenced.

Networks: Employee's social structures.

Noise: In the context of machine learning, noise corresponds to the type of data or features that do not contain meaningful patterns related to the problem of interest and have a possibility of disrupting and harming the learning process.

Overfitting: Corresponds to the event when a machine learning model memorizes the training set data instead of learning the patterns present within it for accurate generalization. When a model overfits data, the model can return high within-dataset performance while it fails to generalize to other data.

Para-Economic Data: Data on anything that are related but not directly subject to economic nature such as ethnicity, marital status, or as stated in this paper, data from daily life collected through Internet of Things.

Public Opinion: Thoughts and ideas expression of the subjects' community, who are connected by the community of interests around a theme.

Self-Categorization: Self-reference of the individual, who recognizes distinctive attributes.

Social Diversity: It refers to the multiplicity of social, cultural, productive, linguistic, organizational, among other characteristics of expressions that distinguish the societies and the subjects.

Social Networks Analysis: Theory or methodology that show employees' social ties within an organization.

Sociopolitical: Social sciences that include Sociology and Political fields.

Text Mining: Search for words in Big Data repositories using algorithms designed for them.

Theoretical Approach: A set of statements or principles devised to explain a group of facts or phenomena can be used to make predictions.

Ties: Connections formed by employees in an organization. These ties form social structures or networks in organizations.

Tuning: The set of operations within machine learning algorithms to improve the performance of classification and prediction. Some of the tuning procedures happen during the learning process, while it is also possible to tune a model after the initial run of the training process.

Two-Step Flow: It refers to the flow of influence between people through only two steps and unidirectionally from the source to the intermediary then to the general.

Underfitting: Corresponds to the event when a machine learning model does not learn the patterns present within the training set properly for reasons such as incorrect parameter selection or a small number of epochs for the case of neural networks. A machine learning that suffers from underfitting would fail to return acceptable results from the within-dataset experiments and the generalization experiments.

Weighting: Estimation or calculation of expected results.

Compilation of References

Abanoz, E. (2020). *The emerge of computational communication at the intersection of communication and computation: Opportunities and challenges*. Academic Press.

Adali, S., & Golbeck, J. (2012). Predicting Personality with Social Behavior. In *2012 IEEE/ACM International Conference on Advances in Social Networks Analysis and Mining (ASONAM)* (pp. 302 - 309). Istanbul: IEEE. 10.1109/ASONAM.2012.58

Adamic, A.L.A., Buyukkokten, O., & Adar, E. (2003). *A social network caught in the web*. Retrieved January 15, 2018 from https://journals.uic.edu/ojs/index.php/fm/article/view/1057/977

Alba, R. D., & Gutmann, M. P. (1972). SOCK: A sociometric analysis system. *ACM SIGSOC Bulletin*, *3*(3), 11–12. doi:10.1145/1103251.1103252

Allcott, H., & Gentzkow, M. (2017). Social Media and Fake News in the 2016 Election. *The Journal of Economic Perspectives*, *31*(2), 211–236. doi:10.1257/jep.31.2.211

Alsop, T. (2021, April 29). *Number of data centers worldwide 2021, by country*. Retrieved from https://www.statista.com/statistics/1228433/data-centers-worldwide-by-country/

Angwin, J., Larson, J., Mattu, S., & Kirchner, L. (2016). *Machine Bias*. Propublica. https://www.propublica.org/article/machine-bias-risk-assessments-in-criminal-sentencing

Annisette, L. E., & Lafreniere, K. D. (2017). Social media, texting, and personality: A test of the shallowing hypothesis. *Personality and Individual Differences*, *115*, 154–158. doi:10.1016/j.paid.2016.02.043

Antons, D., & Breidbach, C. (2017). Big Data, Big Insights? Advancing Service Innovation and Design with Machine Learning. *Journal of Service Research*, *21*(1), 17–39. doi:10.1177/1094670517738373

Antons, D., Joshi, A., & Salge, T. (2018). Content, Contribution and Knowledge Consumption: Uncovering Hidden Topic Structure and Rhetorical Signals in Scientific Texts. *Journal of Management*, *45*(7), 3035–3076. doi:10.1177/0149206318774619

Appel, M., & Richter, T. (2007). Persuasive Effects of Fictional Narratives Increase Over Time. *Media Psychology*, *10*(1), 113–134. doi:10.1080/15213260701301194

Aswini, V. (2019). Big Data Analytics and Transformation of Election Campaign in India. *Proceedings of the 2nd International Conference on Information Systems & Management Science (ISMS) 2019*. 10.2139srn.3511428

Aytaç, S. E., & Stokes, S. C. (2018). *Why Bother? Rethinking Participation in Elections and Protests* (1st ed.). Cambridge University Press. doi:10.1017/9781108690416

Baker, A. J. (2009). *Mick or Keith: blended identity of online rock fans*. Identity in the Information Society.

Balabantaray, R. C., Mohammad, M., & Sharma, N. (2012). Multi-class twitter emotion classification: A new approach. *International Journal of Applied Information Systems*, *4*(1), 48–53. doi:10.5120/ijais12-450651

Baptista, L. (2003). Framing and cognition. In Goffman's legacy. Rowman & Littlefield Publishers.

Barak, M., Watted, A., & Haick, H. (2016). Motivation to learn in massive open online courses: Examining aspects of language and social engagement. *Computers & Education*, *94*, 49–60. doi:10.1016/j.compedu.2015.11.010

Bargh, J. A., McKenna, K. Y., & Fitzsimons, G. M. (2002). Can you see the real me? Activation and expression of the "true self" on the Internet. *The Journal of Social Issues*, *58*(1), 33–48. doi:10.1111/1540-4560.00247

Barrios, H., Díaz, V., & Guerra, Y. (2020). Subjetividades e inteligencia artificial: Desafíos para 'lo humano'. *Veritas (Valparaíso)*, *47*(47), 81–107. doi:10.4067/S0718-92732020000300081

Barry, C. T., Doucette, H., Loflin, D. C., Rivera-Hudson, N., & Herrington, L. L. (2017). "Let Me Take a Selfie": Associations Between Self-Photography, Narcissism, and Self-Esteem. *Psychology of Popular Media Culture*, *6*(1), 48–60. doi:10.1037/ppm0000089

Bastian, M., Heymann, S., & Jacomy, M. (2009). Gephi: An open source software for exploring and manipulating networks. In *International AAAI Conference on Weblogs and Social Media*. Association for the Advancement of Artificial Intelligence.

Bayram, U., & Benhiba, L. (2021). Determining a Person's Suicide Risk by Voting on the Short-Term History of Tweets for the CLPsych 2021 Shared Task. In *Proceedings of the Seventh Workshop on Computational Linguistics and Clinical Psychology: Improving Access* (pp. 81-86). 10.18653/v1/2021.clpsych-1.8

Bayram, U., Pestian, J., Santel, D., & Minai, A. A. (2019). What's in a Word? Detecting Partisan Affiliation From Word Use In Congressional Speeches. In *2019 International Joint Conference on Neural Networks (IJCNN)* (pp. 1-8). 10.1109/IJCNN.2019.8851739

BBVA Research. (n.d.). https://www.bbvaresearch.com/en/special-section/charts/

Behrendt, S., Richter, A., & Trier, M. (2014). Mixed methods analysis of enterprise social networks. *Computer Networks*, *75*, 560–577. doi:10.1016/j.comnet.2014.08.025

Belcastro, L., Cantini, R., Marozzo, F., Talia, D., & Trunfio, P. (2020). Learning Political Polarization on Social Media Using Neural Networks. *IEEE Access: Practical Innovations, Open Solutions*, *8*, 47177–4718. doi:10.1109/ACCESS.2020.2978950

Bell, G., Hey, T., & Szalay, A. (2009). Beyond the Data Deluge. *Science*, *323*(5919), 1297–1298. doi:10.1126cience.1170411 PMID:19265007

Bender, E. M., Gebru, T., McMillan-Major, A., & Shmitchell, S. (2021). On the Dangers of Stochastic Parrots: Can Language Models Be Too Big? In *Proceedings of the 2021 ACM Conference on Fairness, Accountability, and Transparency* (pp. 610-623). 10.1145/3442188.3445922

Berger, P., & Luckmann, T. (2003). *La construcción social de la realidad*. Amorrortu-Murguía.

Bergman, S. M., Fearrington, M. E., Davenport, S. W., & Bergman, J. Z. (2011). Millennials, narcissism, and social networking: What narcissists do on social networking sites and why. *Personality and Individual Differences*, *2011*(5), 706–711. doi:10.1016/j.paid.2010.12.022

Bergstra, J., & Bengio, Y. (2012). Random Search for Hyper-Parameter Optimization. *Journal of Machine Learning Research*, *13*(2).

Bessi, A., & Ferrara, E. (2016). Social Bots Distort the 2016 US Presidential Election Online Discussion. *First Monday*, *21*, 11–17.

Bilal, M., Gani, A., Marjani, M., & Malik, N. (2019). Predicting elections: Social media data and techniques. *International Conference on Engineering and Emerging Technologies (ICEET)*, 1-6. 10.1109/CEET1.2019.8711854

Bineham, J. L. (1988). A historical account of the hypodermic model in mass communication. *Communication Monographs*, *55*(3), 230–246. doi:10.1080/03637758809376169

Biolcati, R., & Passini, S. (2018). Narcissism and self-esteem: Different motivations for selfie posting behaviors. *Cogent Psychology*, *2018*(5). doi:10.1080/23311908.2018.1437012

Bi, Q., Goodman, K. E., Kaminsky, J., & Lessler, J. (2019). What is Machine Learning? A Primer for the Epidemiologist. *American Journal of Epidemiology*, kwz189. Advance online publication. doi:10.1093/aje/kwz189 PMID:31509183

Blodgett, S. L., Barocas, S., Daume, H. III, & Wallach, H. (2020). Language (Technology) Is Power: A Critical Survey of "Bias" in NLP. In *Proceedings of the 58th Annual Meeting of the Association for Computational Linguistics* (pp. 5454–5476). 10.18653/v1/2020.acl-main.485

Boettcher, S., Gonçalves, B., & Guclu, H. (2008). Hierarchical regular small-world networks. *Journal of Physics. A, Mathematical and Theoretical*, *41*(25), 252001. doi:10.1088/1751-8113/41/25/252001

Bonacich, P. (1990). Communication dilemmas in social networks: An experimental study. *American Sociological Review*, *55*(3), 448–459. doi:10.2307/2095768

Bond, J. R. (2007). The Scientification of the Study of Politics: Some Observations on the Behavioral Evolution in Political Science. *The Journal of Politics*, *69*(4), 897–907. doi:10.1111/j.1468-2508.2007.00597.x

Bonetto, R., & Latzko, V. (2020). Machine Learning. In F. H. P. Fitzek, F. Granelli, & P. Seeling (Eds.), *Computing in Communication Networks* (pp. 135–167). Elsevier. doi:10.1016/B978-0-12-820488-7.00021-9

Borgatti, S. P., Everett, M. G., & Freeman, L. C. (2002). Ucinet for Windows: Software for social network analysis. Analytic Technologies, 6.

Borgatti, S. P., & Halgin, D. S. (2011). On network theory. *Organization Science*, *22*(5), 1168–1181. doi:10.1287/orsc.1100.0641

Boulier, D. (2016). *Un classement qui fait un tri correct dans les offres d'opinion mining et de social monitoring*. Hypoteses. https://bit.ly/3kf1LdA

Bovet, A., Morone, F., & Makse, H. (2016). Validation of Twitter opinion trends with national polling aggregates: Hillary Clinton vs Donald Trump. *Scientific Reports*, *8*(1), 8673. doi:10.103841598-018-26951-y PMID:29875364

Boyd, D., & Crawford, K. (2012). Critical questions for big data: Provocations for a cultural, technological, and scholarly phenomenon. *Information Communication and Society*, *15*(5), 662–679. doi:10.1080/1369118X.2012.678878

Brady, H., & Collier, D. (2010). *Rethinking Social Inquiry: Diverse Tools, Shared Standards* (2nd ed.). Rowman & Littlefield Publishers.

Branch, W. A., & McGough, B. (2018). Heterogeneous expectations and micro-foundations in macroeconomics. In *Handbook of computational economics* (Vol. 4, pp. 3–62). Elsevier.

Braun, B., Taraktaş, B., Beckage, B., & Molofsky, J. (2020). Simulating phase transitions and control measures for network epidemics caused by infections with presymptomatic, asymptomatic, and symptomatic stages. *PLoS One*, *15*(9), e0238412. doi:10.1371/journal.pone.0238412 PMID:32911518

Brodersen, K. H., Ong, C. S., Stephan, K. E., & Buhmann, J. M. (2010). The Balanced Accuracy and Its Posterior Distribution. In *Proceedings of the IEEE 20th International Conference on Pattern Recognition* (pp. 3121-3124). 10.1109/ICPR.2010.764

Brooke, J., Hammond, A., & Hirst, G. (2015). Gutentag: An NLP-Driven Tool for Digital Humanities Research in the Project Gutenberg Corpus. In *Proceedings of the Fourth Workshop on Computational Linguistics for Literature* (pp. 42-47). 10.3115/v1/W15-0705

Brundage, M., Avin, S., Clark, J., Toner, H., Eckersley, P., Garfinkel, B., Dafoe, A., Scharre, P., Zeitzoff, T., Filar, B., . . . Amodei, D. (2018). *The malicious use of artificial intelligence: Forecasting, prevention, and mitigation*. Technical report, Future of Humanity Institute, University of Oxford. https://bit.ly/3wA3E6T

Buatoom, U., Kongprawechnon, W., & Theeramunkong, T. (2020). Document Clustering Using K-Means with Term Weighting as Similarity-Based Constraints. *Symmetry, 12*(6), 967. doi:10.3390ym12060967

Buduma, N., & Locascio, N. (2017). *Fundamentals of Deep Learning: Designing Next-Generation Machine Intelligence Algorithms* (1st ed.). O'Reilly Media, Inc.

Bullingham, L., & Vasconcelos, A. C. (2013). 'The presentation of self in the online world': Goffman and the study of online identities. *Journal of Information Science, 39*(1), 101–112. doi:10.1177/0165551512470051

Bunce, V. (2000). Comparative Democratization Big and Bounded Generalizations. *Comparative Political Studies, 33*(6–7), 703–734. doi:10.1177/001041400003300602

Buolamwini, J., & Gebru, T. (2018). Gender Shades: Intersectional Accuracy Disparities in Commercial Gender Classification. In *Proceedings of the 2018 ACM Conference on Fairness, Accountability and Transparency* (pp. 77-91). ACM.

Burke, M., & Kraut, R. E. (2016). The Relationship Between Facebook Use and Well-Being Depends on Communication Type and Tie Strength: Facebook and well-being. *Journal of Computer-Mediated Communication, 21*(4), 265–281. doi:10.1111/jcc4.12162

Burley, T., Humble, L., Sleeper, C., Sticha, A., Chesler, A., Regan, P., Verdeja, E., & Brenner, P. (2020). NLP Work Flows for Computational Social Science: Understanding Triggers of State-Led Mass Killings. In Practice and Experience in Advanced Research Computing (pp. 152-159). Academic Press.

Burscher, B., Vliegenthart, R., & de Vreese, C. H. (2016). Frames Beyond Words: Applying Cluster and Sentiment Analysis to News Coverage of the Nuclear Power Issue. *Social Science Computer Review, 34*(5), 530–545. doi:10.1177/0894439315596385

Burt, R. S. (2017). Structural holes versus network closure as social capital. In Social capital: Theory and research. Routledge. doi:10.4324/9781315129457-2

Burt, R. (1992). *Structural holes.* doi:10.4159/9780674029095

Burt, R. S. (2004). Structural holes and good ideas. *American Journal of Sociology, 110*(2), 349–399. doi:10.1086/421787

Buss, A. (2001). *Psychological dimensions of the self.* Sage Publications.

Cacciatore, M. A. (2021). Misinformation and public opinion of science and health: Approaches, findings, and future directions. *Proceedings of the National Academy of Sciences of the United States of America, 118*(15), e1912437117. doi:10.1073/pnas.1912437117 PMID:33837143

Caffe. (2021). *Caffe.* https://bit.ly/3yPH2km

Caldarelli, G., Chessa, A., Pammolli, F., Pompa, G., Puliga, M., Riccaboni, M., & Riotta, G. (2014). A Multi-Level Geographical Study of Italian Political Elections from Twitter Data. *PLoS One*, *9*(5), e95809. doi:10.1371/journal.pone.0095809 PMID:24802857

Calegari, M. d., & Gegmani, O. H. (2006). *Temperamento e Carreira* (4th ed.). Summus.

Cannon, W. B. (1927). The James-Lange theory of emotions: A critical examination and an alternative theory. *The American Journal of Psychology*, *39*(1/4), 106–124. doi:10.2307/1415404 PMID:3322057

Carvalho, A. C., & Freitas, A. A. (2009). A Tutorial on Multi-Label Classification Techniques. *Studies in Computational Intelligence*, *205*, 177–195.

Carver, R. P. (1993). The case against statistical significance testing, revisited. *Journal of Experimental Education*, *61*(4), 287–292. doi:10.1080/00220973.1993.10806591

Castells, M. (2010). *The information age: Economy, society, and culture*. Wiley-Blackwell.

Celli, F., Pianesi, F., Stillwell, D., & Kosinski, M. (2013). Workshop on Computational Personality Recognition (Shared Task). *Proceedings of WCPR13, in conjunction with ICWSM-13.*

Centola, D., & Macy, M. (2007). Complex contagions and the weakness of long ties. *American Journal of Sociology*, *113*(3), 702–734. doi:10.1086/521848

Ceron, A., Curini, L., & Iacus, S. M. (2015). Using Sentiment Analysis to Monitor Electoral Campaigns: Method Matters—Evidence From the United States and Italy. *Social Science Computer Review*, *33*(1), 3–20. doi:10.1177/0894439314521983

Chang, J. C., Amershi, S., & Kamar, E. (2017). Revolt: Collaborative Crowdsourcing for Labeling Machine Learning Datasets. In *Proceedings of the 2017 CHI Conference on Human Factors in Computing Systems* (pp. 2334-2346). 10.1145/3025453.3026044

Chan, K., & Liebowitz, J. (2006). The synergy of social network analysis and knowledge mapping: A case study. *International Journal of Management and Decision Making*, *7*(1), 19–35. doi:10.1504/IJMDM.2006.008169

Chapelle, O., Schölkopf, B., & Zien, A. (2006). Semi-Supervised Learning. In Adaptive Computation and Machine Learning. The MIT Press. doi:10.7551/mitpress/9780262033589.001.0001

Charoensukmongkol, P. (2018). The Impact of Social Media on Social Comparison and Envy in Teenagers: The Moderating Role of the Parent Comparing Children and In-group Competition among Friends. *Journal of Child and Family Studies*, *2018*(27), 69–79. doi:10.100710826-017-0872-8

Cheng, J., Adamic, L., Dow, P. A., Kleinberg, J. M., & Leskovec, J. (2014). Can cascades be predicted? *Proceedings of the 23rd International Conference on World Wide Web - WWW '14*, 925–936. 10.1145/2566486.2567997

Cherman, E. A., & Monard, M. C. (2009). Um Estudo sobre Métodos de Classificação Multirrótulo. *Proceedings of do IV Congresso da Academia Trinacional de Ciências*, 1, 1-10.

Chou, H.-T. G., & Edge, N. (2012). They are happier and having better lives than I am": the impact of using Facebook on perceptions of others. Cyberpsychology, Behavior, and Social Networking, 15, 117-121.

Chowdhury, G. G. (2005). Natural language processing. *Annual Review of Information Science & Technology*, *37*(1), 51–89. doi:10.1002/aris.1440370103

Claro, C. F., Lima, A. C., & de Castro, L. N. (2019). The Application of Keirsey's Temperament Model to Twitter Data in Portuguese. In Agents and Artificial Intelligence. ICAART 2018. Lecture Notes in Computer Science (Vol. 11352, pp. 408-421). doi:10.1007/978-3-030-05453-3_19

Claro, C. F., Lima, A. C., & de Castro, L. N. (2018). Predicting Temperament using Keirsey's Model for Portuguese Twitter Data. In *Proceedings of the 10th International Conference on Agents and Artificial Intelligence* (vol. 1, pp. 250-256). 10.5220/0006700102500256

Clauset, A., Shalizi, C. R., & Newman, M. E. (2009). Power-Law Distributions in Empirical Data. *SIAM Review*, *51*(4), 661–703. doi:10.1137/070710111

Coble, K. H., Mishra, A. K., Ferrell, S., & Griffin, T. (2018). Big data in agriculture: A challenge for the future. *Applied Economic Perspectives and Policy*, *40*(1), 79–96. doi:10.1093/aepp/ppx056

Coelho, T. A. (2011). Uma estratégia híbrida para o problema de classificação multirrótulo. Universidade Federal de Minas Gerais, Instituto de Ciências Exatas.

Collins, B. (2016). Big data and health economics: Strengths, weaknesses, opportunities and threats. *PharmacoEconomics*, *34*(2), 101–106. doi:10.100740273-015-0306-7 PMID:26093888

Conover, M. D., Ratkiewicz, J., Francisco, M., Goncalves, B., Flammini, A., & Menczer, F. (2011). Political Polarization on Twitter. *Proceedings of the Fifth International AAAI Conference on Weblogs and Social Media.*

Conte, R., & Gilbert, N. (1995). *Artificial Societies.* Routledge. https://www.doabooks.org/doab?func=fulltext&rid=38833

Cornell, X. (2014). *INFO2040X mod1 kleinberg structural holes v1* (video file). Retrieved on January 17, 2018 from https://www.youtube.com/watch?v=GaQLRCaLQG4

Corvalán, J. (2018). Inteligencia artificial: retos, desafíos y oportunidades - Prometea: la primera inteligencia artificial de Latinoamérica al servicio de la Justicia. *Revista de Investigações Constitucionais*, *5*(1), 295–316. doi:10.5380/rinc.v5i1.55334

Cox, M., & Ellsworth, D. (1997). Application-controlled demand paging for out-of-core visualization. *Visualization*, *97*, 235–244.

Creager, A. N. H., Lunbeck, E., & Wise, M. N. (Eds.). (2007). *Science without laws: Model systems, cases, exemplary narratives.* Duke University Press. doi:10.1215/9780822390244

Crosas, M., King, G., Honaker, J., & Sweeney, L. (2015). Automating Open Science for Big Data. *The Annals of the American Academy of Political and Social Science*, *659*(1), 260–273. doi:10.1177/0002716215570847

Cross, R. L., Cross, R. L., & Parker, A. (2004). *The hidden power of social networks: Understanding how work really gets done in organizations*. Harvard Business Press.

Cross, R., Borgatti, S. P., & Parker, A. (2002). Making invisible work visible: Using social network analysis to support strategic collaboration. *California Management Review*, *44*(2), 25–46. doi:10.2307/41166121

Cross, R., Parker, A., & Sasson, L. (Eds.). (2003). *Networks in the knowledge economy*. Oxford University Press. doi:10.1093/oso/9780195159509.001.0001

Cross, R., & Prusak, L. (2002). *The people who make organizations go–or stop*. Networks in the Knowledge Economy.

Currie, J., Kleven, H., & Zwiers, E. (2020, May). Technology and big data are changing economics: Mining text to track methods. *AEA Papers and Proceedings. American Economic Association*, *110*, 42–48. doi:10.1257/pandp.20201058

Cyram. (2003). *NetMiner II*. Ver.2.4.0 [computer software]. Cyram Co., Ltd.

Damasio, A. (2003). *Looking for Spinoza: Joy, Sorrow, and the Feeling Brain*. Harvest.

Daniel, E., Crawford, E., & Westerman, D. (2018). The Influence of Social Media Influencers: Understanding Online Vaping Communities and Parasocial Interaction through the Lens of Taylor's Six-Segment Strategy Wheel. *Journal of Interactive Advertising*, *18*(2), 96–109. doi:10.1080/15252019.2018.1488637

Daraghmeh, H. M., & Wang, C. C. (2017). A review of current status of free cooling in datacenters. *Applied Thermal Engineering*, *114*, 1224–1239. doi:10.1016/j.applthermaleng.2016.10.093

Darley, V. (1994). Emergent phenomena and complexity. *Artificial Life*, 411–416.

Darwin, C., Ekman, P., & Prodger, P. (1998). *The expression of the emotions in man and animals*. Oxford University Press.

Datta, A., Tschantz, M. C., & Datta, A. (2015). *Automated Experiments on Ad Privacy Settings: A Tale of Opacity, Choice, and Discrimination. Proceedings on Privacy Enhancing Technologies*. doi:10.1515/popets-2015-0007

Daud, I., & Himelboim, I. (2018). A Social Networks Approach to Online Social Movement: Social Mediators and Mediated Content in #FreeAJStaff Twitter Network. *Social Media + Society*, *4*(1), 1–14. 10.1177%2F2056305118760807

de Castro, L. N., & Ferrari, D. G. (2016). *Introduction to Data Mining: Basic Concepts, Algorithms, and Applications*. Saraiva.

De Grauwe, P. (2010). Top-down versus bottom-up macroeconomics. *CESifo Economic Studies, 56*(4), 465–497. doi:10.1093/cesifo/ifq014

De Veirman, M., Cauberghe, V., & Hudders, L. (2017). Marketing through Instagram influencers: The impact of several followers and product divergence on brand attitude. *International Journal of Advertising, 36*(5), 798–828. doi:10.1080/02650487.2017.1348035

Delli Gatti, D., Desiderio, S., Gaffeo, E., Cirillo, P., & Gallegati, M. (2011). *Macroeconomics from the Bottom-up*. Springer. doi:10.1007/978-88-470-1971-3

Delli Gatti, D., Gaffeo, E., Gallegati, M., Giulioni, G., & Palestrini, A. (2008). *Emergent macroeconomics: an agent-based approach to business fluctuations*. Springer Science & Business Media.

Deshmukh, J., & Tripathy, A. (2018). Entropy-based classifier for cross-domain opinion mining. *Applied Computing and Informatics, 14*(1), 55–64. doi:10.1016/j.aci.2017.03.001

Deutsche Bank. (2014). *Big Data: How it can become a differentiator*. https://cib.db.com/docs_new/GTB_Big_Data_Whitepaper_(DB0324)_v2.pdf

Devlin, J., Chang, M.-W., Lee, K., & Toutanova, K. (2019). BERT: Pre-Training of Deep Bidirectional Transformers for Language Understanding. In *Proceedings of the 2019 Conference of the North American Chapter of the Association for Computational Linguistics: Human Language Technologies* (vol. 1, pp. 4171-4186). Academic Press.

Díaz, L. (2017). *Soy marca: quiero trabajar con influencers. Influencer Marketing*. PROFIT. https://bit.ly/3yQzuOC

Dick, S. (2019). Artificial Intelligence. *Harvard Data Science Review, 1*(1). Advance online publication. doi:10.1162/99608f92.92fe150c

Diermeier, D., Godbout, J.-F., Yu, B., & Kaufmann, S. (2012). Language and Ideology in Congress. *British Journal of Political Science, 42*(1), 31–55. doi:10.1017/S0007123411000160

Dolata, U. (2017). Apple, Amazon, Google, Facebook, Microsoft: Market concentration-competition-innovation strategies. *Research Contributions to Organizational Sociology & Innovation Studies, SOI Discussion Papers,* (1). https://bit.ly/2VtLGGp

Domahidi, E., Yang, J., Niemann-Lenz, J., & Reinecke, L. (2019). Outlining the Way Ahead in Computational Communication Science: An Introduction to the IJoC Special Section on "Computational Methods for Communication Science: Toward a Strategic Roadmap." *International Journal of Communication, 13*(0), 3876–3884.

Domingos, P. (2012). A Few Useful Things to Know About Machine Learning. *Communications of the ACM, 55*(10), 78–87. doi:10.1145/2347736.2347755

Domingos, P. (2019). *The master algorithm: How the Quest for the Ultimate Machine will Remake our World.* Basic Books.

Dubois, E., & Blank, G. (2017). The echo chamber is overstated: The moderating effect of political interest and diverse media. *Information Communication and Society*, *21*(5), 729–745. doi:10.1080/1369118X.2018.1428656

Easley, D., & Kleinberg, J. (2012). Networks, crowds, and markets: Reasoning about a highly connected world. *Significance*, *9*, 43–44.

Edgar, T. W., & Manz, D. O. (2017). Machine Learning. In Research Methods for Cyber Security (pp. 153–173). Elsevier. doi:10.1016/B978-0-12-805349-2.00006-6

Einav, L., & Levin, J. (2014). Economics in the Age of Big Data. *Science*, *346*(6210), 1243089. Advance online publication. doi:10.1126cience.1243089 PMID:25378629

Ekman, P., Friesen, W. V., & Ellsworth, P. (1982). What emotion categories or dimensions can observers judge from facial behavior? In *Emotion in the human face* (pp. 39–55). Cambridge University Press.

El Alaoui, I., Gahi, Y., Messoussi, Y., Chaabi, Y., Todoskoff, A., & Kobi, A. (2018). A novel adaptable approach for sentiment analysis on big social data. *Journal of Big Data*, *5*(1), 12. doi:10.118640537-018-0120-0

Elkink, J. A. (2011). The International Diffusion of Democracy. *Comparative Political Studies*, *44*(12), 1651–1674. doi:10.1177/0010414011407474

Engelen, J. E., & Hoos, H. H. (2020). A survey on semi-supervised learning. *Machine Learning*, *109*(2), 373–440. doi:10.100710994-019-05855-6

Epstein, J. M., & Axtell, R. (1996). *Growing artificial societies: social science from the bottom up*. Brookings Institution Press. doi:10.7551/mitpress/3374.001.0001

Falleti, T. G., & Lynch, J. F. (2009). Context and Causal Mechanisms in Political Analysis. *Comparative Political Studies*, *42*(9), 1143–1166. doi:10.1177/0010414009331724

Farias, L., & Monteiro, T. (2012). A identidade adquirida nas redes sociais através do conceito de persona. *XIX Prêmio Expocom 2012 – Exposição da Pesquisa Experimental em Comunicação - Intercom - Sociedade Brasileira de Estudos Interdisciplinares da Comunicação*. http://www.intercom.org.br/papers/regionais/nordeste2012/resumos/R32-1497-1.pdf

Farmer, J. D., & Lux, T. (2008). Applications of statistical physics in economics and finance. *Journal of Economic Dynamics & Control*, *32*(1), 6. doi:10.1016/j.jedc.2007.01.019

Farmer, J. D., Shubik, M., & Smith, E. (2005). Is economics the next physical science? *Physics Today*, *58*(9), 37–42. doi:10.1063/1.2117821

Federico, P.-A., & Figliozzi, P. W. (1981). Computer Simulation of Social Systems. *Sociological Methods & Research*, *9*(4), 513–533. doi:10.1177/004912418100900408

Feldman, R., & Sanger, J. (2007). *The Text Mining Handbook Advanced Approaches in Analysing Unstructured Data*. Cambridge University Press.

Ferguson, S., & Hebels, R. (2003). Communications and networking. In S. Ferguson & R. Hebels (Eds.), *Computers for Librarians: An Introduction to the Electronic Library* (pp. 197–226). Elsevier Science. doi:10.1016/B978-1-876938-60-4.50013-6

Fernández, J., Hernández, V. & Sanz, P. (2018). Influencers, marca personal e ideología política en Twitter. *Cuadernos.Info. Comunicación y medios en Iberoamérica*, *42*, 19-37. doi:10.7764/cdi.42.1348

Flores, M. (2020). Empatía y respeto entre otros valores: Análisis de experiencias docentes de colaboración con organizaciones sociales. *Revista Digital de Investigación en Docencia Universitaria*, *14*(1), e1195. doi:10.19083/ridu.2020.1195

Forgas, J. P., & Baumeister, R. F. (2019). *The social psychology of gullibility: Fake news, conspiracy theories, and irrational beliefs*. Academic Press.

Forsyth, E., & Katz, L. (1946). A Matrix Approach to the Analysis of Sociometric Data: Preliminary Report. *Sociometry*, *9*(4), 340–347. doi:10.2307/2785498

Fortuna, P., & Nunes, S. (2018). A Survey on Automatic Detection of Hate Speech in Text. *ACM Computing Surveys*, *51*(4), 1–30. doi:10.1145/3232676

Foster, V., Comini, N., & Srinivasan, S. (2021, May 6). *Improving data infrastructure helps ensure equitable access for poor people in poor countries*. Retrieved from https://blogs.worldbank.org/opendata/improving-data-infrastructure-helps-ensure-equitable-access-poor-people-poor-countries

Fox, J., & Moreland, J. J. (2015). The dark side of social networking sites: An exploration of the relational and psychological stressors associated with Facebook use and affordances. *Computers in Human Behavior*, *2015*(45), 168–176. doi:10.1016/j.chb.2014.11.083

Fredericks, K. A., & Durland, M. M. (2005). The historical evolution and basic concepts of social network analysis. *New Directions for Evaluation*, *2005*(107), 15–23. doi:10.1002/ev.158

Freeman, L. C., White, D. R., & Romney, A. K. (1989). *Research Methods in Social Network Analysis*. George Mason University Press.

Gabaix, X. (2011). The granular origins of aggregate fluctuations. *Econometrica*, *79*(3), 733–772. doi:10.3982/ECTA8769

Garcia, R. (2005). Uses of Agent-Based Modeling in Innovation/New Product Development Research. *Journal of Product Innovation Management*, *22*(5), 380–398. doi:10.1111/j.1540-5885.2005.00136.x

Garimella, K., Morales, G., Gionis, A., & Mathioudakis, M. (2018). Political discourse on social media: Echo chambers, gatekeepers, and the Price of bipartisanship. *Proceedings of the 2018 World Wide Web Conference*, 913-922. 10.1145/3178876.3186139

Garrett, R. K. (2009). Politically Motivated Reinforcement Seeking: Reframing the Selective Exposure Debate. *Journal of Communication, 59*(4), 676–699. doi:10.1111/j.1460-2466.2009.01452.x

Gentzkow, M., Shapiro, J. M., & Taddy, M. (2016). *Measuring Polarization in High-Dimensional Data: Method and Application to Congressional Speech*. National Bureau of Economic Research.

George, G., Hass, M., & Pentland, A. (2014). Big Data and Management: From the Editors. *Academy of Management Journal, 57*(2), 321–326. https://bit.ly/3wwO5Nz. doi:10.5465/amj.2014.4002

Giannoulis, G., Krithara, A., Karatsalos, C., & Paliouras, G. (2014). Splice Site Recognition Using Transfer Learning. In A. Likas, K. Blekas, & D. Kalles (Eds.), Lecture Notes in Computer Science: Vol. 8445. Artificial Intelligence: Methods and Applications. SETN 2014. Springer.

Gilbert, N. (1993). Computer simulation of social processes. *Social Research Update*, 6.

Goertz, G., & Mahoney, J. (2012). *A tale of two cultures: Qualitative and quantitative research in the social sciences*. Princeton University Press. doi:10.23943/princeton/9780691149707.001.0001

González-Bailón, S. (2013). Social Science in the Era of Big Data. *Policy and Internet, 5*(2), 147–160. doi:10.1002/1944-2866.POI328

González-Bailón, S. (2017). *Decoding the social world: Data science and the unintended consequences of communication*. MIT Press. doi:10.7551/mitpress/10271.001.0001

González-Bailón, S., Borge-Holthoefer, J., & Moreno, Y. (2013). Broadcasters and hidden influentials in online protest diffusion. *The American Behavioral Scientist, 57*(7), 943–965. doi:10.1177/0002764213479371

González-Bailón, S., & Paltoglou, G. (2015). Signals of Public Opinion in Online Communication: A Comparison of Methods and Data Sources. *The Annals of the American Academy of Political and Social Science, 659*(1), 95–107. doi:10.1177/0002716215569192

Grace, R., Halse, S., Aurite, W., Montarnal, A., & Tapia, A. (2019). Expanding Awareness: Comparing Location, Keyword, and Network Filtering Methods to Collect Hyperlocal Social Media Data. In *Proceedings of the 52nd Hawaii International Conference on System Sciences* (pp. 2699-2708). 10.24251/HICSS.2019.325

Granovetter, M. S. (1973). The strength of weak ties. *American Journal of Sociology, 78*(6), 1360–1380. doi:10.1086/225469

Greenhill, M., Leviston, Z., Leonard, R., & Walker, I. (2014). Assessing climate change beliefs: Response effects of question wording and response alternatives. *Public Understanding of Science (Bristol, England), 23*(8), 947–965. doi:10.1177/0963662513480117 PMID:23825288

Grimmer, J., & King, G. (2011). General purpose computer-assisted clustering and conceptualization. *Proceedings of the National Academy of Sciences of the United States of America, 108*(7), 2643–2650. doi:10.1073/pnas.1018067108 PMID:21292983

Gruzd, A., & Roy, J. (2014). Investigating Political Polarization on Twitter: A Canadian Perspective: Investigating Political Polarization on Twitter. *Policy and Internet*, *6*(1), 28–45. doi:10.1002/1944-2866.POI354

Guanipa, L., & Angulo, M. (2020). La identidad social en la educación: Hacia una participación ciudadana. *Desde el Sur*, *12*(1), 155–166. doi:10.21142/DES-1201-2020-0010

Guillen, M. F., & Suarez, S. L. (2005). Explaining the Global Digital Divide: Economic, Political and Sociological Drivers of Cross-National Internet Use. *Social Forces*, *84*(2), 681–708. doi:10.1353of.2006.0015

Gundecha, P., & Liu, H. (2012). Introduction Mining Social Media: A Brief Introduction. *INFORMS TutORials in Operations Research*, 1-17.

Hajmohammadi, M., Ibrahim, R., & Selamat, A. (2015). Graph-based semi-supervised learning for cross-lingual sentiment classification. In N. Guyen, B. Trawiński, & R. Kosala (Eds.), Lecture Notes in Computer Science: Vol. 9011. *Intelligent Information and Database Systems. ACIIDS 2015* (pp. 97–106). doi:10.1007/978-3-319-15702-3_10

Hall, C. S., Lindzey, G., & Campbell, J. B. (2000). *Teorias da Personalidade*. Artmed.

Han, G., Bohan, L., Wenbin, X., Yuxin, Z., Donghai, G., Weitong, Ch. & Ken C. (2021). CSIP: Enhanced Link Prediction with Context of Social Influence Propagation. *Big Data Research,* (24), 100217. doi:10.1016/j.bdr.2021.100217

Hao, K. (2020). *A College Kid's Fake, AI-Generated Blog Fooled Tens of Thousands. This Is How He Made It.* https://www.technologyreview.com/2020/08/14/1006780/ai-gpt-3-fake-blog-reached-top-of-hacker-news/

Harding, M., & Hersh, J. (2018). Big Data in Economics. *IZA World of Labor: Evidence-Based Policy Making*, *451*. Advance online publication. doi:10.15185/izawol.451

Harford, T. (2014). Big Data: A Big Mistake? *Significance*, *11*(5), 14–19. doi:10.1111/j.1740-9713.2014.00778.x

Hariri, R., Fredericks, E., & Bowers, K. (2019). Uncertainty in big data analytics: Survey, opportunities, and challenges. *Journal of Big Data*, *6*(44), 44. Advance online publication. doi:10.118640537-019-0206-3

Hasan, M., Rundensteiner, E., & Agu, E. (2014). EMOTEX: Detecting Emotions in Twitter Messages. In *ASE Bigdata/Socialcom/Cybersecurity Conference*, (pp. 1-10). Stanford University.

Hatala, J. P. (2006). Social network analysis in human resource development: A new methodology. *Human Resource Development Review*, *5*(1), 45–71. doi:10.1177/1534484305284318

Hautz, W. E., Krummrey, G., Exadaktylos, A., & Hautz, S. C. (2016). Six degrees of separation: The small world of medical education. *Medical Education*, *50*(12), 1274–1279. doi:10.1111/medu.13102 PMID:27873413

Hawi, N. S., & Samaha, M. (2016). The Relations Among Social Media Addiction, Self-Esteem, and Life Satisfaction in University Students. *Social Science Computer Review*. Advance online publication. doi:10.1177/0894439316660340

Hawi, N., & Samaha, M. (2019). Identifying commonalities and differences in personality characteristics of Internet and social media addiction profiles: Traits, self-esteem, and self-construal. *Behaviour & Information Technology, 38*(2), 110–119. doi:10.1080/0144929X.2018.1515984

Hedström, P., & Ylikoski, P. (2010). Causal Mechanisms in the Social Sciences. *Annual Review of Sociology, 36*(1), 49–67. doi:10.1146/annurev.soc.012809.102632

Heermann, D. W. (1990). *Computer Simulation Methods in Theoretical Physics* (2nd ed.). Springer. doi:10.1007/978-3-642-75448-7

Hey, A. J. G., Tansley, S., & Tolle, K. (2009). *The fourth paradigm: Data-intensive scientific discovery* (Vol. 1). Microsoft Research.

Higgins, E. T. (1987). Self-discrepancy: A theory relating self and affect. *Psychological Review, 94*(3), 319–340. doi:10.1037/0033-295X.94.3.319 PMID:3615707

Hilbert, M., Barnett, G., Blumenstock, J., Contractor, N., Diesner, J., Seth, F., & González-Bailón, S. (2019). Computational Communication Science: A Methodological Catalyzer for a Maturing Discipline. *International Journal of Communication, 13*, 3912–3934.

Hilbert, M., & Lopez, P. (2011). The World's Technological Capacity to Store, Communicate, and Compute Information. *Science, 332*(6025), 60–65. doi:10.1126cience.1200970 PMID:21310967

Himelboim, I., & Golan, G. (2019). A Social Networks Approach to Viral Advertising: The Role of Primary, Contextual, and Low Influencers. *Social Media + Society, 5*(3). Advance online publication. doi:10.1177/2056305119847516

Hirschberg, J., & Manning, C. D. (2015). Advances in natural language processing. *Science, 349*(6245), 261–266. doi:10.1126cience.aaa8685 PMID:26185244

Hodgson, G. M. (1993). The Mecca of Alfred Marshall. *Economic Journal (London), 103*(417), 406–415. doi:10.2307/2234779

Holland, P. W., & Leinhardt, S. (1970). A Method for Detecting Structure in Sociometric Data. *American Journal of Sociology, 3*(3), 492–513. doi:10.1086/224954

Hong, S., & Kim, S. H. (2016). Political polarization on twitter: Implications for the use of social media in digital governments. *Government Information Quarterly, 33*(4), 777–782. doi:10.1016/j.giq.2016.04.007

Huang, P., Copertaro, B., Zhang, X., Shen, J., Löfgren, I., Rönnelid, M., Fahlen, J., Andersson, D., & Svanfeldt, M. (2020). A review of data centers as prosumers in district energy systems: Renewable energy integration and waste heat reuse for district heating. *Applied Energy, 258*, 114109. doi:10.1016/j.apenergy.2019.114109

Hughes, C., Ensor, R., & Marks, A. (2011). Individual differences in false belief understanding are stable from 3 to 6 years of age and predict children's mental state talk with school friends. *Journal of Experimental Child Psychology, 108*(1), 96–112. doi:10.1016/j.jecp.2010.07.012 PMID:20846667

Hu, H., Lin, J., & Cui, W. (2015). Intervention Strategies and the Diffusion of Collective Behavior. *Journal of Artificial Societies and Social Simulation, 18*(3), 16. doi:10.18564/jasss.2872

IBM. (n.d.). *Cognitive Class.* https://cognitiveclass.ai

Ignatow, G., & Mihalcea, R. F. (2017). *An Introduction to Text Mining: Research Design, Data Collection, and Analysis.* Sage Publications.

Issenberg, S. (2013). How President Obama's Campaign Used Big Data to Rally Individual Voters. *Technology Review, 116*(1), 38–49.

Ito, P., & Guzzo, R. S. (2002). Diferenças individuais: Temperamento e personalidade; importância da teoria. *Estudos de Psicologia, 19*(1), 91–100. doi:10.1590/S0103-166X2002000100008

Iyyer, M., Enns, P., Boyd-Graber, J., & Resnik, P. (2014). Political Ideology Detection Using Recursive Neural Networks. In *Proceedings of the 52nd Annual Meeting of the Association for Computational Linguistics* (vol. 1, pp. 1113-1122). 10.3115/v1/P14-1105

Jaakkola, H., Henno, J., Makela, J., & Thalheim, B. (2019). Artificial Intelligence Yesterday, Today & Tomorrow. *42nd International Convention on Information and Communication Technology, Electronics and Microelectronics (MIPRO).* 10.23919/MIPRO.2019.8756913

Jackson, J., Watts, J., List, J.-M., Drabble, R., & Lindquist, K. (2021). From Text to Thought: How Analyzing Language Can Advance Psychological Science. *Perspectives on Psychological Science.* Advance online publication. doi:10.1177/17456916211004899 PMID:34606730

Jacobs, A. Z., & Wallach, H. (2021). Measurement and Fairness. In *Proceedings of the 2021 ACM Conference on Fairness, Accountability, and Transparency* (pp. 375-385). 10.1145/3442188.3445901

Jacobsen, C., & Bronson, R. (1995). Computer-simulations and empirical testing of sociological theory. *Sociological Methods & Research, 23*(4), 479–506. doi:10.1177/0049124195023004004

Jaidka, K., Ahmed, S., Skoric, M., & Hilbert, M. (2019). Predicting elections from social media: A three-country three-method comparative study. *Asian Journal of Communication, 29*(3), 252–273. doi:10.1080/01292986.2018.1453849

Jain, P., Gyanchandani, M., & Khare, N. (2016). Big data privacy: A technological perspective and review. *Journal of Big Data, 3*(1), 25. Advance online publication. doi:10.118640537-016-0059-y

James, W. (1884). What is an emotion? *Mind, os-IX*(34), 188–205. doi:10.1093/mind/os-IX.34.188

Jensen, J., Naidu, S., Kaplan, E., Wilse-Samson, L., Gergen, D., Zuckerman, M., & Spirling, A. (2012). Political Polarization and the Dynamics of Political Language: Evidence From 130 Years of Partisan Speech. *Brookings Papers on Economic Activity*, *2012*(1), 1–81. doi:10.1353/eca.2012.0017

Jeyapriya, A., & Selvi, K. (2015). Extracting aspects and mining opinions in product reviews using supervised learning algorithm. *2nd International Conference on Electronics and Communication Systems (ICECS)*, 548–552. 10.1109/ECS.2015.7124967

Jia, Y., Shelhamer, E., Donahue, J., Karayev, S., Long, J., Girshick, R., Guadarrama, S., & Darrell, T. (2014). Caffe: Convolutional Architecture for Fast Feature Embedding. *arXiv:1408.5093*. https://bit.ly/2VpFUFK doi:10.1145/2647868.2654889

Jordan, K. (2014). Initial trends in enrolment and completion of massive open online courses. *The International Review of Research in Open and Distributed Learning*, *15*(1). Advance online publication. doi:10.19173/irrodl.v15i1.1651

Judge, P. (2021, January 28). *Data centers need to find 300,000 more staff by 2025*. Retrieved from https://www.datacenterdynamics.com/en/news/data-centers-need-find-300000-more-staff-2025/

Julious, S. A., & Mullee, M. A. (1994). Confounding and Simpson's paradox. *BMJ (Clinical Research Ed.)*, *309*(6967), 1480–1481. doi:10.1136/bmj.309.6967.1480 PMID:7804052

Jung, C. G. (2000). Os arquétipos e o inconsciente coletivo (2nd ed.). Perrópolis: Vozes.

Justwan, F., Baumgaertner, B., Carlisle, J. E., Clark, A. K., & Clark, M. (2018). Social media echo chambers and satisfaction with democracy among Democrats and Republicans in the aftermath of the 2016 US elections. *Journal of Elections, Public Opinion, and Parties*, *28*(4), 424–442. doi:10.1080/17457289.2018.1434784 PMID:31231432

Katz, E. (1957). The Two-Step Flow of Communication: An Up-To-Date Report on an Hypothesis. *Public Opinion Quarterly*, *21*(1), 61–78. doi:10.1086/266687

Katz, E., & Lazarsfeld, P. (2005). *Personal Influence: The Part Played by People in the Flow of Mass Communications*. Routledge.

Katz, E., & Lazarsfeld, P. F. (1955). *Personal influence: The part played by people in the flow of mass communications*. Free Press.

Katz, L. (1947). On the Matric Analysis of Sociometric Data. *Sociometry*, *10*(3), 233–241. doi:10.2307/2785073

Katz, L. (1953). A new status index derived from sociometric analysis. *Psychometrika*, *18*(1), 39–43. doi:10.1007/BF02289026

Kauffman, H. (2015). A review of predictive factors of student success in and satisfaction with online learning. *Research in Learning Technology*, *23*. Advance online publication. doi:10.3402/rlt.v23.26507

Keles, B., McCrae, N., & Grealish, A. (2020). A systematic review: The influence of social media on depression, anxiety and psychological distress in adolescents. *International Journal of Adolescence and Youth*, *25*(01), 79–93. doi:10.1080/02673843.2019.1590851

Khan, F., Qamar, U., & Bashir, S. (2016). S WIMS: Semi-supervised subjective feature weighting and intelligent model selection for sentiment analysis. *Knowledge-Based Systems*, *100*(15), 97–111. doi:10.1016/j.knosys.2016.02.011

Khan, N., Alsaqer, M., Shah, H., Badsha, G., Abbasi, A., & Salehian, S. (2018) The 10 Vs, issues & challenges of big data. *Proceedings of the 2018 International Conference on Big Data and Education*, 52-56. 10.1145/3206157.3206166

Kilduff, M., Crossland, C., Tsai, W., & Krackhardt, D. (2008). Organizational network perceptions versus reality: A small world after all? *Organizational Behavior and Human Decision Processes*, *107*(1), 15–28. doi:10.1016/j.obhdp.2007.12.003

King, G. (2017, January 4). *Big Data is Not About the Data!* https://gking.harvard.edu/presentations/big-data-not-about-data-16

King, G. (1986). How Not to Lie with Statistics: Avoiding Common Mistakes in Quantitative Political Science. *American Journal of Political Science*, *30*(3), 666. doi:10.2307/2111095

King, G., Keohane, R. O., & Verba, S. (1994). *Designing Social Inquiry: Scientific Inference in Qualitative Research.* Princeton University Press. doi:10.1515/9781400821211

Kiran, R., & Naik, D. (2021). Novel sensitivity method for evaluating the first derivative of the feed-forward neural network outputs. *Journal of Big Data*, *8*(1), 88. doi:10.118640537-021-00480-4

Kırer, H., & Eren, E. (2015). İktisat-Fizik İlişkisine Tarihsel Bakış. *Ekonomi-tek- International Economic Journal*, *4*(2), 25–60.

Kitts, J. A., & Quintane, E. (2021). Rethinking Social Networks in the Era of Computational Social Science. In R. Light & J. Moody (Eds.), *The Oxford Handbook of Social Networks* (pp. 70–97). Oxford University Press. doi:10.1093/oxfordhb/9780190251765.013.24

Kobayashi, V., Mol, S., Berkers, H., Kismihók, G., & Den Hartog, D. (2017). Text Classification for Organizational Researchers: A Tutorial. *Organizational Research Methods*, *21*(3), 766–799. doi:10.1177/1094428117719322 PMID:29881249

Koehler, J. J. (1993). The Influence of Prior Beliefs on Scientific Judgments of Evidence Quality. *Organizational Behavior and Human Decision Processes*, *56*(1), 28–55. doi:10.1006/obhd.1993.1044

Kozinets, R. V. (2010). *Netnography: Doing ethnographic research online*. Sage publications.

Krasnova, H., Widjaja, T., Buxmann, P., Wenninger, H., & Benbasat, I. (2015). Why Following Friends Can Hurt You: An Exploratory Investigation of the Effects of Envy on Social Networking Sites among College-Age Users. *Information Systems Research*, *16*(3), 585–605. doi:10.1287/isre.2015.0588

Krawczyk, B. (2016). Learning From Imbalanced Data: Open Challenges and Future Directions. *Progress in Artificial Intelligence*, *5*(4), 221–232. doi:10.100713748-016-0094-0

Krebs, V. E. (1998). *Knowledge networks: mapping and measuring knowledge creation and reuse.* White Paper. Available at: www. orgnet. com/IHRIM. html

Krebs, V. E. (2004). *Managing the connected organization.* www. orgnet. com

Kuhn, T. (1962). *The structure of scientific revolutions*. Chicago University.

Kuran, T. (1991). Now Out of Never: The Element of Surprise in the East European Revolution of 1989. *World Politics*, *44*(1), 7–48. doi:10.2307/2010422

Kurien, P. A. (1994). Non-economic bases of economic behaviour: The consumption, investment and exchange patterns of three emigrant communities in Kerala, India. *Development and Change*, *25*(4), 757–783. doi:10.1111/j.1467-7660.1994.tb00535.x

Lambrecht, A., & Tucker, C. (2019). Algorithmic Bias? An Empirical Study of Apparent Gender-Based Discrimination in the Display of STEM Career Ads. *Management Science*, *65*(7), 2966–2981. doi:10.1287/mnsc.2018.3093

Latour, B., Jensen, P., Venturini, T., Grauwin, S., & Boullier, D. (2012). 'The whole is always smaller than its parts' - a digital test of Gabriel Tardes' monads: 'The whole is always smaller than its parts.' *The British Journal of Sociology*, *63*(4), 590–615. doi:10.1111/j.1468-4446.2012.01428.x PMID:23240834

Lauderdale, B. E., & Herzog, A. (2016). Measuring Political Positions From Legislative Speech. *Political Analysis*, *24*(3), 374–394. doi:10.1093/pan/mpw017

Lazarsfeld, P. F., Berelson, B., & Gaudet, H. (1968). The People'S Choice: How the Voter Makes Up His Mind in a Presidential Campaign. In *The People's Choice*. Columbia University Press. doi:10.7312/laza93930

Lazer, D., Pentland, A., Adamic, L., Aral, S., Barabasi, A.-L., Brewer, D., Christakis, N., Contractor, N., Fowler, J., Gutmann, M., Jebara, T., King, G., Macy, M., Roy, D., & Van Alstyne, M. (2009). Computational Social Science. *Science*, *323*(5915), 721–723. doi:10.1126cience.1167742 PMID:19197046

LeDoux, J. (1998). *The emotional brain: The mysterious underpinnings of emotional life*. Simon and Schuster.

Leetaru, K. (2019). A Reminder That Machine Learning Is About Correlations Not Causation. *Forbes*. https://www.forbes.com/sites/kalevleetaru/2019/01/15/a-reminder-that-machine-learning-is-about-correlations-not-causation/?sh=2f44af576161

Leskovec, J., Adamic, L. A., & Huberman, B. A. (2007). The dynamics of viral marketing. *ACM Transactions on the Web*, *1*(1), 5. doi:10.1145/1232722.1232727

Liebowitz, J. (Ed.). (1999). *Knowledge management handbook.* CRC Press.

Lima, A. C. (2016). *Social media mining as a tool for triad analysis of the virtual person* [Mineração de mídias sociais como ferramenta para a análise de tríade da persona virtual]. PhD Thesis.

Lima, A. C., & de Castro, L. N. (2016). Predicting Temperament from Twitter Data. In *Advanced Applied Informatics (IIAI-AAI), 2016 5th IIAI International Congress on* (pp. 599-604). IEEE.

Lima, A. C., & de Castro, L. N. (2012). Automatic sentiment analysis of Twitter messages. *Fourth International Conference on Computational Aspects of Social Networks (CASoN)*, 52-57. 10.1109/CASoN.2012.6412377

Lima, A. C., & de Castro, L. N. (2014). A multi-label, semi-supervised classification approach applied to personality prediction in social media. *Neural Networks*, *58*, 122–130. doi:10.1016/j.neunet.2014.05.020 PMID:24969690

Lima, A. C., & de Castro, L. N. (2019). TECLA: A temperament and psychological type prediction framework from Twitter data. *PLoS One*, *14*(3), e0212844. Advance online publication. doi:10.1371/journal.pone.0212844 PMID:30861015

Lima, A. C., de Castro, L. N., & Corchado, J. M. (2015). A polarity analysis framework for Twitter messages. *Applied Mathematics and Computation*, *270*, 756–767. doi:10.1016/j.amc.2015.08.059

Lim, S., Cortina, L. M., & Magley, V. J. (2008). Personal and workgroup incivility: Impact on work and health outcomes. *The Journal of Applied Psychology*, *93*(1), 95–107. doi:10.1037/0021-9010.93.1.95 PMID:18211138

Li-ping, Y. U. (2013). Big Data and Big Data Economics. *China Soft Science*, *7*, 177–183.

Locke, R. M., & Thelen, K. (1995). Apples and Oranges Revisited: Contextualized Comparisons and the Study of Comparative Labor Politics. *Politics & Society*, *23*(3), 337–367. doi:10.1177/0032329295023003004

López, M., & Sicilia, M. (2014). eWOM as Source of Influence: The Impact of Participation in eWOM and Perceived Source Trustworthiness on Decision Making. *Journal of Interactive Advertising*, *14*(2), 86–97. doi:10.1080/15252019.2014.944288

Lorena, A. C., & Carvalho, A. C. (2008). Estratégias para a combinaçao de classificadores binários em soluçoes multiclasses. *Revista de Informática Teórica e Aplicada*, *2*(15), 65–86. doi:10.22456/2175-2745.7016

Lovari, A., & Valentini, C. (2020). Public Sector Communication and Social Media: Opportunities and Limits of Current Policies, Activities, and Practices. The Handbook of Public Sector Communication. doi:10.1002/9781119263203.ch21

Lup, K., Trub, L., & Rosenthal, L. (2015). Instagram# Instasad? Exploring associations among Instagram use, depressive symptoms, negative social comparison, and strangers followed. *Cyberpsychology, Behavior, and Social Networking*, *18*(5), 247–252. doi:10.1089/cyber.2014.0560 PMID:25965859

Lustick, I. S., Miodownik, D., & Eidelson, R. J. (2004). Secessionism in Multicultural States: Does Sharing Power Prevent or Encourage It? *American Political Science Review,* (2), 209–229. doi:10.1017/S0003055404001108

Lustick, I. S. (2010). Secession of the Center: A Virtual Probe of the Prospects for Punjabi Secessionism in Pakistan and the Secession of Punjabistan. *Journal of Artificial Societies and Social Simulation*, *14*(1), 7. doi:10.18564/jasss.1696

Lycett, M. (2013). 'Datafication': Making sense of (big) data in a complex world. *European Journal of Information Systems*, *22*(4), 381–386. doi:10.1057/ejis.2013.10

Mackenzie, A. (2012). More Parts Than Elements: How Databases Multiply. *Environment and Planning. D, Society & Space*, *30*(2), 335–350. doi:10.1068/d6710

Mahoney, J. (2010). After KKV: The New Methodology of Qualitative Research. *World Politics*, *62*(1), 120–147. doi:10.1017/S0043887109990220

Mahoney, J., & Barrenechea, R. (2019). The logic of counterfactual analysis in case-study explanation. *The British Journal of Sociology*, *70*(1), 306–338. doi:10.1111/1468-4446.12340 PMID:29265335

Mairesse, F., Walker, M., Mehl, M. R., & Moore, R. K. (2007). Using Linguistic Cues for the Automatic Recognition of Personality in Conversation and Text. *Journal of Artificial Intelligence Research*, *30*, 457–500. doi:10.1613/jair.2349

Manning, C. D., Raghavan, P., & Schütze, H. (2008). *Introduction to Information Retrieval*. Cambridge University Press. doi:10.1017/CBO9780511809071

Marin, A., & Wellman, B. (2011). Social Network Analysis: An Introduction. In J. Scott & P. J. Carrington (Eds.), *The SAGE Handbook of Social Network Analysis*. SAGE Publications Inc.

Markovikj, D., Gievska, S., Kosinski, M., & Stillwell, D. (2013). Mining facebook data for predictive personality modeling. *Proceedings of the 7th international AAAI conference on Weblogs and Social Media (ICWSM 2013)*, 1-4.

Marozzo, F., & Bessi, A. (2018). Analyzing polarization of social media users and news sites during political campaigns. *Social Network Analysis and Mining*, *8*(1), 1. doi:10.100713278-017-0479-5

Marres, N., & Weltevrede, E. (2013). Scraping the social?: Issues in live social research. *Journal of Cultural Economics*, *6*(3), 313–335. doi:10.1080/17530350.2013.772070

Marshall, A. (1961). *The Principles of Economics* (9th ed.). Macmillan.

Martínez-Plumed, F., Contreras-Ochado, L., Ferri, C., Hernández-Orallo, J., Kull, M., Lachiche, N., & Flach, P. A. (2019). CRISP-DM Twenty Years Later: From Data Mining Processes to Data Science Trajectories. *Transactions on Knowledge & Data Engineering*, *33*(1), 3048–3061. doi:10.1109/TKDE.2019.2962680

Mason, R. J., Farrow, D., & Hattie, J. A. C. (2020). Sports Coaches' Knowledge and Beliefs About the Provision, Reception, and Evaluation of Verbal Feedback. *Frontiers in Psychology*, *11*, 571552. doi:10.3389/fpsyg.2020.571552 PMID:33041941

Mason, W., Vaughan, J. W., & Wallach, H. (2014). Computational social science and social computing. *Machine Learning*, *95*(3), 257–260. doi:10.100710994-013-5426-8

Matei, S. A., & Kee, K. F. (2019). Computational communication research. *WIREs Data Mining and Knowledge Discovery*, *9*(4), 1–18. doi:10.1002/widm.1304

McCloskey, D. N. (1998). *The Rhetoric of Economics*. University of Wisconsin Press.

McLuhan, M., & Lapham, L. H. (1994). *Os meios de comunicação como extensões do homem*. The MIT Press.

Mebane, W., Pineda, A., Woods, L., Klaver, J., Wu, P., & Miller, B. (2017). *Using Twitter to Observe Election Incidents in the United States*. Midwest Political Science Association. https://bit.ly/2T4YQsB

Mehdizadeh, S. (2010). Self-presentation 2.0: Narcissism and self-esteem on Facebook. *Cyberpsychology, Behavior, and Social Networking*, *13*(4), 357–364. doi:10.1089/cyber.2009.0257 PMID:20712493

Meneses, M. (2018). Grandes datos, grandes desafíos para las ciencias sociales. *Revista Mexicana de Sociologia*, *80*(2), 415–444. https://bit.ly/3wAoPFZ

Menzel, H., & Katz, E. (1955). Social Relations and Innovation in the Medical Profession: The Epidemiology of a New Drug. *Public Opinion Quarterly*, *19*(4), 337. doi:10.1086/266584

Meshi, D., Tamir, D. I., & Heekeren, H. R. (2015). The emerging neuroscience of social media. *Trends in Cognitive Sciences*, *19*(12), 771–782. doi:10.1016/j.tics.2015.09.004 PMID:26578288

Mikolov, T., Sutskever, I., Chen, K., Corrado, G. S., & Dean, J. (2013). Distributed Representations of Words and Phrases and Their Compositionality. In Advances in Neural Information Processing Systems (pp. 3111-3119). Academic Press.

Milgram, S. (1967). The Small-World Problem. *Psychology Today*, *1*(1), 61–67.

Miller, J. H., & Page, S. E. (2007). *Complex adaptive systems*. Princeton University Press.

Miotto, R., Wang, F., Wang, S., Jiang, X., & Dudley, J. T. (2018). Deep Learning for Healthcare: Review, Opportunities and Challenges. *Briefings in Bioinformatics*, *19*(6), 1236–1246. doi:10.1093/bib/bbx044 PMID:28481991

Mitchell, M. (2009). *Complexity: A guided tour*. Oxford University Press.

Montavon, G., Samek, W., & Muller, K.-R. (2018). Methods for Interpreting and Understanding Deep Neural Networks. *Digital Signal Processing*, *73*, 1–15. doi:10.1016/j.dsp.2017.10.011

Mordvintsev, A., Olah, C., & Tyka, M. (2015). *Inceptionism: Going Deeper Into Neural Networks*. https://ai.googleblog.com/2015/06/inceptionism-going-deeper-into-neural.html

Moreno, J. L. (1934). *Who Shall Survive? A New Approach to the Problem of Human Interrelations*. Nervous and Mental Disease Publishing Company. doi:10.1037/10648-000

Moreno, J. L. (1937). Sociometry in relation to other social sciences. *Sociometry*, *1*(1/2), 206–219. doi:10.2307/2785266

Moreo, A., Esuli, A., & Sebastiani, F. (2019). Learning to Weight for Text Classification. *IEEE Transactions on Knowledge and Data Engineering*, *32*(2), 302–316. doi:10.1109/TKDE.2018.2883446

Moro, A. (2016). Understanding the Dynamics of Violent Political Revolutions in an Agent-Based Framework. *PLoS One*, *11*(4), e0154175. doi:10.1371/journal.pone.0154175 PMID:27104855

Morrison, A. (2016, February 23). *Attention governments: Big Data is a game changer for businesses*. Retrieved from https://blogs.worldbank.org/opendata/attention-governments-big-data-game-changer-businesses

Morris, S. (1995). The Common Prior Assumption in Economic Theory. *Economics and Philosophy*, *11*(02), 227–253. doi:10.1017/S0266267100003382

Morton, R. B., & Williams, K. C. (2008). Experimentation in Political Science. In J. Box-Steffensmeier, H. E. Brady, & D. Collier (Eds.), *The Oxford handbook of political methodology* (pp. 339–357). Oxford University Press.

Moyano, J. M., Gibaja, E. L., Ciosb, K. J., & Ventura, S. (2018). Review of ensembles of multi-label classifiers: Models, experimental study and prospects. *Information Fusion*, *44*, 33–45. doi:10.1016/j.inffus.2017.12.001

Muise, A., Christofides, E., & Desmarais, S. (2009). More information than you ever wanted: Does Facebook bring out the green-eyed monster of jealousy? *Cyberpsychology & Behavior*, *12*(4), 441–444. doi:10.1089/cpb.2008.0263 PMID:19366318

Muqaddas, J., Soomro, S. A., & Ahmad, N. (2017). Impact of Social Media on Self-Steem. *European Scientific Journal*, *13*(23), 329–341. doi:10.19044/esj.2017.v13n23p329

Mutoh, A., Imura, Y., Kato, R., Matsui, T., & Inuzuka, N. (2016). A model of friendship networks based on social network analysis. *Artificial Life and Robotics*, *21*(2), 165–170. doi:10.100710015-016-0275-8

Nadjahi, C., Louahlia, H., & Lemasson, S. (2018). A review of thermal management and innovative cooling strategies for data center. *Sustainable Computing: Informatics and Systems*, *19*, 14–28. doi:10.1016/j.suscom.2018.05.002

Nadkarni, P. M., Ohno-Machado, L., & Chapman, W. W. (2011). Natural language processing: An introduction. *Journal of the American Medical Informatics Association: JAMIA*, *18*(5), 544–551. doi:10.1136/amiajnl-2011-000464 PMID:21846786

Nambisan, S., Lyytinen, K., Majchrzak, A., & Song, M. (2017). Digital innovation management: Reinventing innovation management research in a digital world. *MIS Quartely*, *41*(1), 223–238. doi:10.25300/MISQ/2017/41:1.03

NASA. (2020, October 15). *International Cooperation*. Retrieved from https://www.nasa.gov/mission_pages/station/cooperation/index.html

Nasukawa, T., & Yi, J. (2003). Sentiment analysis: Capturing favorability using natural language processing. *2nd International Conference on Knowledge Capture*, 70-77. 10.1145/945645.945658

Neresini, F. (2017). Old media and new opportunities for a computational social science on PCST. *Journal of Science Communication*, *16*(2), C03. doi:10.22323/2.16020303

Nguyen, B., & Wait, A. (2015). *Essentials of Microeconomics*. Routledge. doi:10.4324/9781315690339

Nielsen, F. Å. (2011). *A new ANEW: Evaluation of a word list for sentiment analysis in microblogs*. arXiv preprint arXiv:1103.2903.

Niemann-Lenz, J., Bruns, S., Hefner, D., Knop-Huelss, K., Possler, D., & Reich, S. (2019). Crafting a Strategic Roadmap for Computational Methods in Communication Science: Learnings from the CCS 2018 Conference in Hanover | Commentary. *International Journal of Communication*, *13*, 3885–3893.

Now-Casting. (n.d.). www.now-casting.com

Noyes, E. (n.d.). *Structural Hole Theory: The Relationship between Corporate Ties and Corporate Innovation*. Retrieved on September 02, 2016 from https://www.bu.edu/tech/support/research/visualization/gallery/structhole/

Obermeyer, Z., Powers, B., Vogeli, C., & Mullainathan, S. (2019). Dissecting Racial Bias in an Algorithm Used to Manage the Health of Populations. *Science*, *366*(6464), 447–453. doi:10.1126cience.aax2342 PMID:31649194

Oboler, A., Welsh, K., & Cruz, L. (2012). The Danger of Big Data: Social Media as Computational Social Science. *First Monday*, *17*(7).

Oliveira, S. F., Furlinger, K., & Kranzlmuller, D. (2012). Trends in Computation, Communication and Storage and the Consequences for Data-intensive Science. *2012 IEEE 14th International Conference on High Performance Computing and Communication & 2012 IEEE 9th International Conference on Embedded Software and Systems*, 572–579. 10.1109/HPCC.2012.83

Olteanu, A., Castillo, C., Diaz, F., & Kiciman, E. (2019). Social Data: Biases, Methodological Pitfalls, and Ethical Boundaries. *Frontiers in Big Data*, *2*, 13. doi:10.3389/fdata.2019.00013 PMID:33693336

Otter, D. W., Medina, J. R., & Kalita, J. K. (2020). A Survey of the Usages of Deep Learning for Natural Language Processing. *IEEE Transactions on Neural Networks and Learning Systems*, *32*(2), 604–624. doi:10.1109/TNNLS.2020.2979670 PMID:32324570

Ovide, S. (2021, January 13). The Truth About Your WhatsApp Data. *The New York Times*. Retrieved from https://www.nytimes.com/2021/01/13/technology/whatsapp-data.html

Pañellas, D. (2020). Grupos e identidades sociales en cambio. *Novedades en Población*, *16*(31), 64–84. https://bit.ly/3egvdvI

Paterson, M., & Mc Donagh, M. (2018). Data Protection in an era of Big Data: The challenges posed by big personal data. *Monash University Law Review. Monash University. Faculty of Law*, *44*(1), 1–31. https://bit.ly/3i6YKcG

Pauwels, L., & Mannay, D. (2019). *The SAGE handbook of visual research methods*. University of Antwerp.

Peng, T.-Q., Liang, H., & Zhu, J. J. H. (2019). Introducing computational social science for Asia-Pacific communication research. *Asian Journal of Communication*, *29*(3), 205–216. doi:10.1080/01292986.2019.1602911

Peng, Y. (2018). Same Candidates, Different Faces: Uncovering Media Bias in Visual Portrayals of Presidential Candidates with Computer Vision. *Journal of Communication*, *68*(5), 920–941. doi:10.1093/joc/jqy041

Pennebaker, J. W., Francis, M. E., & Booth, R. J. (2001). Linguistic Inquiry and Word Count: LIWC 2001. Lawrence Erlbaum Associates.

Pennebaker, J., Boyd, R., Jordan, K., & Blackburn. (2015). *The Development and Psychometric Properties of LIWC2015*. University of Texas at Austin. https://bit.ly/3hH9UG5

Peterson, A., & Spirling, A. (2018). Classification Accuracy as a Substantive Quantity of Interest: Measuring polarization in Westminster systems. *Political Analysis*, *26*(1), 120–128. doi:10.1017/pan.2017.39

Pierson, P. (2004). *Politics in Time: History, Institutions, and Social Analysis* (1st ed.). Princeton University Press. doi:10.1515/9781400841080

Poppe, K., Wolfert, J., Verdouw, C. N., & Renwick, A. (2015). A European perspective on the economics of big data. *Farm Policy Journal*, *12*(1), 11–19.

Porcelli, A. M. (2020). La inteligencia artificial y la robótica: sus dilemas sociales, éticos y jurídicos. *Derecho global. Estudios sobre derecho y justicia, 6*(16), 49-105. doi:10.32870/dgedj.v6i16.286

PyTorch. (2021). *From Research to Production*. https://pytorch.org/

Qin, J. (2017). *Biased sampling, over-identified parameter problems and beyond*. Springer. doi:10.1007/978-981-10-4856-2

Radford, A., Narasimhan, K., Salimans, T., & Sutskever, I. (2018). *Improving Language Understanding by Generative Pre-Training. Technical Report*. OpenAI.

Rains, S. A. (2020). Big Data, Computational Social Science, and Health Communication: A Review and Agenda for Advancing Theory. *Health Communication*, *35*(1), 26–34. doi:10.1080/10410236.2018.1536955 PMID:30351198

Ramos, A. G. (2020). 9. Para-economy: Paradigm and Multicentric Allocative Model. In The New Sciences Organizations (pp. 153-165). University of Toronto Press.

Rashidi, T., Abbasi, A., Maghrebi, M., Hasan, S., & Waller, T. (2017). Exploring the capacity of social media data for modelling travel behaviour: Opportunities and challenges. *Transportation Research Part C, Emerging Technologies*, *75*, 197–211. doi:10.1016/j.trc.2016.12.008

Rasmussen, L. (2018). Parasocial Interaction in the Digital Age: An Examination of Relationship Building and the Effectiveness of YouTube Celebrities. *Social Media + Society*, *7*, 280–294. https://bit.ly/3hyPLBN

Rathore, A. K., Kar, A. K., & Ilavarasan, P. V. (2017). Social Media Analytics: Literature Review and Directions for Future Research. *Decision Analysis*, *14*(4), 229–249. doi:10.1287/deca.2017.0355

Recht, B., Roelofs, R., Schmidt, L., & Shankar, V. (2019). Do ImageNet Classifiers Generalize to ImageNet? In *International Conference on Machine Learning* (pp. 5389-5400). Academic Press.

Ribeiro, M. T., Singh, S., & Guestrin, C. (2016). "Why Should I Trust You?" Explaining The Predictions of Any Classifier. In *Proceedings of the 22nd ACM SIGKDD International Conference on Knowledge Discovery and Data Mining* (pp. 1135-1144). 10.1145/2939672.2939778

Rice, D., Rhodes, J. H., & Nteta, T. (2019). Racial Bias in Legal Language. *Research & Politics*, *6*(2), 2053168019848930. doi:10.1177/2053168019848930

Richards, N. M., & King, J. H. (2014). Big data ethics. *Wake Forest Law Review*, *49*, 393.

Richardson, D. C. (2000). *MAGE, Computer Software*. Duke University.

Rogers, E. M. (1983). *Diffusion of innovations* (3rd ed.). Free Press.

Rosnay, M., Pons, F., Harris, P. L., & Morrell, J. M. B. (2004). A lag between understanding false belief and emotion attribution in young children: Relationships with linguistic ability and mothers' mental-state language. *British Journal of Developmental Psychology*, *22*(2), 197–218. doi:10.1348/026151004323044573

RStudio Team. (2019). *RStudio: Integrated Development for R*. RStudio. https://www.rstudio.com/

Sadeh, E. (2013). Cooperation in Orbit: The Evolution of the International Space Station Program. *World Politics Review*. Retrieved from https://www.worldpoliticsreview.com/articles/12803/cooperation-in-orbit-the-evolution-of-the-international-space-station-program

Safari, R. M., Rahmani, A. M., & Alizadeh, S. H. (2019). User behavior mining on social media: A systematic literature review. *Multimedia Tools and Applications*, *78*(23), 33747–33804. doi:10.100711042-019-08046-6

Salganik, M. J. (2017). *Bit by bit: Social research in the digital age*. Princeton University Press.

Samuel, A. L. (1959). Some Studies in Machine Learning Using the Game of Checkers. *IBM Journal of Research and Development*, *3*(3), 210–229. doi:10.1147/rd.33.0210

Savci, M., Turan, M. E., Griffiths, M. D., & Ercengiz, M. (2019). Histrionic Personality, Narcissistic Personality, and Problematic Social Media Use: Testing of a New Hypothetical Model. *International Journal of Mental Health and Addiction*. Advance online publication. doi:10.100711469-019-00139-5

Savoy, J. (2010). Lexical Analysis of Us Political Speeches. *Journal of Quantitative Linguistics*, *17*(2), 123–141. doi:10.1080/09296171003643205

Schelling, T. C. (1971). Dynamic models of segregation. *The Journal of Mathematical Sociology*, *1*(2), 143–186. doi:10.1080/0022250X.1971.9989794

Schlauch, W., Obradovic, D., & Dengel, A. (2012, September). Organizational Social Network Analysis–Case Study in a Research Facility. In *35th German Conference on Artificial Intelligence* (p. 78). Academic Press.

Schmidt, E., & Cohen, J. (2013). *The New Digital Age*. Knopf.

Schwartz, P. M. (2003). Property, privacy, and personal data. *Harvard Law Review*, *117*(7), 2056. doi:10.2307/4093335

Scott, J. (1992). *Social Network Analysis*. Sage.

Seidman, G. (2013). Self-presentation and belonging on Facebook: How personality influences. *Personality and Individual Differences*, *54*(3), 402–407. doi:10.1016/j.paid.2012.10.009

Seidman, S. B., & Foster, B. L. (1979). Sonet-1: Social network analysis and modeling system. *Social Networks*, *2*(1), 85–90. doi:10.1016/0378-8733(79)90013-3

Sen, I., Flock, F., & Wagner, C. (2020). On the Reliability and Validity of Detecting Approval of Political Actors in Tweets. In *Proceedings of the 2020 Conference on Empirical Methods in Natural Language Processing (EMNLP)* (pp. 1413-1426). 10.18653/v1/2020.emnlp-main.110

Shah, D. V., Cappella, J. N., & Neuman, W. R. (2015). Big Data, Digital Media, and Computational Social Science: Possibilities and Perils. *The Annals of the American Academy of Political and Social Science*, *659*(1), 6–13. doi:10.1177/0002716215572084

Sharma, A., & Shekhar, H. (2020). Intelligent Learning based Opinion Mining Model for Governmental Decision Making. *Procedia Computer Science*, *173*, 216–224. doi:10.1016/j.procs.2020.06.026

Sherstinsky, A. (2020). Fundamentals of Recurrent Neural Network (RNN) and Long Short-Term Memory (LSTM) Network. *Physica D. Nonlinear Phenomena*, *404*, 132306. doi:10.1016/j.physd.2019.132306

Sil, R., & Katzenstein, P. J. (2010). *Beyond Paradigms: Analytic Eclecticism in the Study of World Politics (Political Analysis*. Palgrave Macmillan. Stalnaker, R. (2009). Iterated Belief Revision. *Erkenntnis*, *70*(2), 189–209. doi:10.100710670-008-9147-5

Soffer, O., & Geifman, D. (2020). Comparing research topics in European and International Communication Association journals: Computational analysis. *The International Communication Gazette*, *0*(0), 1–13. doi:10.1177/1748048520928334

Sola, S. (2018). Los sentidos e interpretaciones del yo: Un análisis multidimensional. *Dixit*, (29), 20-33. https://bit.ly/2VrLrvt

Soltanshahi, M., Asemi, R., & Shafiei, N. (2019). Energy-aware virtual machines allocation by krill herd algorithm in cloud data centers. *Heliyon*, *5*(7), e02066. doi:10.1016/j.heliyon.2019.e02066 PMID:31372538

Sonia, V. (2020). Opinion Mining Techniques and Its Applications: A Review. In *Proceedings of First International Conference on Computing, Communications, and Cyber-Security* (pp. 549-559). Springer. 10.1007/978-981-15-3369-3_41

Sorokowski, P., Sorokowska, A., Oleszkiewicz, A., Frackowiak, T., Huk, A., & Pisanski, K. (2015). Selfie posting behaviors are associated with narcissism among men. *Personality and Individual Differences*, *85*, 123–127. doi:10.1016/j.paid.2015.05.004

Stockdale, L. A., & Coyne, S. M. (2020). Bored and online: Reasons for using social media, problematic social networking site use, and behavioral outcomes across the transition from adolescence to emerging adulthood. *Journal of Adolescence*, *79*, 173–183. doi:10.1016/j.adolescence.2020.01.010 PMID:31978836

Stoicescu, C. (2016). Big Data, the perfect instrument to study today's consumer behavior. *Database Systems Journal*, *6*, 28–42.

Suttles, J., & Ide, N. (2013). *Distant Supervision for Emotion Classification with Discrete Binary Values*. Computational Linguistics and Intelligent Text Processing. doi:10.1007/978-3-642-37256-8_11

Takhteyev, Y., Gruzd, A., & Wellman, B. (2012). Geography of Twitter networks. *Social Networks*, *34*(1), 73–81. doi:10.1016/j.socnet.2011.05.006

Tamir, D. I., & Ward, A. F. (2015). Old desires, new media. The Psychology of Desire, 432-455.

Taraktaş, B., & Över, D. (2017). When does repression trigger mass protest? The 2013 Gezi protests. *Research in Social Movements, Conflicts and Change, 41*, 207-241.

Taylor, L., Schroeder, R., & Meyer, E. (2014). Emerging practices and perspectives on Big Data analysis in economics: Bigger and better or more of the same? *Big Data & Society*, *1*(2), 2053951714536877. doi:10.1177/2053951714536877

Tesfatsion, L., & Judd, K. L. (Eds.). (2006). *Handbook of computational economics: agent-based computational economics*. Elsevier.

Thelwall, M., Buckley, K., Paltoglou, G., Cai, D., & Kappas, A. (2010). Sentiment strength detection for the social Web. *Journal of the American Society for Information Science and Technology*, *61*(12), 2544–2558. doi:10.1002/asi.21416

Thomas, M., Pang, B., & Lee, L. (2006). Get Out the Vote: Determining Support or Opposition From Congressional Floor-Debate Transcripts. In *Proceedings of the 2006 Conference on Empirical Methods in Natural Language Processing* (pp. 327-335). 10.3115/1610075.1610122

Thorson, E. (2016). Belief Echoes: The Persistent Effects of Corrected Misinformation. *Political Communication*, *33*(3), 460–480. doi:10.1080/10584609.2015.1102187

Tokui, S., Okuta, R., Akiba, T., Niitani, Y., Ogawa, T., Saito, S., Suzuki, S., Uenishi, K., Vogel, B., & Vincent, H. (2019). Chainer: A Deep Learning Framework for Accelerat- ing the Research Cycle. *25th ACM SIGKDD Conference on Knowledge Discovery and Data Mining*. 10.1145/3292500.3330756

Törnberg, P., & Törnberg, A. (2018). The limits of computation: A philosophical critique of contemporary Big Data research. *Big Data & Society*, *5*(2). doi:10.1177/2053951718811843

Travers, J., & Milgram, S. (1969). An Experimental Study of the Small World Problem. *Sociometry*, *32*(4), 425–443. doi:10.2307/2786545

Tsamados, A., Aggarwal, N., Cowls, J., Morley, J., Roberts, H., Taddeo, M., & Floridi, L. (2021). The Ethics of Algorithms: Key Problems and Solutions. *AI & Society*, 1–16.

Tsihrintzis, G., & Jain, L. (2020). *Machine learning paradigms: Advances in Deep Learning-based technological applications*. Springer. doi:10.1007/978-3-030-49724-8

Tsoumakas, G., Katakis, I., & Vlahavas, I. (2006). A Review of Multi-Label Classification Methods. In *Proceedings of the 2nd ADBIS Workshop on Data Mining and Knowledge Discovery (ADMKD 2006)*, (pp. 99-109). Academic Press.

Tsui, A., Egan, T., & O'Reilly, Ch. (1992). Being Different: Relational Demography and Organizational Attachment. *Administrative Science Quarterly*, *37*(4), 549–579. https://bit.ly/3eecilk. doi:10.2307/2393472

Turco, C. J., & Zuckerman, E. W. (2017). Verstehen for Sociology: Comment on Watts. *American Journal of Sociology*, *122*(4), 1272–1291. doi:10.1086/690762

Turrell, A. (2016). Agent-based models: understanding the economy from the bottom up. *Bank of England Quarterly Bulletin*, Q4.

Unckless, R. L., Rottschaefer, S. M., & Lazzaro, B. P. (2015). The Complex Contributions of Genetics and Nutrition to Immunity in Drosophila melanogaster. *PLOS Genetics*, *11*(3), e1005030. doi:10.1371/journal.pgen.1005030 PMID:25764027

United Nations. (n.d.). *United Nations Committee of Experts on Big Data and Data Science for Official Statistics* [UN-CEBD]. https://unstats.un.org/bigdata/

Ureña, R. (2019). Autoridad algorítmica: ¿cómo empezar a pensar la protección de los derechos humanos en la era del "big data"? *Louisiana Law Review*, *2*(2), 99–124. doi:10.29263/lar02.2019.05

Urman, A. (2020). Context matters: Political polarization on Twitter from a comparative perspective. *Media Culture & Society*, *42*(6), 857–879. doi:10.1177/0163443719876541

Utz, S., Muscanell, N., & Khalid, C. (2015). Snapchat Elicits More Jealousy than Facebook: A Comparison of Snapchat and Facebook Use. *Cyberpsychology, Behavior, and Social Networking*, *18*(3), 141–146. doi:10.1089/cyber.2014.0479 PMID:25667961

van Atteveldt, W., Margolin, D., Shen, C., Trilling, D., & Weber, R. (2019). A Roadmap for Computational Communication Research. *Computer Communication Review*, *1*(1), 1–11. doi:10.5117/CCR2019.1.001.VANA

van Atteveldt, W., & Peng, T.-Q. (2018). When Communication Meets Computation: Opportunities, Challenges, and Pitfalls in Computational Communication Science. *Communication Methods and Measures*, *12*(2–3), 81–92. doi:10.1080/19312458.2018.1458084

van der Hulst, R. C. (2009). Introduction to Social Network Analysis (SNA) as an investigative tool. *Trends in Organized Crime*, *12*(2), 101–121. doi:10.100712117-008-9057-6

Varian, H. R. (2014). Big Data: New Tricks for Econometrics. *The Journal of Economic Perspectives*, *28*(2), 3–28. doi:10.1257/jep.28.2.3

Veblen, T. (1898). Why is economics not an evolutionary science? *The Quarterly Journal of Economics*, *12*(4), 373–397. doi:10.2307/1882952

Vernette, É. (2004). Targeting Women's Clothing Fashion Opinion Leaders in Media Planning: An Application for Magazines. *Journal of Advertising Research*, *44*(1), 90–107. doi:10.1017/S0021849904040061

Volpi, J. H. (2004). *Particularidades sobre o temperamento, a personalidade e o caráter, segundo a psicologia corporal*. Centro Reichiano.

Wagner, C. H. (1982). Simpson's Paradox in Real Life. *The American Statistician*, *36*(1), 46–48. doi:10.1080/00031305.1982.10482778

Wallace, L., James, T. L., & Warkentin, M. (2017). How do you feel about your friends? Understanding situational envy in online social networks. *Information & Management*, *54*(5), 669–682. doi:10.1016/j.im.2016.12.010

Wang, W., Chen, L., Thirunarayan, K., & Sheth, A. P. (2012). Harnessing twitter "big data" for automatic emotion identification. In *Privacy, Security, Risk and Trust (PASSAT), 2012 International Conference on and 2012 International Conference on Social Computing (SocialCom)* (pp. 587-592). IEEE.

Wang, L., Wang, S., Yuan, Z., & Peng, L. (2021). Analyzing potential tourist behavior using PCA and modified affinity propagation clustering based on Baidu index: Taking Beijing city as an example. *Data Science and Management*, *2*, 12–19. doi:10.1016/j.dsm.2021.05.001

Wang, Y., Xie, X., Wang, X., Wang, P., Nie, J., & Lei, L. (2018). Narcissism and selfie-posting behavior: The mediating role of body satisfaction and the moderating role of attitude toward selfie-posting behavior. *Current Psychology (New Brunswick, N.J.)*. Advance online publication. doi:10.100712144-018-9795-9

Wasserman, S. & Faust, K. (1994). *Social network analysis: Methods and applications* (Vol. 8). Cambridge University Press.

Wasserman, S., & Faust, K. (1994). *Social Network Analysis: Methods and Applications*. Cambridge University Press. doi:10.1017/CBO9780511815478

Watts, D. J. (1999). Networks, Dynamics, and the Small-World Phenomenon. *American Journal of Sociology, 105*(2), 493–527. doi:10.1086/210318

Watts, D. J. (2002). A simple model of global cascades on random networks. *Proceedings of the National Academy of Sciences of the United States of America, 99*(9), 5766–5771. doi:10.1073/pnas.082090499 PMID:16578874

Watts, D. J., & Dodds, P. S. (2007). Influentials, Networks, and Public Opinion Formation. *The Journal of Consumer Research, 34*(4), 441–458. doi:10.1086/518527

Weaver, W. (1948). Science and complexity. *American Scientist, 36*(4), 536–544. PMID:18882675

Weber, T., Sadri, G., & Gentry, W. (2018). Examining diversity beliefs and leader performance across cultures. *Cross Cultural & Strategic Management, 25*(3), 382–400. doi:10.1108/CCSM-11-2016-0200

Weimann, G. (1991). The Influentials: Back to the Concept of Opinion Leaders? *Public Opinion Quarterly, 55*(2), 267–279. doi:10.1086/269257

Wilensky, U., & Rand, W. (2015). *An introduction to agent-based modeling: Modeling natural, social, and engineered complex systems with NetLogo*. The MIT Press.

Windsor, L. C. (2020). Advancing Interdisciplinary Work in Computational Communication Science. *Political Communication*, 1–10. doi:10.1080/10584609.2020.1765915

Wiszniewski, D., & Coyne, R. (2002). Mask and Identity: The Hermeneutics of Self-Construction in the Information. In Building Virtual Communities: Learning and Change in Cyberspace (Learning in Doing: Social, Cognitive and Computational Perspectives) (pp. 191-214). Cambridge University Press.

Witten, I. H. (2005). Text mining. In *Practical handbook of internet computing*. Chapman & Hall/CRC Press.

Witten, I., Frank, E., Hall, M., & Pal, C. (2017). *Data Mining: Practical Machine Learning Tools and Techniques*. Morgan Kaufmann.

Wolf, A. G., Rieger, S., & Knauff, M. (2012). The effects of source trustworthiness and inference type on human belief revision. *Thinking & Reasoning*, *18*(4), 417–440. doi:10.1080/13546783.2012.677757

Wong, F., Tan, C., Sen, S., & Chiang, M. (2016). Quantifying political leaning from tweets retweets and retweeters. *IEEE Transactions on Knowledge and Data Engineering*, *28*(8), 2158–2172. doi:10.1109/TKDE.2016.2553667

World University Rankings. (2021). World University Rankings 2021. *Times Higher Education*. Retrieved from https://www.timeshighereducation.com/world-university-rankings/2021/world-ranking#!/page/0/length/25/sort_by/rank/sort_order/asc/cols/stats

Wright, J. (2003). *The ethics of economic rationalism*. UNSW Press.

Wu, J., & Srite, M. (2021). Envy on social media: The good, the bad and the ugly. *International Journal of Information Management*, *56*, 16. doi:10.1016/j.ijinfomgt.2020.102255

Wu, L., Morstatter, F., Carley, K. M., & Liu, H. (2019). Misinformation in Social Media: Definition, Manipulation, and Detection. *SIGKDD Explorations*, *21*(2), 80–90. doi:10.1145/3373464.3373475

Xu, S. (2018). Naïve Bayesian Bayes classifiers for text classification. *Journal of Information Science*, *44*(1), 48–59. doi:10.1177/0165551516677946

Xusheng, L., Chengcheng, F., Ran, Z., Duo, Z., Tingting, H., & Xingpeng, J. (2018). A hybrid deep learning framework for bacterial named entity recognition with domain features. *BMC Bioinformatics*, *20*(S16), 1–9. doi:10.118612859-019-3071-3 PMID:31787075

Yadav, A., & Vishwakarma, D. K. (2020). Sentiment analysis using deep learning architectures: A review. *Artificial Intelligence Review*, *53*(6), 4335–4385. doi:10.100710462-019-09794-5

Yu, B., Kaufmann, S., & Diermeier, D. (2008). Classifying Party Affiliation From Political Speech. *Journal of Information Technology & Politics*, *5*(1), 33–48. doi:10.1080/19331680802149608

Yue, L., Chen, W., Li, X., Zuo, W., & Yin, M. (2019). A survey of sentiment analysis in social media. *Knowledge and Information Systems*, *60*(2), 617–663. doi:10.100710115-018-1236-4

Zervoudakis, S., Marakakis, E., Kondylakis, H., & Goumas, S. (2018). OpinionMine: A Bayesian-based framework for opinion mining using Twitter Data. *Machine Learning with Applications*, *3*, 100018. doi:10.1016/j.mlwa.2020.100018

Zheng, C., Liu, & Wong, H. (2015). Iterative term weighting for short text data. *IEEE International Conference on Systems, Man, and Cybernetics*, 1687-1692. 10.1109/SMC.2015.297

Zhou, L., Pan, S., Wang, J., & Vasilakos, A. V. (2017). Machine Learning on Big Data: Opportunities and Challenges. *Neurocomputing*, *237*, 350–361. doi:10.1016/j.neucom.2017.01.026

Zhou, X., & Zafarani, R. (2020). A Survey of Fake News: Fundamental Theories, Detection Methods, and Opportunities. *ACM Computing Surveys*, *53*(5), 1–40. doi:10.1145/3395046

Related References

To continue our tradition of advancing media and communications research, we have compiled a list of recommended IGI Global readings. These references will provide additional information and guidance to further enrich your knowledge and assist you with your own research and future publications.

Abashian, N., & Fisher, S. (2018). Intercultural Effectiveness in Libraries: Supporting Success Through Collaboration With Co-Curricular Programs. In B. Blummer, J. Kenton, & M. Wiatrowski (Eds.), *Promoting Ethnic Diversity and Multiculturalism in Higher Education* (pp. 219–236). Hershey, PA: IGI Global. doi:10.4018/978-1-5225-4097-7.ch012

Adebayo, O., Fagbohun, M. O., Esse, U. C., & Nwokeoma, N. M. (2018). Change Management in the Academic Library: Transition From Print to Digital Collections. In R. Bhardwaj (Ed.), *Digitizing the Modern Library and the Transition From Print to Electronic* (pp. 1–28). Hershey, PA: IGI Global. doi:10.4018/978-1-5225-2119-8.ch001

Adegbore, A. M., Quadri, M. O., & Oyewo, O. R. (2018). A Theoretical Approach to the Adoption of Electronic Resource Management Systems (ERMS) in Nigerian University Libraries. In A. Tella & T. Kwanya (Eds.), *Handbook of Research on Managing Intellectual Property in Digital Libraries* (pp. 292–311). Hershey, PA: IGI Global. doi:10.4018/978-1-5225-3093-0.ch015

Adesola, A. P., & Olla, G. O. (2018). Unlocking the Unlimited Potentials of Koha OSS/ILS for Library House-Keeping Functions: A Global View. In M. Khosrow-Pour (Ed.), *Optimizing Contemporary Application and Processes in Open Source Software* (pp. 124–163). Hershey, PA: IGI Global. doi:10.4018/978-1-5225-5314-4.ch006

Adesola, A. P., & Olla, G. O. (2019). Bridging the Digital Divide in Nigerian Information Landscape: The Role of the Library. *International Journal of Digital Literacy and Digital Competence, 10*(3), 10–31. doi:10.4018/IJDLDC.2019070102

Adetayo, A. J. (2021). Fake News and Social Media Censorship: Examining the Librarian Role. In R. Blankenship (Ed.), *Deep Fakes, Fake News, and Misinformation in Online Teaching and Learning Technologies* (pp. 69–92). IGI Global. https://doi.org/10.4018/978-1-7998-6474-5.ch004

Adetayo, A. J. (2022). Building Civic Engagement in Smart Cities: Role of Smart Libraries. In M. Taher (Ed.), *Handbook of Research on the Role of Libraries, Archives, and Museums in Achieving Civic Engagement and Social Justice in Smart Cities* (pp. 314–333). IGI Global. https://doi.org/10.4018/978-1-7998-8363-0.ch017

Adigun, G. O., Sobalaje, A. J., & Salau, S. A. (2018). Social Media and Copyright in Digital Libraries. In A. Tella & T. Kwanya (Eds.), *Handbook of Research on Managing Intellectual Property in Digital Libraries* (pp. 19–36). Hershey, PA: IGI Global. doi:10.4018/978-1-5225-3093-0.ch002

Adriyana, L., & Fitrina Cahyaningtyas, D. (2022). The Importance of Rural Library Services Based on Social Inclusion in Indonesia. In M. Taher (Ed.), *Handbook of Research on the Role of Libraries, Archives, and Museums in Achieving Civic Engagement and Social Justice in Smart Cities* (pp. 201–218). IGI Global. https://doi.org/10.4018/978-1-7998-8363-0.ch010

Afolabi, O. A. (2018). Myths and Challenges of Building an Effective Digital Library in Developing Nations: An African Perspective. In A. Tella & T. Kwanya (Eds.), *Handbook of Research on Managing Intellectual Property in Digital Libraries* (pp. 51–79). Hershey, PA: IGI Global. doi:10.4018/978-1-5225-3093-0.ch004

Ahuja, Y., & Kumar, P. (2017). Web 2.0 Tools and Application: Knowledge Management and Sharing in Libraries. In B. Gunjal (Ed.), *Managing Knowledge and Scholarly Assets in Academic Libraries* (pp. 218–234). Hershey, PA: IGI Global. doi:10.4018/978-1-5225-1741-2.ch010

Ajmi, A. (2018). Developing In-House Digital Tools: Case Studies From the UMKC School of Law Library. In L. Costello & M. Powers (Eds.), *Developing In-House Digital Tools in Library Spaces* (pp. 117–139). Hershey, PA: IGI Global. doi:10.4018/978-1-5225-2676-6.ch006

Al-Kharousi, R., Al-Harrasi, N. H., Jabur, N. H., & Bouazza, A. (2018). Soft Systems Methodology (SSM) as an Interdisciplinary Approach: Reflection on the Use of SSM in Adoption of Web 2.0 Applications in Omani Academic Libraries. In M. Al-Suqri, A. Al-Kindi, S. AlKindi, & N. Saleem (Eds.), *Promoting Interdisciplinarity in Knowledge Generation and Problem Solving* (pp. 243–257). Hershey, PA: IGI Global. doi:10.4018/978-1-5225-3878-3.ch016

Alenzuela, R. (2017). Research, Leadership, and Resource-Sharing Initiatives: The Role of Local Library Consortia in Access to Medical Information. In S. Ram (Ed.), *Library and Information Services for Bioinformatics Education and Research* (pp. 199–211). Hershey, PA: IGI Global. doi:10.4018/978-1-5225-1871-6.ch012

Alenzuela, R., & Terry, M. A. (2020). Diversity, Indigenous Knowledge, and LIS Pedagogy: Conceptualizing Formal Education in Library and Information Studies in Vanuatu. In R. Alenzuela, H. Kim, & D. Baylen (Eds.), *Internationalization of Library and Information Science Education in the Asia-Pacific Region* (pp. 50–77). IGI Global. doi:10.4018/978-1-7998-2273-8.ch003

Allison, D. (2017). When Sales Talk Meets Reality: Implementing a Self-Checkout Kiosk. In E. Iglesias (Ed.), *Library Technology Funding, Planning, and Deployment* (pp. 36–54). Hershey, PA: IGI Global. doi:10.4018/978-1-5225-1735-1.ch003

Anglim, C. T., & Rusk, F. (2018). Empowering DC's Future Through Information Access. In A. Burtin, J. Fleming, & P. Hampton-Garland (Eds.), *Changing Urban Landscapes Through Public Higher Education* (pp. 57–77). Hershey, PA: IGI Global. doi:10.4018/978-1-5225-3454-9.ch003

Asmi, N. A. (2017). Social Media and Library Services. *International Journal of Library and Information Services*, *6*(2), 23–36. doi:10.4018/IJLIS.2017070103

Attademo, G., & Maccaro, A. (2022). Research Ethics in the Social Sciences. In G. Punziano & A. Delli Paoli (Eds.), *Handbook of Research on Advanced Research Methodologies for a Digital Society* (pp. 54–64). IGI Global. https://doi.org/10.4018/978-1-7998-8473-6.ch005

Awoyemi, R. A. (2018). Adoption and Use of Innovative Mobile Technologies in Nigerian Academic Libraries. In J. Keengwe (Ed.), *Handbook of Research on Digital Content, Mobile Learning, and Technology Integration Models in Teacher Education* (pp. 354–389). Hershey, PA: IGI Global. doi:10.4018/978-1-5225-2953-8.ch019

Awoyemi, R. A. (2018). Adoption and Use of Innovative Mobile Technologies in Nigerian Academic Libraries. In J. Keengwe (Ed.), *Handbook of Research on Digital Content, Mobile Learning, and Technology Integration Models in Teacher Education* (pp. 354–389). Hershey, PA: IGI Global. doi:10.4018/978-1-5225-2953-8.ch019

Awoyemi, R. A., & Awoyemi, R. O. (2021). Beyond the Physical Library Space: Creating a 21st Century Digitally-Oriented Library Environment. In C. Chisita, R. Enakrire, O. Durodolu, V. Tsabedze, & J. Ngoaketsi (Eds.), *Handbook of Research on Records and Information Management Strategies for Enhanced Knowledge Coordination* (pp. 189–203). IGI Global. https://doi.org/10.4018/978-1-7998-6618-3.ch012

Babatope, I. S. (2018). Social Media Applications as Effective Service Delivery Tools for Librarians. In M. Khosrow-Pour, D.B.A. (Ed.), Encyclopedia of Information Science and Technology, Fourth Edition (pp. 5252-5261). Hershey, PA: IGI Global. doi:10.4018/978-1-5225-2255-3.ch456

Bakare, A. A. (2018). Digital Libraries and Copyright of Intellectual Property: An Ethical Practice Management. In A. Tella & T. Kwanya (Eds.), *Handbook of Research on Managing Intellectual Property in Digital Libraries* (pp. 377–395). Hershey, PA: IGI Global. doi:10.4018/978-1-5225-3093-0.ch019

Baker, A. A. (2020). To Whose Benefit? At What Cost?: Consideration for Ethical Issues in Social Science Research. In M. Baran & J. Jones (Eds.), *Applied Social Science Approaches to Mixed Methods Research* (pp. 251–260). IGI Global. https://doi.org/10.4018/978-1-7998-1025-4.ch011

Baker-Gardner, R., & Smart, C. (2017). Ignorance or Intent?: A Case Study of Plagiarism in Higher Education among LIS Students in the Caribbean. In D. Velliaris (Ed.), *Handbook of Research on Academic Misconduct in Higher Education* (pp. 182–205). Hershey, PA: IGI Global. doi:10.4018/978-1-5225-1610-1.ch008

Baker-Gardner, R., & Stewart, P. (2018). Educating Caribbean Librarians to Provide Library Education in a Dynamic Information Environment. In S. Bhattacharyya & K. Patnaik (Eds.), *Changing the Scope of Library Instruction in the Digital Age* (pp. 187–226). Hershey, PA: IGI Global. doi:10.4018/978-1-5225-2802-9.ch008

Baran, M. L., & Jones, J. E. (2020). Developing the Research Study: A Step-by-Step Approach. In M. Baran & J. Jones (Eds.), *Applied Social Science Approaches to Mixed Methods Research* (pp. 262–274). IGI Global. https://doi.org/10.4018/978-1-7998-1025-4.ch012

Baskaran, C. (2020). Altmetircs Research: An Impact and Tools. In C. Baskaran (Ed.), *Measuring and Implementing Altmetrics in Library and Information Science Research* (pp. 1–10). IGI Global. https://doi.org/10.4018/978-1-7998-1309-5.ch001

Bengtson, J. (2017). Funding a Gamification Machine. In E. Iglesias (Ed.), *Library Technology Funding, Planning, and Deployment* (pp. 99–112). Hershey, PA: IGI Global. doi:10.4018/978-1-5225-1735-1.ch006

Bhuda, M., & Koitsiwe, M. (2022). The Importance of Underpinning Indigenous Research Using African Indigenous Philosophies: Perspectives From Indigenous Scholars. In R. Tshifhumulo & T. Makhanikhe (Eds.), *Handbook of Research on Protecting and Managing Global Indigenous Knowledge Systems* (pp. 223–248). IGI Global. https://doi.org/10.4018/978-1-7998-7492-8.ch013

Blummer, B., & Kenton, J. M. (2017). Access and Accessibility of Academic Libraries' Electronic Resources and Services: Identifying Themes in the Literature From 2000 to the Present. In H. Alphin Jr, J. Lavine, & R. Chan (Eds.), *Disability and Equity in Higher Education Accessibility* (pp. 242–267). Hershey, PA: IGI Global. doi:10.4018/978-1-5225-2665-0.ch011

Blummer, B., & Kenton, J. M. (2018). Academic and Research Libraries' Portals: A Literature Review From 2003 to the Present. In R. Bhardwaj (Ed.), *Digitizing the Modern Library and the Transition From Print to Electronic* (pp. 29–63). Hershey, PA: IGI Global. doi:10.4018/978-1-5225-2119-8.ch002

Blummer, B., & Kenton, J. M. (2018). International Students and Academic Libraries: Identifying Themes in the Literature From 2001 to the Present. In B. Blummer, J. Kenton, & M. Wiatrowski (Eds.), *Promoting Ethnic Diversity and Multiculturalism in Higher Education* (pp. 237–263). Hershey, PA: IGI Global. doi:10.4018/978-1-5225-4097-7.ch013

Bohuski, L. (2020). What If Your Library Can't Go Green?: Promoting Wellness in Libraries. In A. Kaushik, A. Kumar, & P. Biswas (Eds.), *Handbook of Research on Emerging Trends and Technologies in Library and Information Science* (pp. 13–26). IGI Global. doi:10.4018/978-1-5225-9825-1.ch002

Boom, D. (2017). The Embedded Librarian: Do More With less. In B. Gunjal (Ed.), *Managing Knowledge and Scholarly Assets in Academic Libraries* (pp. 76–97). Hershey, PA: IGI Global. doi:10.4018/978-1-5225-1741-2.ch004

Bosire-Ogechi, E. (2018). Social Media, Social Networking, Copyright, and Digital Libraries. In A. Tella & T. Kwanya (Eds.), *Handbook of Research on Managing Intellectual Property in Digital Libraries* (pp. 37–50). Hershey, PA: IGI Global. doi:10.4018/978-1-5225-3093-0.ch003

Bradley-Sanders, C., & Rudshteyn, A. (2018). MyLibrary at Brooklyn College: Developing a Suite of Digital Tools. In L. Costello & M. Powers (Eds.), *Developing In-House Digital Tools in Library Spaces* (pp. 140–167). Hershey, PA: IGI Global. doi:10.4018/978-1-5225-2676-6.ch007

Brown, V. (2018). Technology Access Gap for Postsecondary Education: A Statewide Case Study. In M. Yildiz, S. Funk, & B. De Abreu (Eds.), *Promoting Global Competencies Through Media Literacy* (pp. 20–40). Hershey, PA: IGI Global. doi:10.4018/978-1-5225-3082-4.ch002

Browne, N. (2021). The IHS Library and Its Response to the COVID-19 Pandemic. In B. Holland (Eds.), *Handbook of Research on Library Response to the COVID-19 Pandemic* (pp. 298-320). IGI Global. https://doi.org/10.4018/978-1-7998-6449-3.ch016

Chaiyasoonthorn, W., & Suksa-ngiam, W. (2018). Users' Acceptance of Online Literature Databases in a Thai University: A Test of UTAUT2. *International Journal of Information Systems in the Service Sector, 10*(1), 54–70. doi:10.4018/IJISSS.2018010104

Chaudron, G. (2018). Burst Pipes and Leaky Roofs: Small Emergencies Are a Challenge for Libraries. In K. Strang, M. Korstanje, & N. Vajjhala (Eds.), *Research, Practices, and Innovations in Global Risk and Contingency Management* (pp. 211–231). Hershey, PA: IGI Global. doi:10.4018/978-1-5225-4754-9.ch012

Chemulwo, M. J. (2018). Managing Intellectual Property in Digital Libraries and Copyright Challenges. In A. Tella & T. Kwanya (Eds.), *Handbook of Research on Managing Intellectual Property in Digital Libraries* (pp. 165–183). Hershey, PA: IGI Global. doi:10.4018/978-1-5225-3093-0.ch009

Chen, J., Lan, X., Huang, Q., Dong, J., & Chen, C. (2017). Scholarly Learning Commons. In L. Ruan, Q. Zhu, & Y. Ye (Eds.), *Academic Library Development and Administration in China* (pp. 90–109). Hershey, PA: IGI Global. doi:10.4018/978-1-5225-0550-1.ch006

Chigwada, J. P. (2018). Adoption of Open Source Software in Libraries in Developing Countries. *International Journal of Library and Information Services, 7*(1), 15–29. doi:10.4018/IJLIS.2018010102

Chigwada, J. P. (2020). Librarian Skillsets in the 21st Century: The Changing Role of Librarians in the Digital Era. In N. Osuigwe (Ed.), *Managing and Adapting Library Information Services for Future Users* (pp. 41–58). IGI Global. https://doi.org/10.4018/978-1-7998-1116-9.ch003

Chigwada, J. P. (2020). The Role of the Librarian in the Research Life Cycle: Research Collaboration Among the Library and Faculty. In C. Chisita (Ed.), *Cooperation and Collaboration Initiatives for Libraries and Related Institutions* (pp. 335–346). IGI Global. https://doi.org/10.4018/978-1-7998-0043-9.ch017

Chigwada, J. P. (2021). Research Data Management Services in Tertiary Institutions in Zimbabwe. In B. Holland (Eds.), *Handbook of Research on Knowledge and Organization Systems in Library and Information Science* (pp. 419-437). IGI Global. https://doi.org/10.4018/978-1-7998-7258-0.ch022

Chigwada, J. P., & Maturure, R. (2019). Advocating for Library and Information Services by National Library Associations of Africa in the Context of Sustainable Development Goals. In P. Ngulube (Ed.), *Handbook of Research on Advocacy, Promotion, and Public Programming for Memory Institutions* (pp. 219–237). IGI Global. doi:10.4018/978-1-5225-7429-3.ch012

Chiparausha, B., & Chigwada, J. P. (2019). Promoting Library Services in a Digital Environment in Zimbabwe. In P. Ngulube (Ed.), *Handbook of Research on Advocacy, Promotion, and Public Programming for Memory Institutions* (pp. 284–296). IGI Global. https://doi.org/10.4018/978-1-5225-7429-3.ch015

Chisita, C. T., & Chinyemba, F. (2017). Utilising ICTs for Resource Sharing Initiatives in Academic Institutions in Zimbabwe: Towards a New Trajectory. In B. Gunjal (Ed.), *Managing Knowledge and Scholarly Assets in Academic Libraries* (pp. 174–187). Hershey, PA: IGI Global. doi:10.4018/978-1-5225-1741-2.ch008

Chu, S., Tu, S., Wang, N., & Zhang, W. (2020). Information Equity and Cultural Sharing: The Service for Migrant Workers in Hangzhou Public Library. *International Journal of Library and Information Services*, *9*(1), 10–24. https://doi.org/10.4018/IJLIS.2020010102

Clarance, M. M., & Angeline, X. M. (2019). User Opinion on Library Collections and Services: A Case Study of Branch Library in Karaikudi. In S. Thanuskodi (Ed.), *Literacy Skill Development for Library Science Professionals* (pp. 343–375). IGI Global. https://doi.org/10.4018/978-1-5225-7125-4.ch015

Costello, L., & Fazal, S. (2018). Developing Unique Study Room Reservation Systems: Examples From Teachers College and Stony Brook University. In L. Costello & M. Powers (Eds.), *Developing In-House Digital Tools in Library Spaces* (pp. 168–176). Hershey, PA: IGI Global. doi:10.4018/978-1-5225-2676-6.ch008

Cui, Y. (2017). Research Data Management: Models, Challenges, and Actions. In L. Ruan, Q. Zhu, & Y. Ye (Eds.), *Academic Library Development and Administration in China* (pp. 184–195). Hershey, PA: IGI Global. doi:10.4018/978-1-5225-0550-1.ch011

Dhamdhere, S. N., De Smet, E., & Lihitkar, R. (2017). Web-Based Bibliographic Services Offered by Top World and Indian University Libraries: A Comparative Study. *International Journal of Library and Information Services*, *6*(1), 53–72. doi:10.4018/IJLIS.2017010104

Eiriemiokhale, K. A. (2018). Copyright Issues in a Digital Library Environment. In A. Tella & T. Kwanya (Eds.), *Handbook of Research on Managing Intellectual Property in Digital Libraries* (pp. 142–164). Hershey, PA: IGI Global. doi:10.4018/978-1-5225-3093-0.ch008

El Mimouni, H., Anderson, J., Tempelman-Kluit, N. F., & Dolan-Mescal, A. (2018). UX Work in Libraries: How (and Why) to Do It. In L. Costello & M. Powers (Eds.), *Developing In-House Digital Tools in Library Spaces* (pp. 1–36). Hershey, PA: IGI Global. doi:10.4018/978-1-5225-2676-6.ch001

Emiri, O. T. (2017). Digital Literacy Skills Among Librarians in University Libraries In the 21st Century in Edo And Delta States, Nigeria. *International Journal of Library and Information Services*, *6*(1), 37–52. doi:10.4018/IJLIS.2017010103

Emmelhainz, C. (2020). Educating the Central Asian Librarian: Considering the International MLIS in Kazakhstan. In R. Alenzuela, H. Kim, & D. Baylen (Eds.), *Internationalization of Library and Information Science Education in the Asia-Pacific Region* (pp. 1–32). IGI Global. https://doi.org/10.4018/978-1-7998-2273-8.ch001

Esguerra, A. C. (2020). Library Education and Librarianship in Japan and the Philippines. In R. Alenzuela, H. Kim, & D. Baylen (Eds.), *Internationalization of Library and Information Science Education in the Asia-Pacific Region* (pp. 131–157). IGI Global. https://doi.org/10.4018/978-1-7998-2273-8.ch006

Esposito, T. (2018). Exploring Opportunities in Health Science Information Instructional Outreach: A Case Study Highlighting One Academic Library's Experience. In S. Bhattacharyya & K. Patnaik (Eds.), *Changing the Scope of Library Instruction in the Digital Age* (pp. 118–135). Hershey, PA: IGI Global. doi:10.4018/978-1-5225-2802-9.ch005

Fagbola, O. O., Smart, A. E., & Oluwaseun, B. O. (2020). Application of Cloud Computing Technologies in Academic Library Management: The National Open University of Nigeria Library in Perspective. In A. Tella (Ed.), *Handbook of Research on Digital Devices for Inclusivity and Engagement in Libraries* (pp. 135–159). IGI Global. https://doi.org/10.4018/978-1-5225-9034-7.ch007

Fan, Y., Zhang, X., & Li, G. (2017). Research Initiatives and Projects in Academic Libraries. In L. Ruan, Q. Zhu, & Y. Ye (Eds.), *Academic Library Development and Administration in China* (pp. 230–252). Hershey, PA: IGI Global. doi:10.4018/978-1-5225-0550-1.ch014

Farmer, L. S. (2017). ICT Literacy Integration: Issues and Sample Efforts. In J. Keengwe & P. Bull (Eds.), *Handbook of Research on Transformative Digital Content and Learning Technologies* (pp. 59–80). Hershey, PA: IGI Global. doi:10.4018/978-1-5225-2000-9.ch004

Farmer, L. S. (2017). Data Analytics for Strategic Management: Getting the Right Data. In V. Wang (Ed.), *Encyclopedia of Strategic Leadership and Management* (pp. 810–822). Hershey, PA: IGI Global. doi:10.4018/978-1-5225-1049-9.ch056

Farmer, L. S. (2017). Managing Portable Technologies for Special Education. In V. Wang (Ed.), *Encyclopedia of Strategic Leadership and Management* (pp. 977–987). Hershey, PA: IGI Global. doi:10.4018/978-1-5225-1049-9.ch068

Fujishima, D., & Kamada, T. (2017). Collective Relocation for Associative Distributed Collections of Objects. *International Journal of Software Innovation, 5*(2), 55–69. doi:10.4018/IJSI.2017040104

Ghani, S. R. (2017). Ontology: Advancing Flawless Library Services. In T. Ashraf & N. Kumar (Eds.), *Interdisciplinary Digital Preservation Tools and Technologies* (pp. 79–102). Hershey, PA: IGI Global. doi:10.4018/978-1-5225-1653-8.ch005

Gu, J. (2017). Library Buildings on New Campuses. In L. Ruan, Q. Zhu, & Y. Ye (Eds.), *Academic Library Development and Administration in China* (pp. 110–124). Hershey, PA: IGI Global. doi:10.4018/978-1-5225-0550-1.ch007

Guan, Z., & Wang, J. (2017). The China Academic Social Sciences and Humanities Library (CASHL). In L. Ruan, Q. Zhu, & Y. Ye (Eds.), *Academic Library Development and Administration in China* (pp. 31–54). Hershey, PA: IGI Global. doi:10.4018/978-1-5225-0550-1.ch003

Gul, S., & Shueb, S. (2018). Confronting/Managing the Crisis of Indian Libraries: E-Consortia Initiatives in India - A Way Forward. In R. Bhardwaj (Ed.), *Digitizing the Modern Library and the Transition From Print to Electronic* (pp. 129–163). Hershey, PA: IGI Global. doi:10.4018/978-1-5225-2119-8.ch006

Gunjal, B. (2017). Managing Knowledge and Scholarly Assets in Academic Libraries: Issues and Challenges. In B. Gunjal (Ed.), *Managing Knowledge and Scholarly Assets in Academic Libraries* (pp. 270–279). Hershey, PA: IGI Global. doi:10.4018/978-1-5225-1741-2.ch013

Guo, J., Zhang, H., & Zong, Y. (2017). Leadership Development and Career Planning. In L. Ruan, Q. Zhu, & Y. Ye (Eds.), *Academic Library Development and Administration in China* (pp. 264–279). Hershey, PA: IGI Global. doi:10.4018/978-1-5225-0550-1.ch016

Hahn, J. (2020). Student Engagement and Smart Spaces: Library Browsing and Internet of Things Technology. In B. Holland (Eds.), *Emerging Trends and Impacts of the Internet of Things in Libraries* (pp. 52-70). IGI Global. https://doi.org/10.4018/978-1-7998-4742-7.ch003

Halder, D. (2020). A Transitional Shift From Traditional Library to Digital Library. In A. Kaushik, A. Kumar, & P. Biswas (Eds.), *Handbook of Research on Emerging Trends and Technologies in Library and Information Science* (pp. 147–155). IGI Global. https://doi.org/10.4018/978-1-5225-9825-1.ch011

Hallis, R. (2018). Leveraging Library Instruction in a Digital Age. In S. Bhattacharyya & K. Patnaik (Eds.), *Changing the Scope of Library Instruction in the Digital Age* (pp. 1–23). Hershey, PA: IGI Global. doi:10.4018/978-1-5225-2802-9.ch001

Halupa, C. (2022). An Introduction to Survey Research. In A. Zimmerman (Ed.), *Methodological Innovations in Research and Academic Writing* (pp. 41–62). IGI Global. https://doi.org/10.4018/978-1-7998-8283-1.ch003

Hartsock, R., & Alemneh, D. G. (2018). Electronic Theses and Dissertations (ETDs). In M. Khosrow-Pour, D.B.A. (Ed.), Encyclopedia of Information Science and Technology, Fourth Edition (pp. 6748-6755). Hershey, PA: IGI Global. https:// doi.org/ doi:10.4018/978-1-5225-2255-3.ch584

Haugh, D. (2018). Mobile Applications for Libraries. In L. Costello & M. Powers (Eds.), *Developing In-House Digital Tools in Library Spaces* (pp. 76–90). Hershey, PA: IGI Global. doi:10.4018/978-1-5225-2676-6.ch004

Hayes, C. (2022). Methodology and Method in Case Study Research: Framing Research Design in Practice. In S. Watson, S. Austin, & J. Bell (Eds.), *Conceptual Analyses of Curriculum Inquiry Methodologies* (pp. 138-154). IGI Global. https:// doi.org/10.4018/978-1-7998-8848-2.ch007

Hayes, C., & Graham, Y. N. (2022). Phenomenology: Conceptually Framing Phenomenological Research Design and Methodology. In S. Watson, S. Austin, & J. Bell (Eds.), *Conceptual Analyses of Curriculum Inquiry Methodologies* (pp. 28-50). IGI Global. https://doi.org/10.4018/978-1-7998-8848-2.ch002

Hill, V. (2017). Digital Citizens as Writers: New Literacies and New Responsibilities. In E. Monske & K. Blair (Eds.), *Handbook of Research on Writing and Composing in the Age of MOOCs* (pp. 56–74). Hershey, PA: IGI Global. doi:10.4018/978-1-5225-1718-4.ch004

Hoh, A. (2019). Expanding the Awareness and Use of Library Collections Through Social Media: A Case Study of the Library of Congress International Collections Social Media Program. In J. Joe & E. Knight (Eds.), *Social Media for Communication and Instruction in Academic Libraries* (pp. 212–236). IGI Global. doi:10.4018/978-1-5225-8097-3.ch013

Holland, B. (2020). Emerging Technology and Today's Libraries. In B. Holland (Eds.), *Emerging Trends and Impacts of the Internet of Things in Libraries* (pp. 1-33). IGI Global. https://doi.org/10.4018/978-1-7998-4742-7.ch001

Homza, A., & Fontno, T. J. (2021). Supporting Teacher Candidates as Social Justice Change-Makers: A Faculty-Librarian Collaboration for Building and Using Diverse Youth Collections. In D. Hartsfield (Ed.), *Handbook of Research on Teaching Diverse Youth Literature to Pre-Service Professionals* (pp. 398–421). IGI Global. https://doi.org/10.4018/978-1-7998-7375-4.ch020

Horne-Popp, L. M., Tessone, E. B., & Welker, J. (2018). If You Build It, They Will Come: Creating a Library Statistics Dashboard for Decision-Making. In L. Costello & M. Powers (Eds.), *Developing In-House Digital Tools in Library Spaces* (pp. 177–203). Hershey, PA: IGI Global. doi:10.4018/978-1-5225-2676-6.ch009

Huang, C., & Xue, H. F. (2017). The China Academic Digital Associative Library (CADAL). In L. Ruan, Q. Zhu, & Y. Ye (Eds.), *Academic Library Development and Administration in China* (pp. 20–30). Hershey, PA: IGI Global. doi:10.4018/978-1-5225-0550-1.ch002

Huang, J., & Vedantham, A. (2019). Cabot Science Library: Creating Transformative Learning Environments in Library Spaces. In A. Darshan Singh, S. Raghunathan, E. Robeck, & B. Sharma (Eds.), *Cases on Smart Learning Environments* (pp. 284–298). IGI Global. doi:10.4018/978-1-5225-6136-1.ch016

Hunsaker, A. J., Majewski, N., & Rocke, L. E. (2018). Pulling Content out the Back Door: Creating an Interactive Digital Collections Experience. In L. Costello & M. Powers (Eds.), *Developing In-House Digital Tools in Library Spaces* (pp. 205–226). Hershey, PA: IGI Global. doi:10.4018/978-1-5225-2676-6.ch010

Hussain, A. (2020). Cutting Edge: Technology's Impact on Library Services. In J. Jesubright & P. Saravanan (Eds.), *Innovations in the Designing and Marketing of Information Services* (pp. 16–27). IGI Global. https://doi.org/10.4018/978-1-7998-1482-5.ch002

Idiegbeyan-ose, J., Owolabi, S. E., Ayooluwa, A., Foluke, O., Toluwani, E., & Sunday, O. (2019). Digital Library and Distance Learning in Developing Countries: Benefits and Challenges. In R. Bhardwaj & P. Banks (Eds.), *Research Data Access and Management in Modern Libraries* (pp. 220–245). IGI Global. https://doi.org/10.4018/978-1-5225-8437-7.ch011

Ifijeh, G., Adebayo, O., Izuagbe, R., & Olawoyin, O. (2018). Institutional Repositories and Libraries in Nigeria: Interrogating the Nexus. *Journal of Cases on Information Technology*, *20*(2), 16–29. doi:10.4018/JCIT.2018040102

Igbinovia, M. O., Solanke, E. O., & Obinyan, O. O. (2020). Building Influence: Strategising for Library Advocacy. In N. Osuigwe (Ed.), *Managing and Adapting Library Information Services for Future Users* (pp. 221–241). IGI Global. https://doi.org/10.4018/978-1-7998-1116-9.ch013

Iglesias, E. (2017). Insourcing and Outsourcing of Library Technology. In E. Iglesias (Ed.), *Library Technology Funding, Planning, and Deployment* (pp. 113–123). Hershey, PA: IGI Global. doi:10.4018/978-1-5225-1735-1.ch007

Ikolo, V. E. (2018). Transformational Leadership for Academic Libraries in Nigeria. In M. Khosrow-Pour, D.B.A. (Ed.), Encyclopedia of Information Science and Technology, Fourth Edition (pp. 5726-5735). Hershey, PA: IGI Global. doi:10.4018/978-1-5225-2255-3.ch497

Ikolo, V. E. (2020). Doctor's Awareness and Perception of Medical Library Resources and Services: A Case Study of Delta State University Teaching Hospital (Delsuth), Nigeria. *International Journal of Library and Information Services*, *9*(2), 58–71. https://doi.org/10.4018/IJLIS.2020070104

Joe, J. A. (2018). Changing Expectations of Academic Libraries. In M. Khosrow-Pour, D.B.A. (Ed.), Encyclopedia of Information Science and Technology, Fourth Edition (pp. 5204-5212). Hershey, PA: IGI Global. doi:10.4018/978-1-5225-2255-3.ch452

Juliana, I., Izuagbe, R., Itsekor, V., Fagbohun, M. O., Asaolu, A., & Nwokeoma, M. N. (2018). The Role of the School Library in Empowering Visually Impaired Children With Lifelong Information Literacy Skills. In P. Epler (Ed.), *Instructional Strategies in General Education and Putting the Individuals With Disabilities Act (IDEA) Into Practice* (pp. 245–271). Hershey, PA: IGI Global. doi:10.4018/978-1-5225-3111-1.ch009

Kalu, C. O., Chidi-Kalu, E. I., & Mafe, T. A. (2021). Research Data Management in an Academic Library. In J. Chigwada & G. Tsvuura (Eds.), *Handbook of Research on Information and Records Management in the Fourth Industrial Revolution* (pp. 38–55). IGI Global. https://doi.org/10.4018/978-1-7998-7740-0.ch003

Kalusopa, T. (2018). Preservation and Access to Digital Materials: Strategic Policy Options for Africa. In P. Ngulube (Ed.), *Handbook of Research on Heritage Management and Preservation* (pp. 150–174). Hershey, PA: IGI Global. doi:10.4018/978-1-5225-3137-1.ch008

Kamau, G. W. (2018). Copyright Challenges in Digital Libraries in Kenya From the Lens of a Librarian. In A. Tella & T. Kwanya (Eds.), *Handbook of Research on Managing Intellectual Property in Digital Libraries* (pp. 312–336). Hershey, PA: IGI Global. doi:10.4018/978-1-5225-3093-0.ch016

Karagöz, E., Güney, L. Ö., & Baran, B. (2022). The Collaborative Digital Content Library Fostering Faculty Members' Collaboratively Building Learning Sources. In G. Durak & S. Çankaya (Eds.), *Handbook of Research on Managing and Designing Online Courses in Synchronous and Asynchronous Environments* (pp. 196–213). IGI Global. doi:10.4018/978-1-7998-8701-0.ch010

Karmakar, R. (2018). Development and Management of Digital Libraries in the Regime of IPR Paradigm. *International Journal of Library and Information Services, 7*(1), 44–57. doi:10.4018/IJLIS.2018010104

Kasemsap, K. (2017). Mastering Knowledge Management in Academic Libraries. In B. Gunjal (Ed.), *Managing Knowledge and Scholarly Assets in Academic Libraries* (pp. 27–55). Hershey, PA: IGI Global. doi:10.4018/978-1-5225-1741-2.ch002

Kehinde, A. (2018). Digital Libraries and the Role of Digital Librarians. In A. Tella & T. Kwanya (Eds.), *Handbook of Research on Managing Intellectual Property in Digital Libraries* (pp. 98–119). Hershey, PA: IGI Global. doi:10.4018/978-1-5225-3093-0.ch006

Kenausis, V., & Herman, D. (2017). Don't Make Us Use the "Get Along Shirt": Communication and Consensus Building in an RFP Process. In E. Iglesias (Ed.), *Library Technology Funding, Planning, and Deployment* (pp. 1–22). Hershey, PA: IGI Global. doi:10.4018/978-1-5225-1735-1.ch001

Kohl, L. E., Lombardi, P., & Moroney, M. (2017). Moving from Local to Global via the Integrated Library System: Cost-Savings, ILS Management, Teams, and End-Users. In E. Iglesias (Ed.), *Library Technology Funding, Planning, and Deployment* (pp. 23–35). Hershey, PA: IGI Global. doi:10.4018/978-1-5225-1735-1.ch002

Kowalsky, M. (2020). School Librarian Experiences of Learning Management Implementation. In A. Tella (Ed.), *Handbook of Research on Digital Devices for Inclusivity and Engagement in Libraries* (pp. 160–184). IGI Global. https://doi.org/10.4018/978-1-5225-9034-7.ch008

Kumar, K. (2018). Library in Your Pocket Delivery of Instruction Service Through Library Mobile Apps: A World in Your Pocket. In S. Bhattacharyya & K. Patnaik (Eds.), *Changing the Scope of Library Instruction in the Digital Age* (pp. 228–249). Hershey, PA: IGI Global. doi:10.4018/978-1-5225-2802-9.ch009

Kwanya, T. (2018). Social Bookmarking in Digital Libraries: Intellectual Property Rights Implications. In A. Tella & T. Kwanya (Eds.), *Handbook of Research on Managing Intellectual Property in Digital Libraries* (pp. 1–18). Hershey, PA: IGI Global. doi:10.4018/978-1-5225-3093-0.ch001

Lapo, P., Makhmudov, G., & Rakhmatullaev, M. (2020). Internationalization of Library and Information Science Education in Tajikistan and Uzbekistan: Implications in Central Asia. In R. Alenzuela, H. Kim, & D. Baylen (Eds.), *Internationalization of Library and Information Science Education in the Asia-Pacific Region* (pp. 225–245). IGI Global. https://doi.org/10.4018/978-1-7998-2273-8.ch010

Lewis, J. K. (2018). Change Leadership Styles and Behaviors in Academic Libraries. In M. Khosrow-Pour, D.B.A. (Ed.), Encyclopedia of Information Science and Technology, Fourth Edition (pp. 5194-5203). Hershey, PA: IGI Global. doi:10.4018/978-1-5225-2255-3.ch451

Lillard, L. L. (2018). Is Interdisciplinary Collaboration in Academia an Elusive Dream?: Can the Institutional Barriers Be Broken Down? A Review of the Literature and the Case of Library Science. In M. Al-Suqri, A. Al-Kindi, S. AlKindi, & N. Saleem (Eds.), *Promoting Interdisciplinarity in Knowledge Generation and Problem Solving* (pp. 139–147). Hershey, PA: IGI Global. doi:10.4018/978-1-5225-3878-3.ch010

Liu, C., Dou, T., Zhou, H., Zhang, B., & Zhang, C. (2021). Library Service Innovation Based on New Information Technology: Taking the Interactive Experience Space "Tsinghua Impression" as an Example. *International Journal of Library and Information Services*, *10*(1), 71–81. https://doi.org/10.4018/IJLIS.2021010106

Long, X., & Yao, B. (2017). The Construction and Development of the Academic Digital Library of Chinese Ancient Collections. In L. Ruan, Q. Zhu, & Y. Ye (Eds.), *Academic Library Development and Administration in China* (pp. 126–135). Hershey, PA: IGI Global. doi:10.4018/978-1-5225-0550-1.ch008

Long, X., & Yao, B. (2020). The Construction and Development of the Academic Digital Library of Chinese Ancient Collections. In I. Management Association (Ed.), *Digital Libraries and Institutional Repositories: Breakthroughs in Research and Practice* (pp. 78-87). IGI Global. https://doi.org/10.4018/978-1-7998-2463-3.ch006

Lowe, M., & Reno, L. M. (2018). Academic Librarianship and Burnout. In *Examining the Emotional Dimensions of Academic Librarianship: Emerging Research and Opportunities* (pp. 72–89). Hershey, PA: IGI Global. doi:10.4018/978-1-5225-3761-8.ch005

Lowe, M., & Reno, L. M. (2018). Emotional Dimensions of Academic Librarianship. In *Examining the Emotional Dimensions of Academic Librarianship: Emerging Research and Opportunities* (pp. 54–71). Hershey, PA: IGI Global. doi:10.4018/978-1-5225-3761-8.ch004

Lowe, M., & Reno, L. M. (2018). Why Isn't This Being Studied? In *Examining the Emotional Dimensions of Academic Librarianship: Emerging Research and Opportunities* (pp. 90–108). Hershey, PA: IGI Global. doi:10.4018/978-1-5225-3761-8.ch006

Lowe, M., & Reno, L. M. (2018). Research Agenda: Research Ideas and Recommendations. In *Examining the Emotional Dimensions of Academic Librarianship: Emerging Research and Opportunities* (pp. 109–125). Hershey, PA: IGI Global. doi:10.4018/978-1-5225-3761-8.ch007

Luyombya, D., Kiyingi, G. W., & Naluwooza, M. (2018). The Nature and Utilisation of Archival Records Deposited in Makerere University Library, Uganda. In P. Ngulube (Ed.), *Handbook of Research on Heritage Management and Preservation* (pp. 96–113). Hershey, PA: IGI Global. doi:10.4018/978-1-5225-3137-1.ch005

Ma, W. Y. (2022). Supporting Indigenous Education From a Distance: Adjusting Strategies to Maintain Access to a Rare Library Collection During a Global Crisis. In P. Pangelinan & T. McVey (Eds.), *Learning and Reconciliation Through Indigenous Education in Oceania* (pp. 197–209). IGI Global. https://doi.org/10.4018/978-1-7998-7736-3.ch012

Mabe, M., & Ashley, E. A. (2017). The Natural Role of the Public Library. In *The Developing Role of Public Libraries in Emergency Management: Emerging Research and Opportunities* (pp. 25–43). Hershey, PA: IGI Global. doi:10.4018/978-1-5225-2196-9.ch003

Mabe, M., & Ashley, E. A. (2017). I'm Trained, Now What? In *The Developing Role of Public Libraries in Emergency Management: Emerging Research and Opportunities* (pp. 87–95). Hershey, PA: IGI Global. doi:10.4018/978-1-5225-2196-9.ch007

Mabe, M., & Ashley, E. A. (2017). Emergency Preparation for the Library and Librarian. In *The Developing Role of Public Libraries in Emergency Management: Emerging Research and Opportunities* (pp. 61–78). Hershey, PA: IGI Global. doi:10.4018/978-1-5225-2196-9.ch005

Mabe, M., & Ashley, E. A. (2017). The CCPL Model. In *The Developing Role of Public Libraries in Emergency Management: Emerging Research and Opportunities* (pp. 15–24). Hershey, PA: IGI Global. doi:10.4018/978-1-5225-2196-9.ch002

Mabe, M., & Ashley, E. A. (2017). The Local Command Structure and How the Library Fits. In *In The Developing Role of Public Libraries in Emergency Management: Emerging Research and Opportunities* (pp. 44–60). Hershey, PA: IGI Global. doi:10.4018/978-1-5225-2196-9.ch004

Mafube, M. A., & Keakopa, S. M. (2019). Customer Services at the Library Archives of the National University of Lesotho. In P. Ngulube (Ed.), *Handbook of Research on Advocacy, Promotion, and Public Programming for Memory Institutions* (pp. 62–76). IGI Global. doi:10.4018/978-1-5225-7429-3.ch004

Majumdar, S. (2022). Community Engagement Through Extension and Outreach Activities: Scope of a College Library. In M. Taher (Ed.), *Handbook of Research on the Role of Libraries, Archives, and Museums in Achieving Civic Engagement and Social Justice in Smart Cities* (pp. 121–138). IGI Global. https://doi.org/10.4018/978-1-7998-8363-0.ch006

Mangone, E. (2022). The Difficult Joining of Theory and Empirical Research: Strengths and Weaknesses of Digital Research Methods. In G. Punziano & A. Delli Paoli (Eds.), *Handbook of Research on Advanced Research Methodologies for a Digital Society* (pp. 11–23). IGI Global. https://doi.org/10.4018/978-1-7998-8473-6.ch002

Manzoor, A. (2018). Social Media: A Librarian's Tool for Instant and Direct Interaction With Library Users. In R. Bhardwaj (Ed.), *Digitizing the Modern Library and the Transition From Print to Electronic* (pp. 112–128). Hershey, PA: IGI Global. doi:10.4018/978-1-5225-2119-8.ch005

Maringanti, H. (2018). A Decision Making Paradigm for Software Development in Libraries. In L. Costello & M. Powers (Eds.), *Developing In-House Digital Tools in Library Spaces* (pp. 59–75). Hershey, PA: IGI Global. doi:10.4018/978-1-5225-2676-6.ch003

Markman, K. M., Ferrarini, M., & Deschenes, A. H. (2018). User Testing and Iterative Design in the Academic Library: A Case Study. In R. Roscoe, S. Craig, & I. Douglas (Eds.), *End-User Considerations in Educational Technology Design* (pp. 160–183). Hershey, PA: IGI Global. doi:10.4018/978-1-5225-2639-1.ch008

Marrazzo, F. (2022). Doing Research With Online Platforms: An Emerging Issue Network. In G. Punziano & A. Delli Paoli (Eds.), *Handbook of Research on Advanced Research Methodologies for a Digital Society* (pp. 65–86). IGI Global. https://doi.org/10.4018/978-1-7998-8473-6.ch006

Mertens, D. (2022). Designing Mixed Methods Studies to Contribute to Social, Economic, and Environmental Justice: Implications for Library and Information Sciences. In P. Ngulube (Ed.), *Handbook of Research on Mixed Methods Research in Information Science* (pp. 173–189). IGI Global. https://doi.org/10.4018/978-1-7998-8844-4.ch009

Moahi, K. H. (2020). The Research Process and Indigenous Epistemologies. In P. Ngulube (Ed.), *Handbook of Research on Connecting Research Methods for Information Science Research* (pp. 245–265). IGI Global. https://doi.org/10.4018/978-1-7998-1471-9.ch013

Mohapatra, N. (2021). Webrarian: A Librarian on the Web. In C. Chisita, R. Enakrire, O. Durodolu, V. Tsabedze, & J. Ngoaketsi (Eds.), *Handbook of Research on Records and Information Management Strategies for Enhanced Knowledge Coordination* (pp. 458–470). IGI Global. https://doi.org/10.4018/978-1-7998-6618-3.ch027

Munatsi, R. (2020). National Research and Knowledge Systems: Role of Libraries. In C. Chisita (Ed.), *Cooperation and Collaboration Initiatives for Libraries and Related Institutions* (pp. 273–293). IGI Global. https://doi.org/10.4018/978-1-7998-0043-9.ch014

Musimbi, W. L., & Mutuku, P. K. (2019). The Future of LIS and Media Training in the Global Era: Challenges and Prospects. In C. Chisita & A. Rusero (Eds.), *Exploring the Relationship Between Media, Libraries, and Archives* (pp. 82–101). IGI Global. doi:10.4018/978-1-5225-5840-8.ch006

Mwanzu, A. (2019). Economics of Resource Sharing via Library Consortia. In C. Chisita & A. Rusero (Eds.), *Exploring the Relationship Between Media, Libraries, and Archives* (pp. 19–34). IGI Global. https://doi.org/10.4018/978-1-5225-5840-8.ch002

Na, L. (2017). Library and Information Science Education and Graduate Programs in Academic Libraries. In L. Ruan, Q. Zhu, & Y. Ye (Eds.), *Academic Library Development and Administration in China* (pp. 218–229). Hershey, PA: IGI Global. doi:10.4018/978-1-5225-0550-1.ch013

Nagarkar, S. P. (2017). Biomedical Librarianship in the Post-Genomic Era. In S. Ram (Ed.), *Library and Information Services for Bioinformatics Education and Research* (pp. 1–17). Hershey, PA: IGI Global. doi:10.4018/978-1-5225-1871-6.ch001

Natarajan, M. (2017). Exploring Knowledge Sharing over Social Media. In R. Chugh (Ed.), *Harnessing Social Media as a Knowledge Management Tool* (pp. 55–73). Hershey, PA: IGI Global. doi:10.4018/978-1-5225-0495-5.ch003

Nazir, T. (2017). Preservation Initiatives in E-Environment to Protect Information Assets. In T. Ashraf & N. Kumar (Eds.), *Interdisciplinary Digital Preservation Tools and Technologies* (pp. 193–208). Hershey, PA: IGI Global. doi:10.4018/978-1-5225-1653-8.ch010

Ngulube, P. (2017). Embedding Indigenous Knowledge in Library and Information Science Education in Anglophone Eastern and Southern Africa. In P. Ngulube (Ed.), *Handbook of Research on Social, Cultural, and Educational Considerations of Indigenous Knowledge in Developing Countries* (pp. 92–115). Hershey, PA: IGI Global. doi:10.4018/978-1-5225-0838-0.ch006

Ngulube, P. (2022). Using Simple and Complex Mixed Methods Research Designs to Understand Research in Information Science. In P. Ngulube (Ed.), *Handbook of Research on Mixed Methods Research in Information Science* (pp. 20–46). IGI Global. doi:10.4018/978-1-7998-8844-4.ch002

Nicolajsen, H. W., Sorensen, F., & Scupola, A. (2018). User Involvement in Service Innovation Processes. In M. Khosrow-Pour (Ed.), *Optimizing Current Practices in E-Services and Mobile Applications* (pp. 42–61). Hershey, PA: IGI Global. doi:10.4018/978-1-5225-5026-6.ch003

Ocholla, D. N. (2022). A Research Dashboard for Aligning Research Components in Research Proposals, Theses, and Dissertations in Library and Information Science. In P. Ngulube (Ed.), *Handbook of Research on Mixed Methods Research in Information Science* (pp. 629–640). IGI Global. https://doi.org/10.4018/978-1-7998-8844-4.ch029

Ochonogor, W. C., & Okite-Amughoro, F. A. (2018). Building an Effective Digital Library in a University Teaching Hospital (UTH) in Nigeria. In A. Tella & T. Kwanya (Eds.), *Handbook of Research on Managing Intellectual Property in Digital Libraries* (pp. 184–204). Hershey, PA: IGI Global. doi:10.4018/978-1-5225-3093-0.ch010

Okada, D. (2020). 10,000 Newly Certified Librarians, 100 Secure Jobs. In R. Alenzuela, H. Kim, & D. Baylen (Eds.), *Internationalization of Library and Information Science Education in the Asia-Pacific Region* (pp. 78–101). IGI Global. https://doi.org/10.4018/978-1-7998-2273-8.ch004

Oladapo, Y. O. (2018). Open Access to Knowledge and Challenges in Digital Libraries. In A. Tella & T. Kwanya (Eds.), *Handbook of Research on Managing Intellectual Property in Digital Libraries* (pp. 260–291). Hershey, PA: IGI Global. doi:10.4018/978-1-5225-3093-0.ch014

Oladokun, O., & Zulu, S. F. (2017). Document Description and Coding as Key Elements in Knowledge, Records, and Information Management. In P. Jain & N. Mnjama (Eds.), *Managing Knowledge Resources and Records in Modern Organizations* (pp. 179–197). Hershey, PA: IGI Global. doi:10.4018/978-1-5225-1965-2.ch011

Olubodun, O. J., & Oye, P. O. (2019). Library: A Tool for Information Dissemination and Creating Awareness in Conflict-Induced Situations. In E. Nyam & F. Idoko (Eds.), *Examining the Social and Economic Impacts of Conflict-Induced Migration* (pp. 55–63). IGI Global. https://doi.org/10.4018/978-1-5225-7615-0.ch003

Omeluzor, S. U., Abayomi, I., & Gbemi-Ogunleye, P. (2018). Contemporary Media for Library Users' Instruction in Academic Libraries in South-West Nigeria: Contemporary Library Instruction in the Digital Age. In S. Bhattacharyya & K. Patnaik (Eds.), *Changing the Scope of Library Instruction in the Digital Age* (pp. 162–185). Hershey, PA: IGI Global. doi:10.4018/978-1-5225-2802-9.ch007

Onwuchekwa, E. O. (2020). Library Signage and Information Graphics: A Communication Tool for Library Users. In A. Tella (Ed.), *Handbook of Research on Digital Devices for Inclusivity and Engagement in Libraries* (pp. 231–237). IGI Global. https://doi.org/10.4018/978-1-5225-9034-7.ch011

Onyancha, O. B. (2020). Informetrics Research Methods Outlined. In P. Ngulube (Ed.), *Handbook of Research on Connecting Research Methods for Information Science Research* (pp. 320–348). IGI Global. https://doi.org/10.4018/978-1-7998-1471-9.ch017

Oshilalu, A. H., & Ogochukwu, E. T. (2017). Modeling a Software for Library and Information Centers. *International Journal of Library and Information Services, 6*(2), 1–10. doi:10.4018/IJLIS.2017070101

Oswal, S. K. (2017). Institutional, Legal, and Attitudinal Barriers to the Accessibility of University Digital Libraries: Implications for Retention of Disabled Students. In H. Alphin Jr, J. Lavine, & R. Chan (Eds.), *Disability and Equity in Higher Education Accessibility* (pp. 223–241). Hershey, PA: IGI Global. doi:10.4018/978-1-5225-2665-0.ch010

Oukrich, J., & Bouikhalene, B. (2017). A Survey of Users' Satisfaction in the University Library by Using a Pareto Analysis and the Automatic Classification Methods. *International Journal of Library and Information Services, 6*(1), 17–36. doi:10.4018/IJLIS.2017010102

Oyelude, A. A., & Oluwaniyi, S. A. (2020). Managing Future Library Services for the Medical Sciences: A Pharmacy Library Experience. In N. Osuigwe (Ed.), *Managing and Adapting Library Information Services for Future Users* (pp. 200–220). IGI Global. https://doi.org/10.4018/978-1-7998-1116-9.ch012

Özel, N. (2018). Developing Visual Literacy Skills Through Library Instructions. In V. Osinska & G. Osinski (Eds.), *Information Visualization Techniques in the Social Sciences and Humanities* (pp. 32–48). Hershey, PA: IGI Global. doi:10.4018/978-1-5225-4990-1.ch003

Paganelli, A. L., & Paganelli, A. L. (2021). Blockchain and the Research Libraries: Expanding Interlibrary Loan and Protecting Privacy. In D. Gunter (Ed.), *Transforming Scholarly Publishing With Blockchain Technologies and AI* (pp. 232–250). IGI Global. https://doi.org/10.4018/978-1-7998-5589-7.ch012

Patel, D., & Thakur, D. (2017). Managing Open Access (OA) Scholarly Information Resources in a University. In A. Munigal (Ed.), *Scholarly Communication and the Publish or Perish Pressures of Academia* (pp. 224–255). Hershey, PA: IGI Global. doi:10.4018/978-1-5225-1697-2.ch011

Patnaik, K. R. (2018). Crafting a Framework for Copyright Literacy and Licensed Content: A Case Study at an Advanced Management Education and Research Library. In S. Bhattacharyya & K. Patnaik (Eds.), *Changing the Scope of Library Instruction in the Digital Age* (pp. 136–160). Hershey, PA: IGI Global. doi:10.4018/978-1-5225-2802-9.ch006

Paynter, K. (2017). Elementary Library Media Specialists' Roles in the Implementation of the Common Core State Standards. In M. Grassetti & S. Brookby (Eds.), *Advancing Next-Generation Teacher Education through Digital Tools and Applications* (pp. 262–283). Hershey, PA: IGI Global. doi:10.4018/978-1-5225-0965-3.ch014

Perry, S. C., & Waggoner, J. (2018). Processes for User-Centered Design and Development: The Omeka Curator Dashboard Project. In L. Costello & M. Powers (Eds.), *Developing In-House Digital Tools in Library Spaces* (pp. 37–58). Hershey, PA: IGI Global. doi:10.4018/978-1-5225-2676-6.ch002

Perumalsamy, R., & Kannan, S. P. (2019). User Information Needs in the Public Libraries in India. In S. Thanuskodi (Ed.), *Literacy Skill Development for Library Science Professionals* (pp. 25–53). IGI Global. https://doi.org/10.4018/978-1-5225-7125-4.ch002

Phuritsabam, B., & Devi, A. B. (2017). Information Seeking Behavior of Medical Scientists at Jawaharlal Nehru Institute of Medical Science: A Study. In S. Ram (Ed.), *Library and Information Services for Bioinformatics Education and Research* (pp. 177–187). Hershey, PA: IGI Global. doi:10.4018/978-1-5225-1871-6.ch010

Quadri, R. F., & Sodiq, O. A. (2018). Managing Intellectual Property in Digital Libraries: The Roles of Digital Librarians. In A. Tella & T. Kwanya (Eds.), *Handbook of Research on Managing Intellectual Property in Digital Libraries* (pp. 337–355). Hershey, PA: IGI Global. doi:10.4018/978-1-5225-3093-0.ch017

Quintana, A. J. (2021). Ensuring Research Integrity. In K. Elufiede & C. Barker Stucky (Eds.), *Strategies and Tactics for Multidisciplinary Writing* (pp. 192–201). IGI Global. https://doi.org/10.4018/978-1-7998-4477-8.ch015

Qutab, S., Adil, S. A., Gardner, L. A., & Ullah, F. S. (2022). The Role of Libraries, Archives, and Museums for Metaliteracy in Smart Cities: Implications, Challenges, and Opportunities. In M. Taher (Ed.), *Handbook of Research on the Role of Libraries, Archives, and Museums in Achieving Civic Engagement and Social Justice in Smart Cities* (pp. 355–375). IGI Global. https://doi.org/10.4018/978-1-7998-8363-0.ch019

Raj, S. K., & De, K. (2020). Electronic Resource Management and Digitisation: Library System of the University of Calcutta. In A. Kaushik, A. Kumar, & P. Biswas (Eds.), *Handbook of Research on Emerging Trends and Technologies in Library and Information Science* (pp. 231–265). IGI Global. https://doi.org/10.4018/978-1-5225-9825-1.ch017

Ram, S. (2017). Library Services for Bioinformatics: Establishing Synergy Data Information and Knowledge. In S. Ram (Ed.), *Library and Information Services for Bioinformatics Education and Research* (pp. 18–33). Hershey, PA: IGI Global. doi:10.4018/978-1-5225-1871-6.ch002

Rao, M. (2017). Use of Institutional Repository for Information Dissemination and Knowledge Management. In B. Gunjal (Ed.), *Managing Knowledge and Scholarly Assets in Academic Libraries* (pp. 156–173). Hershey, PA: IGI Global. doi:10.4018/978-1-5225-1741-2.ch007

Rao, Y., & Zhang, Y. (2017). The Construction and Development of Academic Library Digital Special Subject Databases. In L. Ruan, Q. Zhu, & Y. Ye (Eds.), *Academic Library Development and Administration in China* (pp. 163–183). Hershey, PA: IGI Global. doi:10.4018/978-1-5225-0550-1.ch010

Rao, Y., & Zhang, Y. (2020). The Construction and Development of Academic Library Digital Special Subject Databases. In I. Management Association (Ed.), *Digital Libraries and Institutional Repositories: Breakthroughs in Research and Practice* (pp. 24-44). IGI Global. https://doi.org/10.4018/978-1-7998-2463-3.ch002

Razip, S. N., Kadir, S. F., Saim, S. N., Dolhan, F. N., Jarmil, N., Salleh, N. H., & Rajin, G. (2017). Predicting Users' Intention towards Using Library Self-Issue and Return Systems. In N. Suki (Ed.), *Handbook of Research on Leveraging Consumer Psychology for Effective Customer Engagement* (pp. 102–115). Hershey, PA: IGI Global. doi:10.4018/978-1-5225-0746-8.ch007

Rothwell, S. L. (2018). Librarians and Instructional Design Challenges: Concepts, Examples, and a Flexible Design Framework. In S. Bhattacharyya & K. Patnaik (Eds.), *Changing the Scope of Library Instruction in the Digital Age* (pp. 24–59). Hershey, PA: IGI Global. doi:10.4018/978-1-5225-2802-9.ch002

Roy, L., & Frydman, A. (2018). Community Outreach. In M. Khosrow-Pour, D.B.A. (Ed.), Encyclopedia of Information Science and Technology, Fourth Edition (pp. 6685-6694). Hershey, PA: IGI Global. doi:10.4018/978-1-5225-2255-3.ch579

Rutto, D., & Yudah, O. (2018). E-Books in University Libraries in Kenya: Trends, Usage, and Intellectual Property Issues. In A. Tella & T. Kwanya (Eds.), *Handbook of Research on Managing Intellectual Property in Digital Libraries* (pp. 120–141). Hershey, PA: IGI Global. doi:10.4018/978-1-5225-3093-0.ch007

Sabharwal, A. (2017). The Transformative Role of Institutional Repositories in Academic Knowledge Management. In B. Gunjal (Ed.), *Managing Knowledge and Scholarly Assets in Academic Libraries* (pp. 127–155). Hershey, PA: IGI Global. doi:10.4018/978-1-5225-1741-2.ch006

Sadiku, S. A., Kpakiko, M. M., & Tsafe, A. G. (2018). Institutional Digital Repository and the Challenges of Global Visibility in Nigeria. In A. Tella & T. Kwanya (Eds.), *Handbook of Research on Managing Intellectual Property in Digital Libraries* (pp. 356–376). Hershey, PA: IGI Global. doi:10.4018/978-1-5225-3093-0.ch018

Sahu, M. K. (2018). Web-Scale Discovery Service in Academic Library Environment: A Birds Eye View. *International Journal of Library and Information Services*, *7*(1), 1–14. doi:10.4018/IJLIS.2018010101

Salim, F., Saigar, B., Armoham, P. K., Gobalakrishnan, S., Jap, M. Y., & Lim, N. A. (2017). Students' Information-Seeking Intention in Academic Digital Libraries. In N. Suki (Ed.), *Handbook of Research on Leveraging Consumer Psychology for Effective Customer Engagement* (pp. 259–273). Hershey, PA: IGI Global. doi:10.4018/978-1-5225-0746-8.ch017

Saroja, G. (2017). Changing Face of Scholarly Communication and Its Impact on Library and Information Centres. In A. Munigal (Ed.), *Scholarly Communication and the Publish or Perish Pressures of Academia* (pp. 100–117). Hershey, PA: IGI Global. doi:10.4018/978-1-5225-1697-2.ch006

Sauti, L. (2020). Social Media and Library Collaboration: Analysis of Government Libraries (Kaguvi Building). In C. Chisita (Ed.), *Cooperation and Collaboration Initiatives for Libraries and Related Institutions* (pp. 312–334). IGI Global. https://doi.org/10.4018/978-1-7998-0043-9.ch016

Schuster, D. W. (2017). Selection Process for Free Open Source Software. In E. Iglesias (Ed.), *Library Technology Funding, Planning, and Deployment* (pp. 55–71). Hershey, PA: IGI Global. doi:10.4018/978-1-5225-1735-1.ch004

Seagraves, K., & Weyand, L. (2021). From Bake-Alongs to Tech Talks: How One Public Library System Pivoted to Virtual Programming. In B. Holland (Ed.), *Handbook of Research on Library Response to the COVID-19 Pandemic* (pp. 447-480). IGI Global. https://doi.org/10.4018/978-1-7998-6449-3.ch023

Segaetsho, T. (2018). Environmental Consideration in the Preservation of Paper Materials in Heritage Institutions in the East and Southern African Region. In P. Ngulube (Ed.), *Handbook of Research on Heritage Management and Preservation* (pp. 183–212). Hershey, PA: IGI Global. doi:10.4018/978-1-5225-3137-1.ch010

Shakhsi, L. (2017). Cataloging Images in Library, Archive, and Museum. In T. Ashraf & N. Kumar (Eds.), *Interdisciplinary Digital Preservation Tools and Technologies* (pp. 119–141). Hershey, PA: IGI Global. doi:10.4018/978-1-5225-1653-8.ch007

Sharma, C. (2017). Digital Initiatives of the Indian Council of World Affairs' Library. In T. Ashraf & N. Kumar (Eds.), *Interdisciplinary Digital Preservation Tools and Technologies* (pp. 231–241). Hershey, PA: IGI Global. doi:10.4018/978-1-5225-1653-8.ch012

Shook, R. (2022). Achieving Balance Through Fundamentals of Digital Librarianship. In P. Pangelinan & T. McVey (Eds.), *Learning and Reconciliation Through Indigenous Education in Oceania* (pp. 185–196). IGI Global. https://doi.org/10.4018/978-1-7998-7736-3.ch011

Shukla, P., & Das, C. (2020). Plagiarism: The Role of Librarian and Teachers in Combating It. In J. Jesubright & P. Saravanan (Eds.), *Innovations in the Designing and Marketing of Information Services* (pp. 148–158). IGI Global. https://doi.org/10.4018/978-1-7998-1482-5.ch011

Siddaiah, D. K. (2018). Commonwealth Professional Fellowship: A Gateway for the Strategic Development of Libraries in India. In R. Bhardwaj (Ed.), *Digitizing the Modern Library and the Transition From Print to Electronic* (pp. 270–286). Hershey, PA: IGI Global. doi:10.4018/978-1-5225-2119-8.ch012

Silvana de Rosa, A. (2018). Mission, Tools, and Ongoing Developments in the So.Re. Com. "A.S. de Rosa" @-library. In M. Khosrow-Pour, D.B.A. (Ed.), Encyclopedia of Information Science and Technology, Fourth Edition (pp. 5237-5251). Hershey, PA: IGI Global. https://doi.org/ doi:10.4018/978-1-5225-2255-3.ch455

Smolenski, N., Kostic, M., & Sofronijevic, A. M. (2018). Intrapreneurship and Enterprise 2.0 as Grounds for Developing In-House Digital Tools for Handling METS/ALTO Files at the University Library Belgrade. In L. Costello & M. Powers (Eds.), *Developing In-House Digital Tools in Library Spaces* (pp. 92–116). Hershey, PA: IGI Global. doi:10.4018/978-1-5225-2676-6.ch005

Sochay, L., & Junus, R. (2017). From Summon to SearchPlus: The RFP Process for a Discovery Tool at the MSU Libraries. In E. Iglesias (Ed.), *Library Technology Funding, Planning, and Deployment* (pp. 72–98). Hershey, PA: IGI Global. doi:10.4018/978-1-5225-1735-1.ch005

Soliudeen, M. J. (2021). The Relevance of Feedback Mechanisms to Library Databases in Academic Libraries. In A. Maake, B. Maake, & F. Awuor (Eds.), *Digital Solutions and the Case for Africa's Sustainable Development* (pp. 116–130). IGI Global. doi:10.4018/978-1-7998-2967-6.ch008

Sonawane, C. S. (2018). Library Catalogue in the Internet Age. In R. Bhardwaj (Ed.), *Digitizing the Modern Library and the Transition From Print to Electronic* (pp. 204–223). Hershey, PA: IGI Global. doi:10.4018/978-1-5225-2119-8.ch009

Sorokhaibam, S. D., & Mathabela, N. N. (2017). Information Needs and Assessment of Bioinformatics Students at the University of Swaziland: Librarian View. In S. Ram (Ed.), *Library and Information Services for Bioinformatics Education and Research* (pp. 188–198). IGI Global. https://doi.org/10.4018/978-1-5225-1871-6.ch011

Staley, C., Kenyon, R. S., & Marcovitz, D. M. (2018). Embedded Services: Going Beyond the Field of Dreams Model for Online Programs. In D. Polly, M. Putman, T. Petty, & A. Good (Eds.), *Innovative Practices in Teacher Preparation and Graduate-Level Teacher Education Programs* (pp. 368–381). Hershey, PA: IGI Global. doi:10.4018/978-1-5225-3068-8.ch020

Stevenson, C. N. (2020). Data Speaks: Use of Poems and Photography in Qualitative Research. In M. Baran & J. Jones (Eds.), *Applied Social Science Approaches to Mixed Methods Research* (pp. 119–144). IGI Global. doi:10.4018/978-1-7998-1025-4.ch006

Stewart, M. C., Atilano, M., & Arnold, C. L. (2017). Improving Customer Relations with Social Listening: A Case Study of an American Academic Library. *International Journal of Customer Relationship Marketing and Management*, *8*(1), 49–63. doi:10.4018/IJCRMM.2017010104

Sukula, S. K., & Bhardwaj, R. K. (2018). An Extensive Discussion on Transition of Libraries: The Panoramic View of Library Resources, Services, and Evolved Librarianship. In R. Bhardwaj (Ed.), *Digitizing the Modern Library and the Transition From Print to Electronic* (pp. 255–269). Hershey, PA: IGI Global. doi:10.4018/978-1-5225-2119-8.ch011

Surendran, B., & Kumar, K. (2020). Implementing Information Literacy Skills and Soft Skills for Better Use of Library Resources and Services. In S. Thanuskodi (Ed.), *Handbook of Research on Digital Content Management and Development in Modern Libraries* (pp. 214–224). IGI Global. doi:10.4018/978-1-7998-2201-1.ch012

Suresh, M., & Ravi, S. (2020). Online Database Use by Science Research Scholars of Alagappa University, Karaikudi: A Study. In S. Thanuskodi (Ed.), *Handbook of Research on Digital Content Management and Development in Modern Libraries* (pp. 86-102). IGI Global. https://doi.org/10.4018/978-1-7998-2201-1.ch006

Tella, A., & Babatunde, B. J. (2017). Determinants of Continuance Intention of Facebook Usage Among Library and Information Science Female Undergraduates in Selected Nigerian Universities. *International Journal of E-Adoption, 9*(2), 59–76. doi:10.4018/IJEA.2017070104

Tella, A., Okojie, V., & Olaniyi, O. T. (2018). Social Bookmarking Tools and Digital Libraries. In A. Tella & T. Kwanya (Eds.), *Handbook of Research on Managing Intellectual Property in Digital Libraries* (pp. 396–409). Hershey, PA: IGI Global. doi:10.4018/978-1-5225-3093-0.ch020

Thobane, M. S., & Jansen van Rensburg, S. K. (2022). Transforming Methods for Research With Indigenous Communities: An African Social Sciences Perspective. In P. Ngulube (Ed.), *Handbook of Research on Mixed Methods Research in Information Science* (pp. 190–203). IGI Global. doi:10.4018/978-1-7998-8844-4.ch010

Thull, J. J. (2018). Librarians and the Evolving Research Needs of Distance Students. In I. Oncioiu (Ed.), *Ethics and Decision-Making for Sustainable Business Practices* (pp. 203–216). Hershey, PA: IGI Global. doi:10.4018/978-1-5225-3773-1.ch012

Titilope, A. O. (2017). Ethical Issues in Library and Information Science Profession in Nigeria: An Appraisal. *International Journal of Library and Information Services, 6*(2), 11–22. doi:10.4018/IJLIS.2017070102

Tutu, J. M. (2018). Intellectual Property Challenges in Digital Library Environments. In A. Tella & T. Kwanya (Eds.), *Handbook of Research on Managing Intellectual Property in Digital Libraries* (pp. 225–240). Hershey, PA: IGI Global. doi:10.4018/978-1-5225-3093-0.ch012

Udo-Anyanwu, A. J., & Alor, A. R. (2020). Library Associations, Leadership, and Programmes: IFLA, AfLIA, and NLA. In N. Osuigwe (Ed.), *Managing and Adapting Library Information Services for Future Users* (pp. 89–102). IGI Global. https://doi.org/10.4018/978-1-7998-1116-9.ch006

Wallace, D., & Hemment, M. (2018). Enabling Scholarship in the Digital Age: A Case for Libraries Creating Value at HBS. In S. Bhattacharyya & K. Patnaik (Eds.), *Changing the Scope of Library Instruction in the Digital Age* (pp. 86–117). Hershey, PA: IGI Global. doi:10.4018/978-1-5225-2802-9.ch004

Wang, W., & Wei, Z. (2021). Tongwei County Library: Practices of Social Cooperation in Grassroots Libraries in Western China. *International Journal of Library and Information Services, 10*(1), 48–60. https://doi.org/10.4018/IJLIS.2021010104

Wani, Z. A., Zainab, T., & Hussain, S. (2018). Web 2.0 From Evolution to Revolutionary Impact in Library and Information Centers. In M. Khosrow-Pour, D.B.A. (Ed.), Encyclopedia of Information Science and Technology, Fourth Edition (pp. 5262-5271). Hershey, PA: IGI Global. https://doi.org/ doi:10.4018/978-1-5225-2255-3.ch457

Watkins, K. E., Nicolaides, A., & Marsick, V. J. (2021). Action Research Approaches. In V. Wang (Ed.), *Promoting Qualitative Research Methods for Critical Reflection and Change* (pp. 119–139). IGI Global. https://doi.org/10.4018/978-1-7998-7600-7.ch007

Weiss, A. P. (2018). Massive Digital Libraries (MDLs). In M. Khosrow-Pour, D.B.A. (Ed.), Encyclopedia of Information Science and Technology, Fourth Edition (pp. 5226-5236). Hershey, PA: IGI Global. https://doi.org/ doi:10.4018/978-1-5225-2255-3.ch454

Wu, S. K., Bess, M., & Price, B. R. (2018). Digitizing Library Outreach: Leveraging Bluetooth Beacons and Mobile Applications to Expand Library Outreach. In R. Bhardwaj (Ed.), *Digitizing the Modern Library and the Transition From Print to Electronic* (pp. 193–203). Hershey, PA: IGI Global. doi:10.4018/978-1-5225-2119-8.ch008

Wulff, E. (2018). Evaluation of Digital Collections and Political Visibility of the Library. In R. Bhardwaj (Ed.), *Digitizing the Modern Library and the Transition From Print to Electronic* (pp. 64–89). Hershey, PA: IGI Global. doi:10.4018/978-1-5225-2119-8.ch003

Wulff, E. (2019). Research Data Access and Management in National Libraries. In R. Bhardwaj & P. Banks (Eds.), *Research Data Access and Management in Modern Libraries* (pp. 1–28). IGI Global. https://doi.org/10.4018/978-1-5225-8437-7.ch001

Xiao, L., & Liu, Y. (2017). Development of Innovative User Services. In L. Ruan, Q. Zhu, & Y. Ye (Eds.), *Academic Library Development and Administration in China* (pp. 56–73). Hershey, PA: IGI Global. doi:10.4018/978-1-5225-0550-1.ch004

Xin, X., & Wu, X. (2017). The Practice of Outreach Services in Chinese Special Libraries. In L. Ruan, Q. Zhu, & Y. Ye (Eds.), *Academic Library Development and Administration in China* (pp. 74–89). Hershey, PA: IGI Global. doi:10.4018/978-1-5225-0550-1.ch005

Yao, X., Zhu, Q., & Liu, J. (2017). The China Academic Library and Information System (CALIS). In L. Ruan, Q. Zhu, & Y. Ye (Eds.), *Academic Library Development and Administration in China* (pp. 1–19). Hershey, PA: IGI Global. doi:10.4018/978-1-5225-0550-1.ch001

Yin, Q., Yingying, W., Yan, Z., & Xiaojia, M. (2017). Resource Sharing and Mutually Beneficial Cooperation: A Look at the New United Model in Public and College Libraries. In L. Ruan, Q. Zhu, & Y. Ye (Eds.), *Academic Library Development and Administration in China* (pp. 334–352). Hershey, PA: IGI Global. doi:10.4018/978-1-5225-0550-1.ch019

Yuhua, F. (2018). Computer Information Library Clusters. In M. Khosrow-Pour, D.B.A. (Ed.), Encyclopedia of Information Science and Technology, Fourth Edition (pp. 4399-4403). Hershey, PA: IGI Global. doi:10.4018/978-1-5225-2255-3.ch382

Yusuf, F., & Owolabi, S. E. (2018). Open Access to Knowledge and Challenges in Digital Libraries: Nigeria's Peculiarity. In A. Tella & T. Kwanya (Eds.), *Handbook of Research on Managing Intellectual Property in Digital Libraries* (pp. 241–259). Hershey, PA: IGI Global. doi:10.4018/978-1-5225-3093-0.ch013

Zhang, Q., Zhang, C., & Zhang, Z. (2021). Open Data Services in the Library: Case Study of the Shanghai Library. *International Journal of Library and Information Services*, *10*(1), 1–17. https://doi.org/10.4018/IJLIS.2021010101

Zhang, W., Zou, W., & Qiu, X. (2019). A Unique Development Road of Urban Public Libraries of China: Practice and Exploration of Pudong Library. *International Journal of Library and Information Services*, *8*(2), 51–71. https://doi.org/10.4018/IJLIS.2019070104

Zhu, S., & Shi, W. (2017). A Bibliometric Analysis of Research and Services in Chinese Academic Libraries. In L. Ruan, Q. Zhu, & Y. Ye (Eds.), *Academic Library Development and Administration in China* (pp. 253–262). Hershey, PA: IGI Global. doi:10.4018/978-1-5225-0550-1.ch015

About the Contributors

Enes Abanoz is an assistant professor in the School for Communication at Ondokuz Mayıs University, Turkey, where he has been a faculty member since 2018. He had worked as an assistant professor at Woosong University, South Korea, in the 2018-2019 academic year. Enes Abanoz completed his Ph.D. at Marmara University and his undergraduate studies at Istanbul Commerce University. During his Ph.D. education, he was a visiting researcher in Digital Media, Networks & Political Communication (DiMeNet) at the University of Pennsylvania and Social Media & Political Participation (SMaPP) at New York University. His research interests lie in the area of Graph Theory, Computational Communication, and Social Media, ranging from theory to implementations.

* * *

Yigit Aydogan is a faculty member at Kirklareli University Department of Economics, Turkey, since 2013. He holds a PhD from Yildiz Tehcnical University, Istanbul since 2019 and currently publishes in the field of microeconomics.

Israel Barrutia Barreto is a Doctor of Administration, graduate of Centrum, Pucp, candidate for a doctorate in education, Universidad Autónoma Benito Juárez, Mexico, master's degree in business administration and management, graduate of master's degree in public management, master's degree in education, degree in administration, collegiate, specialist in cooperatives and logistics, with 25 years of professional experience in public and private entities, university professor, advisor and jury of undergraduate and graduate theses, author of research books, academic books, scientific articles, nominated for the Master of the Year award Unab - Colombia, with excellent grades in teacher evaluation at universities in Colombia and Peru. Lectures on research, production, logistics, entrepreneurship in prestigious companies and universities in Peru and Colombia, consultant to SMEs, cooperatives, public and private companies, diagnostic capacity of productive units. He currently works as General Manager of the Innova Scientific research center.

Ulya Bayram is an Assistant Professor in the Electronics Engineering Department of Çanakkale Onsekiz Mart University in Turkey. She got her Ph.D. from the Computer Science/Engineering Department of the University of Cincinnati in Ohio, USA while working in the Biomedical Informatics Department of Cincinnati Children's Hospital Medical Center. She is currently working on machine learning and complex networks research applications in mental health, biomedical, and social science problems.

Mirella Gavidia Canaquiri is a Professional in Tourism and Hospitality. Ecotourism activities manager. Principal Professor of the Faculty of Ecotourism of the National Amazonian University of Madre de Dios. Researcher on the subject of Ecotourism, Communities, and Environmentally friendly Activities.

Caroline Kiarie's, PhD, research interests include interpersonal communication, social media and social networks among employees. Caroline currently lectures at private and public universities in Kenya in corporate communication and public relations disciplines. She has worked and trained with several organizations both in Kenya and USA. In most of her roles, she's been the communication liaison among the international organizations in both public and private sectors. She holds a PhD from University of KwaZulu Natal in Durban, South Africa (media and cultural studies), a Masters in Science degree in Communication and Marketing from Franklin University in Ohio, USA where she specialized in employee performance and organizational communication. She writes and presents widely on new media influence in organization communication and higher education sector.

Ana Lima is a PhD in Electrical Engineering and Computing (2016) and Master in Electrical Engineering (2012) from Universidade Presbiteriana Mackenzie. Graduated in Computer Science from the Catholic University of Pernambuco (2010). Member of the Natural Computing Laboratory (LCoN) at Universidade Presbiteriana Mackenzie. She was a Scientific Initiation student as a scholarship holder of the PIBIC-UNICAP and CNPq program, working on the following topics: soft sensors, neural networks, fuzzy logic and biosurfactants. Her main interests are in data mining, text mining, social media mining, social media, sentiment analysis, psychological factor prediction and bio-inspired computing. She is currently a senior data scientist at Itaú-Unibanco.

Leandro Nunes de Castro has a B.Sc. in Electrical Engineering from the Federal University of Goias, a M.Sc. in Electrical Engineering from Unicamp, a Ph.D. in Computer Engineering from Unicamp and an MBA in Strategic Business Management from the Catholic University of Santos. He was a Research Associate at the

University of Kent at Canterbury from 2011 to 2002, a Research Fellow at Unicamp from 2002 to 2006, a Visiting Lecturer at the University Technology Malaysia in September 2005, and a Visiting Professor at the University of Salamanca in 2014. He is currently a Professor at the Graduate Program in Electrical Engineering and Computing at the Mackenzie Presbyterian University, where he founded and lead the Natural Computing and Machine Learning Laboratory (LCoN). He is acknowledged by the Brazilian Research Council as a leading researcher in Computer Science, and was recognized in 2011 as one of the most cited authors in Computer Science from the country. His main research lines are Natural Computing and Data Mining, emphasizing Artificial Immune Systems, Neural Networks, Swarm Intelligence, Evolutionary Algorithms and real-world applications. He was the founder and Editor in Chief of the International Journal of Natural Computing Research and member of the committee of several conferences. He has eight books published, from among four were authored or co-authored and the others organized, and has published over 250 scientific papers.

Victor Ruiz Nunura is a professional in administrative sciences. Manager of public and private companies. Master in Education with a specialty in Andragogy. Academic with completed Doctorate studies in Educational Sciences, as well as in Law. Specialist in corporate law.

Renzo Seminario received his master's degree in biodiversity, landscape and sustainable management from the University of Navarra in 2017. In 2020 he was hired as a researcher by the Innova Scientific research center, a position he held until October 2020. He currently works as Manager of Innovation and Development at Innova Scientific. Writes and presents widely on environmental, technology, social science, and education topics.

Basak Taraktas received her Ph.D. in Political Science from the University of Pennsylvania in 2016. Since Fall 2018, she has been working as an assistant professor of political science at Bogazici University. Her research is set in the contexts of regimes, contentious politics, and international finance, where she combines computational methods (such as, agent-based models and network analysis) and qualitative research to unpack the effect of ideology and ideational beliefs on co-operation. Taraktas is particularly interested in adaptations of complexity theory and dynamical systems in social sciences.

Index

L

M

N

O

P

S

T

U

V

W

www.ingramcontent.com/pod-product-compliance
Lightning Source LLC
LaVergne TN
LVHW081329300926
849161LV00008B/1921